Kabbalah
for the
Layman

🦁 © 2012 Kabbalah Centre International, Inc.

Kabbalah Publishing is a registered DBA of
The Kabbalah Centre International, Inc.

For further information:

The Kabbalah Centre
155 E. 48th St., New York, NY 10017
1062 S. Robertson Blvd., Los Angeles, CA 90035

1.800.Kabbalah www.kabbalah.com

First Edition, February 2012

Printed in USA

ISBN: 978-1-57189-780-0

Design: HL Design (Hyun Min Lee) www.hldesignco.com

Kabbalah
for the
Layman

Rav Berg

KABBALAH
PUBLISHING

Table of Contents

Volume One

Note to Reader 2
Introduction 3

Part One: Origins and History of Kabbalah 9

Chapter 1: Kabbalah: A Definition 10
Chapter 2: Origins of Kabbalah 13
Chapter 3: Rav Shimon bar Yochai and the Greater Assembly.. 17
Chapter 4: Golden Age of Safed 22
Chapter 5: A Later Light—Rav Ashlag 33
Chapter 6: Kabbalah and the Age of the Messiah 36

Part Two: The Body of Knowledge 41

Chapter 7: The Methodology of Kabbalah 42
    Conditions for Studying Kabbalah 49
    The Biblical Methods of Kabbalah 52
Chapter 8: The Main Teachings 57
    Yesh Me'Ayin (Something from Nothing) 60
    Shutting Off the Light 63
Chapter 9: The Major Concepts 70
    Giving and Taking—The Purpose of Existence 72
    The Doctrine of Tzimtzum and the Jewish People 76
    The Chosen People 81
    Sefirot 89
    Vessels and Lights 94
    The Middle Point 96

Part Three: Making the Connection—Practical 107
Applications

Chapter 10: Operational Tools 108
Chapter 11: *Devekut*—The Circular Concept 118
Chapter 12: A Contemplation 128

Volume Two

Introduction 136

Chapter 1: The Thought of Creation 139
            How the Circle Became a Line 139
Chapter 2: Making Metaphysical Connections 142
            The Real World 143
            What You See is What You Forget 144
Chapter 3: *Or Ein Sof* 146
Chapter 4: The Seed 148
            Before the Big Bang 149
            Before and After 150
            The Closer the Better 151
Chapter 5: The Illusion of Darkness 152
            Perspectives 153
            The Two Faces of Desire 154
Chapter 6: The *Sefirot* of Straightness 156
            Light 157
Chapter 7: By Any Other Name 160
Chapter 8: The Cause Contains the Effect 162
            Fulfillment 163
            Sympathetic Vibrations 165
Chapter 9: The Circle is Not Attached to the Endless 167
            Negative Expectations 168

Chapter 10: Binding By Striking 170

    The Circular Concept 172

Chapter 11: Intentions 174

    On Becoming a Circle 174

    Inner Light/Surrounding Light 176

Chapter 12: The Essence of Time 178

Chapter 13: Energy-Intelligence 180

    The Source Reigns Supreme 182

    A World Apart 183

    Smoking is Hazardous for Your Health 183

Chapter 14: Bread of Shame 185

    Restriction 186

    Tzimtzum (Restriction) 187

    The Offspring of Restriction 188

Chapter 15: Curtains 192

Chapter 16: Symmetry 194

Chapter 17: The Primordial Man 198

    The Emergence of the Central Column 199

    Straight from the Source 201

Chapter 18: Step by Step 202

Chapter 19: Free Will 208

    Probing the Nature of Intelligence 209

Chapter 20: *Adam Kadmon* (Primordial Man) 212

    Malchut 213

Chapter 21: One Equals Four 216

    Best Laid Plans 216

    The Closed Circuit 218

    Cravings 220

Chapter 22: *Parzuf* 222

    Lasting Impressions 223

Chapter 23: The First Three 225

    The Crown of *Adam Kadmon* (Primordial Man) 226

    Affinity 228

    On a Scale of One to Ten 230

Chapter 24: Density 232
    Less is More 233
    Breaking Through 235
    The Head-Body Dichotomy 236
Chapter 25: The Paradox 238
    Inferiority 240
Chapter 26: Beyond the Common Sense 243
    Insanity 244
Chapter 27: The Line of Most Resistance 248
    Pressure 250
    Diversity of Phase 252
Chapter 28: Brainstorm 253
    The Filament 253
    Illusion 254
    Negative Space 255
    Klipot 256
    Space 257
    Transference 261
    Circuits 261
Chapter 29: If There is a God 265
    Initiative 266
    The Lower Seven 268
    One Step Beyond 269
    The Sparkplug 270
    The Future 271

Volume Three

Introduction 278

Part One: New Age of Reality 283

Chapter 1: Back to the Future 284

Chapter 2: The New Age 289

Chapter 3: Mind Over Matter 297

Chapter 4: Altered States 305

    Faces of Evil 315

    Evil Inclinations 316

Chapter 5: The Speed of Light 317

    Great Discoveries 320

Chapter 6: This Modern Age 322

    Star Wars 323

    Complacency 324

    Sensual Asceticism 326

Chapter 7: Giving and Receiving 327

    Happiness 330

Part Two: The Creative Process 333

Chapter 8: Spiritual Substance 334

    No Disappearance in Spiritual Substance 336

    Space and Dimension 339

Chapter 9: Mirrors of Redemption 341

    The Birth of Desire 343

Chapter 10: *Keter, Chochmah, Binah, Tiferet* and *Malchut* ... 345

    Keter – Crown 345

    Chochmah – Wisdom 347

    Binah – Intelligence 349

    Transformation 352

    Tiferet – Beauty 353

    Zeir Anpin – Small Face 355

    Malchut – Kingdom 356

    The Middle Point 358

Chapter 11: *Keter* Versus *Malchut* 359

    Four Phases 361

Chapter 12: The Outer Space Connection 365

    Ten Not Nine 368

Part Three: Expanding Consciousness 371

Chapter 13: The Line 372
    The Lights of Life and Spirit 373
    The Line Connects the Circles 375
    Here and Now 378
Chapter 14: On Restoring Light to the Circles 381
Chapter 15: Activating the Central Column 385
    Resistance 386
    The Filament 388
    Returning Light 389
    Free Will or Determinism 391
Chapter 16: The Good Fight 392
    The Global Village 394
Chapter 17: *Tikkun, Tzadik,* Coming Full Circle 398
    The Mother of Invention 400
    Growth 401
    Tzadik 402
    Coming Full Circle 405
    A World of Difference 407

Part Four: Art of Living 411

Chapter 18: The One Percent Solution 412
    99.44% Pure 413
    The Shortest Distance Between Two Points 414
    Success and Failure 414
    Permanent and Temporary Remnant 416
    All Vibration is Music 420
    Creative Disengagement 421
    On Death and Dying 422
    Two Points of View 424
Chapter 19: Crime and Punishment 426
    A Fable of Two Brothers 430

Chapter 20: Victim of Circumstance 440

    What is Love? 442

    Lack 443

    Amnesia 445

    Limitation 446

    On Becoming Unreasonable 447

Post Script: I'll Take the High Road 499

Appendix: Glossary of Kabbalistic Terminology 452

Volume

One

A Note to the Reader

I t is of the utmost importance that the reader strives to achieve a clear understanding and comprehension of the basic concepts and terminology of Kabbalah as a foundation for more advanced studies. The reader is urged to read carefully the section on "The Main Teachings" (Chapter 8); without it the terms and concepts used in the text may be misleading. An inclusive glossary has also been provided at the back of the book for further guidance.

It may seem, on occasion, as though definitions and explanations are repeated, but successive readings of the book will reveal increasingly profound levels of meaning as the essential unity of the teachings of Kabbalah becomes apparent.

Introduction

For a long time Kabbalah has remained virtually inaccessible to the average person: Its study has been restricted either to the more Orthodox sects of Judaism or to academic scholars. Orthodox Judaism has always stressed the prime importance of *Talmudic* studies, viewing Kabbalah as suitable only for those who are already knowledgeable in *Talmud* and *Mishnah*, and who have reached an age when they can cope with the secrets of esoteric wisdom. The academic world, on the other hand, sees in Kabbalah the ideal field for research, complete with abstruse texts, colorful personalities and masses of symbolism to be collected, collated and set down in numerous papers. Neither Orthodox Judaism nor the field of academia makes a recognizable attempt to treat the vast literature of Kabbalah as a living and viable system of thought. As a result, little effort has been made to present the material gleaned from research in a format that could be understood by the vast majority of people who lack any specialized knowledge on the subject. The ordinary person who wants to find out more about the nature and content of the study of Kabbalah will find himself facing difficulties. If he approaches "religious figures," he will inevitably be discouraged—either because of the widespread ignorance that exists within religious circles about Kabbalah, or by the stringency of the qualifications that will be demanded before he can undertake even preliminary investigations.

The result of this disregard of Kabbalah—which, as we shall see, signifies a lack of understanding of the position held by Kabbalah on the Torah (Bible)—can be seen in the all-too-frequent degeneration of religion into an insignificant social activity, and in the flight of young people away from religion to the more mystically-inclined eastern religions.

The purpose of this book, therefore, is not just to provide the reader with a taste of the vast world of mystical thought and an experience of how Kabbalah can be brought to bear on the problems facing the world today, but to argue the appropriateness and necessity of returning to the study of the universe and its law that is provided for us by Kabbalah.

There can be no doubt that the recent interest in mysticism among the young has given an important impetus to the resurgence of Kabbalah as a living force in spiritual studies. It has come as a surprise to many to discover the existence of such a full-fledged, complex and absorbing system as Kabbalah—a system, that can deal intelligently with all the problems thrown up by existence in the twentieth century. Religion is frequently experienced by young people as an arbitrary and archaic system of coercive and restrictive rules, fossilized through the arrangements of the sages until the result would seem of more interest to the historian and the archaeologist than to the person facing the problems of finding out what it means to be spiritual in a modern society.

How refreshing, then, to discover Kabbalah. Here we find that all forms of coercion are finally ruled out. It is pointed out that the Almighty, who created each and every one of us, does not force us to "do good." How then, can we justify the use of force and threats to compel one another to certain forms of behavior? According to Kabbalah, no precept should be fulfilled merely in the name of "tradition" or "commemoration," without a deeper understanding of the reasons underlying that precept. The only reason to observe a precept is that by using the understanding of Kabbalah together with the tools and instruments provided for our use by the Bible, one can reconstruct the mystical dimension of a time lost in the past, a time whose energies continue to exist in the universe. These meta-physical energies, which Kabbalah describes in detail, are available for our use each and every day, provided we know how to draw them down and to what use we can put them.

Rav Shimon bar Yochai, the author of the *Zohar* (*Book of Splendor*), the classic work on the hidden understanding of the Bible, made exactly this point in his refutation that religious obligation is a sufficient reason for ritual and the fulfillment of precepts. "Prayer and ritual, devoid of meaning and spirituality, are like straw—the epitome of lifelessness." If religion is not seen as a force in our society, the cause may lie in its current inability to meet the growing spiritual needs of its adherents.

Closer to our own time we have the observation made by Rav Yehuda Ashlag (1886-1955), who translated the *Zohar* and its concepts from the original Aramaic into modern Hebrew: "If the needs of religious observers are not met, then we may expect a totally de-spiritualized and demoralized society, the likes of which has never been experienced in the history of humankind."

It is becoming increasingly clear that what is needed is a genuine moral and spiritual system that will both enable us to redefine such basic terms as "Good and Evil" for a generation to whom they have become meaningless, and help us make sense of a universe that now contains space travel, drug addiction, atomic destruction, television and the laser. It is the contention of this book that knowledge of Kabbalah leads one to a true appreciation of the significance of these problems, and provides the key to their eventual mastery.

The widespread ignorance surrounding the nature and content of Kabbalah has led to the growth of false ideas, fear and mistrust; those few Kabbalists in the past who misused their powers, or misinterpreted their role as the bearers of wisdom, have had a detrimental effect on the popular attitude towards Kabbalah that is quite disproportionate to their numbers. In the absence of arguments to the contrary, it is generally believed that the study of Kabbalah is an unnecessary and dangerous pursuit. It is deemed unnecessary because all that a spiritual person needs to know is contained within the Bible and the commentaries and is dangerous in that it threatens not only the balance and sanity of the individual, but also the well-being of the community. In fact, it was precisely for this reason that Rav Shimon bar Yochai made the vital distinction between *Ta'amei Torah* (Taste of the Bible—the understanding of the Bible that is accessible to all who wish to learn) and *Sitrei Torah* (Secrets of the Bible—available only to those who have reached the point where they can deal adequately with the power contained therein). While the aspects of *Sitrei Torah* are concealed by various means from the sight and understanding of all but a few, the insights of *Ta'amei Torah* are for the benefit of all people. Indeed, Rav Shimon went so far as to claim that the teachings of *Ta'amei Torah* could benefit even a child of six.

However, the fact that some aspects of Kabbalah do contain revelations of the nature and structure of the universe and bring with them an increase in the understanding and power of the individual is not, in itself, a sufficient reason not to study, as has been thought in recent years. A moment's reflection will show that contemporary religion is faced with two choices: It can either continue on its present course, commemorating in its daily life the history of its ancestors, dwindling year by year in both number and influence, or it can reveal its relevance and power in the world today, by demonstrating that it has the power to re-unify the fragmented and scattered people of the Earth. The diversity that we see all around us, which distracts us from the central unity of all existence, resembles the differences found in the branches and twigs of a tree. The overwhelming need today is for a unifying force to counteract this diversity—a knowledge of the structure and the power of the root of all things, which is to be found in Kabbalah.

Rav Shimon indicated that, in response to the crises of our particular era, spiritual meaning and purpose will transcend organizational and schismatic rivalries. By this he meant that involvement in matters of true spirituality takes people away from petty factionalism and allows unity of purpose to emerge. This goal of spiritual unity is best realized through the study of Kabbalah.

An excellent, if unfortunate, example of the widespread malaise that affects all religions is the deep division over questions regarding the letter of the law. Each faction has its own understanding on a subject, and discussions between factions seem to be limited to the spirited defense of particular positions. An obvious and desirable alternative would be to develop an approach that brings out the deeper and unifying dimensions, stressing the experience of the spirituality of the law, and not just its ritualized performance, which becomes possible through an understanding of *Ta'amei Torah*—the reasons for laws found in the Bible that are expounded in the *Zohar*.

The Kabbalah has revealed that science, for so long held to be a refutation of religion, is nothing more than a commentary on the Bible, and that the apparently random and meaningless rules and rituals of the Law are, in fact, expressions of basic laws of the universe, no more arbitrary than the laws of thermodynamics or chemical formulae. The traditional justification of the expression "thus it is written" is no longer needed, for it implies that there is no greater reason for carrying out a precept than that we are told to do so. This, despite the fact that the sages of the *Talmud* were clearly not prepared to take anything on face value and argued strenuously over the meaning of every word in the Bible. In the years to come, with the increasing knowledge and understanding of Kabbalah, we shall witness the very scientists who claimed to have dispensed with the need for religion and belief turning to the teachings of the *Zohar* to find knowledge of the essential structure and laws of the universe. Then "the law" will be seen in its true light—not the convenient focus for factionalism it is today, but the expression of the underlying movement and flow of the cosmos.

Rav Chiya adduced here the verse: "I was asleep but my heart waked, it is the voice of My Beloved that knocks," the Holy One, blessed be He, saying, 'Open to me an opening no bigger than the eye of a needle, and I will open to thee the supernal gates.'"

—Zohar III, P. 95a.

Part One

Origins and History
of Kabbalah

Chapter 1

Kabbalah: A Definition

From the foregoing discussion it should come as no surprise to learn that the definitions of Kabbalah are many and varied, for some Kabbalah will be seen as illuminating a different aspect of history, philosophy or religion. To the Orthodox it might be another commentary on the Bible, albeit a rather exotic one; in less dedicated circles, Kabbalah has been seen as a form of clairvoyance or magic. To those of a mystical inclination, it appears as a key to immortality, the ultimate union of the soul with the Almighty. Yet all definitions fall short of the real meaning of Kabbalah.

The literal meaning of the word Kabbalah is "Receiving." In the opening sentence of the book, *Ethics of the Fathers*, we read that "Moses received the Bible from Sinai" the word used for "receive" being "*kibel*," which is the past tense of the verb "*kabal*." It was clear to the sages that the Bible received by Moses was unique in that it contained the knowledge necessary for all generations. Thus, when Rav Shimon came to reveal the mystical part of the Bible, in the *Zohar*, he related it closely to the written Bible so as to demonstrate that the Bible and Kabbalah are but different aspects of the same essential whole. The Bible itself represents the outer shell while Kabbalah is the inner core, concealed from sight—a relationship similar to that which exists between the physical body and soul. The Bible reveals the word of God, while Kabbalah reveals the hidden and the revealed.

The very fact that the secrets of the universe are revealed through the study of *Receiving* tells us a great deal about the nature of existence. We learn that the Desire to Receive is the basic mechanism by which the world operates; it is the dynamic process at the base of all physical and metaphysical manifestations. The Desire to Receive affects all Creation because it is the basis of all Creation: It affects all four levels of Creation: Human, animal, vegetative and inanimate. In an inanimate object the Desire to Receive is of a lesser quality; a rock or stone is almost independent of the physical world for its existence; it needs nothing to ensure its continuing existence, nonetheless, for it to exist at all it must contain some aspect of the Desire to Receive. As we move up the evolutionary scale, we find an increasing physical dependence upon the external world for survival culminating in Man, who has the greatest Desire to Receive of all Creation—not only for physical things, but also for intangible needs like peace, happiness and satisfaction. The perfection of the Desire to Receive is when it becomes the Desire to Receive for others, which is equivalent to the Desire to Impart.

We see this in its most sublime form in the celebration of the Sabbath, the high point of the Creation, which is the expression of God's Desire to Impart, and humanity's Desire to Receive. It is also at the root of the fundamental instruction of the Bible expressed in the words: "Love your neighbor as yourself." Only when the Desire to Receive is transformed into the Desire to Impart to others is it completed—in loving your neighbor, you are also, in the profoundest sense, loving yourself and, ultimately, your Creator.

The sublime teachings of the wisdom of Kabbalah are also called "The Wisdom of the Truth." The root meaning of the word "wisdom" as it is used here is alluded to by the sages when they ask, "Who is wise?" and reply, "He who sees consequences of actions.:" As soon as he observes an action the wise man perceives what will be born and result from it; he is like a good doctor who can detect the symptoms of a disease at an early stage, and then knows the course that disease will run, and its eventual outcome. Indeed, the mark of a wise person in any trade or profession is that he or she does not have to wait for the future to know what the future has in store; the knowledge that he or she possesses is of the root, from which all subsequent actions can be known. Kabbalah, then, may be understood as the study of wisdom; it allows the individual to understand the true meaning of the Creation, which is the root of all existence, not only on the physical but also on the metaphysical level. By revealing the root of Creation, kabbalah enables us to unravel the mysteries of the working of the universe and shows us the potential consequences of all possible actions.

Yet one should not forget that mysticism is rendered in Hebrew as *chochmot hanistar*, the wisdom of the unexplained, or of the unknown; for we should always remember that all the Kabbalah freely offers us—that knowledge of the original causes of all things—is only a part of its wisdom. Rav Ashlag, by translating and providing commentaries to the classical works of Kabbalah, has stripped away much of the mystique surrounding *Ta'amei Torah*, so that it can be studied with profit by all who wish; *Sitrei Torah*, the concealed sections of Kabbalah, are still—and will always remain—hidden from those who might misunderstand or misuse the knowledge contained therein.

Chapter 2

The Origins of Kabbalah

The first known printed work on mysticism is the *Sefer Yetzirah,* whose authorship has been attributed to the Patriarch Abraham. Containing ideas and concepts of the most sublime and elevated level, this text has not been used by kabbalists of the past due to the difficulty of defining exactly the terms and hidden meanings it contains. The most elaborate and lengthy work to have appeared in the field of esoteric studies is the *Zohar.* Those who have studied it and fully understood the significance of its teachings are unanimous in ascribing it to the saintly sage of the Mishnaic period, Rav Shimon Bar Yochai. The authorship of the *Zohar* is a subject of debate among those who study Kabbalah as an academic pastime. Many scholars maintain that the *Zohar* was written by the 11th century Kabbalist, Moses de Leon, of blessed memory, or by others among his contemporaries. When the Holy *Zohar* is more closely studied and better understood, however, it becomes evident that only someone of the stature and spirituality of Rav Shimon could have composed such a work.

We know that each generation has a lesser understanding of the Bible than its predecessor. To credit a text such as the *Zohar* to any age other than the period of the *Tanna'im,* the compilers of the *Mishnah* who lived from the first to the third centuries C.E., is simply not possible, since this would imply that the level of spiritual consciousness and understanding of Moses de Leon was comparable to, if not higher than that of the saintly *Tanna'im.* When the historians elect Moses de Leon as author of the *Zohar,* they thereby neglect the opinion of such great Kabbalists as Moses Cordovero, Shlomo Alkabetz, Joseph Caro, Isaac Luria, Moses Luzzato and many others— men for whom the *Zohar* was a way of life, rather than a field of study, and who were unanimous in their agreement that Rav Shimon was the author of the *Zohar*. The underlying assumption of these great men was that the man who wrote the *Zohar* must have been on the same level of spirituality as its contents, and that only Rav Shimon fitted that description.

Let us now, therefore, look at the history of this great sage in an attempt to understand the verdict of the famous Kabbalists mentioned above.

When Israel was under the rule of Rome, Rav Shimon was a disciple of Rabbi Akiva, who continued to teach from the Bible despite the Roman decree forbidding its study. Rabbi Akiva was captured and put to death, whereupon Rav Shimon launched a verbal attack on the Romans, accusing them of intolerance and cruelty, and was himself sentenced to death as a result. He fled with his son Elazar to a cave in the mountains near the Galilee town of Peki'in, where he hid in a cave for thirteen years until the Emperor's death made it safe for them to leave.

As to the revelation of the Holy *Zohar*, the sages of blessed memory relate the following legend. The thirteen years that Rav Shimon and his son spent in the cave marked a turning point in the history of the great body of esoteric knowledge. In the seclusion of the cave Rav Shimon was visited twice a day by the prophet Elijah, who revealed to him the secrets of the *Zohar*. The deeper and more comprehensive sections, known as the *Ra'ya Mahemna*, are a record of the discourses that took place between Rav Shimon and Moses himself, the beloved shepherd of the Bible. One should not take this to mean that the secrets of the *Zohar* were revealed only to Rav Shimon. His teacher, Rabbi Akiva, and several others before him were fully versed in all the teachings of the *Zohar*.

In fact, the entire understanding of Kabbalah was presented in its oral form to the Israelites on Mount Sinai; many studied and understood, but few could make others see and understand. For the written text of the *Zohar*, humanity would have to wait for Peki'in and Rav Shimon.

The question still remains, however, as to why was Rav Shimon chosen to set down the teachings of the *Zohar* in preference to his teacher, Rav Akiva, or indeed any of the other giants of the Kabbalah who preceded him. This question has been the source of many commentaries and parables; it is often stressed, for instance, that through his fugitive and solitary life, Rav Shimon was able to overcome the physical constraints and limitations that prevent the attainment of the higher levels of spiritual consciousness. He was thus able to transcend the laws governing time and space, thereby acquiring root knowledge of all existence. Thus we find in the *Zohar* not only discussions of spiritual matters but also fundamental concepts in the fields of medicine, astrology, law, telecommunications and psychiatry. But then the question remains, why was Rav Shimon the one chosen to live in a cave for thirteen years?

Within the physical body of a person we find two distinct motivating factors called the Inner Light and the Encircling Light. The Inner Light is the element of Light contained within a person upon his or her descent into this mundane world at birth. The Encircling Light is the element of Light that the individual merits/earns during his lifetime through good deeds and actions. In other words, it is acquired and is not present at birth. The difference between the two Lights is determined by the degree to which an individual is able to subordinate the physical body to the Light; in effect, the Inner Light that accompanies a person is merely an aid in the pursuit of spiritual ascent. The degree to which an individual is limited by the constraints of time, space and motion—the physical laws of the universe—is dependent on the degree to which he manages to control the Desire to Receive of his or her body, or the evil inclination. Gradually, a person acquires the Encircling Light and ascends the ladder of spirituality.

Rav Isaac Luria (the Ari), (1534–1572), explaining the inner makeup of Moses, states that "Moses encompassed the Inner and Encircling Lights; the inclusion of the Inner Light is alluded to by the verse 'and she saw he was good' (*Exodus* 2:2), and the Encircling Light is denoted by the verse 'the skin of his face shone' (*Exodus* 34:30)." These two qualities were required before Moses could have received the entire Bible including, as I have said, the understanding of Kabbalah and the explanations of its esoteric meanings.

We learn that Rav Shimon was a reincarnation of Moses himself, in reference to which the *Zohar* says, "The son of Yochai (meaning Rav Shimon) knows how to observe his ways; if he ventures into the deep sea, he looks all round before entering, in order to establish how he will accomplish the task in one attempt." From this statement the Ari draws the following conclusions: "One must understand that among the souls of the righteous, there are those who possess the Encircling Light, and who have the capability of communicating the esoteric mysteries of the Bible by means of concealment and cryptic references, so as to prevent those who lack merit from understanding it. Rav Shimon's soul incorporated the Encircling Light from birth; he thus had the power to clothe the esoteric lore and also to discourse on it. Subsequently, permission was granted to Rav Shimon to write the *Book of Splendor*, the *Zohar*: the sanction to write this book of wisdom was not given to the sages who preceded Rav Shimon because, even though they were highly knowledgeable in this wisdom, even to the extent of exceeding Rav Shimon, they lacked his ability to clothe and protect the esoteric lore. This is the meaning of the reference to Rav Shimon made above."

Chapter 3

Rav Shimon Bar Yochai and the Greater Assembly

A valuable method of studying the historical development of Kabbalah is to examine the lives and personalities of the exceptional individuals who were chosen to disseminate its teachings. Among these people the foremost group was that of Rav Shimon and his followers.

It is told that when Rav Shimon emerged from the cave in which he and his son Elazar had spent thirteen years learning the secrets of Kabbalah, his body was covered with sores: his father-in-law, Rabbi Pinchas, wept bitterly when he saw the state of Rav Shimon's body, saying, "How bitter it is for me to see you in such a state!" Whereupon Rav Shimon replied, "I am happy that you see me like this—otherwise I would not be what I am." Clearly he regarded his physical condition and discomfort as necessary for him to have reached the spiritual heights that he had attained. Rav Shimon went on to select eight disciples, who, together with himself and his son, formed the Great Assembly. They chose a location on the road from Meron to Safed in the Galilee and began to discuss the hidden meanings and mysteries of the Bible that had been revealed to their teacher. Rav Shimon taught his disciples both *Sitrei Torah* and *Ta'amei Torah*. He revealed the Divine secrets, going back to the period before even the primal Vessels had been formed. It was necessary for him to transmit ideas—even if they were sometimes unintelligible to his audience—so that they would not be lost to future generations.

Before the Great Assembly was disbanded, however, three of the disciples—Rav Yosi ben Jacob, RavHezekiah and Rav Yisa died. They had absorbed as much spiritual Light as their capacity allowed and had thus moved beyond the physical sphere. Those students who were left saw the three being carried away by angels.

Rav Shimon wept and said, "Is it possible that we are being punished for revealing that which has been hidden since Moses stood on Mount Sinai?" At that moment a voice exclaimed from above, "Praiseworthy are you, Shimon bar Yochai, praiseworthy is your portion and the portion of your assembly. Through you is revealed that which was not even revealed to the Upper Celestial Hosts. Therefore, praiseworthy is your portion; your three students departed because their lives were fulfilled."

The Light that emanated from Rav Shimon was of such intensity that it was said to resemble the reality that will exist at the End of the period of Correction (*Gemar HaTikkun*), the period in which we now live, when we enter the Age of the Messiah. The vessels of the three students came from the lower spheres and consequently could not contain or endure the Light that had entered them, just as ordinary glass cannot withstand boiling water.

Such, was the power of the author of the *Zohar*, a man who had truly transcended the limitations of time, space and motion.

One day Rav Shimon observed that the world was covered by darkness and that the Light was concealed. His son, Rav Elazar, said to him, "Let us try to find out what the Creator means to accomplish."

They found an angel who appeared to them in the form of a great mountain, spewing forth thirty torches of fire, and Rav Shimon asked him what he intended to do. "I am instructed to destroy the world," replied the angel, "because humanity does not contain in its midst thirty righteous individuals." Rav Shimon said to the Angel, "Go before the Creator, and tell him that Bar Yochai is among the inhabitants of the world, and his merit is equal to that of thirty righteous men."

The angel ascended to the Creator and exclaimed, "Lord of the universe, are You aware of Bar Yochai's words to me?" Whereupon the Creator replied, "Descend and destroy the world as you were commanded: take no notice of Bar Yochai!"

Seeing the angel reappear, Rav Shimon told him, "If you do not ascend again to the Almighty with my request, I shall prevent you from ever reaching the heavens again: and this time, when you come before the Creator repeat to Him that if the world lacks thirty righteous men, He should spare it for the sake of ten; if there are not ten such men to be found in the whole world, then ask Him to spare humanity for the sake of two men, my son and I; and if He deem these two insufficient, then preserve the world for the sake of one man and I am that one. For it is written, 'But the righteous is an everlasting foundation.' (*Proverbs* 10:25)."

At that very moment a voice from Heaven was heard, saying, "Praiseworthy is your portion, Shimon Bar Yochai, for the Lord above issues a decree, and you seek to countermand it; surely for you is written the verse: He will fulfill the desire of those that fear Him. (*Psalms* 145:19)."

Here we see Rav Shimon, through the power of his Inner and Encircling Light, going so far as to challenge the authority of the Creator. So firmly did he believe in the justice of his cause. But his power was not only used in this way, to ward off the encroaching darkness. He struggled throughout his life to introduce Light into places where ignorance and superstition reigned, to make the metaphysical as well as the physical world comprehensible, and to link all the levels of existence to reveal a world of true beauty and harmony.

So pure and righteous was the soul of Rav Shimon that the Angel of Death could never utter his name. When the Angel of Death appeared before the Creator demanding the death of an individual, he would cite the evil deeds that necessitated the death penalty. When it came to Rav Shimon, however, he could find no evil deeds to hold against him. Then one day, the *yetzer hara* (the evil inclination) appeared before the Creator and demanded that He immediately recall Rav Shimon from his Earthly abode to his rightful place in the Garden of Eden. This was a strange request, a departure from the normal procedure; the Evil inclination usually demands the recall of an individual for the express purpose of imposing justice, punishment, or even death. But the plea of the Evil inclination for the recall of Rav Shimon went as follows:

"My purpose in the physical world is to divert the individual from a humane and righteous path to one of wrongdoing: but I have never before encountered a man like Rav Shimon bar Yochai. Not only have I been unsuccessful in my attempts to divert him from the proper course of piety and righteousness, but he has actually sought me out that he might be confronted with temptation, in order to turn this temptation to some useful and fruitful purpose. You must remove him from the world: I have nowhere to conceal myself from him and I fear that my objective in this physical world will fail."

For this reason alone, Rav Shimon was summoned to the Garden of Eden. The day of his death, known as the Smaller or Lesser Assembly, was no ordinary day: "On the day that Rav Shimon desired to leave this world, he prepared his final words. To all his friends gathered beside him, he revealed new esoteric mysteries. Rav Aba wrote, 'The Light was so great that I could not approach him. When the Light departed, I saw that the Holy Light (Rav Shimon) had left this world. His son, Rabbi Elazar, took his father's hands and kissed them saying, My father, my father—there were three, and only one is now left.' (The reference is to Rav Shimon, his father-in-law Rav Pinchas, and Rav Elazar.)

"The peoples of the surrounding communities assembled, each demanding that Rav Shimon be buried in their midst; then the bed upon which the body lay rose up and flew through the air, preceded by a torch of fire, until it reached the cave at Meron. Here it descended, and everyone knew that Rav Shimon had reached his final resting place. All this took place on the thirty-third day of the *Omer*, which is the eighteenth day of the month of *Iyar* (Taurus)."

To this very day, tens of thousands of people make a pilgrimage to Meron to connect to Rav Shimon—in the hope of finding an answer to their prayers, and fulfillment of their needs, through the influence of the Holy Light, Rav Shimon bar Yochai.

Chapter 4

Golden Age of Safed

In the year 1492 of the present era, Queen Isabella and King Ferdinand issued a decree of expulsion that sealed the fate of the Jews in Spain—all those who refused to renounce their faith were forced to leave Spain.

In the wake of this spiritual and physical upheaval, many Jews migrated to the Middle East. A number of them settled in the Upper Galilee, drawn to the ancient town of Safed; here a group of Jewish mystics were setting the stage for the numerous mystical movements of the next four hundred years, among them being the resurgence of interest in the study of Kabbalah.

It is certainly true that the idea of the Messiah was closely linked to this migration, but in a radical sense that did not include the imminent arrival of the Messiah among its aims or expectations. It was, rather, the realization stemming from the words of the Kabbalah, that the redemption of humanity as a whole was deeply linked with the land of Israel. In Isaiah's prophetic vision of the future, he states: "For out of Zion shall go forth the Law, and the word of the Lord from Jerusalem." There is an apparent contradiction here, since the Israelites had already received the Law from Mount Sinai, which was not within the boundaries of Israel; nor did the Law go forth from Zion or Jerusalem. What, then, did the Prophet Isaiah mean by this passage?

The *Zohar* compares the Pentateuch, the Five Books of Moses (the Law), to the body of man, and the Kabbalah to his soul; thus the "body" of the law was given on Mount Sinai, but the inner meaning, the "soul" of the Bible in its written form, would wait to be revealed from the Land of Israel. This revelation is the instrument by which Israel and the rest of the world will finally be redeemed, realizing the dream of "peace on Earth, good will to all men." Thus the migration to Israel can be seen as part of the Divine plan, the next step on the road to redemption. The great minds of mysticism were to gather in Safed to prepare the necessary texts that would, in time, enable the world as a whole to comprehend the soul of the Bible—the wisdom of Kabbalah.

In Safed the people lived a simple, religious life, seeking only peace and piety. With Rav Shimon's interpretation of the hidden meaning of Bible as their foundation, Kabbalah flourished as never before. As the Sephardic community spread out, the study of Kabbalah extended to Italy and Turkey. In Salonika, then part of Turkey, Solomon Alkabetz (1505-1584), the composer of the Sabbath hymn "Lecha Dodi" (Come, My Beloved) established a center for the teaching of Kabbalah; shortly afterwards, he, too, was drawn to Safed, to take part in the great revitalization of the Bible then taking place there.

The kabbalists of Safed made a conscious effort to preserve the entire Bible, with its fundamental principles and laws, by extending it so that its relevance to all aspects of life could be seen. They strove to present a religious experience that would provide its adherents with sufficient energy to meet the demands of daily life.

Rav Moses Cordovero was drawn "as by a thirst" to the wisdom of Kabbalah in 1522; he studied in Safed with Rav Solomon Alkabetz, whose sister he married. He proved a gifted teacher and writer, composing the first comprehensive commentary on the *Zohar* called *Or Yakar* (Exalted Light). The manuscript, obtained on microfilm from the Vatican Library, has already yielded many volumes of priceless teachings.

Rav Isaac Luria (the Ari Hakodesh or Holy Lion), was born in Jerusalem in 1534. According to legend the Prophet Elijah appeared at his circumcision ceremony to act as *Sandak* (Godfather), and told his father to take great care of the child, for he would be the source of an exalted Light. After the death of his father, his mother, who was of Sephardic descent, took him to the home of her brother Mordechai Francis, a wealthy and respected man in the community of Cairo. In Egypt he studied with the famous Rabbis Bezalel and David Zimra (the Radbaz). At the age of seventeen he married one of his cousins.

The Ari was a *Talmudic* authority before he had reached the age of twenty, and soon mastered all the material his mentors had to offer him. He then discovered the *Zohar*, and lived as a hermit in a remote place by the Nile for thirteen years, while he studied the secrets of Kabbalah. In 1569, he settled in Safed, where he studied with Moses Cordovero until he became a master in his own right, with a circle of devoted disciples.

The Ari developed a new system for understanding the mysteries of the *Zohar* called the Lurianic method; it focuses on the Ten *Sefirot* or Luminous Emanations, and sheds new light on the hidden wisdom of Kabbalah. His complete understanding of the mysteries of the *Zohar* together with the other great powers that he manifested during his lifetime was a result of his unique spiritual identity.

Anyone familiar with the *Writings of the Ari* will realize that his clarity and depth of thought and understanding could only come from one blessed with the spirit of Rav Shimon; only Rav Shimon's soul would have been capable of the feats of transcendence that are clearly indicated in the Ari's writings.

Some people thought that the Ari was the harbinger of the Messianic Age, and extraordinary legend grew concerning his piety and righteousness. One *Erev Shabbat* (Sabbath eve), the Ari assembled his disciples and declared that he could affect the coming of the Messiah that very *Shabbat*. He stressed to all present the importance of complete harmony, warning them to be aware of the slightest confrontation with one another. So the unique *Shabbat* began, and all went well throughout Friday night and *Shabbat* morning. Towards the close of *Shabbat,* a trivial argument broke out among the children of the Ari's disciples. This quarrel escalated until the parents intervened, leading, in turn, to a disagreement among two of the disciples. *Shabbat* ended without the appearance of the Messiah; the disciples showed their disappointment at being unworthy of his coming, and asked their teacher the reason for this. The Ari replied sadly, "For a small pittance, the arrival of the Messiah was forestalled." Little did his disciples know that Satan resorts to any means to divert people from their noble intentions; knowing all too well the disciples' awareness of the important task of maintaining harmony among themselves, he chose a covert and unsuspected approach to gain his objective of disunity. "Thus," concluded the Ari "the coming of the Messiah does not mean that we must wait for some individual to ride through the Gate of Mercy in the Eastern Wall of the city of Jerusalem, mounted on a white donkey. Rather, the presence of goodwill towards men and peace on Earth, as indicated in the verse 'and the wolf shall dwell with the lamb, the leopard shall lie down with the kid, (*Isaiah* 11:6) this is the Messiah. The Messiah is nothing more than the symbol of world harmony." Hearing this, the disciples departed with bowed heads.

On another occasion, the Ari gathered his disciples together for a journey to Jerusalem in order to spend *Shabbat* there. When they heard his intention they were overcome with bewilderment and asked their teacher how he could contemplate such a long journey when the arrival of the *Shabbat* was only a matter of minutes away. Smiling, the Ari replied, "The elements of time, space and motion are merely an expression of the limitations imposed by the physical body on the soul. When the soul has sway over the body, however, these limiting factors cease to exist. Let us now proceed to Jerusalem, therefore, for our corporeal bodies have lost their influence over our souls." In this way, singing mystical chants, the Ari and his disciples arrived in Jerusalem in time to celebrate the coming of the Sabbath.

At the age of thirty-eight, on the fifth day of *Av* (Leo) 1572, the Ari completed his task on Earth and ascended to the place waiting for him in the Garden of Eden. To his most trusted and favored pupil, Chaim Vital, and to Chaim's son, Shmuel Vital, he gave the task of recording his thoughts and teachings on paper as a record for posterity of the Golden Age of Kabbalah in Safed. These two devoted followers summarized, as far as was possible, the deeds and wisdom of their teacher, producing the volumes that we now regard as the *Writings of the Ari*. Chaim Vital became a legendary figure and a source of wisdom for later Kabbalists, who could now refer to a concise and clear literary work that laid open the heretofore obscure and abstruse contents of the central work of kabbalistic literature, the *Zohar*.

The faculty of human reason has alienated many people from the basic tenets of the Bible, due to the difficulty in accepting as intrinsic truths those teachings that are based on a literal understanding of the Law. A prime objective of the Ari's commentary was that truth should be presented in a logical, consecutive manner. The system devised by Rav Shimon was not immediately apparent to students and scholars of Kabbalah, leading some to claim that the knowledge found in the *Zohar* was irrational and illogical. *The Writings of the Ari*, however, refute this claim completely, in as much as they represent a commentary on the *Zohar* that can be both grasped by the intellect and perceived by the senses. Where ambiguous and figurative expressions and seemingly inconsequential stories in the Bible leave an impression of irrelevancy, the *Writings of the Ari* caution the reader to beware of literal interpretations. Where some aspect of the Bible appears to contradict common sense, the Ari reminds us that the metaphors of the law were originally intended merely to enable the untaught to comprehend to the best of their abilities. To the knowledgeable a deeper interpretation of such stories should present itself. The parables themselves are of no great value until their inner, sublime meanings have been made intelligible by means of the study of Kabbalah.

We have already seen that the "accidents" of history that brought together the great minds of Kabbalah in Safed, were, in fact, part of the eternal scheme leading to the eventual redemption of humanity. The presence of Chaim and Shmuel Vital was a part of this unfolding, and is demonstrated by their unerring grasp of an enormous body of sublime kabbalistic scholarship. They presented concepts that were not perceptible through the five senses and identified truths that could not be attained through the exercise of logic or imagination. The Ari himself implied that his reincarnation on this Earth was largely for the purpose of instructing Chaim Vital in the mysteries of Kabbalah. Furthermore, his presence permitted Vital to rectify faults in the many reincarnated personalities that he contained—among them being Cain, Korach, Yohanan ben Zakai and Rabbi Akiva. In addition, the Ari told Vital that his soul contained sparks of the Divine Essence that were of a higher degree than those possessed by many of the Supernal Angels. ""But more than that I may not reveal; if I were to reveal your essence to you, you would quite literally fly with joy, but I have not been granted permission to discuss your incarnation in greater detail."

One Friday night, Moses Alshich—the most important homilist of the 16th century—came to the Ari and asked him why he should receive the Ari's teachings only through Chaim Vital, who was considerably his junior; the Ari replied, "I have returned to this world solely for the purpose of teaching Chaim Vital, since no other student is capable of learning so much as a single letter from me." When Vital himself put the same question to him, the Ari told him that the study of Kabbalah did not depend on the student's level of understanding, intelligence or active intellect, but rather on his spirit, which is incarnated from a supernal level. He told Vital that he would soon come face to face with the Prophet Elijah and talk of many things with him; also, through repentance and good deeds, that he would complete and amend his *Nefesh* (the Crude Spirit that represents the lowest level of the soul), and would ascend the ladder to a higher level of *Ruach* (Spirit) that would ultimately unite with the *Ruach* of Rabbi Akiva.

One Shabbat, the Ari noticed the following text on Chaim Vitals forehead: "They prepared a chair for Hezekiah, King of Judah." He understood immediately that a part of the soul of Hezekiah had joined that of Chaim Vital through the mystery of *Tosfat Shabbat*, whereby on *Shabbat*, one acquires parts of other souls that may remain for a longer or shorter time, depending on the actions of the recipient. During that *Shabbat*, Vital became angry with a member of his family, and the additional soul consequently left him. After a week of repentance, on the following *Shabbat*, the Ari noticed the embodiment of the *Ruach*, or higher level of soul of both Hezekiah and Rabbi Akiva in Chaim Vital. Having thus attained a majestic level of spirituality, Vital was unable to prevent the influence of the Left Column from distracting him from his path of piety—again he quarreled with a member of his family, and again the spirits of Hezekiah and Rabbi Akiva left him. This time, however, he repented immediately and emended the entire Left Column of anger, whereupon Ben Azzai, the son-in-law of Rabbi Akiva, entered his spiritual realm.

The Ari considered it necessary to reveal Chaim Vital's levels of spirituality to him in this way in order to explain why his exalted Vessel had been chosen and prepared to receive the great Light that would illumine the sublime wisdom of Kabbalah. One day Vital asked the Ari, "How can you tell me that my soul is so elevated when it is well known that even the less pious of former generations were so elevated that I can never hope to reach even their comparatively low level of spirituality?" The Ari replied, "The levels of spirituality are not dependent on a man's deeds or incarnated soul alone, but are in relation to the level of the generation in which he finds himself; thus a minor deed in our generation may be compared to much greater deeds in previous generations, due to the severity and dominance of the *klipot* (the shells or husks of evil) in the world today. Had you lived in an earlier time, therefore, these same deeds of yours would have been superior to those of the most pious of that generation. This is similar to what has been said with regard to Noah: that he was righteous in his wicked generation; (*Genesis* 6:9) had he lived in a generation of righteous men, he would certainly have been a more righteous individual. You should not, therefore, be amazed or confused about your exalted spiritual level."

On another occasion, when Vital implored the Ari to tell him why he did not devote his valuable time to more eminent scholars such as the Ari's teacher, Rabbi David ibn Abi Zimra (the Radbaz), Yosef Caro, or the Alshich the Ari replied, "Do I really need you? Do I derive any benefit from my association with you? On the contrary, your extreme youth, compared with those scholars that you mentioned, should give me reasons to associate more closely with them, so that my reputation might be enhanced; if that were my objective, I would certainly have chosen that way. However, after considering the matter carefully, and reflecting upon these righteous persons, penetrating their innermost recesses, I find no vessel as pure and as spiritually elevated as yours. This should satisfy your curiosity; I have no intention of revealing the secrets of these men, and you should rather rejoice in your share of the spiritual realm."

So it was that Chaim Vital and his son Shmuel labored together to produce the *Writings of the Ari*. Shmuel recorded every word transmitted to him by his father with the efficiency of an accomplished scribe, and the resulting volumes achieved great fame as the classic textbook on the *Zohar*.

Just as in the case of his father, Chaim Vital, Shmuel Vital had also been carefully chosen to perform the tasks allocated to him in his lifetime. If we are to understand the significance of the doctrines of Kabbalah in our own times, it is important to have some understanding of the spiritual development of Kabbalah in past ages. The characters and personalities of the kabbalists of Safed were the channels or cables through which the power of Kabbalah was transmitted, so that complete understanding of its wisdom is impossible unless we are aware of the spiritual composition of those who taught it, or those who set it down for future generations. This is made possible through the sublime teachings of Rav Shimon, later developed and elaborated upon by the Ari, regarding the transmigration of the soul.

In the *Sefer Hagilgulim* (Book of Transmigrations), the Ari describes the developments leading to the exile and migration of Shmuel Vital's soul and their significance in relation to the mission to which he was assigned during his life on Earth. According to the Ari, there were special affinities between Chaim Vital and his son. Chaim's first wife, Hannah, was a reincarnation of Kalba Savua, Rabbi Akiva's father-in-law; because her soul had its origins in a male, she could not bear children. As the Ari explained, "And Hannah will die, and you (Chaim) will marry again when your *Nefesh* (lower aspect of the soul) is corrected, and you join the second level of the spiritual ladder, which is *Ruach*. When your *Nefesh* has enveloped that of Rabbi Akiva, your *Ruach* will become joined to his, and only then will you be permitted to marry your true soul mate. She will be on the same spiritual plane as Rabbi Akiva's soul mate, since your soul and that of Rabbi Akiva are truly united on the levels of *Nefesh* and *Ruach*. Then you will marry Kalba Savua's daughter Rachel, and will be blessed with a son, whom you will call Shmuel."

So far it is clear that Shmuel Vital's spiritual background was of the rarest quality; however, there is as yet no indication of why he was chosen for the specific task of recording the teachings of the Ari, as they were reported to him by his father. For this information, we must turn to Chaim Vital himself: "One day Chaim Vital revealed to his son that he was a reincarnation of Rabbi Meir, the celebrated *tannah*. Later Shmuel had a dream in which the Rabbi himself told him the same. It is stated in the *Mishnah* that Rabbi Meir was the foremost scribe of his generation. Rabbi Joseph Vital, Chaim Vital's grandfather, was also blessed with a spark of the soul of Rabbi Meir, and he too was a noted scribe. Chaim Vital says of his grandfather that he was one of the greatest scribes the world has ever known. "The Ari told me," he said to his son, "that at one time half the world received spiritual nourishment through the merits of our grandfather, because of the accuracy and faithfulness with which, in his position as scribe, he prepared the written portion of Tefillin. You, my son, are incarnated with that spark as well, which is why you are able to record the words of the Ari with such accuracy."

Shmuel Vital was ideally suited to his task, as indeed, were his father Chaim Vital and their teacher, the Ari. Through the spiritual Vessel of Shmuel the world was now prepared to enter the Messianic era, fully equipped with all the necessary material and knowledge to carry out the work required of it; despite the fact that a complete commentary on the *Zohar* was now available, the metaphors and interwoven imagery were still understood only by a select few.

While it is true to say that the Lurianic system provides the necessary background for a full and comprehensive understanding of the *Zohar*, it is nonetheless puzzling that Chaim Vital should have almost totally ignored the commentaries of the master Kabbalist, Moses Cordovero, the Ari's mentor. According to legend the reason lies in a dream that Chaim Vital once had in which Moses Cordovero appeared before him and told him that, although both his own system and that of the Ari were correct interpretations of the *Zohar*, the Ari's would prevail in Messianic era. This in fact, is the case today, as the *Writings of the Ari* have been arranged, organized and published, while those of the Rabbi Moses Cordovero (Ramak) have only recently been rediscovered.

Another famous kabbalist who flourished during the Golden Age of enlightenment that lasted from about 1490 until 1590, was Abraham ben Mordechai Azulai (1570 1643). Born in Fez to a family of kabbalists of Castilian origin, he wrote three treatises based on the *Zohar*: *Or haLevanah* (Light of the Moon), *Or haHamah* (Light of the

Sun), and *Or haGanuz* (the Hidden Light), all three being based primarily on the Lurianic system; he also prepared a volume entitled *Chesed LeAvraham* (the Mercy of Abraham), in which he presented an analysis of the principles of Kabbalah.

The words of his preface to *Or haHamah* resonate with greater force today than ever before. "It is most important from this time on that everyone study Kabbalah publicly and preoccupy themselves with it. For, by the merit of Kabbalah—in fact, solely through Kabbalah—will the Messiah appear and efface forever war, destruction, social injustice and, above all, man's inhumanity to his fellow man."

It may be said, therefore, that the Spanish Inquisition, for all its violence, ushered in the Golden Age of Enlightenment, and that the Lurianic era set the stage for the Messianic age.

Chapter 5
A Later Light – Rav Ashlag

Until the period when Rav Yehuda Ashlag (1886 1955) pioneered a new system for understanding the works of the Ari, Kabbalah remained a mystery to most people. In his sixteen-volume textbook, the *Study of the Ten Luminous Emanations* (*Talmud Eser Sefirot*) Rav Ashlag devised a logical system through which the essence of the transcendent realm was transmitted by means of an array of symbols and illustrations. These, he felt, best described those aspects of the teachings of the Ari that were beyond the grasp of the intellect alone. The *Ten Luminous Emanations* deals with those concepts that have eluded the most determined scholars for centuries. The intimate relationship between the physical and metaphysical realms is presented simply, together with a description of the series of evolutions that culminates in the world we know today, and also a detailed presentation of those motives that may be ascribed to the Creator.

In addition to these volumes, Rav Ashlag's monumental work on the *Zohar* has had a great influence on Judaic studies and marks a turning-point in the attempt to render the wisdom of Kabbalah comprehensible to contemporary students. His was the first translation of the entire *Zohar* into modern Hebrew. Realizing that a comprehensive translation would not be sufficient on its own, he also composed a commentary on the most difficult passages. He also compiled a volume of diagrams describing the process of evolution of the *Sefirot* in all their manifestations down to the level of this world. Generally speaking, kabbalists of the rank and stature of Rav Ashlag receive their knowledge through Divine Revelation. More penetrating, however, was his knowledge of the spectrum of Kabbalah, and his translation of the *Zohar* shows clearly that he was knowledgeable in every known science.

I was told of his life and personality by my master, Rav Yehuda Tzvi Brandwein, who was his disciple. Rav Ashlag was born in Warsaw and educated in Chassidic schools. In his early years, he was a student of Shalom Rabinowicz of Kalushin and of his son Yehoshah Asher of Porissor. He immigrated to Palestine in 1919 and settled in the Old City of Jerusalem. Rav Brandwein told of a man with immense powers of meditation, a man to whom the worlds of metaphysics and mysticism were as familiar as was the world of physics to Einstein. The comparison is not altogether without significance, since it was during Rav Ashlag's lifetime that great advances and discoveries were being made in the world of science, destroying many of the traditional scientific theories of stability, permanence and purpose in the universe. The great monument of that scientific era, Einstein's theory of relativity, confirmed what kabbalists had known to be true for centuries—that time, space and motion are not immutable constants but a function of energy.

The increasing awareness among scientists of the shortcomings of the analytic methodology of science and the growing sense of the unity and inter-relatedness of physical and biological systems has given a fresh impetus to the world of mysticism, and particularly to Kabbalah. In this respect, the works of Rav Ashlag are distinguished by their unique and striking mixture of salient facts concerning the structure of the universe, together with a deep, penetrating description of the purpose of the individual within this system.

The restoration of a mystical approach in the world of Kabbalah, as opposed to the dry study of ritual and ceremony for their own sake, draws a large part of its strength from the link between the concepts expressed and the mystical consciousness of the author. Since the beginnings of Kabbalah, the Prophet Elijah has been closely identified with its profound teachings. He appeared to both Rav Shimon and the

Ari. Rav Ashlag, however, did not claim Elijah as the source of his mystical revelation. A beautiful story, told to me by my master, demonstrates the inner connection that existed between the soul of Rav Ashlag and the levels on high: "One evening," recalled the Rav Ashlag, "following the completion of a volume of the *Zohar*, I dozed off into a very deep slumber. A voice came to me and proclaimed that I would be shown the entire Creation, from the beginning to the very end, including the coming of the Messiah. I then asked why I could not be shown that which the prophets had seen. The reply was, Why should you be satisfied with the visionary level of the prophets, when you can see all?"

The source of his revelation is described in a letter written by Rav Ashlag to an uncle, in which he relates his meeting with his master, and the egocentricity that he developed after learning the inner mysteries of Kabbalah. This element of pride led to his master discontinuing the lessons until Rav Ashlag had adopted the correct attitude of humility, whereupon his master—a stranger whose name he was forbidden to utter—revealed to him a *Sod* (a secret or inner meaning) concerning the *Mikveh* (ritual bath). "This," reports Rav Ashlag, "brought on an ecstasy of such intensity that it literally created a total *Devekut* (a cleaving to the Divine Essence), a complete separation from corporeality, and a tearing asunder of the veil of eternal life." Shortly after this revelation his master passed away, leaving him brokenhearted. As a result of Rav Ashlag's deep sorrow and despair the revelation, too, left him for a while, until he was once more able to devote his life to the Creator, "Whereupon the fountains of Heavenly wisdom suddenly burst forth, (and) with the grace of the Almighty, I remembered all the revelations I had received from my master, of blessed memory."

Today, as in the Golden Age of Safed, the invisible spring of Kabbalah has once again come to the surface; in our times, however, we notice one significant difference—science, for so long the sworn enemy of spirituality, is now seen in its true light as the ally and companion of Kabbalah.

Chapter 6

Kabbalah and the Age of the Messiah

Before delving more deeply into the actual methodology and wisdom of Kabbalah, let us look at the recommendation made as to the appropriateness of studying at this time; in particular the connection between learning Kabbalah and the approach of the Messianic Age.

We have already observed the rising tide of interest in mystical teachings and in the *Zohar*, together with the reawakening of spirituality within and outside of religion. The inevitable question is why the *Zohar* was concealed from earlier generations, since they were undoubtedly of a more conscious and spiritual level than our own and thus better equipped to understand the Kabbalah's profound wisdom.

A clue to the answer is provided by the *Zohar*, in a discourse on the coming of the Messiah: "Rav Shimon raised his hands and wept and said, "Woe unto him who meets with that period; praiseworthy is the portion of him who encounters and has the Divine capacity to be cast with that time." Rav Shimon then explains this paradoxical remark as follows: "Who unto him who meets with that period, for when the Almighty shall remember the *Shechina* (the Divine Presence), if He shall gaze upon those who stand loyal to her, upon all who are found in her midst, and then scrutinize the actions and deeds of each, He will not find among them a single righteous one, as the scripture warns, 'I looked, and there was none to help.' Agonizing torment and trouble lie in wait.

"Praiseworthy, however, are those who shall merit the joy-giving Light of the King. Concerning that time, it is proclaimed. 'I will refine them as silver is refined, I shall try them as gold is tried.'"

Rav Shimon confirmed that the Messianic Era will bring with it a Light representing the infusion of Divine purity through all the Worlds. The dawn of a new world will appear, and with it, the Light will begin to liberate humanity from our ignorance, bringing a spiritual and intellectual awakening. The *Zohar* also states that, in the days of the Messiah, "There will no longer be the necessity for one to request of his neighbor, 'Teach me wisdom,' as it is written, 'One day they will no longer teach every man his neighbor, and every man his brother, saying know the Lord, for they shall all know Me, from the youngest to the oldest of them."

The *Zohar* here expresses the idea that the Messianic era will usher in a period of unprecedented enlightenment; Messianism represents the essence of hope and optimism, which will grow out of the indelible belief that there will be an eventual triumph of harmony over confusion, of love over hate, an ultimate victory of justice and kindness over oppression and greed. This victory, explains the *Zohar*, is bound to *Chochmah* (Wisdom), and dependent upon the dissemination of the knowledge, and wisdom of Kabbalah.

However, taken all together, these explanations still do not reveal the cause of the perplexities involving the Light of the Messiah and the Final Redemption. Neither have they answered the question of why Kabbalah was not revealed in its full glory to earlier generations. Why now? Is our confused generation in some way better suited to receive the abundance of Light, to savor the ineffable beneficence awaiting the souls present in our age?

Such paradoxes regarding the relative merit of earlier and latter generations were dealt with in the *Talmud* by our sages of blessed memory:

> *Rav Pappa said to Abbaye, "How is it that miracles were performed for earlier generations, yet no wonders are produced for us? It cannot be due to their superiority in study, since in the years of Rav Yehuda (a sage of an earlier generation) the aggregate of their studies was confined to the order of Nezikins (only the fourth of six books of the Mishnah) whereas we study all six orders. In fact, when Rav Yehuda came to the tractate of Uktzin, he would say, I see here all the difficulties raised by Rav and Shmuel; we on the other hand, possess thirteen versions of this same tractate. Then again, when Rav Yehuda drew off one of his shoes (before fasting for rain), rain used to start falling immediately, whereas we torment ourselves and cry out, yet no recognition is accorded us." To this Abbaye replied, "The former generations were prepared to sacrifice their lives for the sanctification of the Name of the Lord."*

It was obvious to Rav Pappa and Abbaye those earlier generations were infinitely superior to them from the standpoint of the immortal inner soul; however, from the point of view of the revelations of the Bible knowledge and wisdom, Rav Pappa and Abbaye were the greater beneficiaries of this vast reservoir of Divine literature than were earlier generations.

The discussion in the *Talmud* anticipates the questions being raised in this generation. It is concerned with the nature of spirituality and its change over time. In their discussions the sages show that they are fully aware of the paradox at the center of the issue; the earlier generations, being more spiritual by nature, needed less in the way of spiritual knowledge from books, yet achieved more in the realm of the working of wonders and miracles. Thus we find a situation where greater knowledge and more intensive study appears to be less rewarded. The resolution of this paradox lies in the spiritual level achieved in different generations. The earlier generations were quite simply, closer to the source of spirituality than the later ones; they demanded far less from the physical world—both physically and spiritually, and were on a higher plane of existence. Being thus less dependent on the mundane Vessels of the physical world, they could maintain their elevated status, and indeed exert control over the direction of the world, through their spirituality. The expression of this control was the manifestation of miracles, meaning the display of their power over the natural order of the universe. Later generations have to rely to a greater extent on knowledge from secondary sources, such as the written word; at the same time, their greater dependence—their Desire to Receive—makes them more capable of drawing and receiving the Light, which is of the highest nature. The Vessels to receive that Light are of a coarser material, but the Light, once it has penetrated, is present in a much more explicit form than in former generations. Instead of one book—we require six books. This is why we require the *Zohar*.

Rav Shimon then said, "There are three signs in a man: paleness is a sign of anger, talking is a sign of folly, and self praise is a sign of ignorance."

—*Zohar III, 193b.*

Part Two

The Body of
Knowledge

Chapter 7

The Methodology of Kabbalah

If man loves a woman who lives on a street of tanners; if she were not there he would never go to the street, but because she is there, it seems to him like a street of spice makers where all the sweet scents of the world are to be found. So, "even when they are in the land of their enemies," which is the street of tanners, "I will not abhor or reject them," because of that bride in their midst, the beloved of my soul who abides there.

—Zohar III, 115b.

Stemming from science and technology, increasingly sophisticated and complex techniques are being developed for gathering and analyzing information; yet the further scientific endeavor progresses down its path, the more its methods seem to hinder its objectives. Today we have reached a point where the terminology of the scientist is incomprehensible to the layman, and often to scientists in other fields. Unlike the scientist/philosopher of earlier generations, who understood how his area of study fitted within the structure of the universe, the scientific specialist today, limits his field of view in the hope of being able to master some small corner of the physical world. The hope is in vain according to Kabbalah, because the physical world, to which science has restricted itself, is a world of effects. The true causes lay beyond in the realm of the metaphysical. Even so, there are a number of assumptions made by the scientific method that reveal the lie in its claims of objectivity, by far the greatest being the assumption that the universe is ordered, and that it obeys the law of cause and effect. Neither of these fundamentals, without which science cannot exist, can be substantiated without recourse to knowledge of higher non-physical modes of existence.

The limitation of the scientific method is that it is incapable of generating new ideas. Max Planck, the Nobel Prize winning physicist wrote: "When the pioneer in science sends forth the groping fingers of his thoughts, he must have a vivid, intui¬tive imagination, for new ideas are not generated by deduction, but by an artistically creative imagination."

Without the subjective element of imagination the objectives of science cannot be reached. How "scientific" can science be if it depends on a motivation that, by its very definition, is unscientific?

The question is, perhaps, unfair; we are too ready to categorize ideas and principles, forgetting often that our categories are arbitrarily selected. Thus we think of science as dealing with knowledge, as its etymological root might suggest, and religion or philosophy as being concerned with truth or essence; the reality is not so cut-and-dry, as both science and religion attempt to arrive at a balance of knowledge and truth. This combination is the wisdom referred to by the sages, as "seeing the consequences of action."

At the basis of this quest for wisdom is the question: "How shall I know?" It appears that on this question science and religion part company. Thus, it is the claim of many modern thinkers that advances in science are a result of the decline of religion as a force in the world. A kabbalistic interpretation of history would challenge this assumption on the grounds that the implied distinction between knowledge and faith, together with the implied superiority of the former over the latter, is altogether false.

Contemporary thought on the subject of the "scientific method" reveals that it is not the all-powerful tool that was once hoped. Perception, psychologists have finally realized, is an active process of sorting and interpreting, not the passive, objective absorption of stimuli implied by the scientific method. In other words, we must have a prior knowledge before we can see and understand a concept that comes very close to the idea of faith. According to Kabbalah, there is no rigid distinction between physical and spiritual forms, and the picture presented is of a total, unified, interrelated system. The prior knowledge that casts doubt on the objectivity of science appears in the form of the Desire to Receive, whereby we have a tendency to project onto "reality" what we want to see, rather than what might actually exist. This distinction between the projections of our physical bodies (the outward appearance) and the essence is the difference in approach between science and Kabbalah. Science asks only how something exists within the dimensions or limitations of time, space, motion and causality; whereas Kabbalah goes further and tackles the question of why things exist at all.

Having made this point, it should be said that science is increasingly becoming aware that there are areas of study that are not governed by the laws of time, space and motion. Instead of observation of interactions being supported by formulae and equations, the emphasis is shifting to the study of changes, so subtle and undefinable, that they may not follow the accepted behavior patterns of the physical world. Perhaps, physical reality no longer represents the final word in scientific discovery.

The explanation on the nature of the universe found in the *Zohar* stresses not only the polarities of existence—time and timelessness, motion and motionlessness—but also the role of humanity as a causative factor. Here we find a description of the true scientist, the vital link played by man in the chain of discovery that stretches from the potential of knowledge in the universe down to its manifestation on Earth. In this view, the scientist is as much a part of the universe as is his discovery; indeed, he is a part of what he discovers, since he acts as a channel for the knowledge of his discovery. Thus we can no longer ignore the psyche of the scientist—the searcher after wisdom—and must take this additional variable into consideration when approaching theoretical physical phenomena. This brings up further problems, drawing us nearer to the mysterious unknown. The question remains, however: is it possible to reach the ultimate goal of absolute truth, and if it is, how does one set about it?

We see an apple seed being planted. We assume that the law of the harvest—as you sow, so shall you reap—is reliable, and that the apple tree will eventually bear the fruit in due course. This is similar to the course of events in the realm of metaphysics where, undetected by any physical means, the delicate interplay of cause and effect is at work. Through the precepts, laws, commandments, prohibitions, allegories and tales of the Bible, Kabbalah teaches us about the workings of the unseen world. The outcome of humanity's actions—the consequences of our motivations—are expressed in metaphors of reward and punishment. Kabbalah reveals the mystical interpretation of the Bible's use of retribution, atonement and suffering. The function of this knowledge is radically different from that of science: it allows us to recognize the paths by which all creative processes emanate from God, Who is the root of all Creation—albeit the hidden root. In the physical world, the interaction of unknown elements may at times be revealed to the scientists though the essence of those elements, which creates the interactions, is nevertheless completely obscured from the perception of the five senses. The strings of formulae and equations may describe the interactions—the effects—but these tools can never reveal the innermost secrets of the reasons for the reaction.

It is the task of Kabbalah, especially in its current state of development to provide such bridges and connections between the physical world of How? And the spiritual world of Why?

The language of Kabbalah is the language of humanity; it permits us to experience wisdom at the utmost extent of our capabilities. To a generation that has witnessed numerous advances in every sphere of scientific research, the wisdom of Kabbalah is no longer remote and inaccessible; on the contrary, its most important teachings are becoming increasingly vital to a growing number of people who want to better understand their world. We come now to another area of difference between science and Kabbalah, an area which in itself suggests why many people believe Kabbalah to be even more complicated and inaccessible than science. The difference may be understood by considering the relationships that exist between objects. When we wish to make a distinction between two objects or events, because we can see no connection between them, we say that they are unrelated, that their occurrence or presence together is coincidental. The root meaning of this word "coincidental," however, has quite the opposite connotation; it implies that our two events have occurred together. The teachings of Kabbalah indicate that two events that occur together, in whatever dimension (time, space, thought, etc.), are related to one another. How did this difference in interpretation between science and Kabbalah arise? The answer is that science, however deeply it penetrates into the world of the senses, is still only dealing with external phenomena. The scientist's world is the manifest universe—a universe, in which the outward structures remain secondary in importance. It is the task of the scientist to examine and report the outer surface, whereas the kabbalist is concerned with pointing out the alignments (coincidences) of one world with the other, locating and strengthening the links between the world of appearances and the world of essence.

If, as we have previously said, the fundamental concern of Kabbalah is with the Desire to Receive, it follows from the foregoing that its (Kabbalah's) task must be to reveal the nature of this force, and the ways in which it is connected with the physical world. Not to do so would imply a separation between the two worlds that does not exist. Here, however, is an obvious dilemma; since the inner or supernal world described in the *Zohar* is without form or outer covering—that which we refer to colloquially as "the naked truth—and cannot therefore be described directly by means of the outer coverings with which we are familiar in this material world. This is the secret of truth, the essence of all elements, which is never affected by change or movement but remains the prime causative factor in all interactions. We can more easily understand this concept if we imagine curtains or veils of various colors placed between us and the sun; what we see is a change in the appearance of the light as it is filtered through the different colored curtains, but, clearly, the actual light of the sun is not altered. The essence of anything being without form remains beyond the grasp of rational thought, and as such cannot be communicated through ordinary language or familiar levels of experience; only after it has become interwoven with the external world of material existence can it be perceived, although even then it remains elusive and deceptive.

Mysticism relates to that which is without form. Thus, Kabbalah has become known as "Jewish mysticism," since it attempts to provide us with an understanding of essence and truth through which a clearer perspective of our actions may be reached. Once we have achieved an understanding of the root or essence of any element, the subsequent interactions resulting from these basic elements will of necessity behave within the limits of the root; this follows the principle that the branch (effect or interaction) and the root (cause) will always be in harmony. With this knowledge of the essence of things we can avoid many of the conflicting viewpoints that hinder our progress and understanding, both as individuals and as nations.

With the esoteric teachings of the Kabbalah, we set foot on a path that reveals the essence, the root, the point of view that can lead us to the Absolute. Once we can recognize the realm of the real, where the veils of the material world are stripped away, we may achieve universal oneness; having unveiled the mysteries and enigmas of life, we shall reach total truth. Hence the names *Wisdom of the Mysterious* and

Wisdom of the Truth have been given to the *Zohar* to denote the subject of this great work, the treasury of the mystical world of ideas.

This, then, is the distinction between science and Kabbalah. Even though both claim to be searching for truth, their expectations and criteria—and therefore their findings—are different. Kabbalah posits the existence of two basic levels of life—spiritual and material—and treats them both as proper subjects of investigation and analysis. Kabbalah also suggests that, rather than being separate, there are strong and necessary links between the two, and that the Desire to Receive acts as a common link. The results of the Desire to Receive can, of course, be seen in the external world of appearances to which science has chosen to limit itself. However, the Desire itself cannot be observed scientifically, since the world of the scientist—whether dealing with astronomy or sub-atomic physics, is one of outward effects, the prime causes always remaining hidden. To rely on the findings of science alone is simply to accept the view that the external world is self-contained and self-constructed. Yet the deeper we delve into the mysteries of the physical universe, the more we become aware that such an interpretation just does not fit the information we now have at our disposal. Kabbalah presents an alternative view to this mechanistic philosophy of existence, one that sees humanity as the ultimate missing link between the Upper and Lower Worlds. That link, technically speaking, is in our very blood, which contains not only material substances but also the lowest spiritual level of the Desire to Receive, as it is written: "*hadam hu hanefesh*" (the blood is the soul).

With its central core of symbolism, the *Zohar* reveals the essence of *nistar* (the mysterious) as timeless, changeless, motionless and eternal. Material phenomena, distinguished by the characteristic of being in the realm of reality, are perceived by our physical channels of perception, while those things that are beyond the range of our senses can be observed in part through interaction. This explains why since each individual can either consciously or unconsciously interpret his specific experiences through his own selective reasoning, the interactions of material phenomena may be differently understood.

CONDITIONS FOR STUDYING KABBALAH

The claims made in this book for the study of Kabbalah are admittedly lofty; indeed, it is hard to imagine loftier. This is because Kabbalah deals with the ultimate reality, the ultimate truth of our essence, so that no claim can be too great. On the other hand, the very power generated by this knowledge might suggest that it would be wiser to restrict its availability to those who would best be able to handle it. It is therefore necessary to remind ourselves of the divisions and scope of Kabbalah.

Kabbalists such as Rav Shimon Bar Yochai, Moses Cordovero and Isaac Luria, and many others in days past who possessed the Secrets of the Bible (*Sitrei Torah*) were capable of transcending the physical realm altogether. It was through the power of the Secrets that many of the legendary incidents in their lives were affected. The traditional prohibitions on the study of *Sitrei Torah* should not, however, be seen as placing chains and impediments on man's freedom of thought; on the contrary, there is no place in the Bible for the suppression of inquiry and knowledge. Is it conceivable that a person should be required to observe precepts and "commandments," yet be prohibited from understanding them to the utmost extent of his ability? Why, then, were such stringent conditions imposed before one could enter the portals of study called *Sitrei Torah*?

We must realize that, unless the intellect has been properly trained and prepared, there are areas in which the mind does not and cannot have a total grasp. This could be compared to attempting to explain the concept of light to a man who has been blind from birth—the explanation will have no meaning for him, since the concept, is one of which he has no knowledge. The inner depths of man, the subconscious mind, remain irrevocably sealed to the probing of the intellect; to avoid confusion and frustration, which might eventually lead to negating the precepts of the Bible, our sages' prohibition was in effect a warning to the student that he was incapable of attaining this knowledge, so that the pursuit of *Sitrei Torah* would be pointless.

It would be foolish to rely on human intellect and reason alone as a passport to the Divine mysteries of the Secrets of the Bible, *Sitrei Torah*; the preconditions laid down by the sages are necessary before one can find the entrance to the sanctuary—without them one would wander about lost and groping in the darkness. It is clearly stated that one must be over forty years old to study these secrets, as well as being male and married. The initiate into this realm must also be well versed in all aspects of Bible study, and must have a thirst for the knowledge of the Secrets that makes his life unbearable without it. This knowledge, without Divine guidance, remains hidden. Thus we find some sections of the *Zohar* marked as containing *Sitrei Torah*: this means that unless the conditions have been met and the gates of this knowledge have been opened, the true meaning of these passages will not be perceived.

However, to study the reasons for the precepts and explanation for the rituals of the Bible, known as *Ta'amei Torah*, was not only possible but was even encouraged by the sages because to understand the order and purpose of Creation leads to the very root of one's existence and being. The individual striving to grasp the moral essence of unity with the Divine Spirit was provided with the proper and necessary tools— namely the precepts of the Bible—to achieve this unification with the Divine Light. A precise and methodical system, originating within the framework of the *Zohar*, meticulously researched and compiled by the Ari and accompanied by Divine Revelation from Elijah the Prophet, furnished new dimensions of understanding regarding the precepts of the Bible and concepts of spirituality. The Lurianic system emerged as a way of joining together human emotion, thus providing spiritual nourishment for all those whose natures contained aspects of these two forces. The scientist, in his pursuit of reason and his unfailing faith in logic, will find in *Ta'amei Torah* (Taste of the Bible), the unity of mind and heart that lie at the very centre of the sublime mysteries of the Bible. The genuinely religious person, needing no confirmation that all the teaching of the Bible are both Divinely inspired and true, will now find and understand the inner meaning and purposes of the precepts revealed by God on Mount Sinai. Each prayer and precept will then reveal forces that unite the physical and metaphysical worlds. The pious observant person, constantly struggling with apparent inconsistencies and contradictions when confronting the problem of good and evil, will find solutions in the Taste of the Bible so profound that they will completely satisfy all his doubts. This should not be taken to imply that complete reliance on one's own thought processes will necessarily reveal the totality of this sublime wisdom; however, one need not be apprehensive when considering the variety of questions that may plague the inquisitive rationalist, since it would be unthinkable for the Bible to forbid the acquisition of knowledge through inquiry, containing as it does the answers to all possible questions.

Wisdom is an integral branch of the Bible, despite the limitations that permeate the fibre of man's finite being; closing the doors of Kabbalah because of the few who have followed false paths would be like forbidding the *Kiddush* prayer over wine because of those individuals who have unfortunately become addicted to alcohol. If the profound study of the Taste of the Bible permits and encourages inquiries into and comprehension of the precepts and commandments, then it is incumbent upon each of us to pursue and acquire this knowledge with the utmost zeal. Ignorance of the paths of Bible and of its inner meaning will eventually lead to contempt and neglect. Without wisdom and understanding, religion—and ultimately, life itself—is meaningless. In the same way, abstract knowledge and intellectual attainment alone, divorced from spirituality and the fulfillment of precepts contained within the Bible, cannot provide nourishment for the thirsting soul.

THE BIBLICAL METHODS OF KABBALAH

Though Kabbalah often deals with profound matters, it does so in language that can be easily understood, a process which in itself contains an important lesson. The method of dissemination of knowledge in the Kabbalah points to one of its central teachings, namely that the Divine word of infinity can be transformed into the finite and limited language of man.

This method is not exclusive to the Kabbalah. Its roots are to be found in earlier written texts, particularly in those of *Mishnah*, and even earlier in the writing of the Bible itself. Both of these contain not only directives and imperatives but also, perhaps less expectedly, stories, songs, parables and histories, which would seem at first to have no logical place in such work.

For the kabbalists, the stories of the Bible are merely the outer covering under which exalted mysteries are concealed. They are only the garment for the body of the inner meaning. Kabbalah seeks to imbue the commandments and laws of the Bible with their true, hidden spirit. Indeed, in the view of the *Zohar*, the tales and parables of the Bible are symbolic reflections of the inner metaphysical realm through which one could perceive the hidden, divine mysteries of our universe. Rav Shimon berates those who take these simple tales as relating only to incidents in the lives of individuals or nations.

Rav Shimon said, "Woe unto the man who says that Torah (Bible) merely presents narratives and mundane matters. For, if it is the nature of the Bible that it only deals with simple matters, we, in our day, could compile a superior version; if the Bible comes just to inform us of everyday things, then there are in the possession of the rulers of the world books of greater quality, and from these we could copy and compose a Bible. However, the uniqueness of the Bible lies in the fact that each word contains Supernal matters and profound secrets. When the angels descend they clothe themselves in Earthly garments, without which they could not exist in this world, nor could it bear to co-exist with them if they were not thus clothed. If this is so with angels, then how much more must it be true of the Bible (in as much as the angels were created from the Bible) and all the worlds, the Bible through which all are sustained? The world could not endure the Bible had she not clothed herself in the garments of this world (tales and narratives).

Tales related in the Bible are merely the Bible's outer garments. One who considers the outer garments as the Bible itself and no more is a simpleton, and will not merit a portion in the world to come. King David said, 'Open my eyes, that I may behold wondrous things from your Bible,' (Psalms 119:18) meaning that one should perceive that which lies beneath the outer garment of the Bible.

"The clothes man wears are the most visible part of him; fools, on seeing a well-dressed man, do not see any further, and judge him simply on the basis of his beautiful clothes. They see the attire as a reflection of the physical individual, and the physical appearance as a reflection of the soul itself.

"So it is with the Bible; its narrations relating to the mundane things of this world are but the garments that clothe the body of the Bible; the body of the Bible consists of its precepts. Foolish people see the outer garment—the narrations of the Bible—and ignore that which lies beneath this outer garment. Those who understand more see the body beneath the garment, but the truly wise, however, those who serve the Supernal King and who stood on Mount Sinai, will penetrate to the soul (of the Bible) which is the essence of the entire Bible itself."

When Rav Shimon says, "When the angels descend, they clothe themselves in Earthly garments...," he reveals two significant secrets in relation to the conceptual reality of mysticism. Spirituality, indicated in the *Zohar* by the term "angels," cannot reveal anything of its essence unless it is clothed by a corporeal garment. It is only when it is thus clothed that the outward actions and interactions reveal something of their essence through the five senses. It is largely through these five senses that we develop the formulae and exploratory devices that enable us to evaluate and store data relating to the external world.

The thoughts of man, before being put into the corporeal garment of speech, remain hidden within the mind of the individual. As a thought is revealed through this corporeal garment of speech, a stranger phenomenon takes place, both in relation to the speaker and the listener. The original thought or idea in the mind may emerge in quite a different form, with quite a different sense, when it is passed through the filter of speech. Neither will the words reaching the ears of the listener necessarily correspond to those uttered by the speaker. Indeed, it is remarkable how many divergent points of view can arise among a number of listeners from an idea expressed by one individual. Taken one step further, we might pass a voice through the medium of a telephone or tape-recorder, whereupon the resulting distortion will often appear to the original speaker to be the voice of someone else; thus we see how misleading the forms of the mundane world can be.

However, cautions Rav Shimon, without these Earthly garments—the cables and vessels—metaphysical essence could not co-exist with, or be observed by this world; this is why the *Zohar* concerns itself with the study of essence, providing instant understanding of its characteristics, and thereby avoiding the potential inaccuracies and misinterpretations that inevitably arise from the study of the Earthly garments of action and interaction.

This then is the first secret revealed by Rav Shimon: Metaphysical concepts and essence are, and must be, clothed in corporeal garments, and all actions and interactions that we observe consist of, and are governed by metaphysical forces.

To explain the subtle but penetrating second secret contained in this passage of the *Zohar*, contained in the section: "nor could it bear to co-exist with them if they were not thus clothed," let us consider the case of electricity. We know electric current is an energy force that must be contained within some sort of cable for it to be useful. In the case of a fallen power-line or a broken cable, there is the danger of electric shock or fire, since the flowing current is no longer contained, and anything with which it comes into contact will be unable to contain this naked energy. Within the metaphysical realm, the pattern is identical; there is a great danger here when an imbalance exists between imparting positive forces and receiving negative forces. The overloading of an electrical cable (the overstraining of an individual's mental capacities) signals trouble, since the receptacle or vessel simply lacks the proper insulation and safeguards for the directed output of energy (the flow of ideas). These analogies are relevant at the peripheral areas of angelic or pure essence of spirituality. So how much greater then is the need for a suitable medium or garment in transmitting the omnipotent beneficence and sublime esoteric wisdom of metaphysics.

The *Zohar*, interwoven with profound philosophic views, reveals that the biblical narratives are the vehicles by which the Divine mysteries of our universe can be understood. Furthermore, through a system of laws and commandments, which act as a garment for true spirituality, the same objective is achieved as is seen in the beauty of spiritual meditation clothed in a garment of systemized prayer, or in the holiness of the Sabbath, when its metaphysical implications are fully understood.

The question of how we can be certain of the interpretation of the metaphysical plane that is revealed by the *Zohar* is carefully considered by its author: "And for those persons who do not know, yet have a desire to understand," declares the *Zohar*, "reflect upon that which is revealed and made manifest (in this world), and you shall know that which is concealed, inasmuch as everything (both Above and Below) is the same. For all that God has created in a corporeal way has been patterned after that which is above."

Thus we learn the sublime teaching that when Kabbalah reveals the essence of unseen elements its interpretation of the concealed will not and cannot conflict with subsequent revealing actions and interactions. We are presented by the *Zohar*, therefore, with instant, immediate knowledge of the root of any matter, obviating the necessity of going through the customary procedures of trial and error, action and reaction, and independently of the fluctuations of time, space and motion.

Chapter 8

The Main Teachings

The vast scope and quantity of Kabbalistic literature should not prevent us from examining some of the main ideas and concepts in a concise form, bearing in mind at all times that such a shortening does have its limitations, and is chiefly intended for the newcomer to Kabbalah. It should be noted that the wisdom of Kabbalah is anything but dogmatic; at all times it is left to the reader to make his choice of whether to believe or not. Very little is left to supposition or suggestive thinking, the central aim being always clear understanding and comprehension.

There is one premise in the whole of Kabbalah, and only one. This premise, from which every idea contained in kabbalistic teaching can be evolved, is that God is all-inclusive and lacks nothing whatsoever. The immediate conclusion that we can draw from this statement is that God is good, since as we shall shortly demonstrate, all aspects of evil stem from the root of unfulfillment. We can see this in our own lives, where all our jealousies, anger and hatred are a result of desires for emotional or physical gratification that is not forthcoming.

Having said that God is complete and therefore good we can now go on to describe the attribute through which we are aware of God's existence—His Desire to Share—which is an extension of God's goodness and is described as the Light. Again we know that sharing, or imparting, is an attribute of goodness from our experience in this mundane world. If we consider any object or person that we would call "good," we will realize that the essential quality that all "good" things have in common is that they give us something that we want. That something might be physical, as in the case of a benefactor who gives us physical gifts, or it might be an experience that gives us pleasure. The aspect of fulfilling a part of our desires remains the constant common factor. We call this factor positive energy, since the positive force is always the one that is complete and tends to fill areas of incompleteness, or negativity. This positive energy is also called the Desire to Impart, or the Desire to Share. The word Desire is used because it reminds us that there can be no sharing of something we do not possess; thus we could paraphrase the Desire to Impart in the form of a Want to Give, expressing the sublime principle that the whole of existence is sustained from moment to moment only by the continuous gift of life from the Creator, fulfilling our "want" or Desire so that we can "give" or Impart.

This is the total of all that we can know or say about God: God is complete and lacks nothing; God is good; God's attribute is the Desire to Impart, and that the manifestation of that Desire is called positive energy.

It might be thought that sharing—the only aspect through which the Creator is made known to us—implies diminishing. Our experience in this world is that after we have shared or given something we are left with less than before. In fact, this is often not the case, since sharing is the prerequisite for receiving. When we share, we create the correct metaphysical atmosphere for the drawing down of forces and energies from Above. Nonetheless, we can safely say that a bottle of water from which half the contents are poured into another receptacle will contain less after the transaction than before. Can we then say that the Creator is diminished, Heaven forbid, by his sharing with us? We have already suggested the answer in the example given above. The bottle is inanimate, and although it contains some small degree of the Desire to Receive (without which it could not exist) it does not have the power to draw down metaphysical energy for itself; when it shares therefore it is diminished. When we share, as we have said, we may appear to have lost something but we differ from the inanimate order of existence in that our Desire to Receive is far greater and is even increased each time we share; thus our apparent loss in the physical world is balanced by a gain in metaphysical power. A second example we might consider is that of a candle, whose light when shared can ignite infinite number of other candles without being diminished. To be sure the candle itself will grow smaller the longer it burns, but this is merely the body or vehicle by which the light is transmitted; the light itself remains unaffected. This is because light does not belong in the four levels of existence— inanimate, vegetative, animate and human—but is, like electricity, a force and a source of energy. As such it has a very close affinity to pure metaphysical energy, which in turn gives us an insight into the importance of lighting candles in ritual and celebration.

To summarize, we can say that the concepts of goodness, beneficence, positive energy, the Desire to Impart, Light, all-inclusiveness, total fulfillment and the lack of the Desire to Receive, are all manifestations of one single concept, all interlocking, inseparable, and comprising in their totality the nature of the Creator.

Kabbalah teaches us that the first state of existence of which we can have any knowledge is the *Ein Sof*, the Endless World. As its name implies, this state is without beginning or end, and within it there are no manifestations of the concepts of time, space or motion. Thus when we talk of events taking place within the *Ein Sof* we should always bear in mind that these are merely distinctions we impose, and not discrete operations within the Endless World. It is only through the separation of existence into the modes of time, space and motion that we can bring our limited powers of understanding to bear on a problem, but the unfolding of the process of Creation in the *Ein Sof* is governed purely and solely by cause and effect, with no discernible extension or movement. The Ari says of this stage of Creation that "There were no distinguishable or discernible levels or grades." The modes of thought and perception by which we attempt to understand the external world only came into being after the process of Creation was finished, as we shall see.

YESH ME'AYIN (SOMETHING FROM NOTHING)

We have said that the Creator's attribute is sharing or imparting; however, there can be no sharing unless there is some agent that can receive. We should also note that the Creator's infinite Desire to Impart implies a desire to fulfill every possible grade and quality of desires to receive: whether there was a desire for health, wisdom, money or possessions, its fulfillment was con¬tained in the original desire to impart.

Here we have what the Kabbalah calls the Thought of Creation, the process by which God's infinite Desire to Impart led to the creation of a Vessel to receive His blessings. Although we talk of a Vessel (or *Sefira*), we must remember that, due to the infinite Desire to Impart, the Vessel must also be considered in the aspect of an infinite number of Vessels, each receiving its individual fulfillment from the Creator. The creation of this Vessel, according to Kabbalah, was the beginning and the end of Creation.

If all that existed was the Desire to Impart, then all that was created was the Desire to Receive. The Desire to Impart could not have been created, for the process of Creation implies that something previously non-existent has been brought into existence; yet we have already stated that the essence of the Desire to Impart is that it is full and lacks nothing. It is therefore inconceivable that the Desire to Impart itself should be created, since lacking nothing, existence must be one of its attributes. We find this explained in Nachmanides'—Rabbi Moses ben Nachman's (also known as the Ramban, 1195-1270) commentary on the line from the Morning Prayer, "He forms the light, and He creates the darkness." The Ramban asks why two different words are used— formed and created—and concludes that the Light (which, as we have said, indicates the Force of positive energy) could not be created, since creation indicates incompleteness, and the Light is always whole. Instead, it was "formed," meaning that it was molded and circumscribed so that it could descend from the *Ein Sof.* The darkness, however, can be said to have been "created," since darkness is an indication of incompleteness, of negative energy, and of the Desire to Receive. As such, it was not present in any form whatever within the Creator, but was created as a totally new phenomenon.

The creation of this Vessel called the Desire to Receive is therefore called, *Yesh Me'ayin,* meaning that something (*yesh*) was created from nothing (*ayin*). The "nothing" from which the Desire to Receive was created should under no circumstances be mistaken for such concepts as emptiness or blackness: it is simply a state of non- or pre-existence, devoid of any attribute.

We have now reached a stage in our description of the process of the Creation of the worlds where the actual essence of Creation has already taken place. Kabbalah justifies its claim that the creation of the Vessel of receiving, (*Yesh Me'ayin*), was the whole of Creation on the grounds that all subsequent emanations and unfoldings are essentially no more than the multiplying results of this primal union of cause (positive) and effect (negative).

It is precisely this mystical "nothingness" (*ayin*) from which all manifestations unfold, whether in the terrestrial or celestial worlds; it is known in kabbalistic terms as the "hidden cause." But this "nothing" is in fact immeasurably more real than any other existence, since it is from this stage that the entire Creation sprang. Creation from nothing actually typifies, and is the prime example of the process of emanation (which presupposes a source of emanation) and indeed the very creative process itself which, as we have mentioned, produces something new without involving the processes of logical thinking.

The relationship between the Creator, His beneficence and the *Sefirot,* is comparable to that between the soul and the body, and between the essence and the vessel that contains it; but there is one difference, in that both the soul and the body differ in nature from the Creator. The soul, while symbolizing the imparting aspect of the Creator, nevertheless has equal characteristic of the body—namely a Desire to Receive.

The idea of "nothingness" is not as complicated and mystical as it might seem at first sight; it is merely a convenient conceptual aid to encapsulate the idea of something that results from a thought, an effect that ensued after a prior motivating cause and which, having been non-existent, is considered as "something that emanated from nothingness." This idea is at the same time simple and profound; it states that there is no such thing as "nothingness," for the world is made from the Eternal Substance of the Desire to Receive. The Creation of the world was the radical formation of this substance into what we know as our world.

This basic insight helps us to understand the paradoxes that permeate the entire Kabbalah. It deals with the world as it actually is, revealing the true immutable substance of the universe, as opposed to the changing appearance and transforming realities of the lower levels of existence. Only the underlying truth abides the real substance of the universe, as opposed to the physical substance that we can touch but which decays and fades as the Light in it dies. Viewed in its simplest form, the Desire to Receive therefore signifies Creation in its totality. As a result of the Creator's original Desire to Impart, which was the motivating factor behind the Creation of the Desire to Receive, there arose a new phenomenon—the Desire to Receive, which is said to have sprung from "nothing" to indicate the elemental characteristic of the Creator.

However, there are still many stages of emanation before we can see the eventual emergence of our physical universe.

SHUTTING OFF OF THE LIGHT

Let us return to the original Thought of Creation, which as we said was to share the Creator's boundless blessings. If we consider this concept of sharing or imparting, we shall see that it makes certain demands on the recipient. We know from our own experience that the mere mechanical act of giving is, in and of itself, unsatisfactory. We do not give advice to the trees, nor do we offer money to animals. Clearly there must be a Desire to Receive on the part of the recipient—knowledge of what the gift entails and signifies—before we can say that we are truly giving.

This is true for all levels of giving and receiving. There can be no sharing or imparting unless the recipient both knows and wants what he is being offered. Penetrating even more deeply into the nature of sharing and receiving, we find that these two criteria of knowledge and desire imply a previous possession of that which is sought. Thus in a daydream we may possess our wildest hopes and fantasies, and taste the enjoyment of them just as though they were real; however, on waking, that pleasure fades away. We learn from this that our desires are constantly receiving fulfillment, but that the fulfillment is never permanent because we are unable to complete the circuit by sharing with others. Nonetheless, we can see that the subject of the Desire to Receive—the content of the dream—must be present before we can think of fulfilling it.

It also follows, however, that we must have lost what we possessed before we can desire it. Who desires food when he has enough to eat? Who desires wealth when he has all that money can buy? It is only after we have lost something that we can want it back; while we still possess it, that particular Vessel or Desire to Receive is filled, and feels no sense of loss.

If the Thought of Creation was to create a Desire to Receive, as we have said, then the creation of the Vessel in its initial form in the *Ein Sof* did not completely achieve this end. This Vessel, which we referred to as

Yesh Me'ayin, is completely and everlastingly filled with Light and therefore cannot experience any Desire to Receive in itself. Indeed, its structure is indistinguishable from the Light, which is the Desire to Impart. The arousal of this Desire to Impart by the Vessel is called the second stage of Creation; "stage" being understood in the sense of cause and effect not in terms of time.

There now exists a situation where the infinite number of Vessels all desire to share with one another. This, however, is not possible because each is, at this stage, completely fulfilled. So sensitive are the Vessels to one another's Desire to Share, however, that each one empties itself voluntarily of its Light. This is the only way in which they can enable one another to share. We could compare this to a rich man deciding to get rid of all of his money so that he can provide other people with the opportunity of sharing their wealth with him. While he is in possession of his money, he has all that he wants, and consequently no Desire to Receive. It is only after he has made himself poor that he can enable others to share with him.

Now as soon as the Vessel brings about this shutting-off, it becomes empty, and is referred to as the third stage. This emptiness brings about the fourth and final stage of Creation, for here we find the completion of the original Thought of Creation. Once the Vessel becomes empty, it feels the lack of what was previously contained—the Light of Creation. Here then we find for the first time the criteria for the existence of the Desire to Receive.

This stage completes the world of Creation that is called the *Ein Sof.* In Rav Ashlag's commentary on the Tree of Life, we read: "This last grade, in its complete perfection, is found only in the Endless World, before the creation of all the worlds."

Rav Ashlag describes the next step in the emanation of the Lower Worlds: "The perfect Will to Receive of the Endless World underwent a Restriction or *Tzimtzum*." This is explained as follows: Since the Desire to Receive, which had been established in the *Ein Sof*, was now receiving the Infinite beneficence of the Creator (Fourth Stage), there arose a feeling called Bread of Shame. The Vessel is receiving continuously, but can do nothing in return inasmuch as the Creator, being whole and lacking nothing, has no Desire to Receive. The Vessel feels Bread of Shame because it is unable to earn what it is receiving. Furthermore it is no longer merely a passive recipient as it was in the Second Stage of the *Ein Sof*, before the appearance of the Desire to Receive. Now it actively wants the Light that it lost in the Third Stage of Creation, but cannot take it due to its inability to offer anything in return. The metaphysical energy generated by this situation brings about the Restriction or *Tzimtzum*. It leads by the principle of cause and effect to a voluntary shutting off of the Light so that it can redress the existing lack of balance.

The resultant emptiness and lack of Light gives birth to the infinite Desires to Receive of the physical world, in which we are placed in an incomplete state so that we can eliminate Bread of Shame by sharing with others who are also lacking, and in this way fulfill our own desires.

This is the reason for placing an unfulfilled Desire to Receive in man. The original Thought of Creation was only to impart the Creator's infinite blessings, but we must first learn how to construct the link between giving and taking by means of precepts before we can bring that Thought to completion.

It should be noted that the arousal of Bread of Shame is very different from the arousal of the Desire to Impart in the *Ein Sof* or the emptying of the Vessels. The concept of Bread of Shame only comes into existence after the evolution of the Desire to Receive, which was the last of the Four Stages of Creation in the *Ein Sof*. "The restriction of Light occurred outside the Endless World, and, following this first restraint, the function of limiting became operative in all the worlds below it."

Some might ask why this whole process is necessary. If the Creator is all powerful, as we have said, why could He not have created a Vessel that would have a Desire to Receive without a Desire to Impart? Why was it necessary to bring us down to this mundane world of suffering and hardship? How can we, with our desire for the pleasures and luxuries of our physical existence, ever hope to achieve re-unification with the Creator? The answer to these questions lies in a closer study of the Creation and a deeper understanding of the significance of the teachings of Kabbalah. To those who have understood the explanation given here, it should be clear that the intention of the Creator was only to do good, this being His very nature. The restriction and emptying of the Vessel in the Fourth Stage of Creation, however, was a voluntary act brought about by the Vessel itself. The laws regarding the flow and transfer of metaphysical energy, from which all physical manifestations grow, were established from the beginning of Creation and are an expression of the attributes of the Creator. However, what is established by voluntary means on a high level becomes involuntary on successively lower levels. This is similar to a law that is established voluntarily by a process of debate and decision in the governing body of a state or country and which subsequently becomes binding on all the citizens over whom the jurisdiction extends.

The essential laws regarding the flow of energy in the universe were therefore established in the process of Creation. These laws include the reasons why we are present in this physical world, and why we are subject to the desires that we experience. Unfortunately, we are prone to forget that what was voluntary in the *Ein Sof* becomes involuntary in our universe. The freedom that our souls chose voluntarily by restricting the Light of the *Ein Sof* was intended to give us the opportunity to redress the balance between what we were receiving and what we could impart to others. Nonetheless that freedom is still subject to the higher laws of Creation. While we can now exercise our Desire to Receive for our own gratification, without any thought of sharing with others, the essential structure of the universe (Bread of Shame, restriction) still applies. Gratification, whether it be spiritual or physical, will still last only if there is a balance between receiving and sharing.

This should answer the often-asked question regarding free will. Why could the Creator not merely have commanded us to obey the laws and precepts, instead of leaving us with the overwhelming confusion of choice? From what we have already said regarding the evolution of the universe, it should be clear that the decision not to receive was ours and ours alone. It was taken because of the imbalance that existed, and it was taken with the sole purpose of restoring balance. If the Creator were to order us to receive His infinite blessings, we would be faced with the same unacceptable imbalance that brought about the original feeling of Bread of Shame, which would in turn bring about a restriction, returning us full circle to our present state. Clearly, our first concern should be to eliminate the feeling of Bread of Shame, for this is the cause of the restriction that cuts us off from the Light.

Furthermore, it is as a direct result of the restriction, that was brought about by the Vessel of receiving, that the forces of evil became manifest in our universe. Until there was a lack or emptiness there could be no evil, since the nature of evil is the unfulfilled Desire to Receive. If we examine our desires for the physical benefits of this world, we find that they all stem from this same root—the lack of fulfillment. Whether our desire is for money, status or possessions, the common element is always the Desire to Receive; awareness that we have lost a fulfillment we once had and can regain it by amassing physical objects. It is because we have lost sight of the true purpose of our existence on this physical level that the Desire to Receive has become more real to us than the Light, which is the Desire to Impart. In showing us the forces by which the universe was created, the *Zohar* provides us with the reasons for our existence, and indicates unequivocally the work we have to accomplish during our brief period in this world.

The question of purpose is discussed by the sages of the *Zohar* who provide the simple answer that the Creator might bestow upon it (Creation) His infinite love and abundance. The thought behind Creation was to share with mankind. The effect of this motivating cause was the creation of man as a vessel for that bestowal, thus revealing the true essence of man as the Desire to Receive. Without this Desire to Receive, the creation of the world could not have proceeded, since the concept of positive energy must, out of necessity, come before the concept of negative energy; one could not possibly desire something without the prior capacity to desire.

Consequently we cannot speak of Creation when referring to the Light, which would designate something newly-made or newly-revealed. Creation refers not to the Light but to the newly revealed phenomenon of the Desire to Receive. Within this concept alone were contained all future manifestations of Creation, including the physical world together with its central point, man.

At the time of the revelation of Creation, the Desire to Receive was like the seed of a tree. A tree is made up of roots, trunk, branches and leaves, all evolving indisputably from the seed, yet not discernable to the naked eye. While contained within it the seed gives no sign of its future development into a tree. Through a series of evolutions, man developed from his root or seed, which was the original revelation of the Desire to Receive. As man appears in our world, he is but an emanation or evolution of that Desire. His inner, hidden essence remains the Desire to Receive.

Now it should be clearly understood that this Desire to Receive is not necessarily degrading, nor is it to be considered a liability. On the contrary, as we have seen, it is the vital pivot of Creation. We can modify our Desire to Receive and channel its demands into areas that will strengthen us and draw us nearer to the Light, but we can never destroy it. This is in absolute opposition to those religions that claim man's objective to be the removal or destruction of the ego. According to Kabbalah, this feat is only accomplished with the death of the body.

Only through a complete understanding of the Desire to Receive in all its manifestations will we come to a better understanding of our inner motivating consciousness and its relationship with our physical actions, and far more importantly, a better understanding of our relationship with our fellow-men. All this information is provided for us by the *Zohar*. The *Zohar* shows us the sublime wisdom concerning the metaphysical characteristics of all Creation, which is the Desire to Receive.

Chapter 9

The Major Concepts

N ot all the concepts of Kabbalah are susceptible to direct description. Much of the analysis of the Upper and Lower Worlds is carried out through analogy and metaphor. Through the use of colorful images, an imaginative link is established between the phenomena being described and the tangible world in which we live, otherwise the world described by Kabbalah would remain forever closed and inaccessible. The imagery enables us to discern the reality and helps us understand more surely the consequences that flow from the inner meaning of the image. It is for this reason that the analysis of the concept of *Yesh Me'ayin* is central to the understanding of the purpose of this imagery. We must imagine a world, spiritual in content, which lies beyond the immediate grasp of the senses. It is a world that exists both within and beyond our physical existence, with its own structure, modes of behavior, patterns of identity and communications; it sees without being seen. This metaphysical realm bears the same relation to the sensible world as the Creator does to the Creation, or the soul to the body. The implication of this analogy is that, in order for the transcendent to be known, it must assume the guise of the material. This has obvious echoes of the concept of *Yesh Me'ayin*, but, whereas *Yesh Me'ayin* is a general description of the process of the Creation, Kabbalah in its wider applications also deals with the realities of our physical existence, whether as individuals or as a people.

The most common metaphor used for describing this progress from higher to lower spiritual levels involves the image of Light (the content), and the Vessel (the container). These exist on all levels, whether we are dealing with different types of spiritual Worlds (*Olamot*), their constituent parts (*Sefirot*), or with the major process by which one level is transformed into the next. The configuration of Light and Vessel at any particular stage in their development is called *Partzuf* (Face or Countenance). At the very beginning of this process, is a cosmic event known as "the Breaking of the Vessels" (*Shevirat haKelim*) where the initial Vessels through which the Creation is to be formed and shaped are unable to contain the power of the spiritual Light that pours into them, and so they shatter. Here, too, we have a warning to future generations not to run before they can walk in spiritual matters.

The result of this cosmic explosion necessitates the formation of far more sturdy Vessels that will be able to contain the Light. By virtue of their thickness, however, Vessels tend to hide the Light they contain, and for which they are meant to act as conduits. In the final stage, where the Vessels are coterminous with the tangible world of the senses, the Light is practically invisible.

Yet the very dynamism by which this process operates also contains within itself its own purpose. The Creator veils his *Or Ein Sof* (Eternal Light) in order to allow this world to exist in its present form. This should not be understood to mean that Creation is separated from the Creator—Heaven forbid—but rather that the spiritual end-product of Creation—humanity—has the facility within him or herself to uncover the source and purpose of his or her own Creation. This is to be achieved specifically through the tools of study, prayer and Precepts, the end goal of which is called *Devekut*, (the Attachment or Unification) of man to his Creator, the reunification of all Vessels and Lights.

Let us now examine these concepts in greater detail.

GIVING AND TAKING—THE PURPOSE OF
OUR EXISTENCE

The Purpose of Creation, as we have said, was to impart boundless goodness to all. The existence of an inherent Desire to Receive was also explained as the expression of one of the profound truths by which the Creation was revealed. This Desire to Receive constitutes the Vessel indicating the exact measure of the bounty to be received, since the dimensions of the Light (forces of goodness) are in exact proportion to the Desire to Receive of the Vessel. The Creator in His wisdom imparts to a spiritual, metaphysical entity no more and no less than is desired, if He were to impart more Light than the Vessel desired or required this would in essence contradict the very nature of His infinite love and abundance, for there can be no degree of spiritual coercion in His goodness. To impart or share with others, on any level can only be considered noble and kind when the recipient desires and enjoys that which is offered to him. However, when the recipient rejects the gift yet the donor continues to insist on its acceptance, one can hardly consider this an act of giving, since the response and pleasure of giving lies in the joy of receiving. There can be little true satisfaction to either party in a gift that is neither sought nor desired, and which is consequently misused or discarded.

It follows from this that God's beneficence cannot manifest itself or prevail without an active Desire to Receive on the part of man, despite God's omnipotence that permits Him to demand and exact our obedience. This sublime idea is emphasized with striking clarity by Rav Shimon: "No influence from Above can prevail unless it is preceded by a stimulus from Below." The symmetry and harmony between these opposing forces, whether we talk of them as positive and negative or cause and effect, is necessary for the continuous and uninterrupted flow of energy. This law is ultimately linked with the question of the fundamental purpose behind the giving of the Bible, with its precepts and commandments.

The reason, according to the *Zohar*, is that the world was created for man with all its blessings and problems. God created this world peopling it with Earthly bodies through which the soul must labor and struggle. By prayer and study of Bible we can attain His objective of purification and sanctity; without the struggle this necessitates we would be nothing more than an idle recipient of God's blessing:

Since the Creator has the attribute of all-goodness, He therefore created this mundane world with its human inhabitants. Thus the Creator could now bestow upon them His infinite love and abundance. However, should all this be true, if God indeed desired to bestow His abundance upon humanity, then why did He cast the noble and divine souls to this Earthly, sublunary plane, into bodies built of clay, where they endure sorrow, temptation and the constant trials of the demonic forces of hatred and ruthlessness that the material body imposes on the soul? He might, preferably, have maintained them in His Heavenly sphere where all spirits rejoice in Paradise, where they merit the ineffable goodness of the Divine splendor which is bestowed upon them. The natural consequence of eating unearned bread, of receiving something that is not earned by labor and endeavor," declares the Zohar "is embarrassment and shame! He eats the Bread of Shame.

Rav Shimon, in the *Zohar*, teaches us that in order to permit us to eliminate this feeling of Bread of Shame, God provided us with the means of performing service to Him so that He might bestow His ineffable Heavenly Light upon purified souls while they are still on this Earthly abode. Man thus eliminates all feeling of shame. Upon receiving the Light, the soul experiences the all goodness and perfection of its Creator and recognizes the delight and contentment that follow the successful implementation of exacting labor.

In the *Zohar's* view, the labor and service one exerts in his or her spiritual study and in the performance of the Precepts and good deeds is commensurate with the Heavenly bounty that one is granted. In fulfilling the Precepts of the Creator with love and understanding, one is exerting one's Desire to Impart, and thus removing the Bread of Shame that prevents the boundless and eternal Light from entering the soul.

Reflection on the conclusion of the *Zohar* that "a lifetime of study of Bible, together with performance of its doctrines, equates with the reward of eternal happiness," leads to the question of whether it is possible to earn perpetual bliss with a mixture of corporeal and Divine servitude. We might compare this to a man engaged in manual labor for an hour a day for which he receives an enormous amount of money, far in excess of the value of the job. According to the *Zohar*, inequality of labor and reward, wherever it occurs, results in the aspect of Bread of Shame and leads to the *Tzimtzum* or Restriction.

Tzimtzum is the refusal of the Desire to Receive to receive, when to do so would cause an unacceptable imbalance. We can compare its operation to an overload switch in an electrical circuit that shuts off the power input when it exceeds a certain level; that level being dictated by the ability of the circuit to pass on, or share, the current. In the same way, an increasing metaphysical imbalance (Bread of Shame), where the soul is receiving more Light than it can cope with, leads to a restriction of that Light. *Tzimtzum* is the essential principle through which the *Zohar* traces the entire need for and process of Creation, with its manifold levels of celestial and terrestrial existence.

The Creator's purpose in creating the universe is, as we have said, to bestow his limitless goodness on humanity, and to share with the soul of man the newly-revealed phenomenon of the Desire to Receive. The spiritual substance that emanates from Him is called the Light of the Endless (*Or Ein Sof*). The Light of the Endless' essential characteristic is that It contains the potential of completely satisfying any Desire to Receive by providing the Desire to Receiver's necessary fulfillment. This beneficence flows incessantly, comprising all the varied forms of spiritual nourishment and displaying an infinite degree of Heavenly bliss. It follows from this that innumerable phases of the Desire to Receive ensued as a result of the original Thought of the Creator, each receiving fulfillment from the corresponding degree of bestowal.

Consequently, the first and primary world, which includes our own highly diverse universe, was included in the boundless, integrated, Infinite and Endless World known as the *Olam Ein Sof*, the World of the Endless.

This phase of Creation is shrouded in mystery and remains beyond the grasp of human conception and understanding. In it, we find the co-existence of the Desires to Impart and to Receive, representing together a simple and absolute unity that transcends material expression and the limits of time, space and motion in its diverse and multi-faceted form. This state might be compared to the seed, which contains all future manifestations in potential form, but which remains in complete unity at its source. Only when it begins to unfold and become subject to temporal and physical limitations do the elemental differences of the seed reveal themselves as separate entities—root, trunk, branch, and leaf.

When the exalted light of the *Ein Sof*, the Desire to Impart. the positive or causative factor, had completely and perfectly filled all existence, the Desire to Receive emerged within the World of the Endless. As a result of its emergence, no soul remained unfulfilled in its respective Desire to Receive; no soul required additional correction or perfection. This was eternal bliss at the pinnacle of its glory. The souls bore no trace of defect, lack or inferiority, no jealousy or hatred of one another, since each received complete and instant fulfillment from the Light of the Endless.

Out of His great love of sharing—a boundless love—comes the Essence of the Creator Who ceaselessly bestows His Beneficence, the symbol of His Divine perfection, the Desire to Impart, in which lies the root of His Endless bliss.

THE DOCTRINE OF *TZIMTZUM* AND
THE JEWISH PEOPLE

The ultimate aim of God's Creation is to benefit His creatures, so that even after the Creation, His radiance permeates the universe. As we read in the words of the Prophet Isaiah 6:3: "The whole world is filled with His Glory." Yet how can we substantiate such a conviction? More particularly, how is it possible to maintain that such universal beneficence exists in relation to the one people for whom it is meant to have a "special" significance and purpose?

The logic of religious thought would seem to imply that the Jewish people, more than any other, will bathe in the glory of the Creator's beneficence, are they not called "the chosen people"? But the evidence of history shows quite a different picture. Jewish history is soaked with the blood of martyrdom, continuous affliction and punishment, intolerable sufferings, despairing hearts and languishing unhappiness. Yet even while enduring the bitter pain and humiliation of exile the Jews were expected to remain true to their faith throughout.

Our understanding of the woes that have befallen Jewry since time immemorial is made easier by the doctrine of *Tzimtzum*, the contraction of the Divine Light. The Restriction, according to the Lurianic system, was executed as a voluntary restraint by the Desire to Receive because "there had arisen in His pure Will the intention to create the worlds." This means that, within the Kingdom (*Malchut*) of the *Ein Sof*, which is the Desire to Receive, there was an aspiration towards achieving equality with the Infinite Light of the *Ein Sof*, which is the Desire to Impart. This was made possible and was destined to be revealed through the creation and existence of our universe. The yearning to be identified with the aspect of sharing or imparting, which corresponds to the Essence of the Infinite, grew out of the aspect of Bread of Shame; this, in turn, resulted from the continual receiving of the Kingdom of the *Ein Sof* from the Endless Light. The result of these

76

two stages was the rejection or Restriction of the Light that created a vacuum; this vacuum, in turn, permitted the emanation and creation of all the worlds through the process of progressive revelation.

This vacuum of limitation, which is indicative of the unfulfilled Desire to Receive, gave birth to primordial space and to the limitations of time, space and motion. Prior to the *Tzimtzum* (Restriction), there had been no destructive influences at work in the universe, since there had been no desires left unfulfilled. However, due to the aspect of Bread of Shame brought about by the inability of the souls to earn the Light or to share their blessing with one another, they caused the Restriction. This, in turn, created the physical universe, which is governed by the laws of Restriction. This area of incompleteness and deficiency brought about by the self-imposed restriction of the Light ultimately leads to the chaos and lack of harmony that is called the evil inclination. Just as the physical veiling or screening of the light of the sun blocks its penetration, so the whole of Creation constitutes an enormous process of restriction or rejection brought about by the original *Tzimtzum* that took place in the World of the Infinite.

The involuntary restriction imposed upon man is due to the nature of the soul that is transformed on leaving its domain in the Upper World so that it can live inside a body of flesh and blood. In the higher worlds, the soul experiences both the beneficence of the *Ein Sof* and the feeling of shame that is a result of the inability to impart anything to the all-inclusive Infinite. Thus the soul descends to this world in order to erase the feeling of shame and thereby achieves fulfillment. However, in passing into this world the soul forgets its purpose in coming here, due to the influence of the Evil inclination, and becomes distracted by the Earthly delights of this mundane existence.

In this connection, the story is told of a poor man who found himself unable to support his family. One day, a friend told him of an island so far away that it took six months to reach, where diamonds were said to be so plentiful that he would be able to bring back enough to last him a lifetime. After consulting with his family, he decided that the difficulties of the journey and the pain of separation from those he loved would be amply compensated for by the rewards he could bring back, and so he embarked on a boat bound for the wonderful island.

When the boat eventually landed, he found that his friend's report had been true. Diamonds lay in great heaps wherever he looked. Quickly he set about filling pockets, bags and boxes with the precious stones, but he was interrupted by a man who informed him that there was no need to make such haste, since the boat was not due to return to his homeland for another six months. It now became clear to the traveler that he would have to find some means of earning a living during these six months since the diamonds he had collected, being so common were of no value in this land. He made several enquiries and discovered that wax was a rare and precious commodity on the island, and that a man with the patience and skill to make candles would surely flourish.

Sure enough, he was soon proficient in candle-making, and earned enough for a good and comfortable life on the island, only occasionally thinking with sorrow of the family he had left behind. When the time came to leave after six months, he packed a case full of his precious candles and set off for his homeland. When he reached his native shores he was greeted rapturously by his friends and family and proudly displayed the fruits of his labor—a pile of worthless candles.

So it is with the souls who descend into this world to correct the imbalance of receiving and sharing through the conditioning agent of the Bible, but who neglect this Divine purpose and become preoccupied with the concerns of the body and of this transient world.

Most people are involved only on the physical level of existence, with its ever changing environment of effects and movement. It is easy to see how the apparently varied and complex interactions of the physical world could distract the soul from its true purpose, just as the poor man was distracted from his true purpose by the necessity of earning a living. However in order to maintain a balance between taking and sharing, the concept of restriction became an integral part of our organic mechanisms. Thus in the process of receiving without having merited or earned the benefit, all the involuntary mechanisms intimately connected with our psyche become operative.

In every country where they are permitted to settle, Jews are known to become involved in business, science and the arts. Their capacity for success in the ventures to which they turn is an indication of their strong Desire to Receive—the most powerful of any nation. However, if there is not also an awareness of the importance of balancing this Desire to Receive with an equally great Desire to Impart, the Jew will find, like the poor man in our story, that all he has to show for his time on Earth is the "wax" of a selfish and self-centered existence.

Through his limitless Desire to Receive he can create potent forces of negative energy, causing the Creator to turn his face away from the Jewish people as a father chastises his son. If these negative energies created by the imbalance of the Desire to Receive are allowed to build up, the Angel of Death is given access to the Jews, and his power reigns over them until they eliminate the negativity by balancing the Desire to Receive with one of Imparting, through the medium of the Precepts contained in the Bible.

For one to capture and retain permanent spiritual nourishment or emotional satisfaction, the interaction of giving must at all times be balanced, thus enabling the Light of all-inclusive beneficence perpetually to illuminate each and every corner of our being.

We see this process at work every second of our lives, in the mechanism by which we draw the breath of life into our lungs and then expel it: The drawing in represents the Desire to Receive, the exhaling of air the Desire to Impart. Clearly the two must be in perfect balance at all times. We also notice that we must breathe in before we can breathe out, just as we must have a Desire to Receive before we can share, and we cannot exhale a greater amount of air than we breathe in. Thus the metaphysical symbol of restriction reflects a highly developed conception of the cosmological process and drama of attraction and repulsion, a drama in which the Divine scheme of man's place and function is revealed as corresponding completely to the original *Tzimtzum.*

The phase of receptivity, which forms one part of this dualism, is on a par with the Supreme Light of the Emanator and enables the created being—man—to join with the Creator in perfect union. The totality of these metaphysical forces forms a balanced and harmonious structure that is made manifest by the enveloping of the Light by the Vessel of the Desire to Receive. As long as the relationship remains a directly symmetrical one, as in the *Ein Sof,* the objective of receiving fulfillment of a permanent nature can be achieved.

The Desire to Receive which, as we have seen, was originally created for the sole purpose of drawing down the Endless Blessings of the Creator, is all too often transformed on our physical level of existence into a Desire to Receive for the Self Alone, without any thought of sharing. A great Desire to Receive is not, in itself, harmful in that it contains within it the constant opportunity of an equally large Desire to Share. It is only when the Desire to Receive dominates the individual, so that it is no longer subject to any restraint, that imbalance occurs and the individual, by his selfish acts and thoughts, cuts himself off from the Creator and from the Source of spiritual nourishment. What we find under such circumstances is an increasingly desperate pursuit of pleasure and satisfaction—without the lasting aspect of the union of the Upper and Lower Worlds that comes from an awareness of the circular concept of receiving and sharing—only the Vessels of pleasure are left, without the Light that is pure and everlasting joy. This is the meaning of the sages when they wrote, "He who desires money will not be satisfied with money." In all our feverish pursuit of the good things in this life, we are apt to forget that these are merely the outward forms, or vessels, of pleasure. Even if we have earned them, by the standards of this world, the pleasure they contain is small and transient when compared to the enduring Beneficence of the Creator that is constantly accessible to us through the Bible and its Precepts, which act as a restraint and a channeling of our Desire to Receive.

THE CHOSEN PEOPLE

It is hard for the contemporary Jew to come to terms with his role as one of the chosen people. The term chosen begs so many questions, few of which are answered satisfactorily by traditional sources of learning. By whom were we chosen, and from whom? Why were we chosen and for what task? Is that task the same today as it was when Moses received the Law on Mount Sinai? How can we fulfill this task today, given the apparent difference in circumstances between our time and the time of the Exodus? It is only when we turn to Kabbalah that we begin to understand the reason for this expression—the chosen people—and its implications for Jews throughout the ages.

We must start by understanding the significance of the Patriarch Abraham, who is called the Chariot of *Chesed* (Mercy). Through his spiritual attributes Abraham was the vehicle by which the potential energy that is called *Chesed* (Mercy) was brought down to this Earth. However, to penetrate more deeply into the meaning of this concept, it will help to study the Bible's description of the Creation.

"In the beginning, God created the Heaven and the Earth... And God called the light Day, and the darkness He called Night. There was evening and there was morning, One Day... And God called the firmament, Heaven. There was evening and there was morning, Second

Day... And God said, "Let be there lights in the firmament of the Heaven to divide the day from the night..."

The first question we have to ask is why there appears to be so much repetition in this description; we are told, for instance, that Heaven was created on the second day, yet it is also referred to in the first verse, where we are told that it was created on the first day. In the same way we learn that day and night were established on the first day, yet the process seems to be repeated on the fourth day, when the lights came into being to distinguish day from night. Another strange feature of this passage is that the first day is called *Yom Echad*, meaning "one day," as opposed to all the subsequent days that are called the Second Day, Third Day, Fourth Day, etc.

These problems begin to unravel themselves only when we recall that the Essence of Creation is the progressive transformation of energy levels, which are known as the *Sefirot*. Now we know that this process of transformation does not alter the root of the energy at all; it merely reveals a different aspect of the energy, just as when water is poured into a number of different colored glasses, we see a different color in each glass, but know that the water has not been altered. The *Sefirot* or Vessels, operate in the same way, diversifying the original energy of the *Ein Sof*. On the first day of Creation, the energy level of *Chesed* was brought into being; however, this *Sefira* represents a complete unified whole, like the seed that contains within itself the potential for all future growth and manifestation. This is why the Bible refers to the first day as *Yom Echad* (One Day), stressing its undifferentiated aspect compared to the following days. We can also see now why the differentiation of Heaven and Earth, and of day and night, are mentioned as having taken place on *Yom Echad* as well as on the Second and Fourth Days; the *Sefira* of *Chesed* contains all these elements, but they do not appear as separate entities until further transformations have taken place.

Let us now return to Abraham who, as we said, represents the *Sefira* of *Chesed*. It is in him that the unique spiritual structure of the Jews has its beginning, just as all the manifestations of the Creation had their beginning in that unified day of *Chesed*. The structure is still only in potential form at this stage, needing to progress through successive transformations before it can become implanted into individual souls on the occasion of the giving of the Law on Mount Sinai. It can be compared to a seed that has been planted in the ground—no longer just a potential for growth, as it was before it was planted, but still keeping the same structure of that seed, and not yet showing any form of change or attachment to the Earth. Thus we can say that in relation to previous states, the energy of *Chesed* is brought down onto the physical level by Abraham, while in terms of subsequent transformations, it still remains in the metaphysical realms of potential.

The next step in the revelation of the real meaning of the term, the chosen people, comes from the inheritance that Abraham gives to his son, Isaac: "And Abraham gave all that he had unto Isaac. But unto the sons of the concubines that Abraham had, Abraham gave gifts, and sent them away from Isaac, his son, while he yet lived, eastward unto the east country." (*Genesis* 25:5-6)

The *Zohar* here explains that "Abraham transmitted to Isaac the totality of the wisdom of truth, so that he should be joined to his proper grade." It goes on to discuss the gifts that were given to the sons of the concubines: "What sort of gifts were they? They comprised the sides of the low grades." Isaac's inheritance was therefore the knowledge of the secrets of the structure of the metaphysical world, so as to permit him to connect with the Upper World. Without this knowledge of the Upper World, Isaac would not have been able to establish his ordained link with the *Sefira* of *Gevurah* (Judgment), of which he is the Chariot. The knowledge that was given to Isaac, we must remember, is still in a state of concealment; it is not something that can be passed on among the people but must be transmitted only to the next level of transformation, which is the Chariot of Isaac.

Hence the *Zohar* asks, "What sort of gifts were they?" If the total system in embryo was given to Isaac, what was left to give the other sons? The *Zohar* replies that these were lower levels of understanding. An incomplete system, since the complete system, which is the system of the Three Columns, had not yet been revealed. According to the *Zohar*, because the sons of the concubines received an incomplete system by which to govern their lives, this is the origin of the various eastern religions that seek to amend their lack of a Central Column by denying the value of the Left Column, which is the Desire to Receive:

It is written, "And Solomon's wisdom excelled the wisdom of all the children of the east." (*I Kings* 4:30). This is an allusion to the descendants of the children of Abraham's concubines who, as we have already said, live in the mountains of the east, where they instruct the sons of men in the arts of magic and divination.

Thus we see that the knowledge of the complete system of Three Columns was passed from Abraham to Isaac. But knowledge itself is not sufficient—there must also be tools with which to put that knowledge into practice. The culmination of this gradual unfolding and revealing of the system came with the exodus from Egypt, followed fifty days later by the giving of the Law on Mount Sinai, which we commemorate by the festival of *Shavuot*. It is on this occasion that we are given a direct indication of the meaning of the chosen people.

"And Moses went up unto God, and the Lord called unto him out of the mountain saying, 'Thus shall you say to the house of Jacob, and tell the children of Israel; you have seen what I did to the Egyptians, and how I bore you on eagles' wings, and brought you to Myself. Now, therefore, if you will obey My Voice indeed, and keep My Covenant, then you shall be a special treasure unto Me above all people: for all the Earth is mine." (*Exodus* 19:3-5)

With Abraham we see the concept of the Three Columns contained within the context of *Chesed*, which is positive energy or Right Column; with Isaac the system evolves within the framework of *Gevurah* (Judgment), which is negative energy or Left Column; Jacob being the chariot of *Tiferet* (Beauty) finally brings the system into its appointed place, which is the energy of the Central Column. However, the children of Israel themselves must be aware of the system before they can be said to have freely accepted it. This is the significance of the passage quoted above, "You have seen..."

When the Israelites put the blood on their doorposts in Egypt to ward off the Angel of Death, they were witnessing the operation of an elevated and potent system of laws. That same system was to be presented to them on Mount Sinai. Having had the basic structure of the Law implanted in them by the Chariots of the Patriarchs, the Israelites were now ready to be presented with the operational tools of Bible.

The *Zohar* tells us that, although the Israelites were thus primed for the knowledge of Bible, it was nevertheless first offered to the other nations, who rejected it!

"It is written, 'Lord, when You went forth out of Seir, when You marched out of the field of Edom, the earth trembled.'" (*Judges* 5:4) This refers to the fact that, before God gave the Law to Israel, He offered it to the children of Esau and to the children of Ishmael, but they would not accept it.

The text of the *Zohar* goes on to relate the reasons for this, telling us why the other nations refused the Bible: "He therefore summoned Samael (the ministering angel of Esau) and said to him, 'Do you desire my law?' 'What is written in it?' he asked. The Lord replied, using a passage to test him, 'Thou shalt not kill.' Then Samael said, 'Heaven save us. This Bible is Yours, and let it remain Yours. I do not want it...

If You give it to me, all my dominion will disappear, for it is based on slaughter and on the planet of Mars; if there are no wars, my power will pass away from the world." Samael recommended that the Law be given to "the sons of Jacob," thinking that the restrictions of Bible would eliminate their power. In the same way, the Bible was offered to Rahab (the angel with influence over Ishmael), who rejects the Law on the grounds that his dominion is based on the sexual urge expressed in the blessing given to Adam in the Garden of Eden, "Be fruitful and multiply" (*Genesis* 8:17). Since the Bible forbids adultery, Rahab fears that it will deprive him of the source of his power.

It should be noted that on each of these occasions the offer is made not to the people themselves, but to the angel who presides over their destiny: "He summoned all the Myriads of Holiness who are appointed to rule over the other nations, and they gave Him the same reply."

It is only in the case of the children of Israel that the entire population is brought together and prepared to accept the Law. This tells us something about the special nature of the attachment between Israel and God. The other nations are ruled by prevailing influences—the instincts that are indicated by the angels—while Israel has chosen to bind itself to the Almighty Himself. This binding is symbolized by the Binding of Isaac, indicating the restricting power of the Central Column. This is also symbolized by the Precept of *Tefillin* (Phylacteries), and by the passage already mentioned, "You shall be a special treasure to Me above all people."

To the other nations of the world, Judaism appears to be a fiercely prohibitive religion. The Angel Samael believed that its restrictive force would crush it out of existence. However, for the Israelite, with his unique metaphysical structure, the Bible enables him to elevate every aspect of his existence to the same exalted level that is represented by the lives of the Patriarchs.

The *Zohar* tells us that God was "like a physician who had a vial of some elixir that he wanted to keep for his son. He was a clever man, and he said to himself, 'I have bad servants in my house; if they learn of my intention to give my son this present, they will be jealous of him and try to kill him.' So what did he do? He took a little poison and smeared it round the edge of the vial. Then he summoned his servants and said to them, 'You are faithful servants; do you want to try some of this drug?' They said, 'Let us see what it is. They tasted a small amount and had hardly smelt it before they came near to death. They said to themselves, 'If he gives this poison to his son, he will surely die and we shall gain his inheritance.' They therefore said to him, 'Master, this drug has been merited only by your son...' So God, being a wise physician, knew that if He gave the Bible to Israel without telling the other nations they would every day pursue them every day and kill them for it."

Just as the faith of the children of Israel, when they were slaves in Egypt, enabled them to overcome the opposition of the prevailing influence of that country, which was the Left Column, the Desire to Receive, so adherence to the precepts of Bible will help them to rise above the predominant influences of Esau and Ishmael.

We have stated earlier that what was voluntary in the Upper Worlds becomes involuntary in the Lower; having chosen the Law on Mount Sinai, we bound ourselves forever to that system of operation, knowing it to be our true salvation. If we choose to neglect it, then we once more enter the realm of the Lower Worlds, with their incomplete structures and influences. The choice presented to us, and open to us at every moment, is between the instant gratification that follows the fulfillment of the Desire to Receive if there is no restriction or sharing and the eternal and never-ending blessing that comes from a system that is functioning at all times in accord and harmony with the structure of the Upper World. The difference may be expressed as the contrast between a contact and a connection. Contact allows only momentary flow of energy, which is why physical pleasures are called instant or transitory.

Connection, however, permits the existence of a permanent channel for the flow of energy from the Upper Worlds. The energy here can be passed on via the channels, so that it does not build up in the system and cause a shutting-off. This is why the reward for adherence to the Three Column System is timeless and infinite.

The Hebrew word used for "chosen" in Bible is *segulah*, from the same root as the Hebrew vowel, *segol*, which is shown as three dots. This should remind us of the Three Columns that comprise the structure of the Bible and of all people. On Mount Sinai, where the souls of all Israelites were present, we were shown how to live within the framework of these Three Columns—how to organize our lives so as to connect with these three forces—Mercy, Judgment and Beauty. In this way the energy represented by the Bible was established and connected for all time to this universe by the presence of the Israelites and their exodus from Egypt. Our heritage, therefore, is to channel these energies constructively, avoiding and eliminating clashes and disruptions in the world, in order to bring about the reign of peace and harmony for all peoples. Nor should this role be understood as implying the need for active intervention, any more than the children of Israel intervened actively in their deliverance from Egypt. The structure of the Three Columns that they established by putting blood on the two doorposts and the lintel, which indicated that they were acting within that framework, was sufficient in itself to raise them above the harmful influences that had enslaved them. In the same way, knowledge of the paths and laws of energy that are given to us in Bible is sufficient to enable us to fulfill our purpose in this physical world.

The nature of all the forces of impurity is the Left Column, the Desire to Receive for Oneself Alone. The essential characteristic of the Desire to Receive is lack of fulfillment. It is therefore not necessary to battle with these forces directly. It is possible to resolve conflicts at their source, rather than having to wait for them to manifest themselves through the workings of time, space and motion.

We have given some indication here of the ways in which the *Zohar* throws light on the expression "the chosen people," showing how the concept of the Three Column System emerged through the Patriarchs, to be established finally on the occasion of the giving of the Law. It is in the completeness of this system, compared with the limited method of only Left and Right Columns that were given to the sons of the concubines of Abraham, that we find the true significance of our role as the chosen people.

SEFIROT

The concept of the *Sefirot* has many and wide-ranging implications in the teachings of Kabbalah. The *Sefirot* or Vessels are the system used in Kabbalah to describe the process by which the unified energy of the *Ein Sof* is diversified in its transmission from the Upper World to the Lower Worlds. Each *Sefira* represents a different form of what we might call "bottled-up energy," with different characteristics and attributes.

The purpose of this section is only to introduce the reader in a general way to the system of the *Sefirot*, so that he or she will become aware of their occurrence and significance in subsequent studies. The simplest way to begin to understand the *Sefirot* is through the patriarchs. Each represents a certain form of energy that is characteristic of one of the *Sefirot*, and is the Chariot, or vehicle, by means of which that particular energy is brought down from its potential form in the metaphysical realm into an active form in our universe. Thus by studying the stories told in the Bible about the patriarchs, we can obtain a closer understanding of the sort of energy indicated by each of the *Sefirot*.

The First Three or Upper *Sefirot* are the means by which Light was brought into this world; they are called *Keter* (Crown), *Chochma* (Wisdom) and *Binah* (intelligence). However since they do not in any way affect our physical world, other than by conducting the Light into it, they are considered a part of *Sitrei Torah* and will not be discussed here. Thus the first *Sefira* that we shall consider is *Chesed* (Mercy), which is the energy we associate with goodness and kind actions. As mentioned earlier, the patriarch who brought down this energy was Abraham who, we are told, was always ready to welcome guests into his house; this is why the *Talmud* says that his home had four doors—it was never closed to anyone in need. When Abraham was circumcised and in great pain, we are told that God caused a period of unusually hot weather, so that people would stay at home instead of disturbing Abraham's rest and recovery. The energy of *Chesed* is of the Right Column, which represents the Desire to Impart.

The second of the Seven Lower *Sefirot* that govern our world is called *Gevurah* (Judgment), and is symbolized by the chariot of Isaac, the son for whom Abraham waited a hundred years. The energy of *Gevurah* is called Left Column, because it is associated with the Desire to Receive. On *Rosh Hashanah* (New Year) we read the portion of the Law called *Akedat Yitzak* (the Binding of Isaac), which relates to how the Left Column (Isaac) was tempered or bound by the Right Column (Abraham), preparing the way for the emergence of the chariot of Jacob. Jacob represents the Central Column, the essential balancing factor that enables the Right Column to use the energy of the Left without destroying it entirely. *Gevurah* represents judgment, not in the sense of punishment that we usually understand but in the sense of the inevitable repercussions of the exercise of the Desire to Receive without first removing the aspect of Bread of Shame. Thus we read that "Isaac loved Esau because he did eat of his venison" (Genesis 25:28) Esau represents the Desire to Receive for the Self Alone, without any Desire to Impart. Isaac is the means by which that selfish desire transformed into a Desire to Receive for the Sake of Imparting by means of the "binding" of its harmful elements.

Jacob, as we have mentioned, represents the Central Column, which is the *Sefira* of *Tiferet* (Beauty), as is indicated by the verse, "And Esau was a cunning hunter, a man of the fields, but Jacob was a quiet man, dwelling in tents." (Genesis 25:27) The word for "quiet" in the original Hebrew found in the Bible also has the meaning of "complete" indicating that with Jacob the system of Right, Left and Central Columns was completed. The existence of the Central Column is the aspect that sets the children of Israel apart from all other races and peoples. It is therefore fitting that Jacob, who is also called Israel, should be the father of the twelve tribes of Israel. These twelve sons, in turn, represent the twelve signs of the zodiac that influence our world; a further example of the completeness that we associate with Jacob.

The fourth chariot is Moses, who represents the *Sefira* of *Netzah* (Victory), the energy of the Right Column. The deeper significance of this association will be investigated in a forthcoming book on the significance and meaning of the Festivals, with particular reference to *Pesach* (Passover). For the present it is sufficient to recall the battle between the Israelites and the nation of Amalek, on which occasion Moses stood on a hill and controlled the swing of victory by raising or lowering his hands. (*Exodus* 17:11)

It is now possible to return to the question stated early of why Rav Shimon was chosen to write the *Zohar*, and to the relationship between Moses, Rabbi Akiva and Rav Shimon.

Our sages of blessed memory relate the following; "The entire treasure was seen with his eye. This refers to Rabbi Akiva, for that which was not revealed to Moses was revealed to him." Nonetheless, the *Talmud* states that Moses, through strenuous effort, eventually achieved total comprehension and understanding. A further affinity between Moses and Rabbi Akiva is indicated by our sages as follows: "There were three men who lived 120 years; Moses, Rabbi Yohanan ben Zakkai and Rabbi Akiva." Moses spent forty years in the house of Pharoah, forty years in Midian, and forty years as the shepherd of Israel. Rabbi Akiva's first forty years were spent as an illiterate, his next forty as a student, and his last forty as a teacher. An even more dramatic connection is Moses' plea to the Creator that the understanding of the Bible be transmitted through Rabbi Akiva.

Now it is clear that the soul of Rabbi Akiva, like the souls of all sages past and present, was present at Mount Sinai when God revealed the Bible to Moses why then was it to Moses that the honor of receiving the Word of God was given and not to any of the other noble souls present?

Moses, as we stated, encompassed both the Inner and Encircling Lights. Their power, however, was not sufficient for him to withstand the immense infusion of Light that would be transmitted from Mount Sinai. To understand this requires consideration of the spiritual character of the archetypes of the Bible. The *Zohar* states that while both Cain and Abel had aspects of the Right Column it was the weaker of the two in Cain, who was dominated by the Left Column, whereas Abel had subjected his Left Column to the rule of the Right Column. Rav Isaac Luria (the Ari), in his book the *Gate of Reincarnation*, tells us that the soul of Able was reincarnated within Moses where its good aspects were made manifest. This is the meaning of the verse "and she saw he was good." (Exodus 2:2) Consequently, Moses was deemed fit to act as a chariot for the Supernal wisdom that the Creator imparted to Israel.

On the other hand, while it is obvious that Rabbi Akiva also acquired the necessary degree of spiritual consciousness, the Ari tells us that the root of his soul stemmed from that of Cain. This was to enable him during his lifetime to correct the predominance of the Left Column, so that his inner spiritual capacity could eventually strike a balance with his evil inclination. For this reason he spent the first forty years of his life, as we have said, as an illiterate, despising the scholars and learned sages of his day and building up the power of his Left Column. So great was his spiritual potential, which he realized in the last forty years of his life, that he had to enlarge the capacity of his evil inclination as spiritual anchor to this physical world.

Rav Shimon was a reincarnation of Moses and also being possessed of both the Inner and Encircling Lights was chosen to be the transmitter of the *Zohar* as Moses transmitted the Bible.

The *Sefira* of *Hod* (Glory) is represented by Aaron, who belonged to the tribe of Levites. The energy here is of the Left Column; *Hod* being the manifestation of the total energy of the Left Column in this world. This is indicated by the splendor finery of Aaron's robes when he became *Kohen Gadol* (High Priest)—Although it should be noted that the tribe of Cohen belongs to the Right Column.

Joseph, the son of Jacob, is also a chariot of the Central Column, representing the *Sefira* of *Yesod* (Foundation). It is through him that all the energy of the Upper *Sefirot* is brought down onto this physical level of *Malchut* or Kingdom. He is the storekeeper who dispenses nourishment to the people, just as he was chosen by the Pharoah to control the sorting and distributing of food in the years of plenty and famine in Egypt.

The last *Sefira* is *Malchut* (Kingdom), represented by King David. *Malchut* is the Desire to Receive, and the world in which we live. Thus we see that David was a man of war and conflict, epitomizing the struggle for existence on this physical level. It was because of this warlike nature that he was considered unworthy to build the Temple. More than any other of the Patriarchs, he represented the battle of good and evil that is associated with the "kingdom" in which we live.

The brief exposition of the nature of the *Sefirot* and their connections with the chariots of the Patriarchs should provide the beginner with some new insight into the stories of Bible. On studying them, one should bear in mind at all times the characteristics that we have mentioned here and attempt to understand the events and actions in the light of the aspect of "bottled-up energy" or *Sefira*, that each represents.

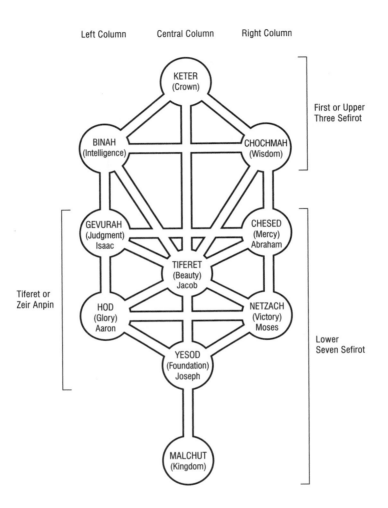

VESSELS AND LIGHTS

The Divine Light of the Creator was not concealed in one action but is gradually transformed in a number of stages; these stages are the Vessels appropriate to the quality and quantity of the Light that exists at each level of *Tzimtzum*.

Vessels are completely the opposite of Lights. The Vessels represent the Desire to Receive, the negative aspect, while the Lights express the Desire to Impart, the positive aspect. The first Vessels to develop after the *Tzimtzum* were those with a greater degree of purity and a consequently lesser degree of the Desire to Receive. This is a law of the metaphysical realm. The opposite is true of the Lights; the first Lights to emerge were those with a lesser degree of the Desire to Impart, and a consequently smaller amount of energy. The emanation of a complete structure is called *Partzuf,* or Countenance. In it are found five *Sefirot* or levels of emanation, known as *Keter* (Crown), *Chochmah* (Wisdom), *Binah* (Intelligence), *Tiferet* (Beauty), and *Malchut* (Kingdom). The fourth *Sefira, Tiferet,* contains the six *Sefirot* of *Chesed* (Mercy), *Gevurah* (Judgment), *Tiferet* (Beauty), *Netzach* (Victory), *Hod* (Glory) and *Yesod* (Foundation).

Keter is the purest Vessel, representing the least amount of the Desire to Receive; *Malchut* represents the epitome and complete manifestation of the Desire to Receive. The various Lights of the soul, commonly referred to as the levels of consciousness are called *Nefesh* (Crude Spirit)—the lowest level, *Ruach* (Spirit), *Neshamah* (Soul), *Chayah* (Living) and *Yechidah* (Individual), this last being the highest and purest level of the Lights. The Lights of *Nefesh,* the lowest level, are first clothed by the highest Vessels, since they are also the first to issue forth from the world of *Ein Sof.* It should be clear that the Upper Lights, which appear later, cannot descend to their proper Vessels until the Lower Vessels have unfolded and evolved to permit the Lower Lights to become clothed in their respective Vessels. This means that until *Nefesh,* the lowest level of spiritual existence, has reached the level of *Malchut* where it is made manifest in the physical world, none of the higher Lights can attain their proper Vessels. The paradox we find in this process, whereby the lofty and elevated must wait for the lowly, is a profound expression of the essential duality of the universe; it also explains in greater depth the question touched on earlier, relating to the nature of the levels of spirituality that have existed through the ages, culminating in our age, which is called the Age of the Messiah.

Our generation represents the lowest and final Vessel of the *Partzuf,* yet it is by virtue of the appearance of this lowly Vessel that the Lights of *Nefesh* can finally achieve their appointed place. In doing so, a vacuum is created in the Upper Vessels allowing the Upper Lights to be drawn down. This is the character of our era, where the gross manifestations of *Nefesh,* the lowest level of spirituality, are revealed in the existence of so many physically-oriented, pleasure-seeking, non-spiritual people while at the same time we witness the re-awakening of spirituality among the young, and advances in the world of science that threaten to destroy— tliterally as well as intellectually—all our established concepts of order and purpose.

The question of why the full meaning of the *Zohar* was not revealed to earlier generations, who were without doubt on a higher level of consciousness and spirituality, and therefore more suited and prepared for it, is no longer a problem. We know that the esoteric mysteries of the Bible and the underlying reasons for the Precepts are derived from the Lights that are contained in the *Sefirot,* while the practical aspects of ceremonial and ritual grow from the Vessels of the *Sefirot* themselves. It follows that earlier generations, whose nature is that of lower levels of soul clothed in higher levels of Vessels, were more complete and developed in the fulfillment of the observances of the practical elements of the Bible, whereas our generation will bear witness to the perfect understanding that results from the complete union of the Lights with their appointed Vessels.

THE MIDDLE POINT

While many of the main teachings of Kabbalah can be stated in a simple form, it is necessary to remember that some of the concepts of kabbalistic technology employs highly intricate explanations and cannot be reduced to simple terms without losing their significance. One such teaching is the concept of the Middle Point, linking in many ways ideas introduced in previous discussions relating to the Creator, Creation and man. More specifically, the concept of the Middle Point sheds light on the difficult problem of "Nothingness," both in the spiritual and physical realms. It is particularly relevant to the contemporary issues being raised in the field of physics.

The unfolding, emanation and evolution of *Yesh Ma'ayin* (Something from Nothing) is frequently described by both the *Zohar* and the Ari. The symbol used to describe the chain of existence from the "hidden cause" is the Middle or Primordial Point. This point is what Rav Shimon bar Yochai and later kabbalists refer to as the Beginning: It is the Source of all being, the concept which led to all subsequent creations. The first word of the Bible, *Beresheet*, usually translated as "In the beginning" bears witness to the supreme and paramount importance of the Point of Creation.

The abstruse and complex *Zoharic* interpretation of Creation, in which it describes the emanation of the Middle Point after the Restriction (*Tzimtzum*), gives a clear indication of the difficulties that will be encountered. It shows here that the entire Bible must be understood on a mystical level if it is to be understood at all. The body of the Bible is no more than a *corpus symbolicum* through which the vast fountain of the Divinity and its metaphysical concepts become revealed.

"Know that before the emanations were emanated and the creations were created," declares the Ari, "that the Supernal simple Light filled the entire existence (within the *Ein Sof*), and there was no empty space or vacuum whatsoever. For everything was filled with the Light of the *Ein Sof,* the Endless World. However, when the simple Desire arose (and restricted itself) to permit creation of the worlds and to emanate emanations and thus bring to fruition the perfection of its deeds, names and appellations, this (Restriction) was the cause of the creation of the worlds. And behold the light and its abundance then restricted itself within the middle point." (*Ten Luminous Emanations*)

The Middle Point is so called because it is the Vessel for receiving the Endless Light, and is also known as the *Sefira* of *Malchut*. However, before the Restriction, the Middle Point (*Malchut* or Kingdom) was completely and endlessly filled with the Upper, Supernal Light, beyond any measure or limit. Consequently, this world is designated as the *Olam Ein Sof*, the Endless World. Here where the Middle Point is united with the Light, encompassed and encircled by it, it is as if the Middle Point were receiving the Light in the exterior of the Vessel and is thus filled infinitely and perpetually. In this manner, it is possible for the Middle Point to hold immeasurable and limitless Supreme Light.

From our discussion of the Thought of Creation, we acquainted ourselves with the purpose of the Desire to Receive which is contained within the Endless Light and the Endless World. While this Desire is called the Kingdom (*Malchut*) of the Endless, nevertheless it did not exert any limitation nor circumscribe any restraint in relation to the Endless Light. At this stage of Creation, the gradations, variations and differentiations of the Desire to Receive were, as yet, unrevealed. Within the Endless World, the Desire to Receive was itself a pure Light and not separated from the Light by any discrimination or severance.

Within this absolute and indivisible unity of the Endless World, there lies a paradox. The Supreme Light has the inherent characteristic only of imparting, lacking any degree of the Desire to Receive—yet this Light co-exists with the Desire to Receive which, by its very essence, should bring about a diversity or severance of some sort. At this stage, however, they are considered indiscernible and are in complete and pure unity. The reader might refer to the concept of *Devekut* for further insight into this problem.

The Infinite Light or Vessel of the *Ein Sof,* according to Kabbalah, belongs to the area that is totally beyond human comprehension. However, the identity of the Desire to Receive with the pure Light can reveal the necessary characteristic of that Desire within the *Ein Sof* from the standpoint of man. It signifies that the Desire to Receive, despite its innate craving for the Ineffable Goodness, is essentially an embodiment of all other positive characteristics as well—imparting, sharing or bestowing—with an admixture of personal desire and ulterior motives. The mystical interpretation of the Desire to Receive that exists concurrently with the Light within the *Ein Sof* is known as the doctrine of the *Sefirot.* This fundamental contemplation of the union between Light and Vessel is the common denominator of sharing. The Desire to Impart of the Light and the transmutation of the Desire to Receive provides us with an indication of the connection between these two opposing forces in the infinite spheres that causes them to be considered inseparable and indiscernible. In this way, we can understand the sublime teaching that the Desire to Receive did not bring about any boundary or limitation upon the Endless Light, inasmuch as no diversity of essence between them had been revealed at that point.

We are more concerned, however, with the second phase of Creation, leading to an understanding of the relationship between God and His Spiritual Substance of Light, that which He created (Creation itself), and the critical part played therein by man, leading to the understanding of our proper objectives in this world.

"Following the Restriction, whereby the Light withdrew around the Middle Point, there remained an empty space, atmosphere or vacuum surrounding the exact Middle Point." (*Ten Luminous Emanations*)

This vacuum after the Restriction should be understood as the First Effect. Here lies the entire secret of kabbalistic thought and I urge the reader to ponder this concept repeatedly: There is no disappearance in Light or energy. This we may more fully understand through an example. A fertile male can procreate life almost all of the time. Whether this procreation actually occurs is decided by the Vessel or female. If she is sterile then when the seed reaches the Vessel (the womb) there is no reaction on the part of the egg. This lack of procreativity we call "vacuum." The energy of the male is not diminished. It is the inability of the female to encompass and thus reveal the Light or energy. A further example of the mysteries and paradoxes that permeate the teachings of Kabbalah is the concept of "speed of light." It is a firm principle in kabbalistic thought that light is motionless. Therefore the speed of movement can only relate to the Vessel—how the vehicle that reveals to us the energy, (light bulb, or lightning), can be measured. The internal energy is immeasurable and timeless. It can be seen as a symbol of profound and penetrating vision that leads to the complete comprehension of the inner meanings and paths of Kabbalah.

Kabbalistic scholars have resorted to figurative terminology in their study of the profound mysteries of Kabbalah, using as references the material objects, ideas and functions of our ordinary world. The nature and manner of this symbolic form has been chiefly responsible for the difficulty of penetrating into the depths of the inner wisdom of Kabbalah. Nevertheless, this intricate and at times confusing maze of symbolism is the very key to its understanding. This paradox can be understood if we consider the use of imagery in other forms of writing and common usage, where we often use one concept to illuminate another. Thus, when we refer to prayers and Precepts as "cables," we are using the image to emphasize the drawing aspect, or their function as paths through which certain sorts of energy can be channeled, just as electricity can be transmitted through a cable. We are not, however, referring to the physical characteristics of a cable, such as its dimensions, shape or color, and anyone who does not realize this is likely to mistake our original intention. It is the same with the use of images and symbols in Kabbalah, where one specific attribute of a physical entity may be referred to by using the image of the whole entity. If we are aware of the precise usage we can learn from the symbol, but if we select the wrong attribute, or impute superfluous attributes, we will be misled. It should be borne in mind at all times that all the words of Kabbalah are but images and symbols, since words alone cannot express the inexpressible mystery of the Creation.

In determining and expressing ideas concerned with the invisible world, the scholars of the Kabbalah have made use of the names of the tangible dimensions of this world. In effect each name symbolizes, explains, and represents its own Upper Entity, which is located in the constellation of the celestial regions. From this we learn that the Lower Realm is patterned after the Upper, preceding Realm, as we read in the *Zohar*: "Nor does the smallest blade of grass on the Earth fail to have its specially appointed star in the heavens."

All that exists in the Celestial or Supernal World will, in time, prevail and show itself in a reflected image on Earth, yet the totality of Upper and Lower Worlds are always one whole entity. This provides the insight and knowledge required for our understanding of metaphysical concepts.

The Upper and Lower Worlds can be compared to a tree when we come to consider the picture of Creation, by which the natural laws and principles of both metaphysical and physical realms operate in our universe. It is the tree of energy, with its feedback of activity—the Tree of Life referred to in the *Zohar* and the book called *Etz Hayim* of the Ari, in which he devised what has come to be recognized as the most comprehensive and lucid interpretation and systematic description of the *Zohar*. The Tree of Life has its roots buried deep underground, beyond the realm of perception; all we see are the results or effects of that root in the form of trunk, branches, and leaves. Thus through the principles of corresponding natures we can observe the unknown areas of the Upper Realm by examining the interactions of that which is Below. With the knowledge of Kabbalah, we can trace the origin and development of those cosmic forces and principles that ultimately influence the behavioral patterns of man, and shape the course of mundane history.

The source of all reality takes place in the Upper, undetected Sphere, (the root) descending and evolving through the process of cause and effect (or imparting and receiving) in an intelligible order down to the level of our existence. The physical universe, with its cosmic elements, is the bodying forth or evolution of the spiritual region (trunk, branches, etc.). There is no wisdom or science to be found whose objects and functions are so closely integrated as in the law of cause and effect, which is the infinite progression of the esoteric knowledge of Kabbalah.

We can now better understand this stage in the evolutionary process of Creation in which, following the restriction of the Middle Point, which is the Desire to Receive, a vacuum or empty space was established.

"At this point," declares the Ari, "there were no distinguishable or discernible levels or grades, despite the withdrawal of the light." Why then, we might be justified in asking, are we witnesses to an undisputedly multi-faceted Creation? "The distinction of a multitude of manifestations," answers the *Zohar*, "is due solely and primarily to our way of perceiving the world, a result of the perception of the Light by finite, created beings." Furthermore, from what we have said regarding the relationship between the Upper and Lower Worlds, it must follow that the infinite manifestations of our terrestrial realm are a metaphorical indication of the yet more remotely hidden worlds of the celestial regions.

The innermost being of the Divinity, the Light as an extension of the Deity, motivated and initiated the creation of the soul and the *Sefirot* or Vessels that would ultimately clothe and benefit from its beneficence. The motivating Thought of Creation, which was to impart beneficence to man, through the Desire to Impart, influenced the emergence of the multiform degrees of the Desire to Receive. This is due to the fundamental characteristic of the Light, which could fill and nourish these Vessels with an infinite quantity of abundance. In other words the Light, in its infinite Desire to Impart, necessitated and caused the manifestation of a correspondingly infinite number of souls that would desire this beneficence. Thus this first and primary world, the world of *Ein Sof* (the Infinite), is given this symbolic name in accordance with the endless variety of degree of receiving that took place within the union of the Light with the Kingdom (*Malchut*) of the *Ein Sof*. In all this it should be remembered that the Divine Light itself remained a total unity, as noted in the passage, "I am the Lord, I do not change." (*Malachi* 3:6)

We can compare this process of undiminished imparting to other varieties of power and energy—the endless waterfall, which can fill an infinite number of vessels without being affected, or an electric current that can supply power for a wide range of appliances that may differ in their subsequent manifestation of that power (light, heat, motion) without affecting the source of the energy. In all these cases, the division that is ultimately seen is a result and dependent on the energy of the source, which is clothed and confined within the vessels. In the source of the energy itself, however, there is no change.

Let us now return to the section of the *Zohar* that deals with the opening lines of the story of Creation, bearing in mind that the "beginning" referred to is the emergence of the Middle Point:

When the desire of the King began to take effect, a hard spark (as from the striking of two stones, one rejecting the other and thus producing a spark, as with the Desire to Receive in its rejection of the flow of Light from the Desire to Impart) engraved engravings in the Upper Supernal Light (thus causing a vacuum, just as in the hewing of a stone, which at the moment of the chisel's stroke, leaves an empty space in the stone and causes a spark, which is otherwise

*known as the spark of friction). This hard spark sprang forth
within the innermost recesses of the mystery of the Olam Ein Sof,
the Endless World, (the final phase of the Endless, which is referred
to as (Kingdom) Malchut of the Endless World) as a potential and
formless concept of aura, indiscernible and undetected, wedged
into a ring. This is the mystery of the Middle Point which, before
the Restriction, was unutterable and inexpressible, but at this
stage, is expressible to the extent of being comparable to a circle in
that it has no beginning or end nor phases by which it can be
detected, so that it is indiscernible. It is neither white nor black,
neither red nor green.*

The *Zohar*, in stressing that it was "not black," seeks to avoid the
misunderstanding that might arise when considering the Restriction of
the Light. Since it is discussing the withdrawal of the Light, it might
seem that the state of "absence of Light" was the same as blackness, this
being its customary definition. However, in its determination to render
the exact nature of the stage that became manifested immediately
outside the Endless World, emerging as the act of Restriction, the *Zohar*
insists that this particular stage, being totally imperceptible, lacks any of
the attributes of color—including the total lack of it.

After the *Tsimtzum* or Restriction, whereby the Vessel of *Malchut*
(Desire to Receive) brought about a separation from and rejection of the
Endless Light, the desire of the Vessel was in no way diminished. We
can see this from the story that appears further on in this book of the
rich man and the poor man, when the poor man refuses the food
(Restriction), he does not thereby affect his hunger in any way, he
merely states that he is unable to exercise his Desire to Receive under
the circumstances, due to his feeling of Bread of Shame. Here too the
desire for spiritual nourishment remains constant.

Since the inherent nature of the Light is to impart, it continues to
attempt to fulfill the desires of the Vessel, as it did continuously in the

Olam Ein Sof. However, at the moment of the Restriction, when the Vessel brought about the separation, the Light withdrew. The *Zohar* talks of the return of the Line of Light from the *Ein Sof* because its return in its entire form would have led to the re-awakening of the feeling of Bread of Shame, since the Vessel had not, at this stage, been able to do anything to share that which it wanted to receive.

The return of a circumscribed and limited measure of Light obviously failed to fill the Vessel completely, as we have said. This paved the way for the Vessel to overcome the Bread of Shame, which is the fundamental purpose for the creation of the worlds, culminating in the creation of our universe. Due to its insatiable desire for the limitless Goodness of the *Ein Sof,* which remained unfulfilled by the limited return of the Line of Light, the Desire to Receive now became recognizable through its exertions to satisfy its desire. Prior to the Restriction, when all desires were instantly fulfilled, the Desire to Receive was motionless and indiscernible due to its union with the Light (*Devekut*). It is only after the separation, after the vacuum and the return of the Line of Light, that an awareness of something lacking comes into being within the Vessel. At this point, movement comes into being, indicating the emanation of the world of time, space and motion in which we exist, prior to our removal of that aspect of Bread of Shame and our subsequent re-unification with the Blessed world of the *Ein Sof.*

Rav Aba was once going from Cappadocia to Lydda in company with Rav Yosi. As they were going they saw a man approaching with a mark on his face. Rav Aba called to him and said. "Tell me, what is that mark on your face?" He replied. "I was once travelling with my sister, and we turned in to an inn, where I drank much wine. All that night I was in company with my sister. In the morning I found the host quarrelling with another man. I interposed between them and received blows from both and was severely wounded, but was saved by a doctor." Rav Aba asked who the doctor was and he replied "It was Rav Simlai." "What medicine did he give you?" asked Rav Aba.. He replied, "Spiritual healing."

—Zohar III, P. 75b.

Everyday below is controlled by a day above. Now an act Below stimulates a corresponding activity Above. Thus if a man does kindness on Earth, he awakens loving kindness Above, and it rests upon that day, which is crowned therewith through him. Similarly if he performs a deed of mercy, he crowns that day with mercy and it becomes his protector in the hour of need.

—Zohar III, P. 92a.

Part Three

Making the Connection

Practical Applications

Chapter 10

Operational Tools

lthough Kabbalah deals with matters of an elevated spiritual
nature, it does so with the sole intention of providing people
with tools of a high enough quality to fulfill our own potential.
The teachings of Kabbalah are not intended to be confined to the
realms of abstract thought processes or disciplines learned for the sake
of discipline alone, but should lead directly to the application of those
elevated thoughts and methods of learning in the realm of action.
Moreover, the intellectual substance of the Bible is of a special and
unique nature providing all people with tools for the soul which,
properly understood, will enable us to articulate in the world of action
what is asked of us in the world of thought and feeling.

A kabbalistic analysis of the Precepts, the commandments of the Bible,
gives a person insight into the essence of all manifestations on the
physical level, by demonstrating how the eternal laws of the universe
manifest themselves in the context of our material world. Those people
who regard the Precepts as outmoded or irrelevant are ignorant of their
true nature, which is that of conduits or cables through which Divine
Revelation, Omnipotent Beneficence, the profound Wisdom of the
Creator, and the metaphysical laws and principles of the universe are
revealed and understood.

The *Zohar*, sensing that the Precepts are but profound symbols filled
with priceless and unused treasures, goes far beyond the customary
approaches to knowledge, as we shall see. Religious authorities have
classified many of the Precepts as statutes, meaning laws that are
ordained by the Bible, and which we are to observe even though a

reasonable or meaningful explanation cannot be given. Some commentators have seen these statutes as an example of the absolute compliance to the decrees of the Creator that is required of religious people as an indication of their faith.

Kabbalah, however, reveals the broader arena of doctrine and statute that flows from the Bible, where strict observance is combined with a fundamental belief in the legitimacy and necessity of inquiry. In explaining the significance and function of each Precept, philosophical discourses that do not have a basis in eternal and universal wisdom of the Kabbalah are bound to lead to divergent, or even opposing points of view, whereas the root knowledge contained in Kabbalah reveals the eternal nature of the unchanging truth that is contained in every word of the Bible. The kabbalistic attitude towards the fulfillment of these Precepts no longer reflects a dogmatic approach whereby the individual is required to demonstrate his allegiance to the Lord by adhering rigorously to the confines of strict obedience. There are many areas, Kabbalah tells us, where our feeble mental capacity is totally unable to grasp the understanding of the mysteries of the universe and of its Creator, but within these limitations there are also many aspects of our world that are revealed through knowledge of the workings of the metaphysical realm.

Kabbalah is a path along which the seeker no longer gropes in blindness and fear; it is a path that has been trodden in the full light of wisdom by the sages of the past, who have foreseen the problems and pitfalls that would face the novice, and have shared with us their knowledge so that their example should be a light for future generations. True spirituality deals with the firm principles and laws of the universe, cognizant of the fact that any deviation from that path might result in physical as well as emotional disturbances. It can be regarded as the system of laws that govern and generate the physical and ethical laws of the world we live in. The spiritual man thus becomes one who has knowledge of the workings of this higher system and of its applications and implications in the lower physical world.

The kabbalistic philosophy regarding Divine commandments and ritual is best described by the legend of Hillel. According to this legend, a student came before Hillel and asked him if it was possible to teach for Hillel to teach him the entire Bible while standing on one leg; Hillel replied, "That which is hateful to you, do not do unto your neighbor. This is the entire Bible. The remaining decrees and commandments are but a commentary on this basic principle."

This exchange raises a great number of intriguing problems. What, firstly, was the intention of this student in asking his question? Was he expressing cynical doubt about religion, seeking a short cut through the wisdom of his teacher or was he sincere in his search for the touchstone of biblical thought and practice? Then we might ask whether Hillel's reply is merely intended to silence a foolish student, or whether it truly contains the essence of the Bible. The difficulty connected with Hillel's answer lies in the fact that the Precepts of the Bible are divided into two categories: Those directed at the relationship between humanity and the Creator, and those concerned with man and his fellow man. How, then, can the one precept of "love your neighbor as yourself" include all the Precepts of the Bible, as Hillel seems to be saying, including even those relating to man and his Maker? Furthermore with regard to the latter part of his reply are we to understand that all the other six hundred and twelve precepts merely explain the one basic ethical law and precept of "love your neighbor"?

A close examination of the dialogue reveals the very essence and purpose of the Bible itself. The student's request refers to the ultimate objectives of the Bible—the termination of the path along which deeds and service lead. The entire content of the Bible, its laws and commandments, are nothing more than instruments for the improvement and development of self control. Therefore Hillel chose the Precept of "love your neighbor" as the one specific idea that can guide men to this final goal. This Precept reveals the inner spirituality of the individual, the incarnation of the truly Divine within him, and thus draws him closer to the Source of Light and beauty. This Source, which we have called the Desire to Impart, is the chief characteristic by which we can come to know the Creator.

We learn from the *Book of Genesis* that "the inclination of man's heart is evil from his youth." (Genesis 8:21) This refers to the essence of man, the Desire to Receive which, until the age of thirteen, dominates all actions in the guise of a Desire to Receive for Oneself Alone. The actions of a child are motivated by this essence, without any regard for others and without any Desire to Impart to anyone else.

Upon reaching the age of thirteen years for a boy, twelve for a girl, the individual is incarnated with a *yetzer hatov*, a good inclination, which is a potential metaphysical form of energy similar to the Creator's Desire to impart. From that age onwards, the concept of "Love your neighbor" becomes the link connecting all that exists in the Celestial Heights with the Lower level of this world. Man is the channel through which the Creator's beneficence and grace flow from the Upper Heavenly Spheres to the corporeal world. The degree and intensity of this union, however, depends on the extent to which human egocentricity transforms itself into the Desire to Impart, since the nature of a channel or cable is to transmit energy, not to absorb it.

We can compare this to the result of placing a curtain in front of the light of the sun; the thicker the curtain, representing the Desire to Receive, the more light it will absorb into itself; while a thin curtain will present less obstruction to the passage of the light. It should be clear from this example that the thinner curtain has a greater affinity with the original source of light—the sun. Although it has no light of its own, it nonetheless has the aspect of the Desire to Impart, which is the essential quality of Light, in that it does not hinder the passage of the light. The thick curtain, on the other hand, through its absorption of light, takes on the opposite characteristic, the Desire to Receive, thus bringing about a separation of function between it and the sun.

If this identity of function is the final destination of the soul, the intimate and permanent union that results from the conformity of Divine and human will, then we must direct our attention to the words of our sages concerning the evil inclination: "The Creator, in addressing Himself to the human will, declares, 'I created an evil inclination, and also the Bible with its commandments and rituals as a means for the transformation of the evil inclination." Bible study and observance of its Precepts gradually nurtures the individual until he is suffi¬ciently disciplined to remove all traces of this Desire for Oneself Alone so that all his deeds are sanctified by a Desire to Impart to others. The ethical and moral commandments that apply between man and his neighbor secure for the individual the structure of the aspect of selflessness which is implied by the Precept of "love your neighbor."

We can therefore understand the words of Hillel to the student more profoundly: By achieving the goal of loving our neighbor, we are transforming our inherent Desire to Receive for Oneself Alone, which separates us from the Creator, into the Desire to Impart which, through its Similarity of Form with the Creator's Imparting aspect, draws us closer to Him and thus fulfills the original Thought of Creation.

A more specific analysis of the Precepts relating to man and his Creator, an area all too often neglected in religious teaching, will reveal a fundamental and extraordinary expression of moral consciousness. To place obedience at the pinnacle of the aims of the Precepts and to interpret ritual and ceremonial observance of the Bible as a revelation of dogmatic precepts leading to unquestioning subservience is to deny the spiritual origin of the Divine commandments. It suffices merely to compare strict religious observance in the course of the last two hundred years with present adherence to Biblical law to realize the result of such an approach. Religion is no longer spiritual and experiential but has developed into a rigid moral code, repellent to all but a small minority of the faithful. The teachings of Kabbalah, in all their many forms, have yet to succeed in establishing once again the bridge linking the fundamental instincts of the individual faced with the demands and strains of daily life with the quest for the inner meaning of the transcendent element of the Celestial World.

The rituals and Precepts that concern themselves with the relationship between man and the Creator would seem to have lost, in our times, their distinctive spirituality. The wisdom of the Kabbalah reveals them again in their original light, however, enabling us to see them not merely as a test of our obedience and faith, but as an active conditioning agent as powerful and vital to spiritual progress as any of the precepts relating to moral and ethical law. One of the clearest examples of the interweaving of ritual and moral instruction is the law concerning *Tefillin* (Phylacteries), which applies to all males who have reached the age of thirteen. A true understanding of this precept, which is given to us in Kabbalah, enables us to see it as a tool by which we can further our journey towards the goal of "love your neighbor," and not as the commemorative or submissive act for which it is all too often mistaken.

One of the most important chapters in the early part of the Bible is that concerning the Binding of Isaac in the *Book of Genesis*. The story itself is too well known to need repeating here, it being sufficient to recall the problems that it raises.

Abraham prayed for an heir, and at the advanced age of one hundred his request had been granted. It is this son, Isaac, who he is now asked to offer up as a sacrifice to God. This seems incomprehensible on a superficial level of understanding. Was Abraham's willingness to slaughter his own son a necessary or justified test of his complete surrender to the service of the Almighty? The Bible would seem to suggest that the supreme test applied solely to Abraham, as it states, "God tested Abraham," (*Genesis* 22:1) yet the strain placed on Isaac's allegiance would seem to be as great, if not greater. Isaac is at this time thirty-seven years old, yet the Bible seems to ignore completely his absolute submission to the Will of the Creator, emphasizing Abraham's selflessness. The *Zohar* explains as follows:

The text requires explanation. We should have expected the verse to read, "God tested Isaac," and not Abraham—after all, Isaac was already thirty-seven years old, and no longer under his father's jurisdiction; he could have easily refused, without rendering his father liable to punishment. Why, therefore, does it say "God tested Abraham" instead of "God tested Isaac?" The truth, however, is that it (the testing of Abraham) was required. In order for Abraham to attain perfection, he had to be invested with the attribute of the Left (negative) Column of Isaac, of which Abraham was not characteristic. Abraham is symbolic of the Right (positive) Column, which is called Chesed (Mercy). But perfection does not exist unless there is a balance of both positive and negative. This we can observe even on our mundane level, where a total unit consists of a harmonious relationship between positive and negative. In this story, water (Mercy or Right Column, represented by Abraham) would be united with fire (Judgment or Left Column, represented by Isaac), through which it would be possible for Abraham to administer justice and make it a part of his character. For whoever saw a father's heart turn from compassion to cruelty? However, the object here was to temper the discord between fire and water so that they should be settled in their places until Jacob (Central Column, the agent of synthesis) appeared. Only then would all be in order and the triad of the patriarchs (the complete system of connections and balance) be completed. It is thus instructive to note that the word 'nisa', usually translated as "tested," also means "lifted up" or "elevated"—meaning, in this context, "brought together at a higher level." The Celestial Level was firmly established on the terrestrial level as a result of Abraham's actions, so that a synthesis could occur.

From this interpretation of the *Zohar*, it would seem that the demand for Abraham's unconditional surrender was not the intent of the Creator. The Binding of Isaac, which represents the focal point of the episode, involves the bringing together of two forces, providing humanity with a system by which we can develop and achieve harmony within ourselves and subsequently connect with the Source of Light, the Creator.

Abraham, symbolizing the Right or Imparting Column, could not achieve wholeness unless he became one with the Left or Receiving Column. This does not mean that he had to negate or destroy the Left Column, as is indicated by the verse, "And Abraham stretched forth his hand, and took the knife to slay his son, whereupon the Angel of the Lord called unto him and said, 'Lay not your hand upon the lad.'" (*Genesis* 22:12)   The binding of the Left (Isaac) by the Right (Abraham) is the procedure through which man achieves perfection by way of his Central Column (Jacob), his thinking or mental capacity, symbolized by the centrally located head.

This, then, was the occasion of the bringing together of these two opposing energy forces, the vehicle through which the metaphysical energy of the binding of the Left Column was connected for all time to the physical level. It is this same harmonizing influence that we connect with when we bind *Tefillin* on the left arm—a ritual observance which, when understood in the light of the Kabbalah, can be seen in its true, profound meaning.

The revelation of the significance of *Tefillin* serves as a model for understanding how Kabbalah comprehends and interprets the Precepts. Another example is provided by the question of *Kashrut*, the dietary laws relating to the separation of milk from meat. All too often this Precept is regarded as an indication of complete submission to the Divine Will, or even as an outward and visible sign of the Jewishness. Kabbalah, however, approaches the subject from an altogether different viewpoint. It distinguishes between meat, which is red in color, and milk, which is white. Is this merely a chance occurrence, or can we assume that an ordered universe will be reflected at all levels of existence? Thus, says Kabbalah, red represents the Left Column, whose attribute is *Din* (Judgment) and whose function is to Receive. The meat of an animal is a result or product of everything that the animal takes into itself, exemplifying the Desire to Receive. Milk, on the other hand, represents the Right Column, the Desire to Share, and the aspect of *Chesed* (Mercy, giving); its color—white—includes all other colors, thereby indicating that it represents in its essential characteristic of giving and nourishment the highest level to which man can aspire. It is clear that the two elements represented by meat and milk are in opposition to one another: One is Judgment, the other Mercy. The outpouring of milk signifies life for the offspring, whereas the shedding of blood signifies death and separation from life. We have seen in the example of Abraham and Isaac, how fundamentally opposed elements can be brought together; here, we see two mutually exclusive elements that we are instructed to separate from one another. The *Zohar* goes on to give the reasons for this difference, too, but such distinctions are beyond the scope of this introductory book.

A similar example of the necessity for the separation of blood (in its aspect of Judgment) from life is found in the laws relating to the menstrual cycle, known as *niddah*. This is traditionally observed by an orthodox Jewish couple. The principle of this precept is to observe a period of separation. During the time of *niddah*, a woman's body is subject to the power of Judgment, signified by the appearance of blood and by other changes in her psychological make-up. Therefore she cannot come into contact with the life-giving forces of the marriage union, represented by the white color of the sperm. There is a clear and grave warning here that death and life must be respected in this world for what they represent—two separate and irreconcilable elements.

It is thus obvious that in each of the six hundred and thirteen Precepts there is an underlying reason that is applicable to everyone—and is not just an outward sign of devotion of a Jew, but an instruction regarding the usefulness of danger of some aspect of the universe. Whereas the Bible gives us a general idea of the nature of these aspects, only Kabbalah reveals their true identity as tools with which we can work to achieve the goal of unity with the Creator. The Precepts exist in order to enable us to keep a balance in the universal forces of energy that resulted from the Creation. The ultimate balance, we learn from Hillel, and the ultimate Precept is the relationship between a man and his fellow man, guided at all times by the principle of "love your neighbor as yourself," the rest, indeed, is commentary.

Chapter 11

Devekut – The Circular Concept

The union of Upper and Lower, the bringing together of opposites brings us full circle in the chain of metaphysical events by which the universe is structured. In relation to the union of man with his Creator, this concept is known as *Devekut* (cleaving or unification).

Union with God is fundamentally a bringing together of metaphysical entities. Just as the separation or union of tangible objects is accomplished by either removing them from each other or by bringing one part closer to the other in space, so it is with metaphysical or spiritual forces. Separation or union is achieved through the transformation of contrasting phases that either sever or unite.

The Creator is, as we have said, purely a bestower; He imparts without being in any way diminished by imparting and receives nothing in return. In this, He is the measure of the perfect donor. Mankind, on the contrary, has a perpetual and unfulfilled craving for the fulfillment of its needs and desires, due to its eternal Desire to Receive; this is the vital intention within the Thought of Creation. The Desire to Receive is thus both a mark of man's essence and also the cause of the separation of his being from that of the Creator. This chasm is widened when man perceives himself as being a receptacle for his own benefit alone, when his Vessel attempts to capture and contain the Light with no thought of sharing or imparting it to others. Thus, while his natural instinct is towards self-reliance rather than reliance on others, he is still aware through the influence of his consciousness that he is very much reliant on the bounty of the Creator. This awareness, however, ultimately leads to the inevitable conclusion that receiving God's Beneficence is only for the purpose of rendering delight to the Creator.

The two alternatives—receiving purely for oneself or accepting God's Beneficence in order to share with others and thus rendering Him great delight—are mutually exclusive. It would appear that we are caught in a trap, for by putting ourselves at the mercy of the Creator's bounty, we experience Bread of Shame because we have received something for nothing and rely on that which we have not earned. This, the *Zohar* teaches, is the complete opposite of what in fact happens. By accepting the Creator's beneficence, we are fulfilling not only the role of our own individual creation, but also of the original Thought of Creation. This can only happen, however, if we are aware of the correct way in which to give and to receive. This, as we have said, is the purpose of Kabbalah, which literally means "Receiving." In the balanced relationship between donor and recipient, the aspect of Bread of Shame is rendered void, since we have created a situation in which, although there is giving and taking, it is equal measure on both sides, so that there is no feeling of lack or shame.

We find this idea elaborated in a treatise of the Bible regarding the laws of the marriage ceremony. It is specified that during the ceremony the man is required to present a wedding ring to his bride, by which exchange she becomes his legal wife. This is the Mosaic law, and the reasons supporting it will be considered more fully in a volume on the concept of soul mates, marriage and divorce. The Bible, however, cites one occasion where the traditional order of the marriage ceremony is reversed. When the bridegroom is a man of great merit, due to his devotion to spiritual study, the bride may give the wedding ring to him, instead of he to her, and on his reciting the traditional formula, "you shall by this become betrothed to me," she then becomes his legal wife. The Bible explains that through his recipiency, the marriage has become legalized by her delight in receiving the pleasure in being honored by virtue of his acceptance of the ring, although the legal procedure has been reversed.

In most marriages, the law is followed the man gives a material token (a ring or coin) as a symbol of marriage. The important point to note here is that the significance of his act is the giving, the token ring or coin being of no intrinsic value. However, in the exceptional case we have just described, we conclude that the bridegroom's act of receiving the ring from his bride is in itself regarded as an act of giving. Instead of giving her a coin or ring, which is a material symbol, he presents her with the far more lofty and spiritual delight of honoring her by marriage. Receiving that is undertaken for the sole purpose of imparting constitutes absolute, complete bestowal. Thus the groom in this instance is considered by the sages to be giving more by receiving the ring than he would if he were to give it. In the case of the Godly man his very marriage is an act of giving, so that the ring, the symbol of consummation, is passed from woman to man. There is also an equivalent heightening in the transference of spiritual energy, since by her act of giving, the bride is receiving and, more to the point, she is receiving far more than she would have done had she merely received the ring from the man. In this heightened dynamic interchange of energy, the relationship is consummated, and the Bread of Shame is totally banished. Indeed, one might argue that the reversal of the normal marriage procedure when the groom is especially learned, since if this were not the case, the bride would be only receiving and would therefore be susceptible to the Bread of Shame. However, when she gives the ring to the man, she elevates her role of recipient to that of donor, and brings the necessary balance to the relationship.

There is a tale told by kabbalists that illustrates this confusing concept clearly. The tale concerns a wealthy man who invited a number of friends to join him on some festive occasion. Just as the company was about to sit down for the meal, the host noticed a poor man passing by.

He felt sorry for the man and instructed one of the servants to invite him in. All the guests could see that the poor man was badly in need of food and clothing, yet when the host cordially invited him to join them and share the meal, they were astonished to hear him refuse. The host, bewildered and mystified by the unexpected reply, urged the poor man to reconsider, only to be told that he (the poor man) had no need for this sort of charity. The host insisted, the poor man politely refused, and so the conversation continued until the poor man finally threw his hands in the air in a gesture of helplessness and said, "Very well, if it really means that much to you, I'll accept your kind hospitality." With a sigh of relief, the company sat down to begin the dinner.

In this story, as in the example of the special marriage, the roles of donor and recipient are reversed, resulting in a heightening and sanctification of the transaction. To the receiver—the poor man—the request that he receive beneficence without due regard to his having earned this kindness appears initially as something degrading; this is identical to the concept of Bread of Shame. Thus what appeared to be simple generosity on the part of the host takes on a new aspect in light of the poor man's inability to share or impart anything and so remove the Bread of Shame. It emerges as something unwanted—not because the poor man is not in need of food, but because there is no way in which he can take it as yet without losing his self-respect. Faced with the choice between humiliation and hunger, it is perhaps no longer surprising that he refuses the food. A receiver who is not prepared to share or who is prevented from sharing will inevitably reject the true intention of the donor. This built-in metaphysical rejection became inevitable after the initial feeling of Bread of Shame was experienced by the souls in the world of *Ein Sof.*

However, once this unexpected refusal of an obviously desired gift has taken place the flow of energy in the situation begins to change. The rich man realizes that he has been deprived of an opportunity to do good, and becomes more insistent and pleading. In effect, he is now no longer offering the poor man food but asking him a favor—that he afford him the opportunity of sharing some of his wealth, and of receiving pleasure from that sharing. The poor man now experiences a situation where he is being asked to impart as well as receive and therefore consents to join the feast. The rich man, too, is both giving and receiving. The cycle has been completed, with flow and feedback now in a state of dynamic balance.

We can apply this example to any form of benevolence. Unless there is this balance between donor and receiver, the original intention of the donor will not be realized. This holds true on all levels, from the original Thought of Creation, which was to impart Ineffable Goodness to man, and which will only be realized finally when we have learnt properly how to receive, and interact on the level of family, friendships and business.

The foregoing analysis reveals the fundamental necessity for this circular concept. It is bound up not only with the redemption of the individual soul, but also with the redemption of all souls that is associated with the age of the Messiah. Through the circular concept, it becomes possible to convert the Desire to Receive into a Desire to Impart, transmuting, we might say, the letter M in "me" to the letter W in "we"; the first points downwards, emphasizing the connection with the physical world, while the second reaches up towards the Heavens, indicating its affinity with the concept of *Devekut* or unification with God. Through this affinity of desires, we are brought closer to the structure of the Creator's Desire to Impart and can free ourselves from the stigma of being able only to receive for ourselves. From our Earthly existence we are led to a higher spiritual level of consciousness, to a liberation from the tyranny of the five senses, and to a higher realm of spiritual existence.

Devekut, in kabbalistic terms, is a profound concept but by no means unattainable. Love of man—or for that matter, love of God—are not merely mystical or theological concepts, but rather a path of life through which the realm of metaphysics can be permanently united with Earthly reality, thus liberating the true spiritual nature of man. It is not a teaching of austerity of asceticism, against which the sages often warned. One is not required to relinquish all the material possessions and physical comforts that are associated with corporeal existence in order to achieve spiritual growth. Indeed, *Devekut* is realized within the framework of the physical world more effectively through social intercourse and commitment to society than by seclusion and self-denial, as Hillel implied in his answer to the student. Precepts, as we have seen, can be divided into two categories: those concerned with the relationship between humanity and the Creator, and those that govern the relationship between man and his fellow man. In working towards the ultimate objective of *Devekut*, the gradual transformation of Receiving for Oneself Alone into Receiving for the Sake of Sharing, those precepts between man and his fellow man are more likely to lead the individual to the goal by reason of their ever-changing role and position in the daily demands of existence. The differentiation of desires that we find in our dealings with those around us forces us to explore, in real terms, the meaning of "loves your neighbor" and to recognize the diversity that has existed since the *Ein Sof*. Through this diversity we shall eventually remove the aspect of Bread of Shame and return to the Blessed Endless.

In the process of spiritual elevation, each person is obliged to express his innermost potential of giving (and therefore, as we have understood, of receiving also), so as to achieve his own elevation, which permits the ultimate measure of beneficence and fulfillment from the Creator. Stated in simple terms, the Precepts that regulate the interactions of men are the ideal conditioning agents for transforming man's basic character. These precepts are designed specifically to re-align the selfish aspect of Desire with the intention of the Creator, Whose fundamental characteristic is that of imparting.

This, then, is the core of Hillel's reply. "Love your neighbor" is, quite simply, the principal and most effective means of attaining *Devekut*, which is the goal and purpose of the Bible. The unifying force of this love, through which the individual may discover and draw on the innermost potential of his or her own positive qualities, assures the continuing progress of human development, inasmuch as the Desire to Receive has been kept in check.

The literal meaning of the word *Devekut* reveals the very essence of man's relationship with God and with his fellow man. It implies attachment, a cleaving of two who while appearing to be a complete unit, nevertheless retain their individual characteristics. The Bible uses the same root to describe the relationship between a man and a woman, a union which is considered as making both parties whole, in that each brings what is lacking from the other to the relationship. The Hebrew word *davok*, meaning "to attach" is used to describe this union, as it is to portray man's union with God.

Thus we find in the concept of *Devekut* a central virtue by which each individual, and thus mankind as a whole, can reach his objective in this world, the goal of transmuting the elemental characteristic of man into the fundamental characteristic of the Creator. The core of man, as represented by his actions, is bound up with the Essence of the Creator, leading to the elimination of the Bread of Shame and thus fulfilling the initial Purpose of the Creation. If the essence of the Precepts is their conditioning ability, providing man with the tools with which to attain his objective, it follows that knowledge and understanding of these Precepts are linked closely to their observance.

This aspect of knowledge in its relation to observance and ultimately to *Devekut* is revealed in the passage from the Bible in which Solomon is advised, "Know the God of your father, and serve him with an entire heart and a willing soul." (*1 Chronicles* 28:9) What is the nature of this "knowledge of God"? Is not the Creator is beyond the scope of understanding and knowledge? A closer analysis of the concept of *Devekut* will enable us to understand the true meaning and application of this injunction.

"And Adam knew Eve his wife; and she conceived and bore Cain." (Genesis 4:25) In this sentence we find a revelation of *Devekut*, the union of man and woman expressed by the verb meaning "to know or understand", succeeded by an attachment. The knowledge of God, is essentially a mental process similar to this physical one—an understanding of His fundamental characteristics, which is followed by cleaving to the Divine Will. The aspect of understanding is related to the transformation of the Desire to Receive into the Desire to Impart, this being the essential nature of the Creator. All we can know about Him is that he is good, and His desire is to share. When we have fully understood this, not just intellectually but with our entire being, it will follow that we will seek to emulate Him in this essential quality, and thus, as we have described, draw closer to Him through an increasing similarity of our nature to His.

While we have repeatedly stressed the unity of the Bible and all its commandments, we seem to be making a distinction here between two sets of Precepts. In fact, it should be clear that there is no distinction to be drawn between the goals of these two aspects of Precepts—any apparent difference is a reflection of the current state of humanity. There are many people who, would nevertheless still claim to uphold the moral and social laws of the Bible—those between man and man. It is the laws concerning ritual, which are seen as a relic of the past, that are rejected. The religious establishment, on the other hand, has sometimes gone to opposite extremes. Having what amounts to a monopoly over the ritual laws that cover the relationship between man and his Creator, they have often abandoned or neglected the moral laws concerning our obligations to our neighbors. Needless to say both tendencies are regrettable, since they indicate a lack of understanding of the true purpose of the whole Bible. The current state of religion is therefore yet another reason for the importance of the revelation for Kabbalah today.

Those Precepts between man and his Creator constitute, for a large number of observers, the central tradition, ceremonial and ritual of religion. For these religious concepts, untold numbers of "faithful" throughout history have fought, suffered and died, placing the freedom to observe these signs of their faith above their own lives. Yet these selfsame Precepts now appear to have caused a dangerous alienation among a large segment, if not the vast majority. Moreover, the barrier between those who adhere to these Precepts and the mass of the people has been constantly hardening.

It would be some consolation if the religious community stressed the spiritual nature of the Precepts so that it could be appreciated by the mass of non-observant or non-ritualistic people. According to our sages, one who performs his ritual obligations correctly will also be a model of supreme moral sensitivity and social awareness. This, regretfully, is not the case at present, since we have witnessed an often alarming separation among humanity of one set of Precepts from the other.

The Precepts between man and Creator are generally expressed and contained within an unchanging formula, unaffected by the varying activities that emerge from the changing texture of desires of society in general and the individual in particular. Prayer, the Sabbath and *Tefillin* are, to a great extent, a private communication between the observer and God, without infringement from external distractions. Yet, even within this area of supposed competence, we find evidence of alienation and division among people.

A story is told of a conversation that took place between Rabbi Israel ben Eliezer (the Besht or Baal Shem Tov) and a congregant. Following a service, the Baal Shem Tov approached the man and extended the greeting of *Shalom aleichem* (Peace be unto you). The man was taken aback at this, and asked the Baal Shem Tov why he had used this form of greeting, since he surely knew that the law obliged one to use it only if one had not seen a friend for three days or more. "You know, Rav" he continued, "that I have never left this town for as much as a single day, and attend morning and evening services here every day, as required by every devout man. So why the greeting?"

"All this is undoubtedly true, my son," replied the Baal Shem Tov, "I do see you every day. However, I should like to know where you are while you are sitting in meditation; it seems to me that your mind, soul and thoughts are elsewhere, perhaps contemplating some new business venture. Placing the *Tefillin* on your hand and head for so many years, day after day has become an automatic habit, apparently exerting little influence over the content of your thoughts and meditations. I therefore extended to you a greeting upon your return from your place of business."

The lack of unity and focus illustrated by this story is merely a symptom of a more widespread disease, namely the continuing separation between ritual and social commandments. We are enjoined to carry out both; each when properly observed leads to appreciation and observance of the other, so that over-emphasis on either is an indication of lack of understanding of the whole. The ritual Precepts, if carried out in their true spirit and understanding, ought to lead to greater charity to one's neighbor, just as the Precepts between man and his fellow man ought to lead to a realization of the Omnipresence and Omnipotence of the Creator, and thence to a desire to celebrate His greatness. The goal of *Devekut*, which is the goal not of one set of Precepts nor of the other, but of both taken and practiced together, can only be pursued through a true understanding of the essential unity of the Bible. Only when that unity has been realized can a true love of one's neighbor come into being.

Chapter 12

A Contemplation

A lthough the knowledge of Kabbalah is discussed and encased in many volumes of writing, both ancient and modern, it should not be thought that its teachings are contained solely in the written word. In previous chapters we have shown that Kabbalah lies at the very heart of the system of actions and deeds known as Precepts; without these actions, the life of a person is considered incomplete and lacking. However, inner devotion is also an important element, and this aspect, too, is emphasized by the teaching of Kabbalah.

The need to center one's inner world with the intention appropriate to the situation is known in Hebrew as *kavanah*, or "direction." While this meditation and the fulfillment of Precepts are essentially inseparable, I feel that many people who may read this book, and who have grown up without knowing the taste of the Precepts of the Bible, will benefit from a contemplation to help link the teachings of Kabbalah with their application in the world of action.

A generation has arisen which, being aware of its spirituality, does not know how to express this aspect of its identity. There is, however, a widespread awareness of the need for inner sincerity and wholeness, which may not find satisfaction in the contemporary teachings of religion. For this reason, it seems fitting to end with a contemplation which, although no substitute for the performance of the Precepts, will, it is hoped, arouse in the reader a deeper appreciation of the intentions of this book, and allow him or her a further insight into the workings and significance of the teachings of Kabbalah.

Rav Aba was one day discussing the teachings of the Bible with the Sacred Lamp (Rav Shimon bar Yochai). "Why is it," he asked Rav Shimon, "that some people of the world always sway back and forth when they are studying spiritual matters; an action that seems to come naturally to them, so that they cannot keep still?"

Rav Shimon replied, "'The spirit of man is the lamp of the Lord.' (Proverbs 12:27) Once this lamp has been lit from the Supernal Bible, its light never stops moving for an instant, like the flame of a wick that is never still. Thus when a spiritual person pronounces studies from the Bible, a light is kindled and he is unable to keep still; thus he sways backwards and forwards like the wick of a candle."

Elsewhere in the *Zohar*, we find a discussion of the two verses of Bible, "For the Lord your God is a consuming fire," (Deuteronomy 4:24), and "But you that did cleave unto the Lord your God are alive every one of you this day." (Deuteronomy 4:4). The apparent contradiction in these words is explained by Rav Shimon:

It has already been established that there is a fire which consumes fire and destroys it, there being fires of different grades of strength. If we extend this concept, we might say that anyone wishing to penetrate the mystery of the Holy Unity should contemplate the flame that rises from a burning coal or candle. The flame cannot rise unless it is attached to some physical substance. Furthermore, within the flame itself there are to be found two lights: One is white and luminous, the other black, or blue. The white light is the more elevated of the two and ascends steadily. The black or blue light is beneath and acts as a pedestal for the white light. The two are inseparably joined to one another, with the white light resting and enthroned upon the blue. The blue lower flame is itself attached to something physical beneath it, which feeds it and makes it join with the white flame above. Sometimes the blue light may become red in color, but the white light above never changes. Thus the lower light, which is either blue or red, forms a connection between the white light above amid the physical substance below, which keeps it alight. The nature of this lower light is to destroy anything that is beneath it or in contact with it; it is the source of destruction and death. The white light above it, however, neither consumes nor destroys, nor does it ever change. This is why Moses said, "For the Lord your God is a consuming fire," meaning that He consumes all that is beneath Him—"your God" and not "our God," because Moses had reached the level of the upper white light, which does not consume or destroy.

By transgressing the Lord's Commandments, the children of Israel have placed themselves in the realm of the judgment of the lower blue flame, whose nature is destruction; but those who obeyed the Holy Commandments, thereby "cleaving to the Lord your God," attached themselves to the upper white flame, whose nature is constant, unchanging, and beyond the realms of destruction. Thus there are different grades of fire, some higher and some lower. There are different aspects to the flame of a coal or candle: That which is attached to the physical realm, draws its life from the physical and ultimately destroys it, and that which is above the realm of destruction is preserved.

"Now observe," continues Rav Shimon: "The motivating force by which the blue flame is kindled, and by which it becomes attached to the white light, comes only from the Israelites, who cleave to it from beneath. Now, although the nature of the blue light is to consume everything that comes into contact with it from below, Israelites can cleave to it from beneath without being destroyed, as it is written, 'But you that did cleave to the Lord your God are alive every one of the you this day.' It is written 'your God' and not 'our God,' indicating the blue flame that destroys all with which it comes into contact from below. Yet you (Israel)

cleave to it and are still alive. Above the white light and surrounding it is yet another light, which can hardly by seen and which symbolizes the Supreme Essence. Thus the ascending flame is a symbol of the most elevated mysteries of wisdom."

The three elements that we can observe in the flame—the wick, the blue light and the white light—symbolize the three elements of man's spirit, and refer to the Three Columns we have discussed throughout this book. The white light represents the Right Column, the Desire to Impart; this is the moral strength that constantly strives to ascend to and unite with the Absolute. While it burns it does not consume, acting rather as an illuminating vehicle permeated with Light through which one can become one with the Eternal Source of Light, the Creator.

The blue or black flame symbolizes the Left Column, the Desire to Receive, and is characterized by its connection with the physical body. It constantly draws up energy from that which is beneath it, and represents the aspect of man that seeks to deny spirituality, pursuing material pleasures for himself alone. Finally, the wick represents the synthesizing and unifying force of both the blue and the clear white flame, which is the Central Column.

How can Israel, the wick of the candle, exist without being destroyed by the "consuming fire" of the blue flame? By the very fact, says the *Zohar*, that Israel, unlike the candle, was created from the Holy Lamp, whose power and energy are infinite and inexhaustible. If we draw only on the energy of the physical world, as the wick draws its energy from the body of the candle, that energy will, in time, be exhausted by the fire of the Left Column, the Desire to Receive. If, however, we connect with the limitless energy of the Creator, through a true understanding of the teachings of the Bible and a fulfillment of its Precepts, then we shall have transcended the destroying influence of the blue flame, and can connect with the unchanging purity of the clear white flame above. This unity is not a negation of the Left Column, any more than the candle can burn without the blue flame. The choice facing us is whether to cut ourselves off from that Endless Source of energy and be consumed by the devouring fire of the Desire to Receive, or to connect with our birthright and cleave to God without being destroyed.

The teachings of Kabbalah are not merely concerned, therefore, with theoretical descriptions of the structure of the universe. They are primarily concerned with preparing man for knowledge of the Almighty through direct awareness of the physical world, and through intuitive connections brought about by a deep contemplation of the relationships between the Upper and Lower Worlds.

Volume

Two

Introduction

The greatest, most advanced, computer ever conceived is not locked within the confines of a massive government vault. Nor is it the jealously guarded secret treasure of some chrome eyed corporate giant. No, the greatest, most advanced and powerful computer that was ever invented is a strange looking thing that weights no more than a few pounds. With the outer casing removed, one might easily mistake it for a creature that just emerged from the depths of some fictional Black Lagoon. You have probably gathered that we are referring to that convoluted mass of nerves and tissue: The human brain.

Why, one might well ask, if I'm so smart, can't I tap into these vast reserves of potential energy and turn them to my advantage?

The answer is, you can. Before you venture into any unknown situation, though, common sense should dictate the wisdom of possessing as much knowledge as possible of the pitfalls and obstacles that might hamper your way.

Through the teachings of the masters we learned that the rational mind represents only a minute fraction of mankind's true potential. The infinitely more powerful, more dynamic circuitry in the human computer remains in suspended animation until such time as it is revitalized through the limited creative process known to Kabbalah as the Line. Consciously or unconsciously we are all searching for the software by which to access those vast reserves. Kabbalah is such a program.

As miraculous as it may seem, the computer operates on a binary system, which means that each of its circuits has but one operation to perform: On or off. Each of the tiny circuits within the computer is conducting electricity or not conducting it, depending on the given commands. On or off, positive or negative, restricting or not restricting, fulfilled or unfulfilled, such was the world view expressed by sixteenth century Kabbalist Rav Isaac Luria (the Ari), the creator of Lurianic Kabbalah. The computer, as remarkable an invention as it is, obviously does not hold a candle to its inventor, the human brain.

The human computer is so far in advance of even the most powerful binary computing machine that comparison is hardly possible. The challenge we face is that of how to access those vast megabytes of potential energy and make them work for us. We have all of the necessary hardware, bits and bytes, all of the "read only" and "random access" systems necessary for our own unique fulfillment, but the conscious mind, a tiny fraction of our true potential, has taken over the controls. The effect is like having access to a thousand NASA computers, but the only disk you have to run them is the home version of Pac Man. Even the most advanced computer in the world is useless without an equally powerful program.

Learning Kabbalah is like slipping a powerful software system into the disk drive of our human computer. One does not become conversant with a program overnight. Depending on the complexity of the software, the documentation, support systems, and so forth, it can take weeks to become familiar with the basics of the system, and years until the various features have been mastered. Eventually, while we may not have the slightest idea of how the computer functions internally, the various functions become second nature so much so that when a new problem presents itself, we can sometimes even second guess the programmer.

Such is the nature of Kabbalah.

Little by little, through the program that is Kabbalah, we begin to grasp the Four Phases and their primary, secondary, and tertiary divisions. By understanding the computerized system, we establish the program which allows us to avoid many of the pitfalls made by those whose lives are ruled by trial and error. Instead of having to find a new solution for each and every obstacle set in our path, the kabbalistic frame of reference allows us to return to the root cause of each matter and thus avoid the constant interruptions presented by life in the material world.

And so it is that while the miracle of the human brain may remain forever beyond the scope of our reasoning abilities, we can, through the careful application of kabbalistic principles, acquire a sense of our own inner workings. For we are models of the universe, as it was, is, and will be, and by understanding the microcosm that is us we connect with the macrocosm that is the *Or Ein Sof,* Light of Creation, the infinite power of the universe.

Chapter 1

The Thought of Creation

In the beginning, before the universe became the multi universe that we live in today, there existed an Infinite "circular" condition of mutual fulfillment between the Light (Emanator/Creator) and the Vessel (Emanated/Created). The Light found completion by giving endlessly of its beneficence and the vessels (though as yet in an undifferentiated state) experienced total satisfaction at receiving endlessly of the Light's supreme positiveness.

This Infinite "circular" condition was disturbed by a stirring within the emanated beings known to Kabbalah as Bread of Shame. No longer could the emanated vessels partake endlessly of unearned benevolence and so, to absolve Bread of Shame, they asked and were granted a share in the give and take of Creation. The Light, whose only desire was to share, saw fit to restrict or withdraw its Infinite illumination so that another desire, the Desire to Receive could manifest.

From this restriction or contraction of the Light, known to kabbalists as the *Tzimtzum* and to modern science as the Big Bang, was born the multi universe with all its variety and individuation, and never again would the vessel find true fulfillment in taking that which was not earned. Hence it is said that the Light gave birth to darkness, the Circle to the Line.

HOW THE CIRCLE BECAME A LINE

For the kabbalist the sphere and the circle are symbols rich in nuance and meaning. The sphere is an example of perfect symmetry, for no matter from which angle it is viewed the image remains the same. The circle, a one dimensional representation of the sphere, symbolizes infinity. Having no beginning and no end, it stands too for the unity, completeness and perfection that was the domain of *Ein Sof* (Endless) before the withdrawal and Restriction (*Tzimtzum*), and which will again be the universal condition when this current age of correction has completed its cycle.

Rav Isaac Luria (the Ari), founder of the Lurianic system of Kabbalah, described in fine detail the ways in which the Ten Circular Vessels (*Sefirot*) were revealed after the *Tzimtzum* and how the *Sefirot* receive Light from the Line. It is important not to limit ourselves to a literal interpretation of the concepts revealed to us by the Ari, but rather to try to draw from them their metaphysical implications. Consider, then, the Circle and the Line as a convenient method by which to metaphorically illustrate that which might otherwise be a difficult or even impenetrable subject.

Unlike the Circle, the Line has a beginning, a middle, and end. So while the Circle represents infinity, the Line serves to conceptually illuminate that which is finite. And whereas the universal condition that existed before the *Tzimtzum* is described as being in circular form, meaning there was complete unity between the Creator and that which He had created, the condition after the Restriction took on a finite, linear dimension, and hence is represented by the Line. The Line, in other words, permits us to have a conceptual idea of limitation which is not possible with the Circle.

In the beginning there was no distinction between the Creator and the Created, the Light and the Vessel, the Circle and the Line. All different concepts, all different entities, all different energy-intelligences were unified. That is not to say there were no differences between them. And herein lies a fine distinction, which we in this fragmented world find difficult to comprehend: There were variables, but they were not yet manifested. The myriad elements, entities, and energies were present in the *Ein Sof* before the restriction but they did not yet express themselves as separate manifestations.

Chapter 2
Making Metaphysical Connections

Hebrew theology was built upon three distinct and equally firm foundations. The first was the law, which was known to all citizens of Israel. The second was the oral tradition, *Mishna*, the soul of the law, which was known only by Rabbis and teachers. The third, Kabbalah, the soul of the soul of the law, was revealed to only a chosen few.

The roots of Kabbalah go deep into the soil of man's primordial past. Certain individuals, it seems, have always sought to reach beyond the grasp of intellect to establish a link with a higher reality; there have always been seekers of an apprehension of the Infinite for whom face value was not enough. Even the most ancient cave paintings, pictographs and petro glyphs attest to man's belief in mystical linkages, myths, and magical transformations. There have always been, and there will always be, those who seek to find the word within the word, the thought within the thought, the meaning within the meaning.

Judging by the preponderance of evidence, it would seem that an excellent case could be made for mystical transcendence being a basic human need. Yet mention an occult or mystical subject to the man on the street today and you are libel to be met with derisive comments, mocking laughter, with perhaps a bar or two of the theme from *The Twilight Zone* tossed in for good measure. "It's not rational," they might be apt to say. "It's not real." If they can't taste it, touch it, see it with their own two eyes, for them it does not exist. Yet what is gravity but an unseen force for which we have no rational explanation? And what of magnetism? We can't see it; we can't explain it; but does that mean it's not there?

When a fool sees a well dressed person, he looks no further. But the thinking man knows that the worth of the clothes has nothing to do with the body that is robed in them. While the kabbalist knows that the worth of the body is in the soul that abides in it. Just as the sheen and ripples on the surface of the water hide that which lies beneath the surface, so too does empirical existence obscure Divine reality.

THE REAL WORLD

"Get real," is an expression one is apt to hear today. It means that the speaker has a better grasp of reality than the person to whom he or she is speaking. It might be followed by other hard line materialist phrases such as: "The truth of the matter..." or "The bottom line is..." and ended with punch lines such as, "It's every man for himself," "They're playing hardball out there," and the old chestnut, "Only the strong survive."

The real world, it seems, is a place of rocks and hard places. Gone is the mystery, the paradox, the irony. Reality is the "thing" today. Nearly everyone these days will hasten to tell us all we want to know about reality and a lot more that we might rather not know. Politicians, businessmen, prostitutes, grocery clerks, and dictators all swear up and down that they live in the real world. Yet when asked for a definition of reality each gives a different answer.

For the rich man it is a place of comfort, refinement, and opulence. For the working man it is a place where one struggles to make a living. For the man who is starving it is a hell from which the only escape is death. The real world is a place where you shut your mouth, do your job, and take the money. It is a place of hard knocks and grindstones to which we must keep our noses, a place where righteous people pull themselves up by the bootstraps and "make something of themselves."

But what is it really?

The confusion arises because there are two real worlds. One is the "real" world of illusion, examples of which are given above. All things of this earthly realm are a part of the illusionary reality. It is a reality that changes with the tides, becoming larger and smaller, harder and softer, faster and slower, depending on how it is perceived. It is a world of symptoms and appearances, starvation and despair, elegance, opulence, and illusionary grandeur. It is many things to many people. In the end it might be said that it is anything you want to make it, and, hence, not real at all. The other real world is the reality of the *Or Ein Sof*, the Light of Creation. This reality is changeless, complete, eternal and infinite. Beyond the realm of struggle and restriction, lies and deceit, illusion, desire and petty machinations—it is a place of peace and perfection, a place of stillness and ultimate, primal truth.

The two realities are separated by a hair's breadth, apart from each other yet together all the same. One, this Earthly realm, is called the Lower World; the other is called the Upper World. One is coarse, the other is fine, one is dense, the other lighter than space. The Upper World, is hidden, the Lower World is revealed. It is said that there are two sides to every story. Kabbalah mediates between them. The kabbalist's task is to resolve them both.

WHAT YOU SEE IS WHAT YOU FORGET

Every North American is familiar with the expression, "I'm from Missouri." It might aptly be translated as, "Show me" or "I'll believe it only if I see it with my own two eyes." It implies that the person who is speaking is a "realist" over whose eyes the wool cannot easily be pulled. Expressions such as these attest to the pride we place in our ability to "see the world as it really is."

In truth, Missouri would certainly be a sorry place if all the people there were to limit their comprehension of existence based solely on what they could see. Words such as faith, hope, love, and intuition would have to be removed from the dictionary. All religions would have to be abolished, for how many of us can attest to having truly seen God? Theories involving quarks, quasars, black holes, and subatomic particles would have to be dropped from the scientific lexicon—not to mention electromagnetism, germs, and atoms. And as if all this were not bad enough, they would even have to repeal the Law of Gravity.

The point is our five senses are notoriously bad judges of the world around us. We all have, no doubt, been in a situation in which a sound is heard and every person in the room believes that sound came from a different place. The sense of taste and the closely related sense of smell can be easily fooled by chemical scents and additives. Nor is the sense of touch any better at gauging actuality, as any number of college pranks involving a blindfold, an ice cube, and the suggestion of fire, can attest. Taste, touch, smell, sight, hearing—all of our senses play tricks on us. Why then do we place so much faith in them? Where do we turn to find the truth?

The physical world is an illusion; the real world is one step beyond. To comprehend the nature of the physical world it is imperative that we begin making perceptual connections with the metaphysical realm. By the same token, to comprehend the nature of the external world, it is necessary to connect with the internal. Just because something is seen with the eyes does not mean that it exists any more than not seeing something is proof that it does not exist. Through Kabbalah we peel away the layers of illusion so that we may connect to the Light within.

Chapter 3

Or Ein Sof

*O*r *Ein Sof,* The Light of Creation, plays at the edges of our consciousness like a dream that cannot quite be remembered. Moments before waking there is a crucial instant when only a loose thread connects the dreamer with his dream. The harder the dreamer pulls on that delicate strand the more quickly does the fabric of the dream unravel and disappear. Try as he might to reattach the thread, his dream fades and the dreamer must resolve himself to a waking "reality" immensely inferior to that of his dream.

We all have experienced some form of what might be called supernatural communication, moments of intense rapture or lucidity that far exceed the run-of-the-mill perceptions with which we normally attend to in our daily routines. For some those brief interludes of expanded consciousness become the fuel of obsessions. Returning to those ecstatic moments becomes the sole focus of their lives. They may search in drugs and vicarious thrills, in war and sexual conquests, in speed, thievery, and other modes of dangerous behavior, but though it is true that brief flashes of cosmic awareness may accompany such activities, those fleeting moments of insight soon evaporate into nothing more than pale recollections. Instead of achieving any lasting result, people who engage in such activities must constantly raise the stakes of their adventures in order to realize a lesser degree of stimulation than that which was attained before.

Metaphysical connections are by their very nature illusory—so much so that most of us acquiesce to a life without them. Though those brief encounters with the next dimensions provide evidence of a world so superior to this phase of existence that comparison is hardly possible, having no words to describe our experiences, and no validation from traditional sources of the existence of the higher realms, we banish the memories of our extraterrestrial sojourns to hidden catacombs deep in our unconscious minds.

Many people attend houses of worship regularly without ever having anything approaching a religious experience. While they may derive some small comfort from a feeling that "something is out there," something magnificent and all-encompassing, their belief in this otherworldly entity, or extraterrestrial intelligence, provides consolation, but not contentment, for it is only something to believe in and not something to connect with. Being unaware of its existence these people have no reason to create a link with the energy-intelligence of the cosmos. The majority of people go through life, unaware that the *Or Ein Sof* could be theirs for the asking, never comprehending the psychological and spiritual discomforts it could quell, the inner needs it would more than gladly fulfill. For them the metaphysical world, if they even acknowledge its existence, seems totally divorced of useful function. Hence, they live their lives; little knowing that it is their lack of attachment with the higher realms of consciousness that is the sole determining factor for the quiet desperation in which they must continually exist.

Like a dream that cannot quite be remembered, the *Or Ein Sof* dances at the fringes of our conscious minds. Kabbalah is a way to connect with that dream, which is a reality. Like a single taste of the most exquisite delicacy, the *Or Ein Sof* tickles the palate of our collective and individual consciousness, and whether we know it or not, our unconscious minds are constantly striving to find the source of that taste and possibly even learn the recipe. Kabbalah is such a recipe. Through Kabbalah we discover the means by which to bring the *Or Ein Sof* to our Earthly table, so that we may partake of a constant diet of unearthly delights.

Chapter 4

The Seed

Any student of Kabbalah will benefit from a metaphorical examination of the seed. Like Jack's magic beans, the seed can serve as a conceptual link with the Upper Worlds; and like the Giant's key, the seed can reveal the jewels of wisdom that can only be discovered by knowledge of the inner truth. And certainly, at least on this physical plane of existence, there can be no better example than the seed for describing the *Ein Sof* (Endless World) before the Thought of Creation.

Within the seed, as with the *Ein Sof* before the Restriction, there exists the potential for roots, leaves, branches, and blossoms. We can look at the seed of an apple and say, here are the roots, here is the bark, here are the branches, the leaves, and the apples. Here is both the Desire to Receive as well as the Desire to Impart, the Light and the Vessel, the Circle and the Line. And just as the unplanted seed replicates in some way the conditions inherent in the *Ein Sof* before the Restriction, the seed, when planted, stands as an example of the conditions as they existed after the withdrawal and resulting contraction.

Only after various conditions are met (moisture, soil, sunlight) can the chain of events begin that will allow the undifferentiated elements within the seed to express themselves as separate entities. Let us, at this stage, examine the prevailing conditions within the *Ein Sof* before the *Tzimtzum* in order that we may better understand the chain of events that allowed the seed of Creation, so to speak, to blossom.

BEFORE THE BIG BANG

All ten of the Divine *Sefirot* or Luminous Emanations (bottled up energy-intelligences) were present within the Endless World from which sprang all future worlds. A perfect balance existed between the endless imparting of the Creator and the endless receiving of his creations—the souls of man. This condition of unity might have gone on forever had it not been for an aspiration towards equality that was inherent in the Desire to Receive. It was this desire to be a part of the give and take of Creation that resulted in the *Tzimtzum*.

The souls of man felt ashamed at the one-sidedness of their relationship with the Creator. This condition, which results from receiving that which is not earned, is defined in kabbalistic terms as Bread of Shame. And as it was the Creator's wish, and sole purpose, to bestow abundance on his creations, and as his creations could partake of His abundance only to the degree to which their sense of shame would allow them, the Creator caused the perfect Will to Receive to undergo a contraction (*Tzimtzum*) thereby causing a diversity of phase (separation) between the Emanator and the emanated, "...severing or discriminating the latter from the Former and causing the emanated one to acquire its own particular name."

Thus, did the Creator withdraw so that the Infinite could give birth to the finite, the Circle to the Line, the Seed of Creation to the Tree of Life. That moment of Divine conception, known to kabbalists as the Thought of Creation, and to scientists as the Big Bang, was the root of Creation, the source from which the Universe expanded complete with all of its phases and diversity, physical and metaphysical, as it was, is, and forever will be. As the seed contains the tree, the Thought of Creation contained the Tree of Life. The effect is always contained within the cause. The end result is inherent at the inception. To grasp this is to grasp a kabbalistic absolute; to master it is to find true wisdom.

BEFORE AND AFTER

Rav Isaac Luria taught us that fulfillment is the cause of desire, not the other way around. Nothing ever comes into existence the roots of which have not taken hold in the Ten Circular *Sefirot*. Desire was born from the Upper Light and to the *Or Ein Sof* it yearns to return. Our inner encircling vessels will find no rest unless and until all of the Infinite (Circular) Illumination which was once revealed in them shines with the same luminous intensity as it did long ago in the place without end.

Having pondered this wisdom, the Ari advanced a concept, elegant in its simplicity, that all phases of existence can be encompassed by a conceptual construct involving only two phases or conditions. The first phase consists of Desire that is fulfilled—as epitomized by the universal condition before the *Tzimtzum*. The second phase includes Desire that is unfulfilled—as exemplified by all that happened after *Tzimtzum*. The condition of fulfillment he called the Endless World. The latter condition of unfulfillment he named the World of Restriction.

By thus limiting the scope of existence, the Ari had arrived at a formula that had validity for every conceivable subject and situation. All of humanity's trials and tribulations, all life and growth, every thought, word, deed, and physical manifestation can be explained and understood according to which phase of Desire (fulfilled or unfulfilled) that is presently being revealed. Desire is constantly seeking fulfillment just as Light is endlessly available for revealment.

From this perspective there seems to be only one question that is truly worth asking: Am I revealing the Light or am I concealing It?

THE CLOSER THE BETTER

The seed is stronger than the tree. The root is stronger than the branch. The Circle is stronger than the Line. The Light is stronger than the Vessel. The thought is stronger than the word. The cause is stronger than the effect. The baby is stronger than the man.

What is meant by all this?

That which is closer to the source is said to be stronger, higher, loftier. The Light contained the Vessel as the cause contains the effect. The seed knows everything about the tree; the roots and branches have a more limited perspective. A baby is born with every brain cell that he or she will ever possess. Spiritually the baby has fewer complications than the man, fewer veils, less *klipot*. It is said that prophecy exists by means of imbeciles and children, and scientists tell us that the physical body begins to die the moment we are born.

So what is stronger?

That which is closest to the source.

Chapter 5

The Illusion of Darkness

When the creator withdrew from the endless so that free will could have expression and we, the emanated, could be absolved of the Bread of Shame, He left a vacuum and the illusion of darkness. For all Earthly intents and purposes, it seemed that the *Ten Luminous Emanations* had disappeared. Yet we know that it is a keystone of kabbalistic thought and theory that every word and every action, every manifestation, internal and external, physical and metaphysical, is imbued with the Light of Creation. How, then, can there be darkness?

In reality, the Light, which had formerly illuminated all phases of the Endless with equal magnitude, had been transformed and made manifest in a finite or linear form. Earlier we described the Light of Creation before the Restriction as existing in circular form, while after the *Tzimtzum* the vessels (*Sefirot*) containing the Light of Creation are said to have taken on the shape of a Line. The Circular *Sefirot* transformed, becoming the *Sefirot* of Straightness.

The Vessels and the Light contained within them became obscured from our view as a result of negativity, which might accurately be described as a by-product of the Desire to Receive. This negative energy, known as *klipot* (husks or shells), encircled the Light and the Vessels at the moment of the Thought of Restriction, producing an effect similar to that of a curtain placed over a lamp. The light is there in all its glory, but the viewer doesn't see it and so is unaware that it even exists. Thus, do the veils or metaphysical barriers cloud our perceptions and limit our spiritual potential.

The Ten Circular *Sefirot*, then, did not disappear. There is no disappearance in the realm of the metaphysical. Radical, essential changes only occur within material objects and in the perceptions of man. The shape of the vessels changed, but not the nature of the "bottled-up energy" within.

The same may be said of the seed that grew into a tree. The same may be said of the Circle that turned into a Line. The same may be said of the Light that transformed into darkness. They are all there—we just don't see them.

PERSPECTIVES

"One man's floor is another man's ceiling."

"One man's trash is another man's treasure."

"One man's art is another man's eyesore."

These old adages speak clearly of perspectives.

Indeed, beauty, ugliness, and everything in between, are in the eye of the beholder. Our reality is shaped to a large degree by our point of view. Take as an example a situation in which three people, a small child, a man of average height, and a man of exceptional height, gaze upon the same statue at a museum. If later asked to describe the statue, the small child might comment on the chin or beard, (assuming the statue was of a man), while the man of average height might comment on the face or eyes, and the exceptionally tall man might comment on the part of the hair.

There that statue sits—a solid, formed, material object of hardest steel or stone, and yet it means something completely different to everyone who sees it.

Is the same not true of all material objects? Taking this argument one step further might not the same be said of the entire material world? Is reality just a matter of perspective? You might arrive at that conclusion. It all depends on your point of view.

THE TWO FACES OF DESIRE

Kabbalah classifies the *Sefirot* into two categories: The Encircling *Sefirot* and the *Sefirot* of Straightness. Before *Tzimtzum*, the circular vessels were eternally satiated with the Light of Creation. The Restriction created a condition in which the Infinite Light contained within the Encircling *Sefirot* would remain concealed until acted upon by the *Sefirot* of Straightness, an aspect of the Line. The Circular *Sefirot* originated within the *Ein Sof* and at the time of the *Tzimtzum*, whereas the *Sefirot* of Straightness were an outgrowth of the subsequent limited creative process, the Line. Therefore the Circular *Sefirot* are considered superior, purer by virtue of their closer proximity to the Endless.

The Encircling Vessels cannot and must not receive Illumination in the Infinite sense, otherwise all Desire (negativity), and consequently all opportunity for correction, would be inundated by the omnipotent Light of the *Ein Sof*. In that event, the original purpose of Creation would be defeated as the Light would engulf the Vessel and the universe would revert to its original condition with the undifferentiated energy-intelligences receiving endlessly of the Light's beneficence, but again experiencing a sense of dissatisfaction at having no way of absolving Bread of Shame.

Desire has two faces. One, the Desire to Receive for the Sake of Sharing, is an attribute of the Circle. The second, the Desire to Receive for Oneself Alone, is a characteristic of the Line. Desire is humanity's most important asset in the struggle for physical survival, but it is also the largest obstacle on the path toward personal and planetary redemption. It is our most negative trait, but also our greatest opportunity for correction. By restricting the negative side of Desire we create a circular concept (an affinity or similarity of form between the Light and the Vessel) and thereby convert the negative aspect of Desire into the positive aspect.

The Circular *Sefirot* provide the impetus for all activity in the World of Restriction. They initiate all of our unconscious yearnings to return to our original Infinite condition. Were it not for those vague, primal memories of our past fulfillment being indelibly etched in our Encircling Vessels we would be totally devoid of all longing and desire— which would greatly hasten the extinction of the human race.

We of *Malchut* can find no peace until the Light contained within the Encircling *Sefirot* has been restored to its former brilliance. That possibility, however, in this phase of existence, is remote in the extreme. The finite nature of the *Sefirot* of Straightness precludes the possibility of them filling our Encircling Vessels to their fullest capacity, for as we know that which is finite can never equal that which is infinite.

Still, true and lasting fulfillment can be attained in this the World of Restriction—but not Infinite perfection. According to the ancient texts the complete illumination of all of the Encircling Vessels will occur only when the corrective process has come full circle.

Chapter 6

The *Sefirot* of Straightness

The Vessels of the Ten *Sefirot* of Straightness are called Pipes because they limit and control with great precision the Light drawn through them. Just as the capacity of a pipe is gauged by its diameter and the volume of water that can flow through it, so too do kabbalists measure the capacity of the *Sefirot* of Straightness. The Light, the *Or Ein Sof,* flows through the Vessels of Straightness in exact proportion to the Vessel's degree of longing, just as water flows through a pipe according to that vessel's capacity.

The Ari, in his description of "The Line as a Narrow Pipe" makes use of two phrases which the student of Kabbalah may find confusing. He refers to "the waters of the Upper Light" and later makes reference to "the more important Light" being "clothed in the purer vessel." As for the former, simply stated, when Light descends from its level in the manner that water descends via gravity, it takes on the image of waters of Light. The "more important Light," in the latter phrase, mentioned as being "clothed in the purer vessel" refers to the Light that is "more important" and the Vessel "purer" by virtue of being closer (having a greater affinity) with the Endless.

In more personal terms, a person who has a great degree of Desire to Receive for the Sake of Sharing will receive of the Light in direct proportion to his longing, whereas the person who has little or no Desire to Impart will receive little or no Light. The latter would not be entirely wrong in stating that there is no Creator or grand design, because for him they do not exist.

In the same manner that children sometimes attempt to hide from their playmates by covering their eyes with their hands, so too does the negative person hide from the Light of Creation. And just as a child who finally wearies of the darkness may peek through the cracks between his fingers, so too can a negative person, in a manner of speaking, open the fingers of his or her being and see the Light—the amount or magnitude of which will be directly proportionate to the size of the opening.

Stress, neuroses, burn-out; these terms from the modern vernacular describe conditions in which the flow of energy is uneven. If the inward flow is too great the pipe is apt to burst, or too little the pipe is apt to burst or become so corroded as to allow no energy to pass through. An even flow of energy is essential to a person's physical, emotional, and spiritual well being.

You will recall that before the *Tzimtzum*, Bread of Shame caused the Vessel to deny the endless flow of Divine Energy and this denial brought about the Restriction that granted a degree of free will to the Vessels. Henceforth, it became the universal condition that the Light would flow according to the instructions given to it by the Vessel. From that moment on it became our responsibility to control the input valves of our own creation.

LIGHT

The Light can be both a shield and a weapon. Not that the Light of Creation can be wielded like a sword or shot like a gun, for no mortal being can presume to actually control the Light of Creation. The Light, however, Whose desire is to share, achieves full expression only in the presence of a Desire to Receive, and should that receiving desire be motivated by the right intentions the true purpose of both Light and Vessel can be achieved.

The Light, the *Or Ein Sof,* accepts the direction of the Vessel in a manner similar to the way sunlight, or artificial light, can be directed through a fine strand, or vessel of fiber optical material. And just as a solar panel either attracts, repels, or magnifies sunlight according to the purpose for which it has been adjusted, so too can we through the "darkness or lightness" of our purpose and intentions, attract, repel, and otherwise give expression to the *Or Ein Sof.*

If a child cannot sleep because he or she is afraid of darkness, the symptomatic solution, of course, is to turn on the lights. That will alleviate the problem temporarily, but to relieve the symptoms permanently it becomes necessary to reveal the source of the problem, the metaphysical cause. Only by bringing the child's fears into the open, can the parent help the child to understand that it is not really the darkness that the child is afraid of, but that which he or she imagines to be lurking in the darkness. Perhaps it is fear of ghosts, goblins boogey men, or the recollections of some horrific television villain, that is causing the child's insomnia. A patient explanation that his or her fears are unfounded, sheds light on the metaphysical root cause of the child's problem, and, in so doing, helps the child effect a permanent cure.

Solar energy harbors great hope for mankind, but there is absolutely no hope of man ever making the slightest change in the sun itself. The same may be said for the *Or Ein Sof.* Light will accept direction, but the eternal circle of Creation cannot be altered in any way by man, it cannot be brightened or dimmed, chemically transformed, genetically grafted, or split like an atom. The reality of its Divine existence is complete, eternal, Infinite; change occurs only in the fleeting perceptions of man.

Darkness, in the material world, cannot exist in the presence of light. Nor can metaphysical darkness exist in the presence of the Energy-Intelligence known as the Light of Creation. Those who attract Light for the sake of sharing attract Illumination of sufficient amplitude to enlighten even the darkest corners of their beings. This method by which Light is attracted for the purpose of imparting, transforms negative into positive, evil into good, darkness into Light.

Chapter 7

By Any Other Name

S tudents of Kabbalah are often confused and exasperated by the seeming plethora of terms used to describe what at first appears to be the same concept. For instance, the expressions: Crown, Wisdom, Intelligence, Beauty, and Kingdom describe the condition in the Encircling *Sefirot* after the Light had withdrawn (*Tzimtzum*) and only the impressions (residues or vibrations) remained. The terms Living, Soul, Spirit, and Individual, on the other hand, are employed to describe the same Vessels after they have been restored with Light. Add to this confusing array, The Five Worlds or Extensions of Emanation: Primordial, Emanation, Creation, Formation, and Action—as well as the Four Phases: Light, Water, Firmament, and One Hundred Blessings, also called Lights of the Soul and Levels of Consciousness, which refer to the four grades of the Desire to Receive.

Thousands more examples could be given, but it is not our purpose to confuse the reader further, but merely to give a brief overview of Kabbalah's rich linguistic heritage and some of the reasons for its development. The highly complex language of Kabbalah evolved slowly over a millennium in response to ever widening, deepening knowledge of the nature of man's intimate relationship with the cosmos. It continues to develop, expand, and ripen to this day.

The kabbalist's task is by no means an easy one: Using illusionary symbols—both in the sense that all languages are symbolic and therefore illusionary, and also in kabbalistic sense that all things of this world are illusion, hence language, too, must be unreal—he attempts to provide a reasonable explanation for that which is beyond reason, to give expression to that which cannot be expressed, to illuminate concepts that are beyond the range of the senses. And, as if that were not enough, he must do all this with words that already have other fixed connotations and denotations that are often the antithesis of the concepts he is trying to express.

Is it any wonder that not everyone can understand what the kabbalist has to say?

Pragmatists criticize the language of Kabbalah as being irrational and illogical, and from their narrow perspective they are, of course, quite correct. In fact, the kabbalist would be the first to admit it, for one of the main purposes of Kabbalah is to transcend what is commonly called "logic" and "rationality" so that the real world can be perceived.

Needless to say, then, the study of Kabbalah is not for those who are extremely literal-minded. Rooted as they are in the illusion we call *Malchut*, the so-called rationalist is incapable of making the conceptual leap to the Divine word of Infinity from the limited language of man. Logic cannot arrive at a conclusion that is beyond the realm of logic. Nor can the kabbalist's language be heard by those who do not know how to listen. Words, thoughts, and ideas amount to nothing unless their meanings are understood.

The language of Kabbalah is of necessity a finite and therefore limited expression, but the concepts of Kabbalah, the indelible truths, can be comprehended by those who read the Language of the Branches with their hearts and not just with their eyes, and who listen with their minds and not just their ears.

It is hoped that the reader now fully understands the need for various nomenclatures to clarify numerous layers of symbolic meaning.

Chapter 8

The Cause Contains the Effect

In the first chapter of the second volume of *Ten Luminous Emanations*, the Ari states, "Everything which is Desire on an Upper Level is Necessity on a Lower Level emanated by its Upper Cause." He was speaking of cause and effect. The words "Upper" and "Lower" do not refer, in this instance, to actual physical relationships, but rather to that which is closer to (Upper) or farther (Lower) from the source. And so it is when the kabbalist says that "not even a blade of grass exists in this world without having its roots in the phase above," he is referring to that which happens at one stage being the result of that which happened one stage before.

Just as the leaf of a maple tree cannot suddenly decide one day to become the leaf of an aspen, nor an apple tree to become an orange tree, a man too must exist within the context of certain predestined genetic and cultural parameters. The tree is the effect contained within the cause, which is the seed, just as a man is the effect contained within the cause that was the "seed" of his parents, just as this world, *Malchut*, is the effect contained within its Upper cause, Formation.

That the effect is contained within the cause is, along with the idea of Endlessness, one of the most difficult metaphysical principles for the rational thinker to comprehend. The answer, as was stated in a previous chapter, is that nothing of a metaphysical nature can be experienced by the five senses. However, it is hoped that the examples given will allow the student to make the proper metaphysical connections. To the examples given, namely the leaf and the seed, and the parent and the child, add one more example, that of the "life" of a baseball which is thrown at a plate glass window.

Momentum, in a way of speaking, is a messenger of the energy-intelligence which, in this case, started the baseball in motion. Energy, as science has proven, has mass. Thoughts are energy, therefore they have mass, therefore they are palpable things. The ball becomes a living thing whose purpose is predestined by the person who threw it. The desire of the thrower becomes necessity on the lower (later) level emanated by its upper (earlier) cause, and somehow this moving energy intelligence telegraphs its trajectory to the object at which it is aimed, and the object in our example a plate glass window, responds by beginning to break up even before the ball reaches it. This phenomenon has been scientifically validated using microscopic photography, but has yet to be explained.

Could it be that the energy-intelligence which caused the ball to be thrown precedes the ball to its destination?

If so, it follows that cause and effect, instead of being considered as two separate entities, must now be considered as two parts of a single entity, one contained within the other. Hence we say that the cause contains the effect, which translates, for modern ears, the ancient, and far more poetic adage: He and His Name are One. He being the Creator or the cause, and His Name, being the Vessel or effect, are inseparable. Like space-time, and mass-energy, cause and effect are one and the same.

FULFILLMENT

Our denial of the Creator's endless imparting, which resulted in the *Tzimtzum*, caused the *Sefirot* of Circles to be left with but a mere impression of their former Illumination. Before the *Tzimtzum* the existence of an independent Desire to Receive was an impossibility, for any desire that might have manifested would have been instantly satisfied. The Light still shines brightly within us, but because of *Tzimtzum* we have lost touch with It. Eclipsed by the negative trappings of physical existence, the Light, the source of that Divine memory, for all worldly intents and purposes, remains latent and only potentially active.

Every one of us, with the possible exception of those who are blessed, or some might say cursed, with a photographic memory, has developed patterns of behavior around important psychological events that we have forgotten. Hidden deep in the sub-consciousness, these memories affect every aspect of our lives. Such is the case with the memory possessed by all mankind of our unity with the *Or Ein Sof.* The effect remains but not the cause.

Like echoes in a canyon, like muffled whispers in some foreign tongue, like phrases that can't quite be remembered, those nebulous impressions of our former unity with the *Or Ein Sof* haunt and sometimes irritate us. Unconsciously, unknowingly, the impressions link us with the supreme fulfillment that was ours before the *Tzimtzum* and keep us on our restless search for contentment.

Fulfillment is illusive. One can search a lifetime and never attain it. As ephemeral as a dream, it hovers near the outskirts of consciousness, barely out of grasp. As rare and priceless as an artistic masterpiece, true satisfaction is something that for most of us can only be appreciated from a distance. Like the Mona Lisa it is not for sale, but even if it were it would be way beyond our current spiritual means.

Lasting fulfillment escapes most of us for the simple reason that we each have but one true calling, one quest, venture, or undertaking that will permanently illuminate our seemingly vacant Encircling Vessels. This unique ordination was revealed to all of us in the *Ein Sof* with the Thought of Creation. The challenge faced by each of us is to rediscover the endeavor or singular activity that will once more establish our affinity with the Light.

The revealment of the latent *Or Ein Sof* within us can be accomplished in one of two ways. One is the trial and error approach in which the seeker tries on new lifestyles, philosophies, diets and spiritual doctrines as readily as a fashion model changes hats. Though not impossible, the odds against finding enduring fulfillment in this manner are monumental. A far less haphazard approach requires an understanding of the process of mental, emotional, and spiritual evolution as taught by Kabbalah.

All that lives and breathes takes part in an identical evolutionary process—every manifestation, physical and metaphysical—advances through the same four stages in the universal quest toward completion. When correctly perceived and applied, the teachings of Kabbalah let us see at a glance the stage through which any entity or manifestation is passing, up to and including ourselves.

This world is an illusion. The real world is hidden from view by veils of negativity, symptoms, and appearances. Through Kabbalah we gain new insights that allow us to trace the Line that is our lives back to our primordial beginnings in the *Ein Sof* where we were once unified with the Circle of Creation. Thus, do we reveal the Light of the Endless anew.

SYMPATHETIC VIBRATIONS

Every vessel has a certain note that causes it to reverberate louder than at any other frequency. Gently encircle the rim of a wine glass with a moistened finger to find that vessel's resonant harmonic. The singer's trick of breaking wine glasses is accomplished by singing that particular pitch at a volume sufficient to cause the glass to explode from the force of its own vibrations. By singing an ascending or descending scale into any container the one resonant harmonic can be readily identified that will cause the vessel to reverberate most loudly in sympathy with the note being sung.

The same can be said for the vessel that is our soul. One note, one activity, one calling, more than any other, can cause our interior Encircling Vessels to come alive with sympathetic vibrations—the same resonant harmonic that once filled our Encircling Vessels when we were all but undifferentiated aspects of the universal music of the spheres. To find this one resonant harmonic is the key to contentment and satisfaction.

Chapter 9

The Circle is Not Attached to the Endless

The previous phrase, attributed to Rav Issac Lucia (the Ari), cannot be taken at face value. As with all of the Ari's teachings, the meaning here cannot be grasped through literal interpretation. The reader is by now aware that Bread of Shame was the first cause of physical creation. The act of *Tzimtzum* dictated that the Circle and the Line would henceforth forever remain separated. From the moment that we, the emanated, asked for and received individuation from the Circle of the Endless, any and all revealment of the *Or Ein Sof* would, and could, only come about as a result of the Desire to Receive which is represented by the Line.

Otherwise, were it any other way, the Circle would embrace the Line, obliterating the essential dissimilarity of form that keeps the emanated separate from the Emanator, the Line from the Circle, the Vessel from the Light. And thus would the universe revert to its former state.

Attachment, from the kabbalistic frame of reference, pertains to similitude of form, or unity, whereas, diversity of phase, refers to detachment, or disunity. The words "not attached" in the above-mentioned phrase refer to this disunity between the Endless and the *Sefira* of the Crown of the Line, which is the "Root" of the extension of the Light to the Four Emanations: Wisdom, Intelligence, Beauty, and this world, Kingdom. As a newborn child is still considered a part of its mother even though the umbilical cord may have been severed so too are the *Sefira* of the Crown of Circles still a part of, though apart from, the Light of the Endless.

NEGATIVE EXPECTATIONS

Why do some men soar like eagles while others must burrow like moles? Why do some seem to drive straight to their destination while others meet with an endless variety of roadblocks and detours? Luck? Fate? Circumstances? Yes, perhaps each of these is in some way responsible. Every day, it seems, we hear of someone, somewhere who has transcended the meanest of circumstances to achieve prominence and prosperity. Though it must be admitted that those fortunate individuals remain the exception rather than the rule.

Why is it that some seem destined to accept their lowly fate while others come much closer to reaching their full potential? Societal and familial obstacles? Lack of opportunity? Peer group pressure? Certainly these all play a part. At one time it was a known fact that the world was flat and anyone who had the temerity to suggest otherwise would be summarily burned at the stake. In more recent times, there were those who predicted, with absolute certainty, that the Wright Brothers would never fly. "If God had meant man to fly he'd have given us wings," went their reasoning. Others warned Henry Ford that his plan to build the Model T would result in a disaster of the highest magnitude. No, they were not worried about pollution and the environment. The problem you see was that the human body would disintegrate at speeds in excess of fifteen miles per hour. There have always been doomsayers and Doubting Thomas's and thank Heaven, there have always been those who refused to listen to them.

For decades, runners strove in vain to conquer the Four-Minute-Mile. Again there were those who claimed that illusive mark to be beyond the scope of human capability. Then came Roger Bannister. Anyone who saw Mr. Bannister's historical record-breaking run will remember the look of agonized anguish etched into the runner's features as he crossed the finish line. Shortly after Roger Bannister broke the Four-Minute-Mile, another runner broke it, and another, and another. Today, we watch runners being interviewed after having run a Sub-Four-Minute-Mile, talking to the commentator as if they had been watching the race from the sidelines rather than having run in it. To what can we attribute the ease with which today's runners break a mark that was long thought impossible? Training? Nutrition? Equipment? Perhaps to some small degree—but a far more plausible reason is that the runners of today are not burdened, as Roger Bannister was, with the added weight of negative expectations.

Negative expectations depend entirely upon the individuals' attachment or detachment from the Circle. The Light contains an energy-intelligence of positivity. The further one is removed from the Light, the closer one is drawn to the power and influence of negativity.

Chapter 10

Binding by Striking

This was the first paradox and the root of every paradox in the universe. Light emanates to this phase, *Malchut*, in response to man's desire, but when that Light arrives it is deflected by the Curtain. Light so repelled is called Returning Light, which is said to bind with the Upper Light, giving Illumination to the Upper Emanations; hence the term: Binding by Striking. The result of this enigmatic phenomenon becomes doubly paradoxical when it is taken into account that this rejection, or casting off, of the Light from this the Fourth Phase, is the sole means by which the Light becomes manifest.

Positive and negative forces can never be reconciled without the aid of an intermediary. Each tendency remains functional in its own respective state until a bridge is made between them. Just as the filament has the potential ability to create a connection between the positive and negative poles of the light bulb, so too can man act as a filament between himself and the Light of Creation. It is only through man's conscious restriction, which is tantamount to a personal *Tzimtzum*, that the Light finds full expression.

The Upper Worlds receive their total illumination, not from the Source, the *Or Ein Sof,* directly, but as a result of this paradox called Binding by Striking. This concept will receive a more detailed analysis in a later chapter. In the meantime, allow the images of the filament of a light bulb and the flint in a lighter, both which illuminate through this process of refusal, to stand as reminders of Binding by Striking. In neither instance would the light be revealed were it not for these elements, the filament and the flint, acting contrary to their natural Desire to Receive.

Only man has the free will to exercise the third dimension which is rejection. Man, and man alone, can act as a filament between the *Or Ein Sof*, the Light of the Endless, and the Encircling Vessels that are within us and all around us, striving for revealment. By his rejection, man duplicates the act of *Tzimtzum* and thereby creates an affinity, or similarity of form with the Light. This is the bridge by which the empty Circular Vessels of man's existence are slowly, yet irrevocably, linked with the Endless Light of Creation.

The Light's sole purpose is to share, but the Vessel's Bread of Shame, which was the cause of the first restriction (*Tzimtzum*), prevents it from receiving the Light of the Endless without first having earned it. Remember, it was the Vessel that asked to share in the give-and-take of Creation, so that it could be absolved of Bread of Shame, but the Emanator, in granting that wish created, of necessity, a dissimilarity of form between the Light and the Vessel—for the finite cannot exist in the realm of the Infinite. This situation preordained a condition in which the Vessel would forever be destined to repeat the act of *Tzimtzum* in order that the mutually exclusive tendencies of the Light, which is to share, and that of the Vessel, which is to receive, can both be satisfied.

A person's Encircling Vessels receive only the Light that they have the capacity to reveal. The Light never says no, that is man's prerogative and his alone. The paradox lies in the fact that while a man may want to accept the Light that is freely offered he cannot do so without deactivating Bread of Shame. A man can bind or reveal the Light to the upper reaches of his being only by striking the Light away. For if he were to receive the Light directly from the Source, the *Or Ein Sof*, neither the purpose of the Light nor that of the Vessel would be served. The Light would envelop the Vessel and the universe would revert to a circular condition that would be contrary to the desire of the Vessel, whose Bread of Shame originally caused the Light and the Vessel to separate.

From the moment of the *Tzimtzum*, it became the universal condition that the Encircling Vessels, which are the hidden animus of all things on this phase of existence, could never again receive Illumination directly from the *Or Ein Sof*, but would have to be manifested via man's restrictive capacity. Thus the Curtain and its effect, that of Binding by Striking, became, and remains, the sole means by which we, the emanated, can reveal the Light that is our essence.

THE CIRCULAR CONCEPT

Some people are connected with the *Or Ein Sof*, others are not. The difference is affinity. Those who wish to live in a circular context with the Endless may do so by creating an affinity with the Light. Affinity is a circular concept. The Light cannot reveal the Encircling Vessels, which are the essence of man and the universe, unless the Vessel desires revealment.

Through the limited creative process of the Line a person can reveal the *Or Ein Sof* that surrounds him, and at the same time awaken the *Or Ein Sof*, the Encircling Vessels, within. The Circle can connect with the Line only when and if the Line makes the connection. We are the Line and only we can link our Inner Light with the Circle of the Endless. Through Desire to Share we create affinity, through affinity we reveal the Light.

Desire to Receive, as the reader is by now quite well aware, has two aspects: One is to Share, the other is to Receive for Oneself Alone. A person possessed by the latter can never know the Light. However much Light he may attract is repelled by the Curtain of his negativity.

Conversely, the person who seeks Light for the Sake of Sharing, creates an affinity with the Light by living within a circular context, and can therefore draw Light in direct accordance with his or her needs.

Chapter 11

Intentions

The final product of any thought or action is a direct result of the intention that first gave it impetus. Intentions, like seeds, contain within them all the potential for the roots, branches, leaves, and blossoms of the tree. A well conceived intention results in a well constructed object. The stronger the original intention, the more completely will the final result be manifested.

The same holds true in the physical world as well as in the realm of thoughts, words, and ideas. Make no mistake, Thoughts are things. So too are words, letters, numbers, and ideas. Just as surely as a chair is a thing, so too is a prayer, and so too, it logically follows, is an intention. It matters not in which realm of existence one seeks to make his mark; he must begin with an intention.

An intention is like a form, or mold, into which the cement of creation can be poured. Every thought, word, act, deed, and gesture begins with an intention, known or unknown, conscious or unconscious. Does it not stand to reason that the Creator had an intention when He decided to withdraw the Infinite and thus impart to his creatures love and happiness?

It was with a single intention that the world began.

ON BECOMING A CIRCLE

In kabbalistic terminology, that which encircles is that which causes, so when it is written that, "The Circle of the first emanation was encircled by the Light of the Endless," it means that the first emanation was caused by the Light of the *Ein Sof.* On a personal level, we find that man is born with inner Encircling Vessels, which, though in a potential state, are capable of manifesting Light. It is possible to bridge the gap between the *Or Ein Sof* and the potential Encircling Vessels by establishing what is known to Kabbalah as a Circular Concept, meaning that the Desire to Receive for the Sake of Sharing outweighs the Desire to Receive for Oneself Alone.

The Light exists within us and without us, it is a part of us and yet apart from us at the same time. The *Or Ein Sof* encircling us (Surrounding Light) exists only for the Sake of Sharing. The Inner Light, which is functional in a potential state, is capable of manifesting Surrounding Light, but only when acted upon by the limited creative process, the Line. The Line is man's only link with the *Or Ein Sof*: It is the filament by which Surrounding Light can fill his inner Encircling Vessels, and thereby reveal through illumination his true, primal nature.

The degree to which we fill our Encircling Vessels depends entirely on the capacity of our filament, which is Desire. There is no legal ordinance stating that we have to live within a circular context. Or, if such a law exists, there is no police force, no body politic or inner dynamic whose duty it is to uphold that law. There is no coercion in spirituality. The Light demands nothing from the Vessel. It is the degree to which the Vessel desires that is the sole determining factor in the manifestation of the Light.

The reasons for striving to live within a circular context are myriad. By linking our interior *Ein Sof* with the exterior *Ein Sof,* we establish communication with the Source of all things. This Source, the *Or Ein Sof,* exists in all phases of time-space, energy-matter, cause-effect. By creating a circular concept with the Light, we can "patch in" to the great universal network in which each phase, each atom and subatomic speck, is in constant and instant communication with every other speck. The more connections the kabbalist makes between his Inner Light and the Surrounding Light, the more readily can he utilize the all pervasive universal system. The stronger is his desire to share, the greater is his power to reveal the Light of Creation.

INNER LIGHT/SURROUNDING LIGHT

Rav Ashlag's interpretation of the Ari's discourse on Inner Light begins as follows: "In each *Sefira* we distinguish two types of Light: Inner Light and Surrounding Light..."

Inner Light does not illuminate the Fourth Phase. If it did there could be no diversity of phase between the Light and the Vessel, for the Light would most certainly nullify the Vessel's inherent negativity by drowning it, so to speak, in the immensity of its positive cosmic energy. This Vessel, *Malchut*, the Fourth Phase, must therefore receive Light "at a distance" in the form of Surrounding Light that encircles everything on this planet, in all of its phases.

Just as the ozone layer of the atmosphere repels much of the light that attempts to penetrate it, so too does the Curtain of *Malchut* repel the Light of Creation, allowing only that Light that is specifically required to enter. The harmful sunlight, the infrared and ultraviolet, is for the most part repelled, for if it were not rejected it would surely nullify all that is alive on this planet. And as every physical law and manifestation has a metaphysical counterpart, it follows that there must also be a cosmic perimeter that blocks out much of the Light of Creation. In kabbalistic terminology the Restriction and the Curtain on the Fourth Phase establishes a boundary that limits the extension of the Light to the Fourth Phase. The total Light received by *Malchut*, not including that which was expelled by the Curtain and restriction, is termed: Limit.

The Earth and all her creatures, with the sole exception of man, have a built-in limiting mechanism. Man and man alone must consciously restrict his input, for it is only by exacting finitude on the Infinite—in other words, by creating a bridge or filament between the Line and the Circle—that the Encircling Vessels that are within him can again be filled.

It is the purpose of Light to be revealed, and the purpose of man to reveal it. The aura of Surrounding Light encircles every atom in the universe, yet it must remain in a potential state until man by his conscious desire makes the necessary connection that allows the Light to manifest. By our restriction, our denial, we act as a filament that brings forth the Light. In this way we fulfill the purpose of both Light and Vessel, Circle and Line. By denying the darkness we reveal the Light, by restricting the negative we release the positive, and in this manner do we absolve the Bread of Shame.

Chapter 12

The Essence of Time

Words like "sooner," "later," "now," and "simultaneous," are relative expressions. What is here and now for one, is there and then for another. From the perspective of a man who is late for an important appointment, time is rushing by at a breakneck pace, while from the point of view of another man who is early for the same appointment, the same time may be dragging by interminably. How time is perceived depends on the perspective from which it is observed.

If the man who is late for the appointment were to be suddenly teleported to his destination, time would immediately be transformed from an angry tyrant into a benign servant, worthy of accolades instead of diatribes for having brought all of the parties together at the same time, in the same place, for the same meeting. Distance (space) plays a part in how we perceive time.

Time, as an entity apart from the space-time continuum, does not exist. Just as height cannot exist without width, and depth cannot exist without the other two linear dimensions, neither can time and space exist independently. Space and time are inseparable. The clock is a man made construct. There is no great clock from which the universe sets its cosmic watch. Nature moves according to the dictates of her own internal, eternal, yet ever-changing, rhythms. Only man marches in time to the beat of a clock. Man, and only man, worships at the altar of time.

While it is true that we cannot stem the tide of the space-time continuum, we can change our perception of it and by so doing significantly alter the course of our lives. Imagine time as a river that runs from the far distant past into the far distant future. Imagine that the flow of the river is controlled by your wants and needs, moods and emotions. When your thoughts are clear, so are the waters of time. When you are "agitated" the waters are also agitated. When you are in a hurry (as was the man who was late for his appointment) the banks of the river are narrow and the waters are white capped rapids. When you are at rest the waters run cool and calm. When you are afraid the waters are dark and ominous. When you are at peace the waters are mirror glass smooth.

What, then, is the essence of time? Is it a friend or an enemy? Is it our servant, a mere convenience by which we measure our lives, or is it a tyrant who rules over us with an iron hand? Do we use it or does it use us? There is no single answer. In the final analysis time is what you make it.

Chapter 13

Energy-Intelligence

At first glance the above two words may seem mutually exclusive, but from a kabbalistic frame of reference they make perfect sense, for without one the other could not exist. Everything has intelligence. Everything is imbued with the Light of Creation. Everything has the potential to influence for good and for bad. Everything requires a Vessel, and Energy is the Vessel that reveals the Light of Intelligence.

Energy-Intelligence is what makes man do what he does: The Energy-Intelligence called the *Sefirot* of the Desire to Receive of *Malchut*, the strongest Desire to Receive. A *Sefira* is a vessel. A vessel is that which reveals. An intelligence must work to reveal.

What makes a rock a rock? As we learned earlier, matter is, if you will, a matter of degree. The Rock of Gibraltar, if it could somehow be compressed into a state devoid of space and atoms, would fit comfortably into a wheelbarrow. The one percent of the rock that gives it shape is the rock's energy intelligence. The other ninety-nine percent is totally oblivious to the shape of the rock and would just as soon be occupying space in a Manhattan office building, a human being, or a tree.

Energy intelligence is manifested according to the degree of the Desire to Receive. The greater the Desire to Receive of the Vessel, the greater will be the manifestation of the Light. Inanimate objects have a lesser Desire to Receive than animate life forms, but all are infused with Intelligence to a lesser or greater degree.

Scientists now tell us what kabbalists have known for centuries: Everything is connected. There is no space in metaphysics, no time as we know it. We are all a part of some grand space-time-mass-energy spectrum, and within every color of that spectrum, from the darkest color to the lightest, lives the potential for influence and communication, give and take. When one energy-intelligence meets another there is potential for attraction or repulsion, collision or merger. When energy-intelligences attract there is said to be an affinity between them. It is this meeting of the minds, if you will, that compels one to pick up a certain rock on a beach instead of a million others. It is the energy intelligence of two people that attracts them to, or repels them from, each other.

Is a rock a living thing?

Yes, but again it is a matter of degree. A rock has a Desire to Receive, but nowhere near as great as that of a man. As you move up the scale of life through the mineral, vegetable, and animal kingdoms you find a greater Desire to Receive. Still, as small as the energy-intelligence of a rock may be, it can still influence, cause a stirring, in the energy intelligence of a man, if the man is susceptible. A Desire to Receive for Oneself Alone can make a person susceptible to the negative influences inherent in the energy-intelligence of that rock. Conversely, a strong Desire to Receive so that One May Impart can allow a person to come under more positive influences, or not be influenced at all, depending on the best interests of the person involved.

If anyone has trouble believing that a rock can influence a man, consider the men and women who have died while climbing Mount Everest. Why do men climb mountains? The standard answer is, "Because it's there..." The kabbalist would answer, "Because my energy-intelligence has an affinity with its energy-intelligence." In effect, they are two ways of saying the same thing. Many a climber has talked with a mountain, and many a mountain has answered, it is just that the climber has no words to describe the experience so he must rely on the standard reply.

Still not convinced? Consider that our literature, films, and television are filled with wild-eyed men and women who have succumbed to the negative influences of the energy-intelligences of diamonds, gold, and precious stones. Remember the thousands of lives lost in the gold rushes of San Francisco and the Klondike. Men have killed for a single stone; others have served half of their lives in prisons.

Ask them why they did it and they will probably answer, "Because it was there."

THE SOURCE REIGNS SUPREME

The kabbalist seeks to return to the seed of his existence, the source of his stream. The seed contains, in potential form, all of the attributes of the Four Emanations that have yet to manifest. From the Source of the stream of life, the kabbalist gazes on a vista that encompasses past, present, and future—the beginning, the middle, and the end. If he chooses to view the stream from the perspective of the First Emanation (Wisdom) the view is not as clear, and from the perspective of the Second Emanation (Intelligence) the view is dimmer still, and so on down to *Malchut*, this world, where the *Or Ein Sof* is completely obscured by negativity.

For the kabbalist, reality, as defined by worldly standards, is unreality, and the real reality, the first cause, the Source, the *Or Ein Sof,* lies one phase beyond. By connecting with the Endless, the kabbalist fills his inner Encircling Vessels, thereby creating a similarity of form between himself and the worlds around him, which in turn sheds Light on every phase of his life. By bridging the gap with the Light around him, he reveals the Light within.

A WORLD APART

Although *Keter* (Crown), the first stage in any manifestation, embodies the potential for all stages of a manifestation, it is not included in the chain of events through which all things must pass in order to find full expression. The Line must act upon the Circle. Desire gives expression to the Light. The *Ein Sof*, the *Keter* of Everything, has no need to become manifested on a physical level. It is we who give *It* expression. By our prayers we give *It* expression, by our thoughts, both positive and negative, by our words, and by our deeds.

A seed, the *Keter* of a tree, would never grow in a vacuum-sealed container. Certain conditions must be satisfied before the seed's potential can be realized, and until those conditions are addressed the seed will remain in the Circular Phase of its existence: Having no desire to grow, it does not grow. This is one example of why the *Keter*, in this case the seed, is not considered a part of the process that leads to manifestation.

The brain, the *Keter* of a man, registers every pain and tactile impulse in the body, and yet it remains blissfully ignorant of its own pain and discomfort. Consider the ease with which we can "read" the character or intentions of another person, and the difficulty we have in coming to know ourselves. The brain we have, it seems, plays the leading role in the drama that is our lives, but only if it is acted upon by outside influences that are brought about as a result of Desire.

SMOKING IS HAZARDOUS TO YOUR HEALTH

Why do we succumb to evil? What is the nature of temptation? Why will some men give up their loved ones and families and even their lives in pursuit of ill gotten gains? We know that smoking, drugs, and alcohol pose serious dangers to our health, and yet we go on using them. Why?

As mentioned earlier, the negative aspect of any energy intelligence has the potential to influence any other, but only if one allows itself to be susceptible to the other. All of us, in other words, are subject to negativity, but only some of us fall under its influence.

Why are some of us seemingly impervious to the effects of these evil influences while others seem endlessly to be caught up in their clutches?

To learn the answer we must go back to the *Ein Sof* before the Restriction when the souls of man asked to share in the give and take of Creation. When the Light granted free will to the Vessel it gave up some of its power so that the Vessel would be allowed to express its Desire to Receive. The Light withdrew, in other words, so that darkness could have expression. In this way did the Creator allow evil *klipot* (Shells or Husks) to encircle both Himself and His creations.

Man allows evil. A man who connects only with the external, a man whose Desire to Receive for Himself Alone outweighs his Desire to Receive for the Sake of Imparting, falls easy prey to the influence of negativity; whereas the man who connects with the internal, a man whose desires are in proper balance with the wants and needs of others, is much less susceptible to the influence of negativity and the temptations constantly posed by evil.

Chapter 14

Bread of Shame

One of the most pervasive of all human traits is guilt. Like fear, guilt produces a magnification of the senses, but unlike fear, which usually incapacitates temporarily—as with a fright of short duration—guilt can be protracted over a significant portion of a person's lifespan. Yet, in the end, no matter how hard the guilty party works to cover the tracks of his or her indiscretions, the truth invariably comes to Light.

To live in a world of guilt is to live in a world of distortion. The guilty man must watch his every move. Fear of discovery lurks in the darkened corners of his imagination. Small becomes large, large becomes larger. The world seems out of proportion. For him the walls have ears. Even a casual comment can send the guilty party into a fit of paranoia. An innocent remark made by another in jest, might, for the guilty one, carry heavy portent: News as to how far his guilt has traveled, a clue as to the traitor who might have revealed his unconscionable deed.

Intense self-scrutiny, such as is engaged in by those whose normal reactions are paralyzed by guilt, causes acute self-consciousness that compels the guilty party to invent an increasingly elaborate network of feints and fabrications in order to explain away his unusual behavior. In time, it becomes impossible to hold up the flimsy foundation of pretenses on which the guilty party has constructed his edifice of lies. He grows weary, depleted of psychic and physical energy. No longer can he abide the need for disguises; no longer can he maintain the charade that has become his life. Like a spider caught in a web of its own creation, the guilty man struggles vainly to escape the net of his illusions, until, at last, the intricate structure, so painstakingly woven from the sticky stuff of lies, closes around him—a predicament from which there is ultimately only one escape: The truth.

RESTRICTION

Early Man devised a method by which to start a fire that consisted of striking a hard rock against a softer rock with the intention of producing sparks. A similar restrictive action, known to Kabbalah as Binding by Striking, must take place in every instance where Light is brought into this world. A contraction must take place, a *Tzimtzum*, so that Light may be revealed.

Revealment begins with restriction.

A woman's uterine contractions precede the miracle of birth. Athletes, and also body builders, have an expression, "Pain is gain," which attests to the exact correlation of results produced with the degree of restriction imposed upon the musculature. Even on a metaphysical or thought level we see that the same principle is valid. Concentration, narrowing (restricting) the focus of our thoughts is necessary to manifest words and ideas of the highest order. Where little restriction is exercised the thoughts produced are of the "like, well... you know" variety.

The more resistance a filament is capable of producing, the greater is the revealment of Light. The restrictive capacity of the filament in a light bulb, the flint in a lighter, or what we will call the life-force of a human being, wears down eventually making it impossible for the Vessel to reveal the universal energy-intelligence—Light.

Of all the creatures on this world the human being alone lacks an instinctive restrictive mechanism. Before the *Tzimtzum*, you will remember, we asked for and received a degree of free will that allows us to reveal the Light or not, as we so desire. Either we must consciously re-enact the *Tzimtzum* and in so doing absolve Bread of Shame or succumb to negativity and remain in darkness. Light never diminishes, only the capacity for restriction.

By our conscious restriction we reveal the Light. If we choose not to restrict we allow for the existence of darkness. By restriction we eliminate Bread of Shame, while not exercising restriction imprisons us in a state of psychological, emotional, and spiritual unfulfillment. When viewed from this kabbalistic perspective the choice presented to humanity on this phase of existence boils down to one absurdly simple solution: Restrict so that the Light may be revealed.

TZIMTZUM (RESTRICTION)

The Restriction created the illusion of darkness. Concealed though It may be, the Light still provides the impetus for our every thought and action. The impressions implanted in the Encircling *Sefirot* will allow us no rest, no peace, no contentment, until the Light has been revealed anew. The Ari, of blessed memory, taught us that the one true purpose of existence is to restore Light, as much as is humanly possible, to its original, Circular, Infinite condition through the limited creative process of the Line.

We falsely believe that our restless search for satisfaction will one day result in the fulfillment of our desires, but in reality we already possess everything that will bring us true and lasting satisfaction. Deluged as we are by an endless stream of sensory stimulation, one might easily be deceived into thinking that the world of appearances, the world we see, hear, taste, touch, and smell, is the be all and end all of existence. That is why the kabbalist seeks not to satisfy the myriad of superficial desires presented by the world of illusion, but to restrict them—for by so doing he or she ignites, through the act of

Binding by Striking, the Infinite Light of Creation and thereby absolves Bread of Shame.

Yet, logically we cannot go back in time to the *Ein Sof* before the Thought of Creation or can we?

The *Tzimtzum* that catapulted us from Infinity into Creation was only the first of untold billions of tzimtzums that were to follow. Countless tzimtzums take place every second. Stopping a car, turning off the ignition, locking the door, switching off a light, closing out a bank account, shutting one's eyes to go to sleep, all are tzimtzums. Every time we say no and really mean it we re-enact the *Tzimtzum.*

The kabbalist resists that which would take him from his mission to restore the Light. He repels temptation, obstructs deception, denies illusion; he restricts pride and vanity, resists fraud and duplicity. He narrows his frame of reference to the root cause, the primal essence of existence, for only from the perspective of the source can all future emanations be seen.

To focus is to restrict, to restrict is to create affinity with the Creator. The longer and more attentively we restrict our focus to the physical or metaphysical manifestation on which our sites are set, the greater is the probability of successful completion. By consciously re-enacting the *Tzimtzum* process we rekindle the ancient spark of Infinity.

THE OFFSPRING OF RESTRICTION

The Ari, in *Ten Luminous Emanations*, described the Curtain as being the "Power of Restriction that is awakened when the Light reaches the Fourth Phase...striking and pushing the Light backwards." The Curtain is the power that prevents the Light from spreading to the Fourth Phase. It is not the restriction of *Tzimtzum per se*, but a further restriction that only happens at the moment when the Light of Creation reaches this, the Fourth Phase. In other words, when *Tzimtzum* acts involuntarily to repel the Light of the Infinite it is called Masach or Curtain.

The *Sefirot* of Straightness, acting in conjunction with the power that is the Curtain, represents a paradox in that both behave in complete opposition to their natural Desire to Receive. In this sense, the Curtain has much in common with the filament of a light bulb that also acts contrary to its natural inclination. The light that manifests inside a light bulb is not, as most people imagine, the result of some harmonious conversion of electricity within the filament. Rather it is the effect produced by a violent resistance or throwing off, restricting the negative pole—the natural inclination of which is the Desire to Receive. This action known as Binding by Striking might be likened to a person who asks another for a gift, but when that gift is given the receiver throws it back into the benefactor's face. The negative pole, in effect, is asking the positive pole for electricity, and the positive pole, whose desire is to impart, readily complies; which brings us to the paradox: Instead of accepting the electricity it just asked for, the negative pole repels it, thereby causing the filament to heat up to red hot intensity and the light to be revealed. In human terms, on a physical level, the involuntary narrowing of the eyes when we walk from darkness into strong light is the Curtain, and such is its contrary, though absolutely essential, nature.

The Curtain, then, represents a duality of purpose and function in that it contains both a quality of restriction and a quality of reconciliation. While it protects us from the Light, at the same time it denies us access to it. What need have we for protection from the *Or Ein Sof* which is, after all, a part of us? Just as the eyes must adjust to changes in light, so too must the "eyes" of the soul be prepared before gazing on the Light of the Endless. Just as a light bulb would be obliterated by the sudden infusion of a million watts of raw electric power, so too would an unwary life-force be vaporized by direct connection with the *Or Ein Sof*.

Pause to consider the unimaginable power that is contained within each of us. The most famous formula in the modern world, $E=mc^2$, expresses this power vividly. Simply stated it means that the "bottled up" energy contained in any piece of matter is equal to the mass of that piece of matter times the astronomical number of the speed of light (186,000 miles per second) squared! What this means, hypothetically, is that a sudden release of the energy held captive within a single strand of hair would produce an explosion of such magnitude as to be felt around the world. Is it any wonder that we need protection from the *Or Ein Sof*?

Conversely, any denial of the Light of Creation, as represented by the Curtain, whether involuntary or not, is a negation of both the Light and the Vessel. The Curtain negates the Light by denying its true purpose, which is to share, and it also denies the Light access to the Vessel whose desire is to receive. Thus does the Curtain prevent both Light and Vessel from living up to their true potential.

If the Creator is all-powerful why does He allow the Curtain to shut Him out?

To answer that question we must go back to the *Ein Sof* before the Thought of Creation. The Vessel asked for the right to share in the give and take of Creation and the Light, whose sole purpose in creating the emanated beings was to impart peace and happiness to them, granted that wish. The Creator then had to withdraw, for no negativity could exist as a separate entity in the Light of Creation, just as no darkness can exist in a place where there is strong light. And so the Creator consciously limited His power so that we, the emanated, could be granted free will, and therefore it is incumbent upon us to purify the selfish desire, wherein lies the Curtain, so that we may complete the cycle of imparting and receiving.

How can this be accomplished?

In the words of the Ari, "...the Surrounding Light then exerts itself to purify the Curtain, according to whatever the amount of longing there is." Longing, of course, is synonymous with desire. The negative energy that is the Curtain can be purified, but only if there is great longing on the part of the Vessel (Soul) to receive the Light for the sake of sharing.

And here again the paradox surfaces: By negating the negative we release the positive and move closer to the Endless Circle of Creation.

Chapter 15

Curtains

There are two modes of restriction, *Tzimtzum* and the Curtain. The first is voluntary, the second, involuntary. Either we restrict our Desire to Receive for Ourselves Alone, meaning we create affinity with the Light by repeating the *Tzimtzum*, or restriction will occur regardless through the activation of the Curtain. This situation was of our own making. The *Tzimtzum* resulted from our desire to be released from the burden of Bread of Shame, and because of that restriction we can no longer receive anything in good conscience that has not been earned.

The thief is an embodiment of Desire to Receive for Oneself Alone. While he may imagine himself in some romantic context, the thief is really in a Catch-22 situation. He can receive no joy from that which he steals unless and until he has dealt with Bread of Shame. Generally a thief will do this in one of two ways. Either he consciously lifts Bread of Shame by spending like the proverbial drunken sailor, or, if he is a more experienced thief who has tired of the cycle of fortunes slipping through his fingers, he invests his money wisely, lays low, lives frugally, and then makes some minor "mistake" while in the middle of one of his ventures such as leaving a single fingerprint on a window or a doorknob that allows him to correct his behavior in a federal prison. And so it goes, around and around on an endless treadmill of unfulfilment.

Of the two methods used by thieves to absolve Bread of Shame, the former is a case of voluntary restriction (*Tzimtzum*), in that no one coerces him into throwing away his money—he makes a conscious decision to "live for today." The latter is an example of involuntary restriction, for even though the frugal thief "tzimtzums" initially, insofar as he restricts himself from throwing his money away, the Curtain descends upon him anyway because he has not dealt with Bread of Shame. Those few thieves who steal and never get caught alleviate Bread of Shame through other means such as living in cells of their own making, prisons of paranoia and self-induced solitary confinement. Never does the thief find anything but transitory pleasure from that which he has stolen. In spite of all his attempts to convert his spoils into some type of lasting satisfaction he can never truly enjoy his ill-gotten treasures because the energy intelligence of those goods belongs to someone else. He may launder the money, but that in itself will never cleanse his dirty conscience.

Habitual thievery is by no means the only negative activity subject to the paradox. Compulsive behavior of any kind is an indication of Desire to Receive for Oneself Alone. Eating, drinking, smoking, drug taking, working, and sexual compulsiveness all have the potential to provoke similar outcomes in terms of the two kinds of restriction. Either the smoker voluntarily restricts his intake of smoke (*Tzimtzum*) or emphysema, or some other involuntary ailment (Curtain), will do it for him. The overeater can consciously restrain his appetite (*Tzimtzum*) or an involuntary Curtain of high blood pressure or cholesterol will create a life threatening situation. The alcoholic either stops drinking or his liver gives out. The workaholic consciously restricts his hours or a heart attack does it for him. And so on. If any habituated individual does not learn to consciously restrict his indulgence of that to which he is addicted, it will, to use an old expression, be "curtains" for him.

It is truly ironic that by consciously rejecting that which we think we want we reveal what we really want—not the avaricious longings of our bodies, or the minor matters that are important to our rational minds, but the true and lasting desire of our inner Encircling Vessels, which is to reveal the Light within.

Chapter 16

Symmetry

An aspect of the grand re-formation that unfolded after the *Tzimtzum* was the emergences of Five Worlds. These Worlds, listed in relation to their proximity to the Infinite, from the highest to the lowest are:

1. Primordial Man - Archetypal
2. The World of Emanation
3. The World of Creation
4. The World of Formation
5. The World of Action

When the Creator withdrew to make room for free will and the Desire to Receive, the circular condition became linear hence the concept of limitation. The Creator gave us the choice to manifest Energy according to our Desire to Receive. The Creator imposed a limitation on Himself (*Tzimtzum*) and from that moment on the Vessel could receive Light or not according to its own free will. We are the Vessel. It is we who must choose whether or not to manifest the Light of Creation.

From the kabbalistic perspective, the Line is Adam. Both represent the first limitation. Here, for the first time, the souls of man that had previously been an undifferentiated aspect of a circular (Infinite) condition now became linear or finite. No longer were the souls of man an unexpressed aspect of the endless wheel of Creation. Now, the pure spirit that was man would be housed in a body whose life was finite, having a beginning, a middle, and an end. Like the veils covering the Ten Divine *Sefirotic* Vessels, henceforth would the souls of man be clothed in flesh and encircled by *klipot*.

CONCENTRIC CIRCLES OF UNDERSTANDING

When we speak of a Vessel without a Curtain we use the term Circle. Negativity can cloud our actions and reactions. A person who is not "weighed down" by husks or shells of negativity (*klipot*) is closer to the Infinite, and hence deemed higher than one who is encumbered by the weight of negative thoughts and emotions. A circular concept is defined as: "The balance between left and right, negative and positive, brought about by the use of restriction." Only man has the option of exercising free will when it comes to his own spiritual evolvement. The closer one becomes with the endless circle of Creation, the less encumbered one is by negativity, and the closer one is to creating a circular concept with himself and the world around him.

A man caught up in his own desires is like a snake eating its own tail. The Desire to Receive for Oneself Alone causes layer upon layer of negativity to build up around a person—the greater the Desire to Receive, the greater is the constriction. Farther and farther does he recede from the circular concept, blinder and blinder does he become to the Light of Creation, until, at last, the connection with the *Or Ein Sof* has been completely severed. Thus, with blinded eyes, he goes through life unaware that the brilliant, endless Light of *Ein Sof* is within him, and all around him, and could be his for the asking.

By transforming our Desire to Receive for Ourselves Alone into a Desire to Receive for the Sake of Imparting we can break the chains of negativity that imprison us. Only by re-creating an affinity with the *Or Ein Sof* can we fill the Encircling Vessel within us all. How can we lift the veils of our own negativity and rise to our fullest potential? Shakespeare wrote that the world is a stage. Yes, it is a stage—this physical world, *Malchut*, is a stage of spiritual development, and only by creating a circular concept can we raise the Curtain of negativity that surrounds us to meld with the circular Light of Creation.

An understanding of the nature of symmetry is essential to a proper understanding of Kabbalah. In fact, it may be said that to comprehend symmetry is to comprehend the very workings of nature itself. Everything strives toward symmetry. Negative seeks positive; cause seeks effect; darkness seeks light. Or, to cite a kabbalistic frame of reference: The Light, the Desire to Impart, seeks the Vessel, the Desire to Receive.

Physicists now believe that all natural forces exist solely to allow nature to maintain an abstract balanced symmetry. This constant striving toward equilibrium, in Oriental philosophy, is known as the Male-Female principle or Yang and Yin. Mystics dubbed it simply, life-force. From a kabbalistic point of view, the spirit-body spectrum is one in which energy, or spirit, is connected with the Light, or Life-giving entity, while the body is the material expression of the energy that results from a melding of the two.

One needs only look into a full-length mirror for a practical demonstration of symmetry at work: Two arms, two hands, two legs, two feet, two ears, two nostrils, two of almost everything. Even our brain is divided into two distinct parts that are often at odds with each other and constantly seeking equilibrium. Scientists have discovered that the left half of your brain operates at a much higher speed than the right. Hence, in order to achieve a balanced mental state it is necessary for either the right side to speed up (which can be accomplished through some forms of dance, music, and active meditation, or, to a lesser and inferior extent through the use of intoxicants) or for the left side to slow down, which is achieved through passive meditation and deep relaxation. This constant striving toward symmetry affects every aspect of our lives. When we are out of balance mentally, emotionally, or physically, an instinctual reflex seeks to balance the scales again.

So to understand the dynamics of balance is to understand the nature of life itself. We live in a world of perpetual correction and Kabbalah teaches us how to achieve what is perhaps the only type of equilibrium of which man is or will ever be capable, the symmetry that is achieved by cleaving with the Infinite.

Chapter 17

The Primordial Man

In the previous chapter, reference was made to recent developments in split-brain research, pointing to the fact that the left cerebral hemisphere operates much faster than the right. Many of us are by now familiar with the characteristic attributes of the right and left hemispheres, the left being in control of language and the more cognitive and scientific skills, while the right houses the more artistic side of our temperament.

Another division should also be noted, the division between the front brain or cerebrum, which is the center of our reasoning faculties, and the back brain or cerebellum, which is the principal organ of the central nervous system. It is said that the cerebrum contains the newest, most human circuitry, while the cerebellum is comprised of circuits that were patterned in primordial times.

The human brain, then, has four distinct divisions and not two as is commonly believed, and these four divisions concur and coincide completely with the Four Phases described in the Kabbalah and indeed with the entire *Sefirotic* system. And it also confirms the kabbalistic contention that man is a universe unto himself, with the history of the world, past, present, and future etched into his circuitry.

That may seem like a tenuous leap of logic to some, until they examine more closely the make-up of the human brain. Consider that our skulls contain an old brain and a new brain. Within the old brain are two brains, an old reptilian brain that was perfected 200 to 300 million years ago and is identical to that of a lizard, and an old mammalian brain that is nearly as ancient. Consider, too, that the very chemicals and compounds of which our bodies are composed are only the most recent metamorphosis of materials that have been around since the beginning of time and will be here long after time as we currently keep track of it has been forgotten.

We are all models of the universe, encyclopedias, living museums of all that is, was, or ever will be.

THE EMERGENCE OF THE CENTRAL COLUMN

Before the universe became the multiverse that we live in today, there were only two inherent aspects in nature. Kabbalah describes them as Light and Vessel. Ancient Oriental cosmogony calls these two opposing, though complementary, forces the Male-Female Principle or Yang and Yin. Like Light in the kabbalistic lexicon, Yang represents the male creative aspect, while Yin, synonymous with the kabbalistic Vessel, represents the female receptive of existence. Everything in the world was, and is, endowed with both Light and Vessel attributes in varying degrees. The following chart will provide the student of Kabbalah with practical demonstration of how the principle of Light and Vessel applied to the physical world.

LIGHT	VESSEL
Desire to Impart	Desire to Receive
Right Column	Left Column
Light	Darkness
Male	Female
Yang	Yin
Positive	Negative
Sender	Receiver
Proton	Electron
Plus	Minus

Intellect	Intuition
White – reflective	Black - absorbent
Alkaline	Acidic
Hard	Soft
Active doing	Passive being
Perfection	Completeness

Many more examples could be given, but it is hoped that these few will help the student better understand the concept of Light and Vessel and just how myriad and all encompassing are their implications. According to adherents of the so-called New Physics, the purpose of nature, all action and reaction in the universe, is a striving towards an abstract symmetry. When this new and futuristic theory is finally proven, science will again be confirming what has been common knowledge to kabbalists for thousands of years.

On an atomic level, hydrogen, the most abundant element in the universe represents a pure example of Light and Vessel. As hydrogen is the only element devoid of a neutron, it alone stands as an example of the world as it was before the emergence of the Central Column. In this sense, it is a throwback to the world of Primordial Man, when there was but a Single Line that was composed of Light and Vessel. Only later, at a lower level did the forces congeal to form a third energy intelligence, the mediating principle known to Kabbalah as the Central Column.

This third factor, described atomically as the neutron, displays two tendencies, one of restriction, the other of reconciliation. When the negative energy of the Left Column which is the Desire to Receive is activated, the Central Column acts to restrain it. The nature of the Central Column is to provide a bridge between the Right and Left columns, allowing the energy of the imparting aspect of the Right to make use of the energy of the Left. Only when all three Columns are in balance does the system operate at peak efficiency.

STRAIGHT FROM THE SOURCE

Straight Light emerges directly from the Source without intervention on the part of the Vessel. That is not to underestimate the Vessel's essential role in the manifestation of the Straight Light. There would be no illumination in any Phase were it not for Desire to Receive, which is an attribute not of Light but solely of the Vessel.

It is an ironic twist of metaphysics that Desire to Receive for Oneself Alone sheds more illumination on others than it does on oneself. The negative aspect of Desire emitted by the greed mongers of this Fourth Phase makes it possible for them to draw a large quantity of Light, but the *klipot* (husks or shells of negativity) allow no Light to enter them. The Light attracted by them is repelled away from the Curtain of their greed by the action referred to earlier, namely, the involuntary restriction of the curtain.

Those, on the other hand, who desire Light for the Sake of Sharing, are blessed with Light for others and rewarded with Light with which to permanently illuminate their internal Encircling Vessels. And therein lies the irony: Though the desire of the avaricious man may be far stronger than that of the unselfish man, it is the man whose desire is to share who is the recipient of the Straight Light inadvertently repelled by the other.

Chapter 18

Step By Step

W hen Rav Isaac Luria (the Ari), used terms such as "pure and impure," "slowly and immediately," "thick and thin," "ascent and descent," "near and far," "head," "floor," "life," "line," and "conclusion," he was conveying meanings for those words and phrases that were entirely different from their dictionary definitions. The sixteen volumes of Rav Ashlag's monumental work, *Ten Luminous Emanations*, are laced through with words and references that when happened upon by the uninitiated reader prove baffling at best, but more likely completely incomprehensible. The reason for this is threefold: On a mundane level, the Ari's extremely complex thought processes (which were recorded not by himself but by disciples) have lost something in their translation from the original Hebrew, and finally into English. Secondly, at that time it was necessary that the teachings of Kabbalah, the soul of the soul of the law, which was passed on only to the most worthy initiates, remained hidden from oppressive governments and monarchies. By far the most important and telling reason that the Ari's teachings are so difficult to understand for the uninitiated reader, is the fact that the Ari was attempting to convey with language concepts and meanings for which no words existed. Therefore, he was forced to adapt common words to convey new meanings. Once this is understood the *Ten Luminous Emanations* becomes much easier to comprehend.

With this new information in mind, let us now examine some of the above-mentioned words and phrases, as well as some that have not yet been mentioned, so that the reader may begin to understand their kabbalistic interpretations. For definitions of the many words and references that have been excluded from this chapter see the section of this book titled: Glossary of Kabbalistic Terminology.

The Ari stated that, "Light that emerges according to the laws of the Four Phases, step by step, from pure to thick or impure, then stops at the Fourth Phase, is called Straight Line."

A detailed analysis of even a single sentence of the Ari's could take a chapter in and of itself. Our intention here, however, is to provide the reader with an overview from which to launch further study. And as it is the purpose of Kabbalah to make internal and emotional connections with the immense power that resides within us all, the reader should allow himself but scant satisfaction at being able to comprehend intellectually these concepts which are reduced to simple terms. The reader should take none of the kabbalistic writings at face value and should always be trying to make the proper metaphysical connections. Read, then, with a certain degree of caution, the following detailed, though greatly simplified, interpretations, keeping in mind the real connection to this material cannot be gleaned merely through the intellect.

The first phrase of the sentence reads: "Light that emerges according to the laws of the Four Phases..." What does this mean? Light, of course, refers to the *Or Ein Sof*, the Light of the Endless, while, emerges through the laws of the four phases, refers to the four stages of Desire to Receive through which all physical manifestations must proceed in their evolvement. These four stages are:

1. Emanation (Wisdom)
2. Creation (Intelligence)
3. Formation (Beauty - which is further subdivided into Mercy, Judgment, Beauty, Endurance, Majesty, and Foundation)
4. One Hundred Blessings (Kingdom or *Malchut*:
   This world - physicality).

The latter part of the sentence reads: "...step by step," (meaning through cause and effect), "from pure to the thick or impure..." (obscured from a lesser to a greater degree by negative shells known as *klipot*) "and then stops at the Fourth Phase..." (this world) "is called Straight Line." As we learned earlier, the Line is a convenient method by which to conceptualize finitude. In other words, before the *Tzimtzum* (Restriction) the Light of the *Ein Sof* was infinite and hence deemed circular, while later, after the *Tzimtzum*, the Light took on a finite quality that is designated as linear, hence the concept of the Line.

The descent of the Upper Light to the impure vessels of the Fourth Phase is described as being straight because just as the Earth's gravity exerts a direct influence on a falling stone, in a similar manner do the Vessels of Straightness whose longing is strong, cause Light to descend "swiftly in a Straight Line." Even the word "swiftly" here means something different from what it seems. By common definition, the word "swiftly" entails the rapid movement of something through time-space. Kabbalistically speaking, Light does not move at all. Only the vessels move, the quanta, and how can something that does not move "descend swiftly"? Compare the slow meandering of a feather as it falls to the ground, with the straight and swift trajectory of a stone as a means by which to connect with the idea behind the phrase "swiftly in a Straight Line." Straight Illumination is direct and finite. Circular Illumination is Infinite.

Let us now examine another of the Ari's observations on the extension of Light into the void: "When the Light of the Endless was drawn in the form of a straight line in the void, it was not drawn and extended immediately downward, indeed it extended slowly—at first the Line of Light began to extend and at the very start of its extension in the secret of the Line, it was drawn and shaped into a wheel."

Here again the language, if taken at face value, would be most confusing. Words like "immediately" and "slowly" refer to time, but as we know, spiritual or holy time has nothing to do with chronological time. "Immediately," in this instance means, "without a change of degrees." In other words, the Light of the *Ein Sof* was changed very little in the first stage of emanation that is known as Primordial Man (*Adam Kadmon*). The word "slowly," on the other hand, means "evolution of degrees," referring to the Four Phases: Emanation, Formation, Creation, and Action, which are necessary for existence on a physical level. When the Ari speaks of Light being "drawn in a straight line," it is possible that the image of a pencil or other writing implement might enter the reader's mind. Of course the Ari was not speaking of drawing a line. Rather, here the word "drawn" is similar to the connotation of that word as it is used in the phrase "drawing water from a well." Desire draws the Light through its phases.

The final segment of the sentence we are analyzing reads: "...the Line of Light began to extend, and at the very start of its extension in the secret of the Line, it was drawn and shaped into a wheel." The word "wheel" refers to a *Sefirot* of Circles, meaning that very little had changed in the First Phase of emanation: Primordial Man. The Light still had a connection with the Infinite. Circular Light reveals no gradations, no "above and below." The four grades of Desire to Receive were present in the world of Primordial Man (as they were in the *Ein Sof* before the Restriction), but they were still not as yet individuated. Hence, the Light of the Line is said to have been "dressed in the Circle" a condition designated as "wheel."

By now the reader is beginning to realize the dangers inherent in a literal interpretation of ancient kabbalistic texts. This should by no means discourage the reader, for just as it is necessary for a reader of a novel or fantasy to suspend his or her disbelief, it is necessary when studying Kabbalah to suspend the normal, habitual thought processes. The kabbalist goes to great lengths in order that this suspension of ordinary reality may be accomplished. Practices that may seem strange, or even ridiculous, to the casual observer, such as the long (though for the kabbalist, timeless) hours spent assiduously rearranging the four letters of the Holy Name into seemingly countless combinations and permutations, is actually done solely with this transcendent purpose in mind.

In an earlier chapter we deliberated briefly upon the emergence of the Central Column. The phase we have been analyzing in this chapter, *Adam Kadmon*, also known as Primordial Man, was a stage at which the Central Column had not yet become differentiated from the Single Line because the Light had yet to be drawn through the four stages necessary for the completion of a *Partzuf* or complete structure. The third column merged, or perhaps it would be better to say re-emerged, only after the four stages, Light (Wisdom), Water (Intelligence), Firmament (Beauty), and One Hundred Blessings (Kingdom), had been completed and the World of Emanation was born.

The reader should be reminded that while the Ari was imparting to his disciples the kabbalistic interpretation of the beginnings of Creation, each and every point that has been mentioned has practical viability here on the physical plane of existence. The process of the four stages discussed in such great detail by Rav Luria is much more than just the process through which the universe came into being. It is the process through which everything emerges from the primordial "stew" of Creation into physical, conceptual, or even theoretical being. The Ari was discussing the Four Phases or stages through which anything and everything must pass so as to become manifested. That process never changes. Whether we are discussing the birth of a child, the growth of a tree, the movement of tides or quantum tendencies, or the development from youth to maturity of a human being or any living thing: The process remains the same. The outer manifestations may differ radically, but not the inner process of the Four Emanations.

The laws of cause and effect—which are equally valid in the metaphysical world—dictate that the process proceed step by step through the Four Phases. One level must be a complete structure unto itself before the next level can come into existence. Thus, the kabbalist might find him- or herself speaking of the fourth phase of the Fourth Phase, or the third phase of the Second Phase. And while to the casual observer this part of Kabbalah may seem complex to the point of unintelligibility, from the perspective of the kabbalist the opposite is true. For by observing the world through the framework of the Four Phases, all things become intelligible. Instead of getting lost in the millions upon millions of outer manifestations, the kabbalist, by observing but a single process, can understand all things.

Chapter 19

Free Will

The Ari taught us: "It is impossible for any desire to be stirred up in existence unless at an earlier time a fulfillment was revealed sufficient to that Desire." This startling revelation might in itself be the subject of a series of volumes. The implications stagger the imagination. It means that material manifestations are more the product of thought than of physical making; that completion precedes fabrication; that every thought, every action, is preceded by an impulse that contains all of the potentialities and possible outcomes; that the carrot follows the donkey; that the cart leads the horse; that the effect is the cause of the cause; that there is no initiative, no free will as that term is generally perceived: It means that the fulfillment precedes the need.

The Vessel, man, has no ability to take initiative. All activity begins with a force that wants to be revealed. Not one conscious move is made by any human being without there first being a reason to make that move. One does not scratch an itch unless there is an itch to be scratched. Longing does not manifest of its own accord, there must be something to long for. Desire does not just pop into existence, there must be a need to fulfill before that desire can manifest. The goal must exist before the means to reach that goal comes into existence.

This kabbalistic tenet has been the subject of derision since the advent of modern science. Yet today, we see a wave of new scientific theories that echo this principle. Quantum mechanics acknowledges that we, by our intentions, create movement in subatomic particles—thoughts create manifestations in the subatomic world. Botanist Rupert Sheldrake, a former director of biochemistry studies at Cambridge

University, has created a series of experiments that strongly suggest there are "invisible organizing structures that mold or shape things like crystals, plants and animals, and also have an organizing effect on behavior." A complete description of Dr. Sheldrake's radical new theory of morphogenetic fields would not be appropriate in this volume, but should his theory be proven it would verify what kabbalists have known for centuries: Thoughts and intentions create metaphysical molds into which we can pour the cement of physical manifestation.

Kabbalah is a goal-means system—the goal-means, like space-time and energy-matter, are inseparable. By knowing the process, by living the process, one can understand the process from beginning to end. The more fully something is established in the mind, the better is the chance for a successful completion. The entire process manifests first in the mind. Even in potential state there must be a completion of the creative process in advance. Channels exist in nature, but not in man. By initiating the channels we establish the process. Once we have established the channels we know the secret of how to remove the *Tzimtzum* and Curtain and thereby enhance our chances greatly for creating enduring manifestations that benefit ourselves and all mankind.

PROBING THE NATURE OF INTELLIGENCE

What constitutes intelligence? Is it the capacity to acquire and apply knowledge? The faculty of thought and reason? The ability to adapt to new situations? The faculty of perceiving and comprehending meaning? The inherent ability to seize the essential factors of a complex matter? The ability to learn from experience? Mental quickness? Active intellect? Superior powers of the mind?

The answer, of course, is all of the above, and much more. Scientists have identified as many as two hundred different types of intelligence. Still, science has a long way to go before accepting the kabbalistic definition. Intelligence, kabbalistically speaking, is nothing more or less than Desire, the Desire to Receive. Everything, animate and inanimate, from the lowest order to the highest, is possessed with Desire to Receive to a greater or lesser degree and is therefore also endowed with energy-intelligence.

Why does one child do well in school while another who is as intelligent, or even more so, do poorly? One might answer that the child who does well in school has a better memory than the one who does poorly and is therefore more intelligent. In fact, the opposite is closer to being true. Memory has been proven to be a poor indicator of intelligence. People with excellent memories tend to rely on them to the detriment of their more cognitive and creative abilities. Would not a better explanation be that one child simply has a greater desire to do well in school than the other?

How else, but for desire, can one account for an obvious mathematical genius such as Albert Einstein being seemingly incapable of learning mathematics? Did his brain undergo some miraculous transformation? Did he discover some miraculous diet that helped to strengthen his brain cells? Does it not seem more likely that he had little desire to learn mathematics in his early years and an inordinately strong desire to learn the subject later in his life?

Let us now consider the method by which intelligence is currently measured in our society, IQ tests. And because Desire is the kabbalistic criterion for judging intelligence, it would follow that the only reason one person achieves a higher score on an IQ test than another is because that person has either a greater desire to have a higher IQ or has a greater desire to possess the knowledge that will give him or her a higher IQ. In neither case does the higher score indicate true intelligence as IQ examinations measure but a modicum of a person's mental acuity and potential. However much insecurity a high score may alleviate, however self-aggrandizing it may be, in the end a high IQ is the measure of next to nothing.

One has only to attend a meeting of Mensa, or another of the mutual admiration societies for people with high IQ's, to realize that the average genius, as measured solely by scores on IQ examinations, is probably no more intelligent, and probably less interesting than, say, the average man on the street—though it must be admitted that the geniuses can most likely regurgitate more rote-learned facts and information.

What, then, is the nature of intelligence? What is the true measure of genius? The answer may be stated in a single word. That word is Desire.

Chapter 20

Adam Kadmon
(Primordial Man)

W hen we speak of *Adam Kadmon* (Primordial Man), we are referring to the first stage of the first stage of emanation and hence the first level of limitation. From a cosmological standpoint it was the interval immediately following the *Tzimtzum* (known to science as the Big Bang) when Light and Vessel, energy and matter, were still intimately related by similarity of form. The universal condition extant at that time so closely resembled the state in the Upper Light, where Light and Vessel were fused, that any distinction between them was almost imperceptible. Only later did the Light—from the standpoint of the Vessel—withdraw and vanish completely and the universe evolve to its present dis-unified form.

As with all phases of emanation, Primordial Man is subdivided into Ten *Sefirotic* components so as to clarify subsequent stages of development. The first of the first Emanations, the Crown (*Keter*) of Primordial Man, is described by the Ari, as being "the first circle—closely bound up with the Endless." According to the Ari: "Afterwards, the line was drawn a bit more and then turned back so that a second circle was formed within the first. This is called the Circle of Wisdom (*Chochmah*) of Primordial Man. The Line continued and within the third circle emerged another that is referred to as the Circle of Intelligence (*Binah*) of Primordial Man, and so on until the tenth circle, the Circle of the Kingdom (*Malchut*) of Primordial Man, was formed. Thus is explained the concept of the *Ten Luminous Emanations* or *Sefirot* that emanated in the mysterious form of ten concentric circles."

Of course all of these primordial goings on have corollaries here on *Malchut* in the present time. The immutable process of the Emanations does not change to suit the fashion of the planetary seasons. We can see it in the stages of growth from a seed into a tree. The Crown of Primordial Man is the stage immediately after the seed has been planted but has not yet begun to grow. Only the slightest stirring of life has commenced, but it is as yet undetectable to the naked eye because the Desire to Receive has not yet become established.

Rather than being in a stage of unrevealment, as common logic would argue, the seed, from the kabbalistic perspective, having all of its inherent potentialities, is the most revealed state—for that which is most revealed in the physical world is illusion, and the greater the manifestation the greater the illusion. Only later, when the seed begins to grow, does the totality of the seed become obscured, and, as the old saying goes, "we can't see the forest for the trees."

The seed contains all of the future tree's stages, root, trunk, branch, leaf, and fruit. Each stage must be complete before the next one can begin, and yet, in a sense, each acts independently of the others. With each new embellishment the degree of separation is visually reinforced and the unity of the complete manifestation is further obscured. This is why, the kabbalist argues, it is essential for anyone seeking to understand the totality of nature to always return to the source.

MALCHUT

Malchut, this lowest, most negative, of all worlds, is the only level capable of revealing Light of the highest order. Light, the absolute epitome of positiveness, illuminates man's Encircling Vessels to the exact degree to which the Desire to Receive is exercised. Light is revealed in the presence of the Desire to Receive in direct proportion to the power of the intention, or force of will, by which it is drawn.

The greater is the Desire to Receive, the greater is the potential to reveal. Having by far the most powerful Will to Receive, this world, *Malchut*, is the level at which the greatest degree of Light is manifested.

We constantly remind the reader against literal interpretations of kabbalistic concepts. Here we should point out that while it is a normal reaction to attach disapproving connotations to terms such as "negative" and "lowest," which are used to describe *Malchut*, the kabbalistic definitions of these words serve meanings not found in the dictionary. These terms refer to the degree to which *Malchut* differs from the *Or Ein Sof*—*Malchut* having the greatest dissimilarity is said to be lower and more negative than any of the other phases of existence.

Having little negativity (Desire to Receive) the first three evolutionary Phases, known variously as: Wisdom, Intelligence, and Beauty; Spirit, Soul, and Living; and also as Emanation, Creation, and Formation, manifest not *Or Ein Sof*, the Light of Creation. Here the cycle proceeds spontaneously with no effort on the part of these three Phases. The first three grades of vegetal evolvement, namely, the roots, the trunk-branch complex, and the leaves are stages in an automatic process, the purpose of which is to fulfill an inner need. In the plant kingdom it is the fruit that represents the fourth stage of evolvement. Only here is the purpose of the plant to procreate revealed in the seed contained within the fruit.

Just as a child must advance to a certain stage before realizing the nature of his or her existence, so must all things evolve involuntarily through the first three stages of growth, without awareness of their ultimate purpose. The Desire to Receive is revealed solely in the Fourth Phase. This Fourth Phase, *Malchut*, is the stage at which the *Or Ein Sof*, having only a Desire to Impart, can find complete fulfillment.

When examined from this perspective, *Malchut*, this most negative of worlds, begins to take on a new meaning. This Fourth Phase of *Malchut* and we who reside here are responsible for manifesting the Light of

Creation. Does it not follow that rather than being the lowest stage of evolvement, *Malchut* is really the highest phase? Kabbalistically speaking, the answer is both yes and no. That which is lowest always has the potential to be highest and vice versa. Negative reveals positive, the Vessel reveals Light. It is a kabbalistic principle that revealment comes about exclusively via the lowest, or fourth level, and what higher purpose can there be than revealing the Light of Creation?

The purpose of all worldly and otherworldly activity is to manifest Light, and this Fourth Phase, *Malchut*, is the phase of revelation. Despite its drawbacks and the extreme negativity by which it is surrounded, *Malchut* reveals Light. We dwellers on this lowest of all levels can take some small comfort in the knowledge that through our Desire to Receive we trigger this revealment.

The Fourth, it may be said, is the only phase that has to work for a living. The other phases evolve automatically, without intervention on the part of the Vessel, but the Curtain of the Fourth Phase must repel Light so as to bring Illumination not only to its own phase, the Fourth, but to the higher phases by way of Returning Light. We, of the Fourth Phase, have to exert effort if we are to reveal Light. This condition was of our own making. We tried the easy way, but Bread of Shame caused us to relinquish our acceptance of the Creator's endless beneficence in favor of being able to exercise a degree of self-determination. Now, like it or not, we cannot return to the way we were, and we will not return until the great life cycle is complete.

Chapter 21

One Equals Four

A thought that seems to spring into our mind from out of nowhere is actually the end result, the *Malchut*, of a four phase process that has already happened in our unconscious mind. From another perspective, as strange as it may seem, that same thought is also the first stage, Crown (*Keter*), of a new Four Phase process that has the potential to become a physical reality. The *Malchut*, or final revealment, is the fulfillment of a process that occurred in the stage above and it is also the *Keter* of the next stage below.

A simple example will serve to illuminate this concept. Being the least revealed aspect of a fruit, the seed is considered the fourth stage or *Malchut* of that fruit, but if we remove the seed from the fruit, in effect revealing it, the same seed becomes the First Phase or *Keter* of a potential new manifestation.

BEST LAID PLANS

A man may spend years organizing a new project or business venture, accounting for every detail and decimal point, mapping out every possible pitfall and contingency. He may have all of the necessary capital and qualifications, tools and expertise. He may have surrounded himself with top notch lawyers, planners, and financial advisors, and still his enterprise fails. Another man, meanwhile, possessing none of the former's qualifications, may jot on a napkin the blueprint for what will prove to be a multinational empire.

Examples abound of ventures that were planned to perfection but ended in failure. The Titanic and the Hindenburg stand out as conspicuous reminders of the best laid plans straying in most tragic ways. Both were marvels of planning, ingenuity, and technological achievement, yet both ultimately ended in disaster. Our own projects and investments may seem modest by comparison, but for us, of course, they are of utmost importance. We are all striving, with various degrees of intensity to make our hopes, dreams, and ambitions into tangible assets.

Bread of Shame is the difference between dreams and realities. Consciously, or unconsciously, the one who succeeds must alleviate Bread of Shame, which prevents the dream from linking with physicality. Possessions, whether they are physical or metaphysical, such as learning and knowledge, will not truly manifest without conscious effort, they must be earned. Those who do not take account of this fact may amass huge sums of money or other worldly possessions, but the energy-intelligence of that merchandise will not be owned by him, only the negative material trappings. The thief receives only the paper, but not the buying power of the money he steals. Never will he derive the same enjoyment from those commodities as the man who earned them.

The Curtain must be lifted before any plan can manifest on this phase. The Curtain is the built-in safeguard without which the world would disappear. Were it not for the Curtain there would be no need for a physical existence. We would revert back to the undifferentiated state of perpetual giving on the part of the Emanator and taking on the part of the emanated in which we existed before the *Tzimtzum*. The Curtain and *Tzimtzum* (Restriction) are the reasons why some ideas come to fruition, while others do not. It is essential for anyone who is intent on creating physical reality from the stuff of dreams to come to terms with the negativity that prevents the connection of his dream with the nature of his intentions.

The difference between a dream and actuality is the Curtain that does not permit the energy-intelligence of the Light to enter this phase unobstructed. The Curtain keeps us honest. It reminds us of our limitations. It is the force that prevents us from enjoying ill-gotten gains, the obstacle that stands between the planner and his plan, the dreamer and his dream. By removing the Curtain one allows the connection between his dream and the reality to be made. This is done by converting the Desire to Receive into a Desire to Receive for the Sake of Sharing. Only a clear conscience can lift the Curtain and thereby absolve us of Bread of Shame.

THE CLOSED CIRCUIT

That Desire is the root of all corruption is a kabbalistic principle, a keystone on which the foundation of Kabbalah was constructed. Yet Desire, in and of itself, is not a sinful malediction. True, it is the root of all corruption, but it is also the source of all correction. No change, no friction, no correction of any kind, could take place without the Desire to Receive. The Light is still the *Or Ein Sof,* is Infinite and perfectly constant. Desire creates movement.

The Earth has a tremendous Desire to Receive (the force of gravity) that it exerts in an endless effort to draw to itself anything and everything within a wide radius of its field of influence—yet no one would accuse the Earth of avarice. This is because the Earth's Desire to Receive exists within a circular context. The Earth and all of her creatures—with the single exception of man—have an inborn restricting mechanism that seeks to balance cause with effect and compels them to take only according to specific needs and to give equal measure in return. Having no built-in restrictive mechanism, man falls easy prey to a debilitating malady peculiar only to his species: The Desire to Receive for Himself Alone, which might be loosely defined as greed.

Laws are ways by which we seek to remedy this situation, but laws, no matter how strictly enforced, do not prevent crime. Advocates of capital punishment and stringent judicial penalties may argue that crime rates are statistically lower in those jurisdictions where so-called law and order policies are in effect, but that argument holds little water in view of the fact that thievery still exists in those countries where the penalty is the amputation of a hand, and murder is still committed in those places where the penalty is death.

Nor are morals and ethics—no matter how noble their intentions—any better at curbing the greedy appetites of man. Even the efficacy of the Ten Commandments must be questioned with respect to their attributable results, if any, on the actions of the human race. Man still lies, he cheats, he steals, he kills—in the three millennia that the Ten Commandments have been with us, his greed has not abated one iota, if anything it has increased. There seems to be no upper limit to man's inhumanity to man.

Yet all men are not imprisoned by avarice. A few are free of compulsions; a few can do without habitual crutches; a few are not self-absorbed to the point of self-destructiveness; a few are not so wrapped up in negativity as to be suffocating; a few are blessed with a clear conscience: A blessed few.

Why are some of us serving life sentences in a kind of negative purgatory, while others seem to roam free?

The simple answer is that some people live within a circular context—meaning that they have managed to transform the Desire to Receive for Themselves Alone into a Desire to Receive for the Sake of Imparting—while some have not. Some are able to combine their balanced best interests with the balanced best interests of others—some are not. This Fourth Phase, *Malchut*, is steeped in negativity and we are all subject to its influence. We cannot escape it, but we can, by our positive thoughts and actions, turn it to our best advantage.

CRAVINGS

Desire stems from an inner longing that has already experienced its ultimate fulfillment. As we learned earlier, "it is impossible for any Desire to be stirred up in existence unless at a previous time a fulfillment was revealed sufficient to that Desire." Now the Ari teaches us that, "Desire in the Upper Worlds becomes potential and a necessity in the Lower Worlds."

Any physical effect is initiated by a cause on the metaphysical plane. As the *Ein Sof* was the cause of everything, it follows that It also encompassed every desire and every fulfillment that was, is, or ever will be. Every desire one may have is already fulfilled in a potential state, every sculpture has been sculpted, every building built, every wish has already been potentially granted. Fulfillment precedes desire. The effect is contained within the cause.

Having known fulfillment is it any wonder that we can have no rest, no sense of completion, until our inner encircling vessels have been restored to their former splendor?

We could not possibly long for anything of which we have no conception. A native of the rain forest is no more likely to suddenly develop an urgent craving for chocolate truffles than a westerner is likely to be seized by a desire for the live grubs that the native treasures as a delicacy. Cravings do not spring up of their own volition; the taste must have been tasted before.

The very stuff of which the human body is composed—the atoms in our blood, the electrons that spur the impulses in our brains, the chemicals that make up our tissue and our bones—have roots in the *Ein Sof* before the Thought of Creation. All of the various natural forces and energy intelligences, all physical matter, anti-matter, and subatomic tendencies have existed since before the dawn of time.

We have all known the Endless One. We have experienced unity with the Force of Creation. We have tasted of the sweet fruit of perfection. Why do we not remember? The answer is we do. Only our minds have forgotten. The rest of us remember, our blood, our genes, our bones. The memory lingers in our soul. It is impressed into our circular vessels. The Force is a part of us, but the Curtain and the *Tzimtzum* prevent us from remembering. It must be so. Otherwise, we would have no opportunity for correction, no way of absolving Bread of Shame.

Chapter 22

Partzuf

The emanation of a complete structure is called a *Partzuf,* meaning "face" or "countenance." Each *Partzuf* embodies all five *Sefirot* or levels of emanation: Crown (*Keter*), Wisdom (*Chochmah*), Intelligence (*Binah*), *Tiferet* (Beauty), and Kingdom (*Malchut*). The fourth *Sefira, Tiferet,* includes the *Sefirot*: Mercy (*Chesed*), Judgment (*Gevurah*), Beauty (*Tiferet*), Victory (*Netzach*), Majesty (*Hod*), and Foundation (*Yesod*). It should be noted that a *Partzuf,* as does every manifestation, physical and metaphysical, is made up of a full complement of Ten *Sefirot,* and that each *Partzuf* is caused by, yet distinct from, the structure that emerged one stage before.

The root of a plant must take hold before the trunk can manifest; the trunk before the branches, the branches before the leaves. All things—animal, vegetable, and mineral—evolve through this same, never-varying process of Four Emanations. Each of the Four Emanations is a *Partzuf,* a complete structure, distinct from the stages that precede it and follow it, yet almost identical and thereby related by way of Similarity of Form. Just as each of the four seasons plays a distinct role in the completion of a solar cycle, so too must each person proceed through four distinct, yet interconnected, evolutionary seasons so as to complete the cycle of his or her existence.

Nothing can come fully into the Light without the emanation of four distinct stages. Each *Partzuf* must be complete before the next one can emerge into being. Of all the creatures on this planet only man has the ability to bring this process to a conscious level and to adapt it to serve as a means for cosmic awareness and personal awakening.

LASTING IMPRESSIONS

Before the great restriction known to kabbalists as the *Tzimtzum*, we, the emanated, asked for and received the eternal and inalienable aspect of free will that allows us to reveal the Light or not reveal It as we so choose. The Light that once filled our inner Encircling Vessels restricted and withdrew, but certain "impressions" or "residues" remained in them. These echoes of our former completeness allow us to find no rest, no fulfillment, until the now seemingly vacant *Sefirot* again sparkle with Infinite Illumination.

Bread of Shame caused us to close our eyes to the Light of Creation. The *Tzimtzum* made the Vessel blind to the Light. No longer would the Vessel receive the Light's boundless beneficence. From that instant onward it became the Vessel's task to reveal the Light. Only a minute fraction of the former Illumination remained in the Ten Circular *Sefirot*. These almost unperceivable reverberations stir a longing in the Vessels that prevent them from resting until they draw in all the Light that once filled them.

The Ari called this lingering Illumination "impressions" or "residues." More recently some kabbalists have adopted terms such as, "vibrations," "echoes," and "reverberations" in reference to the connotation of the power inherent in the *Sefirot* as being "Music of the Spheres." All of these terms indicate that the Circular Vessels are empty of revelation, but the "impression" remains, and, as always, the reader is advised to adopt the words that create the strongest internal connections.

The impressions act as a constant unconscious reminder that we once were an undifferentiated aspect of the Infinite Light of Creation. While we may not know it these faint reverberations of our former unity with the *Or Ein Sof* launch our every move and maneuver, decision and desire.

In actuality, all of our desires are aspects of only one desire. We have but one aspiration and that is to restore to our inner Encircling Vessels the full measure of Infinite Illumination with which they once were blessed. The Circular *Sefirot* and the impressions etched into them are the driving force behind our very existence.

Only by reestablishing communication with the Light through the limited creative process of the Line can our singular fulfillment again be revealed—the same aspect of Illumination that satiated all Desire before Bread of Shame was alleviated through the withdrawal and Restriction. Through the conscious application of restriction (the Line) we reconnect our cables with the Light of Creation. This is the method by which the kabbalist restores Light to the inner Encircling Vessels and sheds Illumination on all that enters within his or her circle of influence.

Chapter 23

The First Three

Kabbalah recognizes four distinct, though interrelated, phases of emanation. The evolution of any physical entity or non-physical emanation is a Four Phase process. There is a further division of each phase into ten subdivisions (named after the Ten *Sefirot*) and each of those stages is again divided by ten, and so on into infinity. Every manifestation must proceed through the same four-phase process to complete the cycle of its existence.

Any manifestation, whether physical or metaphysical, that does not advance according to the laws of cause and effect through all four stages and all the myriad sub stages cannot possibly reach completion. The interruption of the Four Phases accounts for seeds that do not come to fruition, plans that go astray, thoughts that get sidetracked, and enterprises that fail to get off the ground.

The stage on which we are now focusing, the first of the first, is actually Three Phases: *Keter* (Crown), *Chochmah* (Wisdom), and *Binah* (Understanding). These three energy-intelligences together are known as the Head, and also as the First Three. The First Three precede both physical and metaphysical emanation by connecting with the potential of each new phase. The reason they are grouped together is that they operate beyond the realm of everyday consciousness and precede the observable phases of physical manifestation. Having great affinity with the Light and little similarity with the world of restriction, The First Three exist in an almost totally purified state, remaining, like the inner operation of a seed, invisible to the naked eye and beyond the realm of normal waking consciousness.

For purposes of clarification, the First Three can be likened to the point of a pencil. Before a person picks up a pencil The First Three must have already made a connection on a metaphysical (thought) level with the end result of whatever it is that the person hopes to manifest. A subconscious activity has taken place in which the completed drawing or writing has already in some sense been completed in the mind. This no observable action is called the First Three. The moment the tip of the pencil touches the paper a new phase begins, that of the physical process. Again the First Three are active, making the potential connections, but this time on the fourth (physical) level of emanation. When the tip of the pencil begins to move the world of restriction becomes manifest, beginning the next phase of the ten stage process.

The First Three, *Keter, Chochmah,* and *Binah,* play a vital behind-the-scenes role in every thought and physical manifestation. Though active only in the potential state they must still be considered a part of every creative process. They are active, connecting potentialities. The beauty of potential is that it has affinity with potential everywhere. Potential is not a part of the World of Restriction, but rather an attribute of the Endless. All of us are blessed with an almost infinite abundance of potential that can connect with potential in any dimension. This act of connecting potentialities is the first step in any thought, growth, or physical manifestation.

THE CROWN OF *ADAM KADMON* (PRIMORDIAL MAN)

Adam Kadmon is the first frame of reference after the *Tzimtzum.* When we speak of the Crown (*Keter*) of Primordial Man we are referring to the root of the root, the seed of the seed, the first world, the first level of fulfillment in the Circular Vessels. This is an unseen world, closely aligned with the Infinite, the operation of which takes place beyond the realm of the common senses.

Why then should we bother to study it?

Physicists are the first to inform us that we see but a fraction of what goes on around us. Even with the most powerful telescopes we can see but a tiny portion of the universe and, conversely, even the strongest electron microscopes reveal only an infinitesimal fraction of the entire spectrum of atomic activity and absolutely nothing of the subatomic realm. An apple would have to be expanded to the size of the Earth to see one of its atoms with the naked eye, and beneath that atomic world is another world, the ratio of which is even greater than that of the atom with the physical world. So when kabbalists tell us that the vast majority of what goes on in this universe is beyond the realm of finite understanding they know well of what they speak.

Still that does not answer the question of why it is necessary or even prudent to consider that which we can never see.

Simple observation should tell us that the final manifestation of any event has nothing to do with the truth. History is full of examples of governmental machinations that pull the wool over the eyes of the populace. A recent example of diversionary tactics was the ruse concerning terrorism by which a frightened populace stays home, adding huge sums to the domestic treasury, while at the same time diverting the public's attention from domestic issues such as poverty and unemployment—when in fact four times more Americans die annually of being struck by lightning than are killed by terrorists.

This isolated incident is not cited here to denigrate politicians, for they are by no means the only parties guilty of hiding the truth in order to achieve some self-serving end. Advertisers gloss over the bad features of the often shoddy merchandise they are peddling. Lawyers pile lie upon lie so that the truth will prevail. Doctors prescribe drugs that hide the symptoms without affecting a cure. In fact, in this the observable world, this tiny fraction of the spectrum of existence, one would be hard pressed to find anything with even the faintest resemblance to the truth. Indeed, the kabbalist will tell you that looking for truth in this the world of illusion is like trying to find a subatomic particle in a haystack.

The kabbalist seeks to understand the source of all things. To accept the observable world as the totality of existence is to cheat oneself out of the vast majority of life's possibilities. The term used earlier "pull the wool over the eyes" as well as other expressions from the common vernacular such as "snow job" and "smoke screen" imply a covering over of the truth. To the kabbalist's way of thinking this entire phase of existence is covered over by negativity (*klipot*) and is hence deemed illusionary.

The Ari gave us a system by which to penetrate the crust of illusion that surrounds this world and find the Infinite reality within. We no longer need to accept at face value the lies that pose as truth. Instead of being enslaved by deception we can become, to some degree, the masters of our fates. Through the Lurianic system we can plant the seeds of our own creation in the vast fields of our potential that now lie fallow. By taking part in the process of our own spiritual evolution, we learn to resist that which is illusion in favor of that which is at the source of existence, the real truth, the metaphysical truth.

AFFINITY

Only the First Three *Sefirot* (*Keter, Chochmah,* and *Binah*), of the *Sefirot* of Straightness (Line), can meld and be encircled by the Ten *Sefirot* of *Keter* of the Circular Vessels (Circle). The First Three, you will remember, exist in a non-observable state of potential. Potential has affinity with potential. Like attracts like. Hence, the affinities in the First Three of the Line can connect with the affinities of Ten Circular Vessels. This blending of similarities is the first of many stages in which the finite and the infinite unite for the sake of mutual revealment.

The frame of reference is Primordial Man (*Adam Kadmon*), which has Ten *Sefirot*, but more specifically we are dealing with only the First Three *Sefirot* (*Keter, Chochmah, Binah*), of the Ten *Sefirot* of Primordial Man. *Adam Kadmon* represents the highest possible state of finite existence, the totality of all that was created. If Primordial Man were any closer to Infinite perfection He and we would revert back to the original condition in which it is said that, "He and his Name were One." It is for this reason that Primordial Man, who should not be confused with the First Man (*Adam HaRishon*), the mythic man of the Garden of Eden, is considered within a Circular (Infinite) context.

As Kabbalah is a multi-layered study, the reader should be aware that while we are discussing the emergence of the World of Creation we are also speaking of the first emergence of self-awareness. Through our conscious re-enactment of the *Tzimtzum*, known as the Line, we send out tenuous, potential "strands" of affinity to the First Three *Sefirot* of our own unique, unrevealed perfection, the inner Encircling *Sefirot*. Only when the *Keter, Chochmah, Binah* of the Line, is encircled by the ten *sefirot* of our Circles, can the process begin by which the unrevealed Light within our inner Encircling (Infinite) Vessels can again be illuminated.

Only the first three *sefirot* of the Ten *Sefirot* of the Crown (*Keter*) of the Line are embraced by all ten *Sefirot* of the Circles. The First Three *Sefirot* of the Line have complete affinity with all of the Ten Encircling *Sefirot*, whereas the Seven Lower *Sefirot* of Straightness (the Line) have no affinity with the Ten *Sefirot* of *Keter* of the Encircling Vessels. The result is that the Encircling Vessels, whose Light is unrevealed, can never be fully illuminated through the limited process of the Line. The simple explanation for this is that the Straight Vessels are a product of finitude while the Circular Vessels are a part of the Infinite. Always there must be a dissimilarity of phase between the two. Otherwise we return back to the condition before *Tzimtzum* in which we the emanated had no opportunity for correction.

ON A SCALE OF ONE TO TEN

The moment a baby is born the doctor or midwife in attendance counts the toes and fingers. If the total in each case is ten the child is declared "perfect." Mathematics, our most perfect invention (in the sense of being absolute), is based on ten. A physically attractive person is apt to be declared a "Ten" by members of the opposite sex. From hit parades to movie and restaurant reviews, it seems that almost everything in this physical realm of existence is measured on a scale of one to ten. Ten is also the number of totality in the dominions of the metaphysical.

Every thought, every manifestation, physical or metaphysical, must advance through four phases, each with ten stages, the Ten *Sefirot* or Luminous Emanations. This aspect of ten exists whether we are considering empty Circular Vessels or the Ten *Sefirot* of Straightness. Earth (solids), sea (liquids), sky (gasses), it matters not of what we speak, the ten attributes, or *Sefirot*, each of which is comprised of infinite permutations of ten within ten within ten, are present in every star and planet, every speck of cosmic dust in the universe.

The root must take hold before the trunk can manifest, the trunk before the branches, and so on. The root is a product of a ten stage process, as is the trunk, the branches, the leaves, and the fruit. Each stage is a necessary component in the completed manifestation. In the same manner as a person learns through experience and, it is hoped, from mistakes, so does each thought, word, deed, and evolving entity acquire a certain residual knowledge of the essence of each *Sefira*. Those characteristics are carried forward until a full aggregate of ten qualities has been accumulated. Thus do we acquire the requisite attributes for a completed physical or metaphysical existence.

Each *Sefira* has what might be described as a unique "atmosphere" that distinguishes it from the other nine *Sefirot*. *Keter*, the first stage, is deemed the highest, purest phase by virtue of being closest to the source, the *Or Ein Sof.* Like the other *Sefirot* and phases of emanation, *Keter* must also pass though ten stages, but being closely aligned with the Infinite, its inner workings occur completely beyond the range of the senses.

Keter, having almost no Desire to Receive, has virtually nothing in common with the Seven Lower *Sefirot,* but a great deal of affinity with *Chochmah* and *Binah,* whose workings also transcend the realm of finite understanding. And it is for this reason, as we learned earlier that *Keter, Chochmah,* and *Binah* are considered as a single stage known as the Head or the First Three. From *Keter* through *Chochmah* and *Binah, Chesed* and *Gevurah,* and so on the density of the atmosphere, or negativity, or thickness, or dissimilarity with the Endless, increases until the evolving thought or entity finally arrives at the tenth and last *Sefira,* which has the least affinity with the Endless—this Fourth World of Resistance, *Malchut.*

The process of ten within ten repeats four times—once for each of the Four Phases of Emanation—before the entity or manifestation reaches completion. In other words, Wisdom, the first phase of emanation, advances through the same ten stage process of *Keter, Chochmah, Binah, Chesed, Gevurah, Tiferet, Netzach, Hod, Yesod,* and *Malchut* before the next phase of emanation, known as Intelligence, can begin. After Intelligence, the second phase of emanation, has completed its ten stage cycle, the third phase of emanation known as Beauty advances through its ten stage cycle, and finally the fourth and last phase of emanation, Kingdom, evolves through ten stages at the end of which the preceding stages of evolution are at last revealed on the physical level.

Chapter 24

Density

When the Ari taught us that all vessels and material of Creation are drawn from the World of Restriction he was not alluding to a situation in which the Vessels and material of which he was speaking were actually drawn or moved through space-time. In the kabbalistic lexicon, the word "drawn" refers to that which becomes "thickened" or "impure" by virtue of being farther from the *Or Ein Sof.*

Just as the air becomes thinner as we rise through the strata of Earth's atmosphere, so too may it be said that the "atmosphere" of the metaphysical levels becomes less dense, and is hence deemed purer and higher as we withdraw from the World of Restriction. That which is farther from the Light is defined as being thicker and less pure than that which is closer to the Endless. The greater is its dissimilarity of form with the Endless, the greater is the degree of impurity, and this world, *Malchut*, the World of Restriction, being possessed with a tremendous Desire to Receive is, in the kabbalistic frame of reference, negative or impure to an extreme degree.

A person's purity, or lack of it, is measured according to the degree of affinity he or she has with the Light. Those manifesting great Desire to Receive for Oneself Alone are considered by Kabbalah to have little affinity with the Endless and are hence deemed lower and less pure than those who convert the Desire to Receive into a Desire for the Sake of Imparting.

LESS IS MORE

If there is one word that could define advanced technology, the concept of reductionism would say it all. The race for small components in hi-tech is in full swing. The smaller the product, the chance for success is so much greater. Smaller microchips that can transfer larger amounts of information are a primary objective for today's scientist.

What we are witnessing today is the realization that the landscape of computers has been radically transformed by the loss of corporeal matter. Microchips become smaller and density greater. The new work has focused not on the power of mathematical computation but on its size.

In a mere 25 years, computers have become so fast at processing information—a third of a billion times faster than they could in the early 1960s—that their powers numb the comprehension.

They have also changed our lives by permitting instantaneous worldwide telecommunications, miniaturization of integrated circuits permitting sophisticated home computers, to name a few examples.

Common sense tells us that a communications cable's capacity should shrink with its diameter. In the case of fiber optics, common sense is wrong. Today's hair thin glass fibers can carry more information farther than metal cables thicker than a man's arm.

Generally speaking, an elaborate excuse for failing to live up to some expectation is less believable than a short, concise explanation. Speeches long on words, but short on substance, are less likely to sway the listener than those that stick to the issues. Complex international espionage thrillers brimming with tricky sub-plots, extraneous characters, globe hopping, and needless elaborations may engage the reader's interest and even keep him turning pages furiously, but in the end the reader is often left with the feeling that he has somehow been had. More effective is a story told in a straight forward manner with sympathetic characters and an identifiable theme.

Less is more.

A simple song is likely to be more accessible to the average listener than a complex one. A lawyer with a strong case will present the simple facts, while the lawyer with the weaker case uses the buckshot approach that attempts to impress the jury with the sheer bulk of inconsequential evidence. The truth needs no embellishment. Scientists search for a simple solution by which to explain the workings of nature. Artists in the movement known as "minimalism" affirm the power of visual images that have been "stripped to the bone."

Less is more.

This concept takes some getting used to. Today, in modern industrialized societies, bigness has become synonymous with quality. "The bigger the better" is the catch phrase of the day. Young people, both male and female, are "bulking up" as never before. Today, we adulate that which is "larger than life." Sports stars with nicknames such as "The Refrigerator" decorate our TV screens. Large, poorly designed, shoddily constructed; gas guzzling cars are making a comeback. People flock by the millions to have their eardrums split by enormous trucks with ten foot high tires and thousand horse-power engines that crush cars while spewing mud and pollution.

Today's modern society judges people by the bulk of their possessions, envying those with the most and pitying those with the least. Yet history is filled with stories of men like Howard Hughes and women like Hettie Green (who lived like a pauper while possessing millions) who were imprisoned by their riches. A fast food factory may serve more food than any other distributor in the world and yet no one who has tasted real food would say that the quality of fast junk food is in any way the equal of good home cooking. Skyscrapers, though they may be the tallest buildings in the world, and even beautiful in their own right, cannot compare in quality with the Taj Mahal or other handmade structures that are minuscule by comparison.

Less is more.

This metaphysical paradox goes against the grain of contemporary popular culture. Undoubtedly it will be some time before the kabbalistic notion that physicality is unreality—the denser the physical matter the greater the illusion—is understood much less accepted or embraced,

Yet were they to compare the energy produced by dynamite with that produced by the splitting of an atom—the lesser corporeal matter producing infinitely more energy—it is possible that they might begin to break through the conceptual barrier that prevents such a transformation from being feasible. And were they to consider the limited sending capacity of copper wire with the far superior ability of much less fiber optical material, they might acquire still more understanding of this principle. And were they to compare the taste of a fruit picked at the peak of season with a much larger fruit that was left too long on the vine, they might suddenly find themselves actually agreeing with the idea that less really is more. True this possibility is remote in the extreme, but then again anything is possible.

BREAKING THROUGH

It is said that when Rav Isaac Luria studied the *Zohar* the flame of his desire burned so intensely that perspiration would quite literally pour off him. Through his studies he absorbed, converted, and transformed negativity (*klipot*) and thus became a channel for the *Or Ein Sof.* That his efforts were rewarded is evidenced by the fact that Lurianic Kabbalah has survived intact for over five centuries.

Rav Ashlag, the twentieth century Kabbalist, philosopher, and translator of the classic sixteen volume work based on the Ari's teachings, *Ten Luminous Emanations,* contended that breaking through to self awareness required only one prerequisite—a quality for which Rav Luria was obviously not lacking, and that attribute is desire.

THE HEAD-BODY DICHOTOMY

The First Three *Sefirot* (*Keter, Chochmah,* and *Binah*) are called the Head. It stands to reason, then, that the Lower Seven *Sefirot* of Mercy (*Chesed*), Judgment (*Gevurah*), Beauty (*Tiferet*), Victory (*Netzach*), Glory (*Hod*), Foundation (*Yesod*), and Kingdom (*Malchut*), should be called the Body. And so they are.

The Body, like us, is a part of the World of Restriction. The human body is a shaft of material substance, a Line that stands up from the Earth. From birth to death it struggles against gravity. All the body's life it must exert an outward force of 14.7 pounds of pressure per square inch to combat the effects of air pressure. The Body has a beginning, middle, and an end. The Body dies.

The Head operates outside the scope of rational comprehension, beyond logic, beyond the senses. The Head is Endless, it is part of the Infinite. And being of a Circular or Infinite nature, it is not affected in the least by restriction and negative constraints. The Head can merge with anyone or anything. It never dies, but continues on in Circles of Return.

Being finite, then, it follows that the only information we finite beings can possibly glean concerning the Infinite First Three *Sefirot* must be through observing the Body, the Lower Seven *Sefirot.* Also, as Kabbalah is an edifice of many stories, it must be true that this concept of three and seven can be viewed from a personal perspective—meaning the Body (the human body), being of a finite nature, can have no affinity with the Head (the human head).

Yet previous chapters assured us that every *Sefira* is comprised of all ten attributes and therefore even the *Sefirot* that make up our bodies must also include the Infinite Head or First Three *Sefirot*, which would mean that the First Three in our heads and in our bodies do have affinity with the Light. How, then, can it be that our bodies have no affinity with something that is an integral part of them?

The answer is that the Head and the Body are separated by a Curtain that prevents the two from communicating, but only in the Body or Lower Seven *Sefirot*. The Curtain does not hinder the operation of the Head, the reason being that the Infinite is never affected by that which is finite. The Light never changes. The Light eclipses darkness whenever the two come into contact—the Infinite holding that which is finite in a state of suspended animation.

Chapter 25

The Paradox

Many, if not all, hunter-gatherer societies believed in a mythical trickster deity. The Indians of the Northwest coast had the Raven. In the southwest and other places it was the Coyote. Thor, the Norse god was a trickster. Brier Rabbit, Reynard the Fox, and the Joker in the deck of playing cards are all pale continuations of this ancient, venerable theme. The hunter-gatherers recognized the paradox and found pleasure in it. They could not solve the riddle of life, so they celebrated it!

When the hunter-gatherer's settled down to more sedentary lives of farming and raising livestock everything changed. No longer could people find humor in the tricksters of old. The Coyote, instead of being a clever, laughable little fellow became a hated, hunted animal that stole chickens and killed sheep. The Fox, in merry olde England, became the subject of cruel hunts on horseback by which "civilized man" could attempt to express his superiority over the trickster, the mystery, the uncertainty of life.

Slowly, the paradox that was the trickster deity was covered over with new theories, validations, and beliefs. Religions sought to protect us from the paradox. Philosophies sought to white wash it. And over the years the mystical relationship that early man enjoyed with life's uncertainty was eroded, replaced by mountains of impossible explanations, ridiculous precepts, rules, regulations and superstitious beliefs. At last, science, with its false promise that all things would one day be explained, sounded the death knell for the trickster.

And a sad day it was for us all.

Of course the trickster never died, the paradox remains as unexplainable, as irreconcilable as it ever was. Still religions try to protect us from it, but it pops up between the words of even the most charismatic evangelist. New scientific theories still seek to explain it, but they never will. Television attempts to homogenize it, but the moment we press the off button the paradox returns.

The paradox is dead. Long live the paradox!

The only light we see is reflected light. Light is darkness until it is revealed through the process of Binding by Striking. The Light is there, but because of the *Tzimtzum* and the Curtain our eyes are blind to its Infinite brilliance. Were it not for Binding by Striking no light would be visible to us. The paradox is that through restriction we create affinity with the ultimate in non restriction, the Light of the Endless. And the greater the capacity for resistance the greater is the revelation of the Light.

In this the World of Restriction, which is also the World of Revelation, it is a physical and a metaphysical truth that the greater the degree of resistance, the brighter will be the revelation of Light. Strike one rock against another and a spark will be produced, strike it again, this time with more force, and the spark will be larger. When we focus the light of the sun through a magnifying glass (restriction) onto a sheet of paper, eventually it bursts into flames. The smaller is the point of focus (the greater the restriction), the more forceful will be the revealment or release when the paper begins to burn. The larger the capacity for resistance of the filament of a light bulb, the more light that bulb will manifest. In every instance light is the product of resistance, and the greater the restriction the greater is the revealment of Light.

The harder one concentrates on something (restriction on one train of thought) the more notable will be the breakthrough in terms of one's thinking. Take as another example the production of sound. The harder a string is struck with a plectrum, the louder will be the note. The greater the force of compression on a membrane, the more forceful will be the percussive effect. No sound can manifest, no light, no thought, nothing at all in this World of Restriction, without resistance, and the greater the resistance the greater is the manifestation.

Art, literature, music, philosophy, no matter what the field of endeavor, the larger the capacity for restriction, the more magnanimous will be the outpouring of Light. The paradox arises even when we are doing the dishes or mowing the lawn. Sometimes, when we are bored with our work, or have other more important things to do, time drags by and our energy becomes so drained that it is almost impossible, it seems, to go on. Yet the moment we decide to apply ourselves to the same task something happens. By concentrating, restricting our focus we release new energy, the job goes faster, and when it is accomplished we have energy enough to take on the world.

By resisting we create affinity with the original Restriction and the first act of Creation, *Tzimtzum*. When we restrict our Desire to Receive for Ourselves Alone we create a Circular affinity with the Light. This is how our original desire, which was a negative characteristic of the Line, is converted into the Desire for the Sake of Sharing. Through resistance we manifest that which is Endless, peaceful, and perfectly still. By saying "no" we arrive at "yes." This is the paradox. And may it always remain a mystery.

INFERIORITY

The Curtain, as mentioned earlier, is inoperative in the First Three of the Encircling *Sefirot*. It is, however, fully activated in all Ten *Sefirot* of the Lower Seven. Imagine a family of ten sitting in a circle on a sunny day when a black curtain descends from the sky, dividing the circle into groups of three and seven. The group of three is on the sunny side of the curtain while the other seven are shaded by the curtain. The family is still in a circle, but now, from the perspective of an observer on the shaded side, it appears as if there are only seven people, and from the point of view of the sunny side it appears as if there are only three.

The group of three is still bathed in sunlight. For them the light is of identical intensity to what it was before. From the perspective of the group of seven, however, who have come under the influence of the curtain, it appears as if the light has dimmed. Imagine now that the curtain is soundproof, creating a situation in which the two groups cannot communicate in any way. The two groups of three and seven cannot perceive with their common senses the people on opposite sides of the curtain, but they know full well that nothing has changed. Each group experiences a sense of loss at having their circle divided and the only way to alleviate that feeling is by lifting the curtain thereby restoring the family to its original circular condition, which is exactly what they would set out to do.

What the Ari meant when he taught us that the seven *sefirot* that follow the Curtain are inferior to the first three, then, was not that there was any internal difference between them. The inferiority of which he was speaking is in no way connected with the *Sefirot* themselves, just as the seven people behind the curtain are not inferior to the other three, nor has anything of their essential nature been changed or lessened. The only difference between them is the result of the negative (darkening) power of the Curtain.

Whether we are speaking of sunlight or the metaphysical Light of Creation, the intensity of Light never changes. In the kabbalistic frame of reference the light on the sunny side of the curtain is identical to the light on the shaded side. The Light is everywhere. It glows with equal intensity in the center of the Earth as it does in the center of the sun. The Eternal Light of Creation can never be diminished any more than painting a light bulb black can in any way lessen the energy produced by the bulb. The difference arises only as a result of the illusion presented by the Curtain from the perspective of all that comes under its negative influence.

The purpose of Kabbalah is to remove that illusion.

Chapter 26

Beyond the Common Senses

We stake careers on common sense decisions. Cars and houses are purchased. Investments are made. Schools and colleges are chosen. Diets are planned. Debts are paid. Laws are passed and broken. Contracts are signed. Work is undertaken. Vacations are arranged. Moves are made. Contacts are developed. The ties of friendship and even marriage are initiated and maintained.

Common sense rules our very lives.

What is common sense? This question will elicit as many different responses as there are people of who it is asked. Common sense is one of these relative expressions that everyone takes for granted as having a common connotation, but which really means different things to different people. For in fact what may seem perfectly sensible to one person may seem illogical or even totally nonsensical to another.

All of us can cite examples in our lives when some action we took that seemed sensible in the beginning led in the end to a less than positive result. Often we go against the grain of our natural inclinations to do what common sense dictates, only to discover that our natural instincts were right. Common sense, it seems, has an almost hypnotic quality. It lulls us into following it down the proverbial garden path and just when we are smelling the flowers of what we thought were our correct decisions we fall into a hole at the bottom of which is a metaphorical alligator or a sharp stick. Common sense is a trap into which many of us fall.

Kabbalah teaches us ways to get out of that trap. Just as the principles of Kabbalah cannot be perceived by the five common senses, nor can logic, reason, and common sense lead us to find the source of the river of our being. The Light cannot be learned, it must be experienced. Metaphysical connections cannot be made by means of the intellect; the tentacles of cosmic awareness proceed from the heart. That is not to imply that common sense and logic do not have their place, for they do. It is only when trial and error methods have failed that one begins— some might say through common sense—to understand that in spiritual matters the five common senses are not enough.

The purpose of Kabbalah is to remove the chains of logic and reason so that we may be released from the cage of our five common senses, for it is only by transcending the limits of these self-made linear boundaries that a direct link with the cosmic forces can be made. Only then can the real inner journey begin.

INSANITY

Pity the madman. He lives in a world of fantasy and make believe. He knows nothing of the world of "what is." The poor fellow, it is said, has no conception of reality. Yet, perhaps in his imagination he is the ruler of a great nation; perhaps in his delusions he lives in a castle where servants attend his every need; perhaps, in his world of perpetual fantasy, he winters in Switzerland and spends sunsoaked summers languishing on the sandy beaches of St. Tropez.

For this he should be pitied?

Now pause to examine a man who by contemporary social standards, is judged sane. Anything but happy, our so-called sane man fights a constant, losing battle with the imagined forces that seek to destroy him. Life is an endless struggle for dominance over the material plane.

A workaholic with an ulcer, he keeps twice weekly appointments with a psychiatrist who does his best to assure him that it is not really a dog-eat-dog world, but as far as our sane man is concerned life boils down to one decision: Kill or be killed, eat or be eaten. For him, "it's a jungle out there." He claims to be, "swimming in shark infested waters." And though his psychiatrist may not know it, the world imagined by our friend, the sane man, is truly his reality. By choosing to live by the laws of the jungle he has become a creature of the jungle. By adopting a shark's mentality he has become a shark. For him it is a dog-eat-dog world of eat or be eaten, and little by little the dogs of his own imagination are chewing him down to the bone.

Meanwhile, our madman, who "in reality" lives in a mental institution, falls asleep the moment his head touches the pillow and he dreams peaceful, kingly dreams. When morning comes, the orderly who wakens him is not a hospital worker. In his demented state of mind, the entire staff of the hospital exists for the sole purpose of giving him pleasure. The breakfast served to him by his personal entourage of servants and handmaidens, while probably quite bland and tasteless by ordinary worldly standards, is, for him, a smorgasbord of royal delicacies. And after breakfast, depending on the season, he is off once again to the sunny slopes of Switzerland, or roaming the sandy shores of St. Tropez.

Back to our friend the sane man. At night he arrives home, one of the world-weary walking wounded, defeated by another day. Two small strangers, his children, barely manage mumbled greetings while staring blankly at the TV screen. A hastily scrawled note from his wife reminds him that the TV-dinners are still kept in the freezer. He has a drink while his dinner is cooking and daydreams about the vacation he needs so desperately, the vacation for which he has been saving all year. After supper he has two more drinks to calm him down. Later he goes to bed, but so filled is he with anxiety, that he cannot sleep. He takes some pills, but even the strongest prescription medications do little to alleviate the worries that haunt him night and day. From the drawer of the nightstand beside his bed he removes the itinerary for his vacation. For an hour he stares at the glossy, four-color pictures of the sun-drenched sands of St. Tropez, where, in only a matter of months, he will at last escape the worries of his stress filled life—if he lives that long.

The madman, in the meantime, has decided to become a movie star and in his imagination he has landed the leading role in the latest Woody Allen movie. Modesty prevents him from talking much about the recent Olympic gold medal he won for downhill ski racing. Nor does he boast about the time he addressed the United Nations. People would think he was crazy.

The long-awaited day of departure has at last arrived for our sane man and his family. This vacation is going to be the best one they have ever had, even if it bankrupts him. After a seven hour flight they deplane in Europe, exhausted. He and his wife are not speaking. The children are in foul moods. An hour long ride at high speed on rain soaked cobblestones brings them to the expensive hotel at which they will be spending the next three weeks. A hurricane is blowing. The taxi lurches off with some of their baggage. Our sane man's mood becomes even darker when he and his family arrive at the suite, which instead of overlooking the Mediterranean, as expected, has a good view of the airport that is no more than a five minute walk away.

By coincidence our madman happens to be staying in the same hotel. Of course all this is happening only in his imagination, but not being there in person has its advantages. For instance, upon arrival in a limousine driven by his own personal chauffeur; our madman was spirited by attentive servants directly to the penthouse suite from which the view of the Mediterranean is beyond compare. The weather is perfect. And to top it off, all this extravagance is not costing him a penny because he owns the hotel and the mile-long stretch of sundrenched beach on which it stands.

By morning, the sane man's ulcer is acting up. His night was a nightmare. A wild party in the suite above precluded any possibility of sleep until sometime after four a.m. And when at last it ended, he and his family received a series of courtesy wake up calls that they did not order. Still, he struggles out of bed, determined that this vacation will be the best he has ever had—even if it kills him.

And, sadly, it nearly does.

The next three weeks are no better. Try as he might our sane man cannot escape the pressurized cabin of his mind. And when his vacation is over, when all is said and done, the sane man returns to the world of stress and strain, the dog-eat-dog world in which so many of us have chosen to live, the jungle where only the strongest survive, the shark infested waters in which it is always a case of eat or be eaten; a world in which only a madman could be happy.

And what ever happened to our madman? The poor fellow is still a man to be pitied. He cannot seem to rid himself of the insane notion that he is a king. He continues to imagine himself skiing the Swiss Alps, starring in movies, winning gold medals, and occasionally addressing the General Assembly of the U.N. His doctors hold little hope for him. The prognosis is bad. They say if something is not done soon, our poor madman is in imminent danger of being overcome by delusions of peace and happiness.

Chapter 27

The Line of Most Resistance

Temptation comes at us in a constant barrage. Advertising leaps out from billboards and television screens, tempting us to buy that which we do not need and cannot afford. Attractive models beckon from the glossy pages of books and magazines, enticing us to drink, smoke, gamble, consume drugs, and act licentiously. Some of us surrender rarely to those temptations, others regularly, some continually. Habitual surrenders, in contemporary Western cultures, are absolved of responsibility for their vices by use of a convenient, but erroneous, catch all concept: Addictive personality.

The idea of resistance takes some getting used to. Today, in a modern sophisticated society, "instant," "new" demands have become synonymous with quality. Have a headache? "Fast, fast relief" is the catch phrase of the day. Let's face it who wants a lingering, painful headache.

No matter how successful the remedy, the price is still "temporary" relief. We have, in effect, traded in permanent relief for the so-called instant benefit, thereby abandoning our inherent right to a pursuit for health and happiness.

In desire for more pain lies its removal.

This metaphysical paradox goes against the grain of contemporary popular culture. Undoubtedly it will be some time before it is understood much less accepted by those who refuse to let go of their illusionary lifestyle.

However, the Age of Aquarius will pressure those whose life pursuits are for momentary pleasure into an astonishing realization that the good life of permanency is theirs for the asking. A clear understanding of our cosmos will dictate that happiness, energy and peace of mind operate in a similar fashion as the light bulb. The more the desire of the negative pole, the greater is the necessity for the filament to restrict this fulfillment. For only then is the reality of circuitry achieved.

Take for example the common toothache. At the onset of pain, we have been programmed to immediately begin pill-popping thus seeking and acquiring temporary relief. And when the pain returns, we revert to pill-popping again.

How does the kabbalist react to a toothache? At the first onset of pain, he is overjoyed by this unique opportunity to restrict the demand of that negative (pole), illusionary physical body for instant relief and fulfillment. He knows the benefit of pain; its cleansing and therapeutic cures for some of his *tikkun*. The soul, our 99% of reality, becomes ecstatic with fulfillment as she observes a depressed and devastated corporeal body, which only represents 1% of our reality.

This is precisely the objective of the filament; reject the demands of the negative pole in the bulb for fulfillment of electrical current. The result! Circuitry.

Who does, in essence, feel pain if not our 1% corporeal body? She demands energy to erase the lack of a physical well- being. Essentially pain is the warning signal that our free-flowing energy system has been disrupted. However, if we were to react to this free-universal demand of things-for-nothing without restriction, we shall inevitably suffer the consequences of the poor light bulb. When the filament permits the negative pole to make her simple demands for electric current and Mr. Filament is either asleep or non functional, a short circuit develops.

What seems to emerge from our insights into reality is that there are two opposite ways to deal with pain. The kabbalist, while awaiting professional assistance to remove the pain, is in the interim enjoying his illusionary misfortune. Who knows, he may never require medical attention in as much as he may have restored his system to a circuitry of energy by his art of restriction. To restore temporary physical relief is an illusionary corporeal entity of the 1% reality.

The usual toothache sufferer, meanwhile, is frantic and suffering, pill-popping until relief arrives. Then who knows what may be in wait for him. So taking the path of least resistance may not necessarily result in the betterment of our physical and mental well being. Maybe the kabbalist knows something we do not.

We each have a pool of knowledge from which to draw recollections of past indiscretions. Luckily, for most of us, those reminders of sojourns away from the straight and narrow are enough to keep us on our chosen paths. It is the man who resists the negative side of his nature who is to be commended and who will be blessed with the addition of new light into his circle. Instead of choosing the line of least resistance, the quick fix, instant gratification, the kabbalist chooses the line of most resistance, for it is resistance against the forces of darkness through the process of Binding by Striking that brings Illumination to this world.

PRESSURE

Since the earliest days of civilization we have been under pressure— psychological pressure, pressure to perform at peak efficiency, pressure to live up to the expectations of others. Humanity has always had to fight for survival. We have always had to struggle to make ends meet.

Fourteen pounds of air pressure per square inch has been pressing down on us since the dawn of time. Gravity has always created a burden that we have had to bear. Yet never before has the pressure been so great as it is today. Now, more than at any other time in history we have stretched the thin thread of our existence to the breaking point. We have come, it seems, almost to the end of our evolutionary rope.

The world is verging on a precipice of ecological disaster. Pollution and nuclear proliferation threaten the survival of every living thing on this Earth. Rape, murder, terrorism, crime is on the rise. No longer can we travel in safety; no longer is it safe to walk the streets. Violent images come at us in a constant barrage, pushing us to the limits of emotional and psychological endurance. Stress, tension, urgency—the heat is on. This pressure cooker we call *Malchut* is about to explode.

Why now, of all times, is this happening?

The Light, the *Or Ein Sof,* is the pressure we feel. It is telling us to realign our values to be in keeping with the new age. Now, in this Age of Aquarius, *Malchut* is under more pressure than ever before. The times demand a new social dynamic if humanity is to keep pace with technology. The greed of this phase of our evolution, the waste and rampant materialism scream out for an outpouring of spiritual energy of equal or greater magnitude if balance is to be restored. From this day onward no peace will come to us, no tranquility revealed—there will be no rest until the Light has been revealed.

No longer can we close our eyes to the Light of Creation. The Light is pressing in, instilling us with a sense of urgency, exhorting us on to greater and greater heights of consciousness, impelling us toward planetary consciousness. Now, more than ever, the Light of Creation demands revealment. There is only one way to relieve the pressure: Reveal the Light.

DIVERSITY OF PHASE

We take pride in our differences. We preserve and cherish them. We celebrate them, and commemorate them, and drown them in sorrow. We keep different customs, different habits and beliefs. We practice different religions and speak different languages. Our body types are as different as the colors of our skin. We have personal differences, differences on principle, different political systems and philosophies in which to express our differences of opinion.

Men die defending their differences, cities fall, empires crumble. So great are our differences and so myriad that it would seem that they are insurmountable. Even in our wildest flights of fantasy it is hardly possible to conceive of a world without differences. And if there were to be such a world what a boring place it would be.

We love our differences. We thrive on them. They are our joy, our hope, our one salvation. *Vive la différence!*

There are differences between us to be sure, but comparatively speaking they are minuscule. Consider that the space between the particles in an atom is proportionately greater than the space between the Earth and the sun, and add to this the further consideration that the human body is made up of one percent matter—the rest is space and atoms. And of that one percent, the vast majority—perhaps ninety-nine percent—is comprised of the exact same chemicals and elements that go into making every other person.

So the next time you hear someone say, "the difference between you and me..." remember that the grand sum total of the differences between one human being and another amounts to one-one hundredth of one percent. And the next time words become heated or push comes to shove, think about the one-one hundredth of one percent in which we differ and the ninety-nine point ninety-nine hundredths of a percent in which we are the same.

Chapter 28

Brainstorm

A flash, a brainstorm wakes us up from a sound sleep. Suddenly some idea or aspect of our lives comes into perfect focus. We are everything; the whole picture is clear. Then the Curtain sets in and begins to cloud our perception and we must hurriedly create mental connections in the hope of retaining something of the essence of the inspiration. Sometimes we are able to grasp a fair portion of the flash's essence, while other times we are lucky if we retain even a pale recollection of what only seconds ago was an absolute certainty.

How can something that is an absolute certainty one moment be a pale recollection the next?

Flashes are expressions of the Infinite; glimpses into our own unique and complete fulfillment which we carry with us from birth through death and beyond. They are gifts, and like gifts of any kind they can be fully appreciated only by those who are deserving of them. The flashes that remain with us are ones for which we have restricted and thus alleviated Bread of Shame. When we are not prepared to accept the gift of a flash from the Infinite an illusionary installation of the Lower Seven *Sefirot* creates a situation in which the flash of Light is said to be "drawn" below, meaning that it has come under the influence of the Curtain.

THE FILAMENT

In our discussion of the filament of a light bulb we have learned that the negative pole and not the positive pole initiates any and all circuits of energy. The Line makes contact with the Circle thereby creating the circular condition necessary for the Light's revealment. The resulting circuit satisfies both the desire of the Line, to receive, as well as that of the Circles, which is to share.

The brightness of a light bulb is determined solely by the size of the filament, not by the current that runs through the wiring system. The current is the same no matter what appliance is plugged into it, whether it is an air conditioner, the demands of which are great, or a five watt bulb, the desire of which is small. Like a light bulb that produces only that amount of light which its filament is capable of generating, so too can we manifest only that exact amount of Light which our filament (our capacity for restriction) allows our inner Encircling Vessels to reveal.

ILLUSION

From the kabbalistic perspective, that which is Infinite and eternal is real and that which is finite, including this world and all that is a part of it, is illusion. Our Encircling Vessels are of an Infinite nature, timeless and eternal; our bodies, conversely, are finite and therefore said to be of the illusion. Bodies come and go, but that which is real, the Infinite Encircling Vessels within us carry on into Infinity.

How can man, liar, thief, rapist, murderer, pillager or plunderer in any way be deemed perfect?

Caught up as we are in outward appearances and the worldly struggle for survival it is difficult to imagine much less embrace any concept contending that man, despite of his myriad flaws, faults and infirmities, is at his core an expression of primal perfection.

The *Tzimtzum* created a space or vacuum between our illusionary (finite) physical aspect and our real Circular (Infinite) nature. That space, the gap, the illusion caused by the Curtain in the Lower Seven *Sefirot*, conceals the perfection of our existence. When we, the emanated, said no to the endless beneficence of the Light we chose a situation in which a Curtain would forever remain between the illusionary aspect (Body) and the real aspect (Soul). From that moment on it became incumbent upon us to consciously bridge the gap of illusion called the Curtain through the act of restriction, thus earning the Light's blessing while at the same time removing our own Bread of Shame.

Our bodies, these Lines of limitation, along with this world of resistance and revealment, provide us with a set of circumstances by which we can amend, so to speak, our finite constitutions. The physical and mental ailments and conditions from which we suffer are aspects of the Curtain—obstacles, it is true—but also opportunities for correction and karmic adjustment. The real aspect of ourselves (the eternal aspect) though concealed, is perfect in every detail.

The rest is an illusion.

NEGATIVE SPACE

Earlier we learned that the Ten *Sefirot* of the Crown of *Keter* encircle (cause) only the Head or First Three *Sefirot* of the Crown of the Line. The Curtain, located directly beneath *Binah*, the third *Sefira* of the Line, divides the Lower Seven *Sefirot* from the Upper Three *Sefirot* thus preventing the Crown of the Circles, which is of an Infinite nature, from melding with the Lower Seven *Sefirot*, which are finite. The Curtain and its inherent Desire to Receive is fully active in the Lower Seven *Sefirot* but not in the Upper Three *Sefirot*. This creates a situation whereby there is a space or gap in each of the Circular *Sefira*.

Many students, when this point is introduced, ask how is it possible that our inner Encircling Vessels, which are said to be an Infinite expression of our primal perfection, can be flawed by the presence of a negative space?

The negative space found in the Encircling *Sefirot* is not a flaw within the *Sefirot* themselves, but rather an aspect of the Line alone. The gap in the Line that is filled by the Curtain is firmly installed in the Lower Seven *Sefirot* of the Line, but not in the First Three *Sefirot*. The situation created when the Line connects with the Circle is such that the space or gap in the Line is transferred to the Encircling *Sefirot*. This situation creates a condition in which there is the illusion of a space or gap in each and every Circular *Sefira* to the extent that the Line transposes the negative space into the Encircling Vessels.

KLIPOT

The word "sin" is derived from the concept of passing over. To sin is to intentionally overlook that which we know is right in favor of that which we know to be wrong. *Klipot* are a product solely of the linear aspect of Creation, the Line, and has nothing whatever to do with the Circular aspect, the all-embracing Light. There is no evil, no duplicity in the Light of Creation. There never was nor will there ever be.

On this point Kabbalah differs from many other spiritual teachings in that it does not acknowledge evil as a separate force of existence, but rather evil is an aspect of Desire that stems from a deliberate disregard for the Light of Creation.

The *Zohar* expresses the view that the illusionary space separating the Emanator from that which He emanated creates a condition whereby *klipot* or evil can manifest, but the Light, whose only purpose is to impart joy and endless abundance, had not the slightest intention of allowing Its Infinite beneficence to be transferred to anything other than the original purpose for which It was intended, namely, the restoration of Light to the Encircling Vessels.

The Energy Intelligence known as *klipot*, the evil husks or shells that permeate this Phase of existence, are really concealments or "passing over" of Light. When the Creator withdrew to give free reign to our desire to alleviate Bread of Shame, a gap or vacuum was created between Itself and that which It had emanated. This negative space allowed for the entrance of *klipot*, a product of the Vessel's premeditated abuse of the Infinite life force of Creation.

Klipot (evil) is a misappropriated vessel where there is no aspect of Desire to Share, a black hole that knows only an all consuming Desire to Receive for Itself Alone. The Light has but one harmless intention, which is to reinstate Illumination to the Encircling Vessels, but the receiving Vessel, *klipot* captures the Light and thus prevents It from fulfilling Its Infinite purpose. *Klipot*, then, becomes a negative force, animated by the Vessel's (man's) active and obdurate passing over of that which he knows to be the truth.

SPACE

Confusion sometimes accompanies the introduction of the following concept for it contradicts every known scientific, philosophical and mathematical construct and stands firmly opposed to all that is normally perceived to be logic and common sense: Space, the separation between people, mental, emotional and physical; the distance between objects, even the seemingly endless void between stars and planets are all illusions. According to Kabbalah there is no limitation of any kind in the real world, no time, no space, no friction or gravity, only the eternal presence of the *Or Ein Sof*. Space, then, from the kabbalistic perspective is an apparition, albeit a necessary one, still an illusion none the less.

A previous chapter advanced the kabbalistic axiom that the Circular *Sefirot*, being of an Infinite nature, possess no phase of the Curtain other than the illusionary space that is transferred to the Circles through the Lower Seven *Sefirot* of the Line. The illusion of space in our Encircling Vessels has nothing to do with the Infinite Light itself. The First Three *Sefirot* on the Curtain's Light side experience no diminishment of the Light's endless abundance. The Line imposes limitation on the Circle, but only from the perspective of that which is on the dark side of the Curtain.

Only the First Three *Sefirot* of the Line entirely resemble and have total affinity for all Ten Circular *Sefirot* that comprise our Infinite primal energy-intelligence. Hence, the First Three *Sefirot* of the Line are said to be "encircled" (caused) by all Ten Circular *Sefirot*, while the Lower Seven *Sefirot* are said to be "drawn below" into the shadow of the Curtain. Unhampered, as they are, by the phase of the Curtain which encumbers the Lower Seven *Sefirot*, the First Three *Sefirot* or Head of the Line are in complete accord with all Ten Encircling *Sefirot* and thus capable of instantaneous communication with the all embracing Circular aspect of existence.

The Encircling Vessels have Infinite ability and potential for revealment, but as their Illumination is restored through the finite straight Vessels, they too give the illusion of being flawed by the identical deficiency, the space that is displayed by the Line. Hence, between the last Phase of the Crown (*Keter*) of Circles and the first Phase of the Wisdom (*Chochmah*) of Circles, and so on through the ten subdivisions, we find an empty space or vacuum, which though illusionary in terms of the our Infinite aspect, is all too real with respect to the human condition as it exists in his or her Fourth Phase.

Hence, our Circular, Infinite selves have the potential to be in constant instantaneous communication with all phases of the universal life force, while the Lower Seven *Sefirot*, our physical presence, falls under the influence of the Curtain that is firmly installed beneath the Head of the Line. This space in the Lower Seven *Sefirot* prevents us from experiencing our true unified relationship with the world and the cosmos and prohibits us from penetrating the vast body of metaphysical knowledge that lies hidden beneath the negative trappings of finite existence.

We are comprised of infinite variations on this theme of Ten *Sefirot* with the Lower Seven *Sefirot* having no affinity for the Upper Three *Sefirot*. So while we find that the true, real, Infinite aspect of humanity has the potential to merge with the Circle, travel through space-time, engage in telepathy and astral projection, and even visit past incarnations, the Lower Seven *Sefirot*, which is separated from the Infinite First Three *Sefirot*, have no such potential unless and until Bread of Shame is relieved through an act of restriction.

Being separated from a good friend or loved one is an intensely traumatic experience for some while for others it can be nothing more than a mere inconvenience. After a year's separation, some couples return to the company of a seeming stranger, while others pick up the tempo of their relationship, so to speak, without losing a beat. The difference does not necessarily have to do with varying degrees of affection. The kabbalistic interpretation of this phenomenon is that those who feel the greater sense of loss are those for whom the Curtain has greater influence.

When we asked for a method by which to absolve Bread of Shame, we took upon ourselves the responsibility of revealing the Light. Only by creating the illusion of separation between the Emanator and that which He had emanated was it possible to retain the illusion of separateness necessary for the emanated, to relieve Bread of Shame by re-initiating the connection with the Light.

Through restriction we can narrow the gap in the Lower Seven *Sefirot* and thus lessen the mental, and emotional space between ourselves and others, and because the *Or Ein Sof* knows no separation or boundaries, it is possible for our Infinite Encircling Vessels, which are a part of the Endless, to merge with the Infinite Light of Creation and thus traverse infinite light-years of illusionary space in a single instantaneous leap of consciousness.

The illusionary space between the First Three and the lower seven in the Line causes not only personal alienation, but also the separation we feel with regard to the earth and the cosmos. Kabbalistically speaking, the Light is eternal, all pervading, never changing, while separation, space, and distance, being of a temporal nature, in that they change according to how they are perceived, are said to be illusions. In the real world, the *Ein Sof*, there is no room for negative space, separation being a characteristic only of the World of Illusion.

The illusion of space was inherited by our Encircling Vessels to give us the opportunity of absolving Bread of Shame by revealing the Light through restriction. Our ability to restore this Endless Illumination depends entirely on the extent to which we can transcend the limitation, the space, the illusion of negativity that is the Curtain.

Kabbalah provides us with a method by which to reconnect the Seven *Sefirot* of the Line with the Ten *Sefirot* of the Circle. The Line is the channel by which to restore Light into our Circular Vessels. Through a regimen of well tempered resistance we narrow the space between the finite and the Infinite, in effect squeezing out the space between ourselves and the Endless nature of the universe.

This restrictive action, known to Kabbalah as "purification of the Curtain" is the method by which the Curtain's influence is made less dense and hence the burden of its negative influence is nullified. The student of Kabbalah should be aware, however, that because the Curtain reasserts itself continually those who seek to lessen its darkening influence must act with equal diligence in revealment of the Light, for that is the method by which the illusion of space between our finite and Infinite aspects is reduced, making it possible to merge with the Circle of Creation.

TRANSFERENCE

Now it should be understood that because the Line feeds the Circle, so to speak, (the Circle remains in a state of unrevealment until it is acted upon by the Line), it is a reasonable and accurate assumption that the negative space, the Curtain, which is an inherent aspect of the Line, should be transferred to the Circle. Therefore, because the space in the Line is transposed to the Encircling Vessels, the Circles (Encircling Vessels) appear to have the same negative space as the Line, when in actuality they are defective only to the extent that the Line is incapable of restoring their full Illumination.

The Light of the Encircling Vessels cannot be fully restored to its former brilliance through the limited creative process of the Line. The Light being of an Infinite nature, can never be completely fulfilled by that which is finite. Still, all of the Illumination received by the Encircling Vessels must manifest as a result of the action of the Line, which is why our Encircling Vessels appear to have the same linear deficiency as the *Sefirot* of the Line when, in fact, they themselves are perfect. The only reason they appear to be flawed is that they inherited the space, along with its negative influence, the Curtain, from the Line.

CIRCUITS

Gravity, Earth's primal motivating force, provides ample evidence that the essential Energy-Intelligence of this the Fourth Phase, *Malchut*, is the Desire to Receive for Oneself Alone. The great universal Energy-Intelligence, the Creator, conversely, has but one aspiration and that is to share. At first glance these two aspects of Desire might appear to be in opposition, but closer observation reveals that actually this universal duality serves the balanced best interests of both phases of existence, for the separation of these two opposing forces prevents this Fourth Phase from reverting back to the unified condition extant before the *Tzimtzum.*

The fusion of these two seemingly opposite aspects is called a circuit, and whether we are speaking of the poles of a battery, or those in a filament, or of the revealment of the Circular Light of Creation, this circular condition must be met in every instance where energy is manifested.

Actually, it is somewhat of an error to say that opposites attract. The opposition between these seemingly opposing natural forces is, like everything of this world, an illusion. The universal Energy-Intelligence is circular. From a circle It was born and to a circle It will one day return. Thus, there being no opposition inherent in the Emanator—no space, no vacuum, and hence no opportunity for Desire to Receive (negativity) to enter—the attraction of opposites, though readily evident on this phase of existence may be said to represent an artificial and hence illusionary condition in that the circuit is only temporarily disconnected.

The *Ein Sof,* Endless Energy-Intelligence of the universe, is eternal, beyond even the space-time continuum, and therefore that which is temporary—including the attraction of opposites—is said to be an illusion.

In fact opposites do attract, but only in the physical world that is itself an illusion. In the real world, the changeless, Circular World of the *Or Ein Sof,* opposites do not exist. Here in this Fourth Phase one may point to the positive and negative poles of a magnet as proof that opposites indeed do attract, however when one allows the two magnets to connect with each other, thus creating a circuit or circular condition, like magic the magnetic polarities disappear.

The reason for this, from a kabbalistic perspective, is that once the circuit is complete the true, universal condition becomes re-established. Each aspect of desire needs the other to complete its own unique fulfillment. Neither phase of the seeming dichotomy can rest until it is once again connected with its counterpart; neither can truly be consummated until it is once again mingling as an undifferentiated aspect of the unified force of which it is an aspect.

The kabbalist's firm conviction that fulfillment always precedes desire leads him to many conclusions that stand contrary to so-called logic, scientific precepts and rational thinking. He has accepted that the true nature of the universe is Circular and that, therefore, any and all separations, all expressions of finitude must be illusionary. Further, he reasons that as no space existed and therefore no room for negativity in the *Ein Sof* before the Thought of Creation there must be no space or separation in this world either, other than that which is illusionary, for the only difference between before and after the *Tzimtzum*, then and now, is that the Restriction created a condition in which the Vessel would no longer be aware of its connection with the Light. So we find that nothing whatever changed after the Restriction other than the Vessel's perspective of events.

The *Tzimtzum*, in other words, for reasons well established, made us blind to the true Circular condition of the universe, but the Restriction did not alter in the least the timeless, spaceless nature of the Light of Creation, merely our finite, hence flawed, perceptions of It. The completed circuit was the original universal condition before the *Tzimtzum*, and therefore the same condition must exist today, for as has often been repeated, the Light never changes. It is eternal, timeless, and perfectly still.

How can the Light, which is infinite, suddenly become finite?

The answer is It cannot. The Light still shines in all its Infinite glory—the only difference being that the illusion of separation, the Curtain, inherent in this Fourth Phase, makes us blind to Its Endless majesty. Therefore, the kabbalist concludes that Circular fulfillment must be included in all aspects of the seeming universal dichotomy and that the accepted edict that opposites attract is, on the universal level, really an illusion. In other words, the circuit is complete.

Still, however well this revelation may serve the kabbalist in terms of his or her conceptual perception of reality, it does little in and of itself to dispel the problems and difficulties of the life of fragmentation that we finite beings must continue to lead. Hence, though it is true that the universal condition is Circular, we, as finite beings, must still cope with our linear existence.

When the Emanator withdrew He created the illusion of a vacuum, a gap, a space where none had existed before. That negative space, the Curtain, which allows us the opportunity of restricting voluntarily and thereby reestablishing a circuit of energy and absolving Bread of Shame, is destined to remain an integral part of this illusionary Fourth Phase of Creation until such time as the great circuit of existence is again re-established as a unified whole.

The kabbalist seeks to operate on a conscious level of restriction so as to always have affinity with the Light. This is what is meant by a Circular Concept. By creating a circuit of energy he or she establishes a circuit of energy through Binding by Striking that not only serves the Light's purpose, which is to share, but reveals his or her own unique fulfillment as well. Thus does the kabbalist achieve affinity with the Light of the Endless.

By completing the circuit we complete ourselves.

Chapter 29

If There is a God...

Kabbalah provides an answer for the frequently reiterated question as to why, if there is a Creator, does He allow so many bad things to happen?

The Energy Intelligence of the Universe has nothing whatever to do with the negativity that permeates this fourth layer of cosmic experience. It was not the Creator's intention to allow negativity to rule the world. The purpose of Creation was to provide an opportunity for those whom the Creator had emanated to earn the Light's blessing by lifting Bread of Shame. This was the reason for the Creator's withdrawal and subsequent restriction.

In the *Ein Sof* before the Thought of Creation the existence of negativity was an impossibility. As was pointed out in a previous chapter, any Desire to Receive that might have manifested would have been instantly satiated. When we, the emanated, requested an element of free will sufficient to allow us to reveal the Light or not as we so desire, the Creator, who aspires only to share, was compelled to restrict Itself (*Tzimtzum*) in order to give expression to our desire to become individuated.

The Light's restriction, known to science as the Big Bang, created the fragmented situation in which we, as finite beings, find ourselves, and henceforth, from that moment on, it became incumbent upon humanity, the emanated Vessels, to continually reestablish the connection with the Light through the limited creative process called the Line.

Desire to Receive for Oneself Alone, evil, *klipot*—all expressions of negative space—are energy-intelligences, born not from the Creator, but from the metaphysical "distance" that was, of necessity, placed between the Light and the Vessel to differentiate between them.

As with everything connected to this Fourth Phase, even this is an illusion. The Creator did not disappear. The Supreme Being is everywhere, without us and within us, permeating every phase and facet, every cosmic speck in the universe. The Creator is willing to impart Infinite majesty to any and all who would care to pay homage to the original act of Creation, which was Restriction. The only difference between the present universal state and the condition that prevailed before the *Tzimtzum* is that we, the emanated, can no longer perceive with our five senses the Endless Presence without first relieving Bread of Shame.

Hence it may be said that *klipot* (evil) is the price we pay for our separate identities.

INITIATIVE

Unlike the *Tzimtzum* that is totally resolute, the Curtain represents a flexible form of restriction. Like a window curtain, it allows more light into the given space, or less, depending on the degree of resistance with which it is confronted. A small gust of wind, for instance, will open it only a little way, a larger gust still further, whereas the hand of a person might pull back the curtains completely, allowing light to stream unobstructed into the room. In a similar manner as one opens curtains with an extended hand, so too can the Curtains of negativity that surround everything on this Fourth Phase, *Malchut*, be opened through metaphysical linear restriction, an act of will.

The Curtain is active below the Head or First Three *Sefirot* of the Line. Between the Head or First Three *Sefirot*: Crown (*Keter*), Wisdom

(*Chochmah*), and Intelligence (*Binah*), and the Lower Seven *Sefirot*: Mercy (*Chesed*), Judgment (*Gevurah*), Endurance (*Tiferet*), Victory (*Netzach*), Majesty (*Hod*), Foundation (*Yesod*) and Kingdom (*Malchut*), there is a negative space or vacuum in which no Light can manifest. That dark gap is filled by the Curtain.

It was the contention of Rav Isaac Luria (the Ari), that the true nature of existence is unified, timeless, and perfectly still. What the kabbalist means when he or she tells us that this world is illusion is that the Circular aspect of existence is Infinite, but all aspects of worldly existence, having a beginning, middle, and end, are finite and therefore imperfect. Hence anything that is not an aspect of the Circular nature of existence is said to be an illusion, including the Line and all of its myriad implications.

The need of the emanated to absolve Bread of Shame compelled the Emanator to restrict Its Infinite power so that the Vessel's wish could be granted. Of course the Creator did not have to grant the wish of that which He had emanated, but to not do so would have precluded all possibility of the Light's revealment. As we know the Light has only one aspiration, to share, which is an impossibility without a receiving Vessel.

This inalienable and eternal right of first refusal granted us by the Emanator is only a blessing for those who have mastered the art of resistance and restriction. Those who fail to exercise the option of restriction place themselves at risk of being inundated by the Curtain's negative influence, for they allow the Curtain to arbitrarily choose when, where, and how much Light the Vessels will or will not receive; whereas those who restrict voluntarily have control over the power of the Curtain and are virtually impervious to its negativity.

In any event, it is infinitely more rewarding to take the initiative of restriction. Through restriction we reveal the Light and we also reveal ourselves. Though it is never the kabbalist's intention of using Light for anything other than unselfish ends, still he or she walks always on a well lighted path.

THE LOWER SEVEN

It is said that the Lower Seven *Sefirot* of the Line are greatly inferior to the Head or First Three *Sefirot*. This concept seems to conflict with an earlier teaching that all of the *Sefirot* are identical. The reason for this is that the inferiority or impurification referred to has nothing whatever to do with the Vessels themselves, but to the quality of Light contained within them. The Lower Seven *Sefirot*, being on the dark side of the Curtain, are capable of revealing far less Illumination than those on the Light side and are therefore deemed to be inferior.

The Ari further taught us that the Lower Seven *Sefirot* of the Line are inferior even to the Lower Seven *Sefirot* of the Circles. Again by examining the two types of Vessels, relative to the Curtain and the degree of Illumination that each is capable of manifesting, we can ascertain that Rav Luria, of blessed memory, was referring to the lesser revealment of which the Lower Seven *Sefirot* of the Line is capable of producing. The Lower Seven *Sefirot* of the Line reveal far less Light than the Lower Seven *Sefirot* of the Circles for the simple reason that the Curtain is active in the Lower Seven *Sefirot* of the Line, whereas the Lower Seven *Sefirot* of the Circles are devoid of that liability. Thus, the Lower Seven *Sefirot* of the Encircling Vessels is deemed superior to the Lower Seven *Sefirot* of the Line.

We live in the Lower Seven *Sefirot* of the Line. The Curtain is firmly installed above the Lower Seven *Sefirot* in the Fourth Phase, *Malchut*, creating a void between ourselves and our fulfillment. It is for this reason that our bodies have so much difficulty communicating with our minds and our minds with our souls.

We are not in touch with ourselves because the Seven *Sefirot* of the Line have no affinity with the Ten Encircling Vessels. There is only one method by which to bridge the gap, thus circumventing the Curtain and restoring affinity with the Light, and that is by effectively nullifying the Desire to Receive for Oneself Alone, a condition which can only be brought about through an act of restriction.

ONE STEP BEYOND

To get caught up in the physical illusion is to cheat oneself out of the better part of life. Like talking without listening, eating without tasting, reading the words in a book without making any attempt to understand the meaning. To accept only what is presented to us on the physical level is to negate reality in favor of an illusion.

Because our physical aspect is destined to struggle for survival in the world of the Seven denser *Sefirot* it does not mean that we have to accept this linear physical world as the be all and end all of existence. We contain, after all, an aspect of Infinity. The better part of us is continually connected with the Infinite Energy-Intelligence of the cosmos. The fact that our five senses are not aware of this cosmic connection is of consequence only in terms of our limited perceptions; it has nothing to do with the Infinite picture, the grand scheme of things. By seeing our actions within the context of the great universal network we create affinity with the Circle of Creation.

Does a hammer pound in a nail or is it the mind?

The kabbalist will tell you that the mind pounds in the nail. The hammer and nails are mere material manifestations of that which was first perceived, undertaken, and completed on a metaphysical (thought) level. All that happens on a physical level has its roots in the metaphysical. Every effect has a metaphysical cause. If one accepts only the physical aspect of any endeavor, for instance if one sees oneself as only a nail pounder, is it any wonder that he or she will feel bored and unfulfilled? If, on the other hand, one sees his or her actions as channels, bridges between thoughts and finished products or manifestations, he or she will experience a sense of satisfaction at being an essential element in a circuit of fulfillment.

We are what we think. If it were possible to deal only with the physical aspect of existence, which fortunately it is not, life would be a one dimensional and utterly boring grind. By traversing the negative space between ourselves and our true Circular nature we reveal Light. Through resistance we bridge that gap—in effect squeezing out the negativity that fills the empty spaces. Thus do we complete the circuit of our own fulfillment and come to the realization that the real world is one step beyond.

THE SPARKPLUG

Consider from a kabbalistic perspective the spark plug:

The spark plug is a device used to introduce the spark directly into the cylinder of a gas engine. Notice the gap between the positive and negative poles. Take note also of the linear dimension of the spark plug and the vaguely humanoid form. Energy, the spark, must traverse that space to complete the circuit. Care is taken to calibrate the width of the gap to the distance that is most conducive to the spark plug's efficient operation.

The spark plug is designed for Binding by Striking on a rapid-fire schedule. As you will recall, a circular condition is always required for the revealment of energy. When, for any reason, the spark plug is unable to complete the circuit no connection is made and hence no energy can be revealed. When the poles become worn, for instance, the space increases to such an extent that the spark is unable to leap the gap. Another problem that can impede the performance of the spark plug is corrosion, which causes a situation whereby sparks can no longer be initiated. When either of these conditions is allowed to persist, the spark plug and hence the entire machine fails to operate.

THE FUTURE

Man's rampage against Nature seems all but complete. A massive, concerted, worldwide effort would have to be undertaken immediately if imminent dangers to our physical existence were to be avoided. Billions of dollars would have to be spent to clean up the air, billions more to purify the water. Laws would have to be enacted to prevent giant multinational corporations from plundering land and sea. Alternatives to nuclear energy would have to be aggressively researched and developed. The problem of world hunger would have to be alleviated. Measures to reduce the birthrate would have to be adopted by countries all over the world. And it would not suffice to relieve only one or two of these life-threatening situations—they must all be solved. Each is so tightly interwoven with the others that the mesh is like threads of the finest cloth.

A case in point: The rapid expansion of the world's population contributes largely to the problem of hunger. Hunger, in turn, is the sole cause of the annual annihilation by slash-and-burn agriculture of hundreds of thousands of acres of rain and cloud forests. Also known as jungles, rain forests support over sixty percent of the Earth's plant and wildlife in addition to absorbing vast quantities of carbon dioxide and providing a significant share of the world's oxygen supply.

Ozone, a form of oxygen, comprises a thin protective layer of the atmosphere that filters the sun's harmful infra-red and ultra-violet rays. A serious depletion of the ozone layer, as will occur with the decimation of the rain forests, will cause a condition of global overheating known as the Greenhouse Effect that will complete the destruction of the rain forests and ultimately sound the death knell for the human race.

It has been predicted that the rain forests, those life-giving natural wonders, those precious storehouses of untold knowledge, will virtually disappear as early as the year 2000.

The full consequences of man's undeclared war against nature are already being felt throughout the world. Each day, several more varieties of plant and animal life disappear from the face of the Earth, some not yet named much less studied. We will never know what possibilities these extinct species might have held in store, what medicines may have been distilled from them, what tastes or esthetic pleasures they could have provided.

Precious plant life is disappearing at an unprecedented rate and the wholesale slaughter of endangered animals continues unabated. Elephants butchered only for their tusks, whales pushed to the brink of extinction and beyond to provide a variety of products that can be produced better and cheaper using synthetic methods—the evidence of man's selfish destruction is incontrovertible. He has run out of excuses. Now, at last, he must pay the price for his myopia and greed.

The future is here today, in the air we breathe, the food we eat, the water we drink. Hardly a day goes by when we are not reminded of the dangers of acid rain, PCB'S, and other unnatural pollutants. Everywhere we turn we are witness to man's inhumanity, stupidity, cruelty, and even genocide. At last we are beginning to understand what the indigenous cultures have known all along: That any serious wound to nature is a wound to ourselves; that the balance of nature is delicate and tenuous; and that everyone and everything is interdependent.

Yet understanding is not enough. Now, before it is too late, we must take immediate steps to dress the wounds of the damage already done. The hunger of the Third World populations is our hunger, their pain is our pain, their fate is ultimately our own. Only a small minority of the world's population is capable of doing anything to alleviate the world's problems—the vast majority being locked in circumstances of raw, bone-of-need survival. No longer is it sufficient for those of us who live in the more affluent societies to hide behind our relative comfort. No longer can we close our eyes to the havoc we have been wrecking. No longer can we choose to remain ignorant of the dangers we are facing.

There was a time in recent memory when if a man spoke out against technology he was condemned as either a religious fanatic or, even worse, as an enemy of progress. Technology was our savior and it was almost sacrilege to suggest otherwise. Proponents of nuclear energy claimed that by the 1960s we would be living a life of ease and comfort with robots and computers taking care of all of our "menial tasks" and daily chores. Sleek, clean, nuclear powered monorails would sweep us to our destinations. Nuclear energy, it was touted, would be ours in abundance, electrifying cities for a cost of pennies per day. Those bright, hopeful voices are silent now and their brazen dreams of a nuclear tomorrow have dissipated into a cloud of radioactive dust.

Perhaps now the voice of reason can be heard.

Each generation has a responsibility to the preceding and subsequent generations. Our burden is perhaps greater than any our ancestors were forced to bear. Our duty is no less than to shed Light on our own ignorance so that future generations may have a world in which to live. Now, today, we must begin to look at overpopulation, world hunger, and ecology from a global perspective.

Vast reserves of cosmic energy surround us, energy which far outshines that produced by the splitting of atoms that the comparison is like holding a penlight up to the sun.

The potential energy of the *Or Ein Sof* is within us and all around us, but to release these vast reserves requires an act of restriction.

The initial step in creating any bridge of understanding is a conscious decision. Men of conscience have always struggled against the forces of darkness. Kabbalists understand that resistance, the conscious re-enactment of the *Tzimtzum* and the Curtain are ways by which to bridge that gap and re-illuminate the primal purpose of Man.

It is time to draw the Line.

Volume

Three

Introduction

I n earnest defiance of one of the great certainties of modern times—that nothing can travel faster than light—Rav Isaac Luria (the Ari), put forward a new comprehension of our universal and the speed of light. Indeed, only within the illusionary physical reality of our universe are we confronted with corrupt theories concerning light.

True light, as the kabbalist pointed out is motionless and timeless. All physical forms of light are merely limited manifestations of the true nature of light. Connecting with light itself permits an instant and practical intergalactic telegraphic system. This indicates travel of thought energy intelligences travelling at a pace faster than the speed of light.

No reasonable definition of the reality of light could he expect to permit, faster than messages or thoughts.

Probably the most bizarre and incredible story of cosmic miracles is the one that marked the career of the successor of Moses, Joshua Ben Nun. Joshua, by instant cosmic communication, stopped the movement of the sun. While pursuing the Amorites at Beth-Horon, he directed the sun and the moon to stand still, and they did it, we are told, for the course of a whole day so that an Israelite victory could be assured (*Joshua*, 10:14).

Are we then to assume, on the basis of the *Book of Joshua*, that at some time during the middle of the second millennium, the Earth's rotation around the sun was interrupted by the command of a mortal man? Joshua, speaking to the Lord, implored this startling cosmic disruption before the eyes of Israel, and these celestial bodies, whose cosmic DNA of energy dictates that they move along their precise, predestined, orbital paths, obeyed as if this very interruption was cosmically present in their computerized program from the time of their creation, and indeed it was. Joshua's halting of the sun and the moon was no different than Moses' parting of the Red Sea.

This story certainly is beyond the belief of even the most pious in today's world. We all have experienced the solar year, consisting of 365 days, during which the moon circles the Earth and the Earth rotates around the sun. So, the sun and moon should come to a complete standstill simply is an incomprehensible cosmic event, unless we can face the realization that celestial intelligences, otherwise known as celestial internal cosmic energy forces, can be and are directed by man in his altered state of consciousness.

If this sort of revolutionary thinking is acceptable then we can proceed to investigate and ultimately understand how there can exist the possibility of motion and communication faster than the speed of light. Most physicists consider the philosophical implications of these theories incompatible with their understanding of space and time.

Considering the distances of 93,000,000 miles between the Earth and the sun, Joshua's command to the sun, travelling at the speed of light, would still take eight and a half minutes. Scripture indicates this command to have immediately made contact with the sun, a tantalizing, absurd possibility that scripture maintains took place.

Consequently when the Ari presented his doctrine of motionless, timeless Light, essentially he advanced the theory that Light was the all pervading constant element of the all-embracing unified whole. Therefore, connecting with and tuning into this integrated, cosmic network system provided instant consciousness of the entire universe.

Most recently, physicists have been obsessed with trying to unify or find connections among the known fundamental forces of nature. Rav Isaac Luria already promulgated the teachings of a grand unification theory. Kabbalah taught that the Ten *Sefirot*, or ten energy-intelligent forces, expressed and made manifest the all-embracing unified force known as the Light. All subsequent physical manifestations were and are the direct result of a universe that started out with ten dimensions.

The billion upon billions of dollars that are to be invested in new Genesis accelerator machines will produce nothing more than a fragmentary view of our universe. Today, some scientists even complain that theorists have ventured into a realm so remote from what can be verified that science is in danger of reverting to something like kabbalistic mysticism and unseen dimensions.

The kabbalist has always known who we are, how we came to be and where we are going. His teachings have one decisive advantage over the teachings of science. Whereas in physics and other fields of science, the layperson has always been left behind in its revelation, Kabbalah with all of its existing truths shall become the domain of all Earth's inhabitants.

Unfortunately, the way the present scientific establishment is growing it is becoming increasingly fossilized by its own particular world view, super-string included. One cannot continue to create formulas and inject the ever increasing aspect of uncertainly and a fragmented view at the same time. This begins to limit our growth and increase a specialization that threatens the sense of wholeness. The purpose of our being also has been severely fragmented by individual egos, which come to make the scientific empire an individual power base created by the owners of scientific knowledge they, themselves, have created.

When the majority of the people are placed beyond grasp of true knowledge, then we are truly awaiting the Messianic or Aquarian Age in which knowledge shall be the domain of all, not a select few.

The wisdom of Kabbalah, itself, has been a jealously guarded secret, but the time has come for it to reach the masses with its simplicity, because in the final analysis, knowledge that is simple is true knowledge.

As stated in Jeremiah, :"And they shall teach no more every man his neighbor, and every man his brother, saying, know the Lord. Rather everyone shall know Me, from the smallest to the oldest." (*Jeremiah*, 31:33).

Part One

New Age of Reality

Chapter 1

Back to the Future

The reader is by now aware that the philosophy of Kabbalah stands firmly opposed to many scientific theories and commonly held beliefs. One such example is the kabbalist's insistence that light has no speed, another is the kabbalist's belief that opposites do not attract, and yet another is perhaps the even more startling assertion that space is an illusion. It should come as no surprise, then, that the kabbalist's understanding of time is also contrary to the standard interpretation. Time, from the kabbalistic frame of reference, is an aspect of the creative process, the Line along with everything else connected to the Lower Seven and this world of limitation, must be considered illusionary.

From the perspective of the Infinite aspect of existence—the First Three, the space-time continuum is an illusion. Time, as we know it, the separation of the space-time continuum into metronomic increments, may be a convenience and even a necessity in the Lower Seven, the world of illusion, but it has no merit or utility in terms of the Infinite First Three.

Concerning the illusionary nature of time, Kabbalah, in this rare instance, finds corroborating evidence in the most recent scientific findings. Physicists now tell us that time cannot be separated from space nor space from time, that gravity influences time, that clocks run slower at ground level than high in the atmosphere, that the speed of a clock is faster when flying in one direction around the Earth than it is when flying in the other, that time stands still at the edge of a black hole, and also it hypothetically comes to a dead stop at the speed of light. These scientific findings, while certainly at odds with what is commonly referred to as logic and common sense, are well in keeping with the kabbalist's long standing assertion that the commonly held presumption of time adhering to some vast, unerring universal rhythm, is a complete fallacy. If time marches on it does so to ten trillion—or thereabouts—different drummers.

Space-time exists only in the Lower Seven, the dimension of the Line. Only in the Line do we find hearts beating, lunar cycles, bio-rhythms, seconds, minutes and hours, planets orbiting stars in regular-as-clockwork cycles, pulsars pulsing with uncanny accuracy, and electrons revolving around protons according to rigidly defined schedules. In fact, the entire visible universe and even much that is invisible operates in an obviously cyclical and measured manner. Thus, from our limited perspective here in the Lower Seven it is only natural that we view the world of fragmentation, the illusionary world of time, space, and motion, as the "be all and end all" of existence. So ensconced are we in the concept of time as a linear, never varying absolute that to even consider other possibilities requires a seemingly illogical state of mind.

It is not surprising, then, that when the kabbalist tries to tell us that time exists as an integral aspect of an unchanging infinitely-dimensional (or undimensional) plane, that the past, present, and future are all present in the same time-space at the same space-time, we are apt, from our limited perspective, to consider him or her to be a perfect candidate for a mental institution. The idea that the past, present, and future are all parts of some unchanging, space-time spectrum is a logical impossibility, the domain of science fiction not of science; of fantasy not of fact. Yet Einstein himself admitted that if anything could travel faster than light it would also be possible to exceed the speed of life, as it were, and hop backward in time, the reasoning being that as time stands still at the speed of light it would presumably begin going backward after that speed was achieved. This could never happen in Einstein's view because nothing could ever exceed the speed of light. In recent years, however, many sub-atomic particles that do exceed the speed of light have entered the scientific lexicon, though in fairness it should be noted that the existence or non-existence of these sub-atomic particles or tendencies has not as yet been factually established.

The kabbalist is not overly concerned whether or not the knowledge of Kabbalah will or will not ever be scientifically validated other than for the fact that were the teachings of Kabbalah to be scientifically proven more people would gravitate to and benefit from the mental, emotional, and spiritual rewards that are gained through the study and practice of Kabbalah. However, kabbalists are certainly not holding their breath awaiting scientific verification for the simple reason that they have ample personal proof that the teachings of Kabbalah are unquestionably valid.

Kabbalah teaches that the thread of our lives is woven inalterably into the entire fabric of Infinity and that we have the capability of tracing that line backward or forward, traversing time and space, leaping from one age, one lifetime, to the next at the speed of thought. For the kabbalist, past, present, and future are indistinguishable aspects of the grand Infinite continuum. The real world is unified. There is an aspect of unification within the atmosphere, within us, within everything that exists in this world. This Circular condition is indicated on the physical level by the planets that are approximately spherical, the atom, air bubbles, the concentric circles that form around a pebble in the water, as well as the human eye, head, and face. The paradox is that the real world must, as has been well established, remain concealed.

Energy intelligences transcend space, time, and motion. Only our finite aspects are caught up in the quagmire of illusion. Our Circular aspect, the First Three, is connected with the great Circle of Infinity. The Lower Seven alone is susceptible to the friction and pitfalls of finite existence. Communication between energy intelligences is instant, transcending both space and time. By bridging the gap between the three and the seven a circuit of unification is achieved by which the kabbalist becomes sensitive to the entire space-time spectrum.

Just as the seed contains the past, present and future of the tree, so too, do we embody the entire spectrum of humanity from our earliest primordial beginnings right up to the ultimate physical demise of humankind. The real world is unified. Through the attitude and practice of conscious resistance it becomes readily possible to achieve an altered state of consciousness through which the time-space continuum can be transcended completely, making telepathy, astral travel, and past life regression not mere possibilities but readily available realities.

From our limited finite perspective time appears to be absolute. We are so used to gauging our perceptions according to the ticking of a clock and the seemingly rigid schedule of birth, life, and death, that we accept the tyranny of the world of resistance as a foregone conclusion. The kabbalist asks us to remember that the Endless is beyond the jurisdiction of that which is finite and that by connecting with the Endless aspect of ourselves we can open the gates of Infinity.

Kabbalah teaches us a way by which to remove ourselves from the spiritually impoverishing cycle of negativity, struggle, failure, and ultimate defeat—which is what people ensconced in the consciousness of limitation consider death to be—and leads us to a state of mind in which we are connected with the Infinite continuum where time, space, and motion are unified, where past, present and future are entwined, where everyone and everything is interconnected, where here is there and then is now.

Be alert, then, and ever wary of the illusion that poses as reality on this negative phase. It is a trap, perhaps capable of ensnaring a hapless animal, but not a thinking, feeling human being. It is a prison, but like any prison it is one from which some, if only a few, will always be able to escape. It is a wall, one hundred meters thick and a thousand meters high, but when one looks more closely one sees that its bricks are made of illusion. It is a house of mirrors that perhaps at times can best be navigated with the eyes closed and the heart open.

Chapter 2

The New Age

Whatever happened to the much-touted age of Aquarius, with its promise of harmony and understanding, sympathy and love abounding? Where are the King Davids, the Joan of Arks, the Knights of the Round Table who held high the banners of peace, justice, and altruism? Whatever became of the young rebels who created the great social upheaval of the 1960s? Have they all, as the media would have us believe, traded in their rainbow of dreams for navy blue worsted, pinstripes and plastic?

True, on the surface it might seem as if the idealistic fervor that fueled the fire of social upheaval in the past has been swallowed up by the ego generated machinery that powers the so-called Me Generation. If we believe what the cultural icons tell us, then this is an age of rocks and hard places, bottom lines, and money market funds. Hard economic realities rule this world, not some silly idealistic dream of world peace. The fad mongers tell us that we are part of the Now Generation, and that this is the age of fast cars, fast food, and fast fun. Live for today, is their advice. Take what you can get, then take some more. The evangelical Bible thumpers paint another picture, a bloody, gloomy portrait of death, pestilence, and divine retribution for any and all who do not toe the fundamentalist line.

Who are we to believe?

Kabbalah teaches that there is no disappearance in Spiritual Substance (Light). Everything that is, ever was, or ever will be was present in the *Ein Sof* before the Thought of Creation, hence everything must also be here today, but unrevealed. Light, the eternal aspect of existence, is not subject to change without notice, it does not fade in and out according to the time of day or the change of seasons. The same is true of the great social upheavals that seem so ephemeral. In truth, important changes in the sociological fabric do not disappear, but remain indelibly etched in the collective consciousness. Like the Light that permeates every speck of material reality those changes in the social macrocosm are merely obscured, hidden behind the myriad disguises that mask the Infinite face of reality.

The New Age is here. We are beginning to witness, and, indeed, some of us are already participating in, a people's revolution of enlightenment. This spiritual insurrection will be made possible as a result of the efforts of individuals who are dedicated to bringing about a metaphysical understanding of the cosmos and man's relationship and place within it.

Consciousness is a matter of revealment, a matter of simply stepping out of the darkness into the Light. The New Age was born with the Thought of Creation, and like all of creation it will be here until the cycle of correction has run its course. Man, perhaps, can change some of the footnotes of history by his thoughts and subsequent actions, and perhaps, he can also slow down or speed up the process of correction, but like any finite existence, the life of the human species must of necessity have a beginning, middle, and end. Hence, we, as a species, must one day shed our physical appearances and merge once again with the Endless.

King David has become synonymous with the advent of the Age of Aquarius and the Messiah. The prophet, Jeremiah, foresaw this abandonment of ignorance and its replacement by an overwhelming visceral comprehension of the very nature of existence. The *Zohar* states, "In the days of the Messiah, there will no longer be the necessity for one to request of his neighbor, 'teach me wisdom,' as it is written, 'One day they will no longer teach every man his neighbor and every man his brother, saying know the Lord. For they shall all know Me, from the youngest to the oldest of them.' (*Jeremiah* 31:34)."

As tenaciously as some people who are ensconced in Desire to Receive for Oneself Alone will cling to outmoded, violent, macho, ego laden frameworks of consciousness, the fact is that the New Age cannot be avoided. It is etched in the cosmic blueprint, the map, the DNA of consciousness that was born with the Thought of Creation and will not disappear until the cycle of correction has come to an end. Like any living entity, the collective consciousness of man is destined to undergo a transformation before passing to the Great Beyond. The only difference between the Age of Darkness in which we are living and the Age of Enlightenment which is yet to come, is that in the Age of Enlightenment all entities and energy intelligences will have total cognizance of their part in an eternal oneness.

By way of illustration, perhaps it might be useful to imagine a scenario in which alien spacecraft suddenly threaten to exterminate all life on Earth. Immediately, all petty quarrels and differences would be forgotten and the sanctity and wholeness of the human race would rush to the surface of each individual's consciousness. Another apt comparison might be drawn between the New Age of humanity and the moments of supreme lucidity that often precede the physical passing of an individual.

The Light is here in all of its glory, the still, timeless, peaceful, infinite unity is present even in this world of greed and violent upheaval, but like all things that are real it must remain concealed to allow us the opportunity of removing Bread of Shame. Thus, kabbalists do not cower in fear of the coming apocalypse, hoping and praying that they might be among the chosen few who will prosper in the New Age that is to follow. One need not, after all, look to the future for something that is already here today. Kabbalists gaze not into the future for the beginning of the

Age of Enlightenment, they look within. The New Age is here today, as is the apocalypse, as is the pestilence, as is the final emendation.

All things physical have their roots in the metaphysical. Consciousness, not science, religion, or public opinion, is the harbinger of what is to come. There is no disappearance in Spiritual Substance. Nothing of value disappears. Shapes change, appearances, the body changes, but the energy intelligence never diminishes. The illusion changes constantly, but the truth beneath the illusion is constant and never varying. Each stage of biological, social, and cultural evolution is impressed into the collective consciousness. In a like manner, each person's important mental and emotional lessons are remembered through the course of each lifetime, and his or her pivotal spiritual lessons are carried over from life to life. Nothing is lost. No great truths fall irretrievably between the cracks of existence, no great crimes go unpunished.

According to kabbalistic wisdom, the physical world is just a blip on the endless screen of reality, a temporary static disruption, a minor disturbance of the Endless peace, a pattern of interference that has existed only for the flash of an instant that we have lived as physical entities and will be here only until that time at the end of the process of correction when the universe fine-tunes itself out of existence.

What proof can the kabbalist offer to substantiate such seemingly outrageous claims in light of the fact that we seem no nearer to resolving our problems than were our primal ancestors when they first began to contemplate the Great Mystery? Indeed, if anything, the situation seems to have gotten worse. Never before has the ecological balance of nature been so seriously threatened, never have we hovered so near to the brink of nuclear disaster. How can the kabbalist's faith and optimism remain undisturbed with the specters of war, genocide, terrorism, and nuclear proliferation looming like dark clouds on the horizon of human consciousness?

Kabbalah teaches that we must ever be wary of appearances—for things in this physical world are never what they seem. Now, as always, the physical universe gives every impression of being in a state of perpetual darkness and chaos. The Light is here, but so obscured by the negative trappings of finite existence that a sensitive eye and a compassionate soul are required to perceive It. The kabbalist is constantly scanning the human horizon for signs of the Light's Endless luminosity. He sees It in the trend toward miniaturization. Where previously a cable carried four hundred conversations, a fiber optic strand can transfer four hundred thousand. He sees It in the computer that once required a large room but is now housed in a package that can be comfortably lifted with one hand. He sees It also in the quantum physicist's rediscovery of the so-called "featureless ground state," which closely corresponds with the ancient kabbalistic contention that the true nature of reality is never changing and perfectly still.

The struggle of science to achieve more with less is seen by the kabbalist as a reflection of man's striving to shed his garments of darkness and step once again into the Light. Thus, these developments, when seen from a kabbalistic perspective, reveal an inborn tendency in man to strip from himself the stifling raiment of physicality and to embrace the Infinite which, after all, we are all destined to do when the cycle of correction has come full circle and we are liberated from the harsh illusion that disguises itself as physical reality.

The Light never rests. It is forever compelling us toward the culmination of the cosmic process, the final emendation, the re-revealment of the true Reality, the *Or Ein Sof.* It incessantly urges us toward that heightened state of consciousness that will allow us to remove *klipot* and end, for all time, the need for Bread of Shame. The greater is the Light's revealment, the greater is the pressure on us to reveal It. What the kabbalist sees today is an increase in the pressure, a hastening of the corrective process that augurs the beginning of the end of a long, arduous process of spiritual adjustment and rectification, and the dawning, for many individuals, of a New Age.

Kabbalah, as the reader is by now aware, describes the physical as illusionary, and only that which is eternal and never changing as real. Even today, the astute observer can detect trends within Western culture that seem to indicate a swing away from the corporeal illusion. Einstein's theories of general and special relativity caused a re-evaluation and ultimately the abandonment of rigid classical constructs involving energy and matter, time and space. Explorations into the subatomic world are revealing the dynamic interplay within the unbroken cosmic oneness.

From the kabbalistic perspective, the fundamental importance of these new scientific findings is that they provide a conceptual framework, a jumping off point, if you will, for realizing altered states of consciousness through which all separate manifestations can be experienced as components of a vast, intimate, and integrated continuum. For its part, Kabbalah furnishes the mental and emotional apparatus by which an elevated awareness of the interconnectedness of past, present and future, space, time and motion, can be achieved.

"Praiseworthy are those who will be in that age," states the *Zohar*, "and woe unto those people."

A common theme in apocalyptic literature is that of the New Age belonging to those who prepare for it. Some of the doomsayers predict that only those who have purified themselves will flourish in the New Age; the rest will, at best, suffer the throes of eternal damnation. When examined from a kabbalistic perspective this same scenario is seen as having not just one but several layers of meaning.

The kabbalist guards always against literal interpretations of ancient esoteric texts, and is especially watchful when interpreting biblical writings. This is not to suggest that a literal interpretation of the Bible does not make good reading, it does. And, indeed, it cannot be denied that the Bible provides a most valuable historical record. Rather, the reason the kabbalist probes beneath the surface of biblical interpretation is the result of an unshakable conviction that the real meaning of the Bible is not to be found in the "outer garments," the stories themselves. The meaning of the Bible, like the Light, must remain concealed.

The Bible, according to kabbalistic wisdom, is a cosmic code that must be deciphered. Every word, line, and passage harbors a sublime hidden meaning. Thus, to lift from the Bible certain passages concerning the apocalypse and interpret them literally is, in the kabbalist's view, to engage in an exercise in futility.

Those who purify themselves have always reaped the rewards of a New Age, a new life, a new level of consciousness; just as those who lurk in the shadows of negativity have always had to suffer. From the kabbalistic perspective, the Age of Enlightenment is not some distant, pie-in-the-sky vision of a new and better tomorrow. The New Age is here, today. It begins the moment each individual chooses Light over darkness, good over bad, life over death.

As for the hellfire and pestilence predicted by the evangelical soul savers, yes that too is with us. Those who choose to live in darkness have always suffered a damnation, which, to the kabbalist's way of thinking, is every bit as insidious as any imagined by the Bible fundamentalists. The apocalypse happens when one has reached rock bottom, when one's life is in shambles, when some wrong has been committed that must be set right. The metaphysical equivalent of hellfire and brimstone consumes the mind, the thoughts, the consciences of those who have chosen to walk on a path of darkness. The world is strewn with the victims of self hatred, those who have perished as a result of the atrophy of their consciousness, those who are the grim reapers of the hatred they themselves have sown. The New Age does indeed belong to those who prepare for it, but not in the sense that the evangelists might have us believe. Those who do not work to purify themselves must certainly suffer the spasms of self-inflicted damnation. Those who cling to antiquated hard-line material views and values, the war mongers, the brass tack materialists who mistake themselves for realists, the power merchants, the ego driven prime movers and shakers of the physical environment, will not, without major adjustments in their spiritual modus operandi, reap the rewards of higher consciousness. That, it seems to the kabbalist, is punishment enough.

Such is the age-old order of things, as it was, as it is, as it should be.

Chapter 3

Mind Over Matter

A dark cloud looms upon the horizon of classical scientific thought and theory. Its name is Quantum Mechanics. New findings in the field of quantum mechanics challenge the scientific method and threaten to evaporate a mirage that has for centuries been generally accepted as reality. Physicists now tell us that in addition to the Cartesian paradigm, the foundation for modern science, which acknowledges as real only that which is subject to scientific verification, we must now consider a subatomic level of existence in which the scientific method is not effective, a world in which the consciousness of the experimenter cannot be separated from his experiment, a world which some say is actually shaped and possibly even initiated by the power of thought.

Newtonian and Einstein physicists must now, in light of quantum discoveries, confront the proposition that there is no such thing as true objectivity in any but a limited frame of reference. This, almost needless to say, strikes deep into the heart of the Cartesian paradigm, not to mention the ego of conservative physicists, everywhere. Objectivity is possible only when one can remain a safe distance from that which is being objectified. However, when dealing with the subatomic spectrum, the experiment and the experimenter operate as a single entity (process). One cannot be disengaged from the other. The experiment becomes an extension of the experimenter, and the results of the experiment are strangely dependent upon the experimenter's thoughts. Hence, we find a situation in which the standard *modus operandi* of science is invalid.

The kabbalist has long known that thought shapes what we perceive as reality every bit as much as that reality shapes thought. We are what we think. More than simply a means of perceiving reality, thought has the ability to create the reality we perceive. We are more than observers of reality, more even than participators in our Earthly conception of what is real. Thought, according to kabbalistic wisdom, not only determines the nature of the Earthly reality we choose to create, but also molds the way in which we choose to interact with it. That self created, tacitly agreed upon reality is the field upon which we play out our cycle of correction. However, again according to the Kabbalah, there is, in addition to this tumultuous physical reality, another timeless, spaceless Reality that operates according to an infinite set of criteria, beyond the machinations of the physical world. This is the Reality to which the kabbalist aspires.

So well has quantum theory stood the critical test of time that all manner of accolades have been showered upon it, one of which has gone so far as to describe it as being the most perfect theory yet devised by man. The trouble is, quantum theory defies what for the past three-plus centuries has been the dominant mode of Western consciousness, the Cartesian paradigm. Named after its progenitor, the French philosopher and scientist, Rene Descartes (1596 1650), the Cartesian paradigm accepts as members into the exclusive club called reality only that which is subject to verification by the scientific method—which quantum reality is not.

This turn of events, of course, leaves the classical Newtonian and Einstein physicist, whose work is rooted in the Cartesian paradigm, in a very awkward situation. Either he must attempt to ignore the quantum theory and assume that the subatomic spectrum, and the rules that govern it (quantum mechanics), are not real—which, in view of the mountain of evidence in favor of quantum findings, is a practical impossibility or, he is forced to admit that the framework upon which his work is based, is not, as has been long believed, infallible. Small wonder, then, that many traditional physicists see it as being in their best interests to disregard, harangue, reject, repudiate, and discredit quantum mechanics in the hopes that it will shrivel up like a dead flower and blow away—a fate for which, fortunately or unfortunately depending on your point of view, quantum physics is showing not the faintest sign or aptitude.

Unable to explain the efficacy of quantum mechanics, unable even to explain it away, the traditional scientist is faced with the unsettling prospect that there must be two realities, one that operates above in the atomic level, which can be explained according to Cartesian criteria, and another that operates below in the subatomic realm and is ruled by a separate set of subatomic dictates. Slowly, the scientist is being obliged to accept the fact that the laws of science do not apply to the metaphysical realm, and that, perhaps more importantly, he is being forced to abandon his cherished conceit of an objective reality, so arduously perpetuated because the Cartesian reality is no more real, no more convincing than the Quantum reality. Each is valid in its own respective framework; each is real in its own right.

The mainstream scientist stands as one tottering at the edge of a black hole. If he falls back into the Cartesian reality of comfort and safety, he will never know what miracles might await him on the other side, but if he takes the plunge into the unknown quantum reality he might be forced to forever abandon logic and rationality and all he holds dear. There he hovers, on a tightrope between two worlds, two realities, one rational the other non-rational, one in which the scientific method is valid, the other which seems to be governed by thought. No longer can he cling to the misconception that he is a cool, impartial observer of nature. Quantum theory tells us that inside and outside, nature and man are one and the same. No longer can he maintain an aloof, holier-than-thou attitude toward the world. To do so would mean having to adopt the same attitude toward himself. And who can be impartial about oneself? Now, in light of quantum discoveries, the classical physicist must leave his ivory tower, re-evaluate the very framework upon which his thinking is based, adjust to a new set of variables, sort through and piece together all of the new data, and finally try to mold it into a viable and livable paradigm.

The kabbalist has no such problem to contend with. Kabbalists welcome quantum developments and even celebrate them. Certainly, to the careful observer, the quantum phenomena appears to represent a trend toward a return to metaphysical values, and in many ways seems to foreshadow the weakening of the centuries old death grip by which science has dominated its inventor, man. However, lest the reader be left with the mistaken impression that the kabbalist gazes in awe upon the quantum physicist's discovery that thought molds, alters, and ultimately creates reality, it should be noted that this amazing leading edge discovery has been known to metaphysicians for as many as twenty centuries. Kabbalists have always engaged in what has popularly come to be called the power of mind over matter, but as mentioned earlier, kabbalists take the concept one step further than the quantum physicist, suggesting that more than mere participators in the metaphysical (quantum) scheme, man, utilizing the power of thought, can act as a determiner of both physical and metaphysical activity.

The kabbalistic conception of mind-over-matter, nonetheless, does not necessarily correspond or comply entirely with the popular connotation of that subject. Telekinesis, for example, the physical movement of objects through the power of thought alone, bending keys, stopping and starting broken watches, while certainly within the realm of practical possibility, are not, to the kabbalist's way of thinking, worthy pursuits—the reason being that to engage in such activities is to play, so to speak, into the hands of the Cartesian paradigm. What, after all, is the purpose of bending a key or guessing symbols on a card, if not for self aggrandizement, entertainment, or to prove to some so-called objective observer, (who we now find is objective only within a limited, physical frame of reference), the power of the mind over matter? A far more productive use of thought-energy, it seems to the kabbalist, is to power the mechanism by which one becomes engaged with the Infinite reality mentioned earlier, for by doing so one becomes impervious to the physical realm and its machinations.

When the kabbalist speaks of mind over matter, he or she is speaking of undergoing an alteration of consciousness, a transformation of the mind, from the rational, logical mode to the non-rational, cosmic mode that allows for the conscious transcendence of physical constraints. Thought can traverse great distances, can affect people and objects, and is indeed a tangible factor in the world around us. That traditional science cannot yet recognize this is no fault of Kabbalah.

The concept of mind over matter is given expression and defended in the ancient esoteric text of the *Zohar* in an important passage pertaining to astral influences. When Abraham, the first astrologer, gazed up at the stars he foresaw that he would not have children. The Creator told Abraham not to gaze any longer into the wisdom of the stars for he would have a son if he attached himself to the Upper Realm and not to the stars. Abraham, knowledgeable in the wisdom of astrology, recognized the impelling nature of the influence of the stars and planets on man. Using his knowledge, he deduced that he was destined not to have a son, but the Creator revealed a paradox regarding man's existence in this world. While man is influenced by external forces he also possesses an element of free choice. The stars impel but they do not compel.

It is possible to remove oneself from the impelling influence of the celestial bodies, and even to transcend, altogether, external constraints. All things physical and metaphysical including humanity, are possessed of two aspects, one finite the other Infinite. The kabbalist's task is to rise above normal, rational consciousness, which means removing him or herself from the confines of physicality, the finite Lower Seven, so as to connect with the Infinite First Three.

Humanity's finite aspect, what might be described as the flesh and bones, is subject to Cartesian rules and regulations; the other, the infinite characteristic operates beyond limited physical jurisdiction. Only the former is subject to pain, discomfort, and death. The latter is part of the Eternal. And whereas the former is rooted to the physical world, the latter, being part of the Infinite is free to merge at will with the Infinite. By consciously connecting with one's Infinite aspect—which is done by paying constant homage to the original act of Creation, which was restriction—it becomes practicable to transcend space, time, matter, along with which comes the potential for presentience, astral travel, and the instant alleviation of physical and mental pain and suffering.

Legions of people of all ages, from all walks of life, have reported out-of-body experiences. In fact, we have all engaged in astral projection, whether or not we remember our sojourns into the ethereal realms. Science, however, has no way of validating astral projection, or any of the other so-called mystical experiences, because the phenomenon of out-of-body travel, like quantum reality, cannot be grasped using the scientific method. Thus, the scientist, given the inherited rigidity of his consciousness, is forced to conclude that astral projection does not exist. Yet, for any of the many thousands of people who have experienced astral travel there is no question that astral reality is every bit as real as the one we experience in our everyday lives.

It is hoped that the reader will forgive a slight digression for the sake of clarifying why the scientific method is incapable of revealing astral, metaphysical, and quantum phenomena. The scientific method, despite its notable success in exposing certain aspects of the physical world, has, as quantum physics has demonstrated, proved incapable of evaluating that which is metaphysical. The simple reason for this can be found by examining an underlying principle of the Cartesian paradigm that is based in the mistaken belief that nature can be browbeaten, so to speak, into revealing her secrets through a method of willful harassment. The Newtonian scientist, in other words, jars, jolts, and otherwise interferes with that which he or she is experimenting upon and then measures the reaction. A similar technique is used by certain large-scale fruit farmers who utilize bulky shaking machines to compel the trees to relinquish their ripe fruits. Thus, we find that while practical in the world above the atomic level, the scientific method has proved ineffectual when dealing with the subatomic (quantum) world—the reason being that the very act of inciting the subatomic particles causes a fundamental transformation in the phenomenon that the scientist is attempting to measure. To determine the position of an electron, for instance, it would be necessary to illuminate the electron using light of the shortest known wavelength, namely a gamma ray, but the gamma ray, upon striking the electron, would catapult the electron out of its orbit, thereby making verification of the electron's position impossible.

Does this in any way prove that the subatomic world is nonexistent? Not for an instant. Such is the case with all metaphysical phenomena: Just because they perhaps cannot be verified using the scientific method does not mean that they do not exist. All that it does prove is that the method of measurement is faulty. By a similar token, as was hinted at earlier, scientific verification is of little importance to those who have been on the receiving end of a mystical experience. Astral and non-rational encounters require no scientific validation. Those who have astral projected generally need no one to assure them that what they have seen or experienced is real. Those who have witnessed fire-walkers stepping calmly and with complete impunity through white hot coals need no empirical validation that the mind can exercise power over matter—as is certainly also the case with those who have undergone painless, bloodless surgery with no anesthetic other than a hypnotic trance.

Not everyone, of course, is given the opportunity of examining the feet of a fire-walker; or has undergone surgery while under the influence of hypnosis; or has total recall of each one of his or her sublimely liberating out-of-body experiences. Quite naturally, then, those people are apt to remain unconvinced as to the mind's ability to temporarily bypass cause-effect relationships and connect with higher levels of consciousness. For those who have no direct experience with—or simply no recollection of—the uncharted regions of consciousness, it is suggested that the tangible verification of the power of mind over matter may be simply acquired by directing one's full attention to the back of a stranger's neck. Almost invariably the subject will react instantly and often will turn to zero-in on the power plant from which the beam of thought originated.

Kabbalistic wisdom holds that we are comprised of two aspects, finite and Infinite. The finite aspect, synonymous with the body, is subject to the laws of Cartesian science; the Infinite aspect operates beyond the laws of science and, thus, may be compared in some respects with the subatomic realm. Physically, we are creatures of the Earth; spiritually we are perpetually connected to the Endless. The finite part of us is subject to change, turmoil, pain and suffering, the other, higher aspect remains beyond the jurisdiction of physicality. Through the kabbalistic attitude of positive resistance a connection can be made by which the Infinite self is, so to speak, illuminated. By attaching with the infinite aspect, a transformation of consciousness takes place that allows one to rise temporarily above the time-space continuum, beyond pain and physical discomfort, above the machinations of the physical world.

Chapter 4

Altered States

T he drug problem spans the entire socio-economic spectrum. Doctors, lawyers, athletes, corporate executives, workers, students, housewives—young and old, rich and poor, black and white—no one, it seems, is immune to this all pervading menace. Staggering numbers of people from all walks of life are addicted to prescription drugs, uppers, downers, valium, quaaludes, diet and sleeping pills. Millions smoke marijuana or take cocaine on a daily basis. Alcoholism continues to be an international disgrace. An estimated 365,000 people die each year in the United States alone of diseases related to cigarette smoking. At least as many are hooked on black market drugs like heroin, crack, angel dust, amphetamines, barbiturates—just name your poison MDA, PCP, LSD, STP street corner pushers dispense an A to Z of chemical corruption.

School children dying with needles in their arms, junkies stealing and killing to support hundred-dollar-a-day habits, mothers selling their babies—incidents such as these have become so commonplace that news of them hardly so much as raises an eyebrow.

As if the problems were not already bad enough, the black market is now being inundated by a new menace, the so-called designer drugs. Concocted by amateur chemists from ingredients available at any local drugstore, these drugs are chemically comparable to illegal anesthetics, hypnotics, and psychedelics, but altered in such a way as to make them legal—so while the law regarding the sale of a drug such as heroin might carry a term of life imprisonment, the penalty for marketing a closely related designer drug with effects and side-effects that are equally as dangerous is tantamount to a light slap on the wrist, or worse, the law provides for no sentence at all. The judiciary and law enforcement officials are hard-pressed in their race to even identify these new, highly addictive and often lethal substances much less to pass laws against them.

Small wonder, then, that the hysteria accompanying the drug epidemic has reached epidemic proportions. Everyone from the president of the United States right down to the man on the street is jumping onto the "War on Drugs" bandwagon and woe to those who are unwilling to go along for the ride. Debates rage on Capitol Hill. Blustery, self-righteous congressmen and senators challenge each other to submit to urinalysis. TV editorials decry the shame of drug-related crime. Letters to the editor endorse the death penalty for drug dealers. Feminists vow to "Take Back the Night" from the users, thieves, and dealers. "Experts" voice conflicting opinions. Hardly a week goes by, it seems, when a newspaper headline does not proclaim the most recent "Largest Drug Bust in History." Rhetoric flows like water from a bursting dam. In the meantime more drugs are bought and sold than ever before, more money changes hands, more lives are wasted.

Since the early years in the twentieth century—and probably much earlier—politicians have been vowing to clamp down on drug traffic, vice, and other blights on the landscape of humanity. Police chiefs have been declaring new crack downs and get tough policies. Supreme court judges have been passing laws designed to curb drug traffic or otherwise legislate morality. Perhaps the most notable example was the fiasco known as Prohibition. But the combined services of the government agencies, the police, the border patrol, and the military have been dismally ineffective in combating the drug problem, as is evidenced by the fact that the use and the importation of illegal drugs has sky-rocketed with each passing year. Crusades against drugs come and go, but the drugs, it seems, go on forever.

Not surprisingly, then, the latest congressional proposals that will vow billions of dollars to cut off drugs at their sources, to crack down on dealers, to administer drug tests to millions of government employees, and to equip the military and border patrol with high-tech radar systems and state-of-the-art helicopters, have been met with more than a grain of skepticism

Perhaps we should pause to consider some of the possible implications attached to these new mandates. Where will the billions of dollars come from that will be needed to administer these grandiose schemes? Social programs? Tax increases? The fund for environmental protection? Perhaps we should also ask ourselves how these programs might affect our personal, legal, and civil liberties. Will every employer be legally bound to administer drug tests? Will narcotics officers be empowered to set up roadblocks and to conduct house-to-house searches? Will all of our phones be tapped? Will we be interminably delayed at border crossings while every car is searched, every suitcase scrutinized, every pocket turned inside-out? Will we be forced to undergo spot checks or strip-searches every time we board an airplane to or from a foreign country? Will the Constitution have to be amended to make legal this new wave of paranoid oppression?

Of course no politician in his right mind would ever propose measures as stringent as these for the simple reason that no democratic population would abide by them. Yet, given the pervasive and pernicious nature of chemical dependency, and the tremendous profit incentive for those who deal drugs, measures at least as oppressive as these would be required to bring a problem of the present magnitude under control. Countries such as Turkey and Russia have relatively minor problems with illegal drugs compared to Western countries—yet, fortunately, few Westerners would willingly pay a price in personal liberty equal to that exacted in those countries even if it meant a completely drug free environment. Given the prevailing conditions, then, it seems that the best we of the Western world can hope for are stop-gap solutions such as those represented by the latest government measures.

As is the case with so many of the predicaments that Western societies face today, no one, it seems, is even considering, much less addressing, the cause of the drug epidemic. Instead we look for symptomatic solutions. With our jails already filled to the bursting point we should be attempting to uncover the underlying causes of addiction, instead we spend vast sums to make more jails. With the criminal justice system already tremendously overburdened we should be trying to find cures for chemical dependency, instead we incarcerate more young users and small time dealers and relegate them to a life of crime.

Imagine a system where a drug addict is cured of his addiction by addicting him or her to another, stronger, more addictive drug. It happens every day a heroin addict is put onto a methadone maintenance program. Does it not seem counter-productive to attempt to cure heroin addiction by prescribing methadone, an even more addictive drug? Should we not try to find out what is causing these people to turn to heroin in the first place? Imagine a rehabilitation program that turns away those it specializes in treating. Drug dependence clinics regularly turn away addicts who are seeking treatment because of restrictive policies, red tape, or overcrowding. Imagine a society that allows people to be jailed for ingesting a relatively mild, physically non-addictive substance while allowing for the promotion and open sale of—and actually collecting taxes on—other far more addictive and debilitating substances. Such is the situation pertaining to marijuana versus alcohol and tobacco.

With hypocritical laws and Neanderthal policies such as these (no offence to the Neanderthal who were more intelligent than is commonly believed) is it any wonder that millions of young people have lost respect for the laws and the judges who make them? With elected officials seeking temporary, easy-to-swallow solutions is it any wonder that the people who elect them do the same? With modern doctors prescribing medications to ease symptoms even when they have not the slightest idea as to the nature of the sickness, is it any wonder that their patients attempt to solve their own psychic discomfort with similar symptomatic quick fixes?

As an exercise in futility, let us now examine some of the recent proposals which are under consideration concerning the battle in the seemingly endless War on Drugs.

1. Throw billions of dollars at the problem and hope it will go away.

    This, of course, will do nothing. The Law Enforcement Assistance Administration doled out $8 billion to combat local crime, yet in those years crime increased at a record pace. Federal spending against narcotics has doubled in the last five years, but more drugs flow into the country than ever before.

2. Undertake a massive propaganda campaign.

    This will serve only to glorify drugs still further. Besides, such announcements have been on the air for years with little or no effect.

3. Increase the number of street arrests.

    This will create a greater problem in our already overburdened prison and judicial system.

4. Stop drugs at their source.

> This method, though currently in favor among certain law makers and politicians, is doomed for a variety of reasons, not the least of which being that the United States has no diplomatic ties with many of the supply-side countries. Hence, many of the world's main drug sources will always remain beyond U.S. jurisdiction. Also, it will raise the price of illegal drugs, thus increasing drug related crime as addicts will have to steal that much more to support their habits. Locally grown and produced "designer drugs" will fill the gap. Even in the highly unlikely event that these measures did manage to destroy every jungle drug factory and stop the importation of all illegal drugs there would still be legal alcohol to fall back on, prescription drugs, cough medicine, airplane glue, sniffing the last few whiffs at the bottom of aerosol containers, and inhaling gasoline fumes, which was, until recently, the drug of choice among certain natives indigenous to the Amazon region.

5. Follow the lead of countries such as England and Holland and legalize drugs and dispense them at low cost.

> This is by far the sanest, practical, and humane solution mentioned so far. This fact alone, given the prevailing belligerent fervor of our brave political crusaders, condemns it to obscurity. Still, though while it has little or no chance of ever being enacted, we will give it a cursory examination anyway, for it would certainly do a great deal towards stopping drug related crime. Addicts would not have to steal to support their habits. The drug kingpins would go out of business overnight because who would buy illegal drugs at expensive prices if they could have legal drugs at low cost? Fewer people would die of overdoses because the quality of

the drugs would be carefully controlled. The inmate population would be cut in half and the burden on the judicial system would be instantly alleviated. However, drug legalization has one major drawback; it would not stop people from taking drugs and, unfortunately, would probably promote more addiction.

Simple logic should tell us that extravagant measures, no matter how well meaning they may be, will do nothing to curb the drug epidemic. Burning fields, spraying crops, assassinating Bolivian drug barons, cutting off aid to various impoverished Third World countries, increasing the border patrols, activating the military, throwing billions of tax dollars at the problem, propaganda, radar equipped, nuclear powered helicopters, vigilante patrols, more laws, stiffer sentences, larger jails, packs of drug sniffing dogs—none of these proposals will have the slightest effect unless and until we can identify and address the underlying cause of the problem:

Why do people take so many drugs?

Simply stated, the transcendence of normal, rational thought consciousness is a basic human need. People will do practically anything to remove themselves from this negative realm of existence—and that is as it should be. The conscious, rational mind is a trap, a prison from which our higher consciousness knows it must escape. Our Encircling Vessels are crying out constantly to be delivered from this world of illusion and to be reunited with the real world of the Light, the *Or Ein Sof.* Transcendence of this dense world of restriction and negativity is as basic as eating, as natural as walking, as necessary as the elimination of bodily waste.

Since time began people have sought ways to transcend ordinary rational thought processes. Early man was aware of this need and instituted culturally condoned methods by which this transcendence and unification with the higher realms of consciousness could be accomplished. There was the Vision Quest of the Native Americans, the Dream Walk of the Eskimo, each of which consisted of long periods of time spent alone in the wilderness. Through socially accepted ritual ceremonies, prayers and meditations such as these, people young and old convened with the spirits of their ancestors, achieved unity with Mother Earth, made peace with the forces of nature and deepened their understanding of themselves.

Primal cultures have always practiced methods of transcendence, songs, dances, and ceremonies by which they achieved altered states of consciousness. We, of the modern world, have no such methods, or rather we do but they have been forgotten, obliterated by rationality, covered over by the trappings of material life, oppressed to such an extent that few of us are even aware of their existence. What was once a rich social, cultural, and spiritual fabric has been eaten away by empty material concepts, false technological promises, and finally digested by the great, blind myth, Progress. Today, that once intimate relationship we had with nature has been replaced by crass illusions provided by a cornucopia of so-called recreational drugs.

Thus, drugs, at least those of the recreational variety, should be avoided, but not for moral, religious, health, or even legal reasons. The problem with drugs is not the motivation behind taking them, but merely the fact that they are totally ineffective. The most important grounds for abstaining from drugs, then, is that they are grossly inadequate for the purpose of transcendence—which, after all, is the underlying motivating factor for taking them in the first place.

From the kabbalistic standpoint that which is temporary is considered illusionary and only that which is permanent is considered real. Drugs provide only a crude delusion of transcendence. The high wears off leaving the user in a lower state of consciousness than he or she was in before. The physical world is illusionary-thought-consciousness is real.

Fortunately, reality cannot possibly be negatively influenced by that which is illusion. Our Encircling Vessels are connected with the Higher Realms, the Super-Conscious *Or Ein Sof,* which is Infinitely superior to the false reality inhabited by our normal waking consciousness. To connect with this higher world—which is our inalienable right (some might say our *duty*) to accomplish—normal, habitual thought processes must be transcended.

From earliest childhood we are subjected to tantalizing images of so-called beautiful people smoking and enjoying the pleasures of alcohol. Is it any wonder that young people emulate what they see?

Although there are numerous methods of achieving altered states of consciousness, Western societies have replaced them all with intoxicants. It is unfortunate that more people are not aware of other, more effective, methods of transcendence, such as those provided by Kabbalah. If everyone were to study Kabbalah no laws against drugs would be necessary. The growers would stop growing drugs for there would be no one to buy their deadly harvest. Smugglers would stop smuggling. The mafia dons would abandon the drug trade because it would no longer be profitable. Perhaps then the Bolivian peasants could return, without fear of retribution, to their traditional use of coca leaves that have been chewed for energy in a manner similar to the way people of western societies drink coffee—a practice that has gone on for thousands of years with few deleterious effects.

Addicts are slaves of illusion, but for this they should not be condemned. In fact, perhaps the addict might exact some small comfort from the fact that even after prolonged exposure to television, media, advertizing, the stultifying confines of our educational system—barely to mention the illusionary reality provided by a constant diet of drugs—his or her instincts are not so eroded as to at least aspire to some kind of union with a higher consciousness. This is more than can be said for some of the politicians, law makers, and bureaucrats who are concocting some of the grandiose, symptomatic schemes mentioned earlier. They too are slaves, the legislators of morality, the servants of rationality, the worshippers of the false security provided by *Malchut*, totally and irrevocably imprisoned by the illusion of a singular, stiflingly narrow perspective of Reality. At least the drug taker's soul cries out to transcend this negative realm. Many so-called realists have lost even that capacity.

Negative human activity does not extend beyond *Malchut*. Humanity, thankfully, cannot cause chaos in the Upper (inner) Realms. Thus, our thoughts, if tempered by positive resistance, are virtually impervious to the petty machinations of those who are possessed by Desire to Receive for Oneself Alone.

Kabbalistically speaking, being in an altered state of consciousness means having no need for the creative illusion provided by the Lower Seven. It means connecting with the *Or Ein Sof* for the purpose of seeing what is born. By transforming the Desire to Receive for Oneself Alone into Desire for the Sake of Sharing one rises above the confines of the Lower Seven and connects with the First Three. Through conscious restriction one can conquer the negative aspect of Desire and achieve an altered state of consciousness that is above and beyond the negativity of this phase.

The illusion of negative space is here for a very real purpose, and that is to allow us the opportunity of bridging the gap between ourselves and the ultimate reality of the Light, the *Or Ein Sof.* Through conscious resistance and restriction one can transform the Desire to Receive for Oneself Alone into Desire for the Sake of Sharing.

What is needed, then, are not new laws or stricter policies, but sane, socially condoned and approved methods of transcendence. Music can be such a method, writing, study, sports, certain forms of meditation, dance—in fact almost any activity can help us to transcend this negative realm of existence, but only if it is accompanied by the correct state of mind, namely, an attitude of resistance such as that which is provided by Kabbalah.

FACES OF EVIL

Evil has a thousand faces, and yet it has only one. From the perspective of the Lower Seven *Sefirot*, evil is like one of those miracle-do-all plastic devices as advertized on late night TV. It can be sculpted, bent and twisted, adjusted, amended, edited and revised, converted, corrected, modified, reversed and flip-flopped. Mold it, shape it, wear it like a mask. Toss it like a salad. Shoot it from a gun. Con with it, cheat with it, hoodwink, rob and swindle. Tease it like a beehive hair-do. It lusts! It envies! Evil—what a versatile product! And, of course, it comes with a limited sixty second money back guarantee.

Those are but a few of the false faces of evil. In reality evil has but one face, the thought energy-intelligence of Desire to Receive for Oneself Alone. Everything that revolves around that deceptive, ever-changing face of Desire, everything that emanates from it, everyone who allows that negative aspect of Desire to prevail, falls under its influence.

Yet, evil has no life of its own. Like a puppet, it is a lifeless, bloodless entity onto which we paint the faces, and for which we pull the strings. We animate evil and give it substance through our negative thoughts and actions. As a result, we also have the prerogative of painting evil with an attractive face. Yes, despite its myriad dubious characteristics, even evil may be seen in a positive light. In fact, it may be said that evil is an Earthly necessity, for it is only through restriction of Desire to Receive for Oneself Alone that the Light is revealed. Perhaps, then, we of *Malchut* owe a small debt of gratitude to evil for allowing us the opportunity of absolving Bread of Shame.

Then again, perhaps we don't.

EVIL INCLINATIONS

As strange as it may seem, it can be more difficult for a person who has few evil inclinations to connect with altered states of consciousness than it is for one who is constantly inundated by evil urges. The reason for this is simple. The person who gravitates toward evil has more opportunities for restriction. Whereas the one who has no propensity for evil is apt to be complacent and thus be offered seemingly few chances to resist the Desire to Receive for the Self Alone, the person who gravitates toward evil has many opportunities to restrict and thus earn the Light's blessing by removing Bread of Shame.

Chapter 5

The Speed of Light

Imagine that you are a twenty-third century astronaut and that you have a device called, let us say, a "Lightning Speed-O-Meter" that gives you a readout of the speed of light as it relates to your vehicle. Logic dictates that if you are heading toward the sun the readout will be the speed of light plus the speed of your vehicle, whereas if you were heading away from the sun the readout will logically be the speed of light minus the speed of your vehicle.

"Wrong!" shouts the scientist. "Not so!" adds the kabbalist.

In this rare instance the kabbalist and the scientist are in complete agreement—but for totally different reasons.

The scientist points to the Michelson-Morley experiment of 1887 that proved, to their satisfaction, as well as, presumably, to Einstein's and a few million others, that light travels at a speed of 186,000 miles per second regardless of the motion of the observer. This means that as an astronaut you might as well throw your handy-dandy Lightning Speed-O-Meter down the waste disposal chute and eject it into outer space because no matter at what speed your spaceship is traveling toward or away from the sun the readout will always be the same, 186,000 miles per second!

This fascinating fact of science defies logic and so-called common sense and for this reason alone the kabbalist would dearly love to embrace it, because as the student is by now aware, one of the main reasons for studying Kabbalah is to break free from the stifling net of illusion that passes for reality on this Fourth Phase. Unfortunately, though, the kabbalist cannot accept this concept for the simple reason that the kabbalist does not believe in the speed of light, period.

A number of kabbalistic concepts are at odds with current accepted scientific theories and the speed of light happens to be one of them. As far as the kabbalist is concerned there is no such thing. The essence of Light is everywhere, timeless, all pervading, perfectly still. Which brings us to a question that almost asks itself:

If light doesn't move, then what is it that the scientists have been measuring all these years?

An excellent question, for which Kabbalah provides an equally satisfactory answer. While Kabbalah does not even entertain the possibility of the movement of Light itself, it does make ample room for the probability that there is movement within the Light on the part of the Vessels, the *Sefirot*. The kabbalistic perspective, in this respect, is more in keeping with the new branch of physics that deals with sub-atomic particles or packets of energy called quanta and hence has been given the name Quantum Mechanics. Quanta are more accurately described as "tendencies" rather than "packets," or "bits and pieces" because they are not really "things" at all, but rather more like Aristotle's concept of *Potentia* which stands somewhere between the physical and the metaphysical, potential and reality. In any event, quantum mechanics advances several concepts that startled the scientific community when they were first introduced, two of which placed before us the possibility that the true nature of existence is beyond the scope of reason, and a second possibility, namely that certain particles travel faster than the speed of light.

Einstein himself believed that light is a rapid-fire stream of photons. In fact it was his paper concerning the quantum nature of light for which he was awarded the Nobel Prize. He drew the line, however, at the concepts expressed by quantum mechanics, that a complete understanding of reality was beyond the realm of rational thought, and that certain particles could travel faster than the speed of light. Thus he felt compelled to refute their findings, though he reluctantly agreed that they seemed to hold up, at least where the sub-atomic realm was concerned, with his now famous announcement that, "God does not play dice with the universe."

Subsequent generations of Einstein physicists have held firm to Einstein's beliefs and are also loathe to allow for either possibility because in the event that these quantum theories were to be proved correct it would punch great holes in the beautiful illusion that they have worked so diligently to construct. Their theories, you see, are based on the idea that light has a fixed speed of 186,000 miles per second.

Michelson and Morley, ironically, were attempting to prove or disprove the existence of ether winds—ether being a hypothetical inert and totally motionless substance which, for many years was believed to permeate every square millimeter of the universe—when they stumbled upon their ground breaking discovery concerning the speed of light, which laid the mathematical foundations for Einstein's theories of general and special relativity, the first of which was to emerge some twenty years later in 1905 to set the scientific world on its ear. Michelson and Morley's experiment did also temporarily disprove the theory of ether winds, and the idea of ether itself subsequently fell out of favor until the quantum field theory, which was spawned by Einstein's theories of relativity, presenting a new variation on the old ether theme, giving it the title of "featureless ground state," a hypothetical vacuum of such perfect symmetry that a velocity cannot be assigned to it experimentally.

In any event it is not our purpose here to present a treatise on the new physics versus the old, but merely to show the dissention among the ranks of science as it relates to different perspectives of reality. Quantum mechanics veers away from the Newtonian position that the universe is governed by laws that are susceptible to rational understanding, and places it in the framework of the study of consciousness—and for this the kabbalist is grateful. It sees man as a participator rather than merely an observer of reality—which has been a major tenet of kabbalistic thinking for the past two millennia.

And as for the idea, which though rejected by the mind of that most benign and brilliant mathematical genius, Dr. Albert Einstein, of blessed memory, quantum mechanics presents us with the possibility that something travels faster than the speed of light, which is yet another concept wholeheartedly embraced by Kabbalah. Yes! Most definitely something travels faster than the speed of light: Thought and consciousness both have that distinct capability. Kabbalistically speaking this is possible for the reason stated earlier that the Light is perfectly still. The Light is one. Every aspect of the universal Energy-Intelligence is in constant, instantaneous communication with Itself, everywhere. Hence, by creating affinity with the Light, by establishing a circuit, a circular concept, the distance of a trillion miles can be traversed instantly, which if placed in terms of time, space, and motion would translate to the speed of light squared ad infinitum.

GREAT DISCOVERIES

When one thinks of discoverers, inventors, explorers, it is difficult to avoid the Hollywood stereotypes such as that of a serious, single-minded Madame Curie, working tirelessly alongside her husband Pierre, to discover radium, or Thomas Edison, the brilliant inventor whose seemingly superior mind produced over one thousand patents. In fact, more often than not, great ideas, thoughts and discoveries come about seemingly by adducing, apparently out of nowhere.

Columbus was looking for a passage to India when he discovered America. Of course this is the wholly erroneous European slant on the story as Native Americans had been living in America for thousands of years. Then there is Newton whose theory of universal gravitation is said to have come to him when an apple fell on his head as he sat under an apple tree. And let us not forget the famous cry of "Eureka!" shouted by Archimedes when, while bathing, he discovered the means by which to measure the volume of an irregular solid by the displacement of water and thus was able to ascertain the purity of a gold crown belonging to the tyrant of Syracuse.

The vast majority of discoveries were the result not of research and dogged determination but stumbled upon, apparently, without the slightest effort on the part of the discoverers. The reason for this, kabbalistically speaking, is that there is, as the old saying goes, "...nothing new under the sun." Therefore, it is impossible to discover or invent something from nothing—all we can do is reveal that which already exists on the metaphysical level.

Why, then, are some people chosen to make evident the great universal truths while others reveal nothing? Simply stated, those who become channels for the Light are those whose motivating energy-intelligence is the Desire to Receive for the Sake of Sharing.

Chapter 6

This Modern Age

The Kabbalist seeks to separate the wrong from the right, the fraudulent from the true, which is not an easy task in this era of symptoms and false fronts, after thoughts and second guesses. The voice of the kabbalist is lost it seems, amid the clatter and the clutter of TV and media brainwashing. Facades, illusion, outward appearances are the trademarks of the electronic age. Social conscience has been replaced by image consciousness. No longer do we purchase a home—today we buy the neighborhood. No longer do we purchase a car—today we buy the hood ornament. No longer do we purchase clothing—today we buy the designer labels.

Enough is no longer enough. In this era of fast food, fads, and changing fashions we will not be satisfied until we "have it all."

One might perhaps imagine that kabbalists must get discouraged at times facing, as we do, the constant barrage of greed, hypocrisy, deception, and illusion that passes for life in this modern age. Nothing could be further from the truth. One of the main purposes for studying Kabbalah is to remove ourselves from limited frames of reference and this epoch of hype and supercilious conceit offers more opportunities for karmic correction than perhaps any other; which is precisely what the kabbalist loves about this illusion we call modern life—there is so much to reject!

FEAR OF FLYING

Students sometimes voice concern about becoming too Infinite, too Circular, and perhaps losing themselves entirely in the study of Kabbalah.

Of course there is no possibility of removing ourselves from this illusionary phase of existence. Even an ascetic who lives in a cave must come down from his interplanetary voyages for an occasional meal. Finite life has always been and will always be plagued by interruptions. We can never withdraw from this world, the reason being that our self-imposed exile from the Creator makes us constantly subject to the influence of the Curtain. Hence we find that no matter how assiduously we apply ourselves to transcendence of this Fourth Phase the Curtain will always intercede on behalf of limitation, and therefore there is no danger in trying to rise, as much as is humanly possible, above this illusion that we call *Malchut* and thus meld with the Light of Creation.

STAR WARS

It is a virtual impossibility for an uninitiated outside observer to comprehend the ancient kabbalistic texts. Little wonder then that when a skeptic scans the *Sefer Yetzirah* (*Book of Formation*), *Ten Luminous Emanations*, or the *Zohar* he or she will almost undoubtedly come to the conclusion that the philosophy of Kabbalah is, at best, an anachronism, at worst merely mystical poetry of no value in this modern age. What, the skeptics wonder; can an antediluvian spiritual system like Kabbalah possibly have to offer to this great scientific era of quarks and quasars, laser beams, black holes and star wars?

Yet when these same skeptics begin to study Kabbalah, when they begin to realize that the *Zohar* speaks of star wars and explains black holes more succinctly than any physicist; that Kabbalah advanced valid explanations of gravity, the neutron, evolution, and relativity hundreds of years before their discovery by science; that kabbalists have been engaging in interplanetary travel for thousands of years, and that the most futuristic scientific theories such as the possibility of going back to the future, alternate universes, string theory, and the featureless ground state are old hat as far as Kabbalah is concerned, how quickly and radically their skepticism changes to astonishment and admiration.

Now, instead of wondering how something so old could be valid, they wonder how can something so old be so new?

COMPLACENCY

Kabbalah is not a go-with-the-flow philosophy. Kabbalists do not necessarily believe in turning the other cheek, sharing for the sake of sharing or charity for the sake of charity. For the kabbalist, complacency is a state of mind that must be guarded against, comfort is a condition to be viewed with a certain disdain. This uncompromising outlook is sometimes mistaken for severe asceticism or simple mulish obstinacy until it is viewed from the correct perspective.

The kabbalist's seemingly implacable attitude is not the result of rebelliousness or rampant iconoclastic fervor, rather it might better be described as a temperament of positive resistance that results from the knowledge that no true rest, no peace of mind, can be secured until the soul's *tikkun* or corrective process has been completed.

The natural inclination of humanity's finite aspect, the Body or Lower Seven, represented by all that is physical including, of course, the human body, is to succumb to gravity, which is the manifestation of Desire to Receive for Oneself Alone. Our Infinite aspect, however, the Head or First Three, which is synonymous with the soul, is not influenced by that negative, finite aspect of Desire (Gravity) and thus the natural inclination of humanity's Infinite aspect, the energy-intelligence known as the First Three, is to perform whatever tasks that may be required to fulfill the soul's Infinite cycle of correction.

The kabbalist, then, denies the body's natural inclination, which is to remain passive, as well as the craving of the rational mind, which is to remain complacent for the simple reason that the restoration of Light to the Encircling Vessels cannot be accomplished by following the directives of that which is finite, including the body, but only by obeying the Infinite mandates of the soul.

Thus the person who seeks cosmic awareness finds him or herself in the paradoxical situation of having to deny the body's inclination, which is to rest, in favor of achieving true spiritual respite, the Infinite stillness that can only be achieved by merging with the Endless. True spiritual unity, the stillness of the Endless, can only be attained by following the Line not of the *least* but of the *most* resistance.

Comfort, the basic energy-intelligence of which is the Desire to Receive for Oneself Alone, serves no purpose other than to isolate us from ourselves and from others; complacency only sidetracks us from our true mission, which is to reveal the Light. The kabbalist, then, gives thanks for the opportunity of discomfort, not to satisfy any masochistic tendencies, but rather to give the soul the opportunity for correction, which is, after all, the ultimate purpose of finite existence. Only by rejecting the desire of the lower seven for comfort and complacency can the purpose of existence, the revealment of the Light of the Infinite First Three, be effectuated.

Hence we find that it is not lack that the kabbalist seeks by denying that which he or she most desires, but the ultimate fulfillment that results from fusing with the Infinite. The kabbalist's attitude of positive resistance serves a very tangible purpose, for it is resistance alone that causes the disappearance of the illusionary world and the revealment of all that is real.

SENSUAL ASCETICISM

The natural inclination of all things physical is to succumb to gravity, the energy-intelligence of which is the Desire to Receive for the Self Alone. Our Infinite aspect, the opposing force that energizes the mind and gives light to the eyes, has no aspiration other than to share in the completion of its circle of fulfillment. Thus the kabbalist finds him or herself in the paradoxical circumstance of having to deny the body's tendency to surrender to the essentially "negative" force of gravity, and adhere instead to the more "positive" agenda of the eternal consciousness, which is to return to the Light from which it originated.

As mentioned earlier, the *tzadikim* (the righteous ones of old), did not resist that which they most desired because of any masochistic need to punish themselves. Self depravation plays not the slightest part in the kabbalist's resistance and denial. It is simply that by reenacting the original act of Creation, the *Tzimtzum*, one creates affinity with the Light and achieves the peace of mind that results from reunion with the *Or Ein Sof.*

Only transitory contentment can be achieved by succumbing to the body's every whim. Thus, the kabbalist chooses instead the path not of the least but of the most resistance, for only by paying homage to the original act of Creation (*Tzimtzum*)—which means rejecting the selfish desires which haunt our finite existence—can our infinite Light once again be revealed.

Chapter 7

Giving and Receiving

"Giving," says an old adage, "makes life worth living." What could be nobler and more spiritually uplifting than helping the destitute, the hungry, the homeless? Surely one can achieve no greater reward in life than sharing with those less fortunate than oneself. True, helping those in need can be one of life's most gratifying experiences, as can receiving that which has been long sought and justly deserved, yet it is by no means difficult to cite numerous instances in which neither the giver nor the receiver derives any lasting sense of achievement.

Concerning the aspect of sharing, for instance, one is hard pressed to imagine a more thankless and wholly futile proposition than lavishing gifts upon someone who does not want, need, or deserve them. Examples abound of older men, who are played for fools while attempting to buy the love of younger women with diamonds and furs, and of divorced parents endeavoring to alleviate their guilt by competing with expensive gifts for the love of their children. Such strategies, of course, inevitably lead only to heartbreak and alienation.

A gift means nothing if it is wrapped in a selfish ulterior motive. Contributing, even to the worthiest of causes, becomes a self-defeating gesture unless the giver is motivated by a certain sense of altruism. A business tycoon, for example, will find no satisfaction in donating even a sizable sum to a building fund if it is merely for the purpose of having a new wing of a hospital bear his name. Nor will a rich widow who gives one of her twenty-eight Rembrandt's to a museum retain any lasting reward if the gift is given for the purpose of receiving a tax deduction, or simply because a brass plaque etched with an inscription such as, "From the Collection of Mrs. Moneybags" will be placed alongside the painting. A gift worth giving transmits something of the giver. If the giver does not experience some sense of loss or personal sacrifice, even an act of seeming beneficence is viewed, from the kabbalistic perspective, as a manifestation of greed.

Conversely, with regard to the aspect of receiving, no fulfillment can be gained by receiving something that is neither wanted, needed, nor deserved other than that of the most transitory nature. Consider the many sizable inheritances that have been squandered, and the fortunes that have been hastily acquired and impetuously lost through gambling. Easy money has wings—it departs as effortlessly as it arrives. Nor does hard work or even unfeigned sincerity necessarily guarantee protection from the pitfalls of conscience insofar as this topic of receiving is concerned. No matter how arduously one struggles to achieve some goal, he or she will gain no lasting gratification if the underlying motivation is purely Desire to Receive for Oneself Alone. Such is the circumstance concerning someone who steps on the necks of others, so to speak, as he or she claws up the ladder of success, or the thief who steals millions, or anyone who achieves wealth or high standing with no purpose other than greed, ego gratification, or material acquisition.

Thus we discover that the motive or intentions of both giver and receiver must somehow conform and coincide if mutual satisfaction is to be achieved. Giving is a two way street. A millionaire who donates a penny to charity will not benefit from the act of giving any more than will a poor man receive lasting value from a gift of something he does not want or need from someone he loathes. The gift, then, must please and benefit both the giver and the receiver if either is to derive fulfillment.

The truth of these examples becomes abundantly evident when we examine giving as it relates to the condition that existed in the *Ein Sof* previous to the Thought of Creation. There the state was such that the as-yet-undifferentiated Energy Intelligences within the great Circle of the Endless began to feel a sense of disquiet at receiving the Creator's Infinite abundance while having no ability to give anything in return. It is pointless to give unless that which one is giving is well received. The Creator felt obliged to restrict His outpouring of beneficence in order to satisfy His Desire to Share of Endless affluence while at the same time allowing the emanated the opportunity of absolving Bread of Shame. Henceforth, after the restriction, it became the prerogative of the emanated to accept the Light, or not, as was so desired, which is precisely why sharing, charity, and philanthropy, in and of themselves, do not necessarily benefit either the giver or the receiver unless those acts are accompanied by restriction, which pays homage to *Tzimtzum*, the first act of Creation.

Mere sharing does not bring one to an altered state of consciousness. Nor does receiving necessarily impart any lasting benefit unless it is accompanied by an attitude of resistance. For the giver, resistance takes the form of giving that which he or she really values and wants to retain, while the receiver, contrarily, creates a circular condition by wanting to receive but rejecting that which is offered.

This concept of giving away valued possessions, whether physical or metaphysical, and denying the same, is utterly alien to most people and quite beyond the scope of what is normally considered by us to be rational comprehension. Thus it will never be understood, much less embraced, by those who are ensconced in the Desire to Receive for Oneself Alone. For those few, however, who seek a more meaningful existence than is offered by the materialistic precepts and dictates of Western societies it is suggested that this idea of resistance, as it relates to giving and receiving, be experimented with on a limited basis so as to experience its spiritual rewards.

The Desire to Receive for Oneself Alone can and must be transformed into the Desire to Receive for the Sake of Sharing if a circuit or circular concept is to be achieved—and, of course, as has often been reiterated, the only way to establish a circuit is through resistance, which in this instance translates to denying that which is most desired.

This is not to imply that the student of Kabbalah is hereby advised to give away all of his or her money and worldly possessions or necessarily to reject an Academy Award or a Nobel prize should one be offered. It is important to understand that the kabbalist's denial of that which is desired is not done with the intention of creating personal suffering or as an exercise in self-negation. Rather the kabbalist restricts that which he or she most wants precisely because he or she desires to receive all that life has to offer. This seeming contradiction is explained, kabbalistically speaking, by the knowledge that since *Tzimtzum* the only way to achieve fulfillment is through resistance. Kabbalah, when seen in this light, becomes not a negation of life but a celebration of it. Hence we find that even this concept of denying that which is desired must be tempered with restriction, for such is the nature of the paradox of resistance.

HAPPINESS

Given the circumstances under which most of us have chosen to play out our drama of correction, is it any wonder that many people are of a pessimistic frame of mind? To even suggest to many people, in this stress filled age, that we have all the makings of our own unique fulfillment here, now, today, within ourselves; that we do not have to reach some financial or material goal or educational plateau to be complete—that our dream homes by the sea and all of the baubles of our illusionary fantasies, when once acquired, will do little or nothing in and of themselves to make us happy and truly satisfied; that all of our on-the-job training, experience, seniority, tenure, and university degrees play only walk-on roles in the quest for personal fulfillment, and in fact, in many instances, serve only to separate us still further from our real selves—brings cries of, Blasphemy! Heresy! Lunacy!

From the kabbalistic perspective, merely acquiring more and more money and material possessions in the hope of achieving happiness is like washing a car that is not running well in the hope of fixing the motor, or like polishing a rotten apple in the hope of making it fresh— and other futile gestures.

So what is the key to happiness and satisfaction in this world of resistance and restriction?

The answer is to change your mind.

Part Two

The Creative
Process

Chapter 8

Spiritual Substance

A n important and often repeated Kabbalistic axiom concerns the fact that there is no disappearance of Spiritual Substance (Light), which means that it is impossible that the Straight Light that passes through the Circles disappears. And yet from the perspective of the Fourth Phase, the Light of the Endless becomes fainter and dimmer until by the time the Light reaches *Malchut* it is almost totally eclipsed.

If the Light does not disappear, what happens to It?

The vast majority of this Endless Illumination is held in a state of suspended animation, so to speak, by the phases of the Circles. By far the greatest portion of this suspended Light, which is in a state of potential, remains in *Chochmah*, less in *Binah*, less still in *Tiferet*, until by the time It finally reaches this Fourth Phase, *Malchut*, It is almost totally devoid of Illumination. The small amount of remaining Straight Light that breaks through to this Fourth Phase is repelled by the Curtain of this phase by the action known as Binding by Striking. The resulting reflected Illumination is called Returning Light, the effects and implications of which are explained in a subsequent chapter. The final act of revelation occurs when Returning Light fuses with the Light that is suspended in the Upper Worlds and all of the Light in all of the Phases is at last revealed.

Rav Isaac Luria (the Ari), describes the action by which the Straight Light descends to this phase in the following terms: "...the Line, a straight illumination, acts as if it breaks the roofs of the Circles and passes through them (the Circles), and descends, drawn to the end, which is the Middle Point." Of course we know that the Ari was not referring to space and dimension and nor do the Circles have roofs that might be physically broken.

The Middle Point is the Fourth Phase, *Malchut*, which awakens the Desire to Receive for Oneself Alone. In terms of the natural forces this negative aspect of Desire is likened to gravitation as it relates to the human condition; it is equated with greed. The Desire to Receive for Oneself Alone acts like a magnet to draw Straight Light through the Line that intersects the Circles.

Concerning the Light's descent through the Phases of Emanation, the Ari reminds us that, "there is no revelation of Light in the Worlds (Phases of Emanation), whether Above or Below, without It being drawn from the Endless." Again, here the terms above and below have nothing whatever to do with physical comparisons but only to the degree of purity or impurity present in each Phase. The Restriction referred to is the result of the Curtain of the Fourth Phase, *Malchut*, which is also known as the World of Restriction.

The Straight Line Vessels, the Lower Seven, intersect the Circles, creating an illusionary separation or gap in each of the *Sefira* of Circles. Although it does intersect each of the Circles, the Line also, at the same time, serves to unite all Phases of the Circles, for were it not for Straight Light each of the Circles would remain separated in a similar way as each of the concentric circles that form around a pebble dropped in water stays connected to and yet sequestered from each of the adjacent waves.

Since the *Tzimtzum* reality has become revealed solely through the creative process called the Straight Line Vessels, the Lower Seven of the Line are the only way by which we can make connections with the Circular World of Reality. Insofar as we who presently dwell in the

Fourth Phase are concerned, the Light of the Line (Light of the Spirit) precedes the Light of the Circles (Light of Life) the reason being that the Circles receive their illumination only via the Line. Therefore Straight Light, the Light of the Line, is considered more important than the Light of the Circles.

The analogy used by the Ari concerning how Light can descend from one Phase to the next without any of the Endless Illumination being lost was that of the lighting of one candle with another, the first candle losing nothing at all. Furthermore, the Light descending might be compared to a lamp being covered with several layers of cloth. To the observer, it seems as if the Light becomes dimmer with each additional layer of cloth. In essence, however, the light of the lamp has not been altered in any way. In a like manner, the Light which enters this world, the World of Action, has already illuminated all of the levels in the Worlds above.

Thus, we find that the Light of the Endless does not disappear as it passes through the Phases of Emanation, it merely undergoes an illusion of concealment. Nothing is lost. The Straight Light must pass through each of the Circles, for as the Ari reminds us, "the Vessels of the Circles came out at once with the Restriction, but the Vessels of Straightness came out afterwards with the Line. Therefore this Illumination that passes between them never really moves from its place, since as was stated, there is no disappearance of Spiritual Substance." The Vessels of Straightness merely give an appearance as the revealer of Light of the circles.

NO DISAPPEARANCE IN SPIRITUAL SUBSTANCE

That which is spiritual in nature is not subject to adjustment or modification. This is what the Ari was referring to when he declared that, "it is impossible that the revelation of renewed Light, which devolves through the various degrees, disappears from the first level when it comes to the second..."

This poses a problem in view of what we know about the lessening of Illumination between the Levels of Emanation. *Chochmah's* Light of Wisdom, for example, is infinitely more powerful than *Binah's* Light of Mercy. The Endless Illumination is further reduced within each of the subsequent stages, until, by the tenth stage, *Malchut*, virtually all of the original Illumination has disappeared.

As convincing as the above statement may or may not have sounded, kabbalistically speaking it is accurate only from the finite (illusionary) point of view. From the Infinite perspective the preceding statement was a complete illusion. From the Infinite viewpoint, the essence of the Light's Endless Presence is not changed, reduced, or in any way transformed by the process of Emanation. Only from the dark side of the Curtain does the Light seem to have disappeared.

The Vessel is capable of only one function and that is to reveal Light on the finite level. Each Vessel's Desire to Receive determines the amount of Light that it is capable of revealing. Light is manifested in direct proportion to the Desire to Receive of the Vessel. The Three Uppermost Vessels—the Phases of Emanation—*Keter*, *Chochmah*, and *Binah* (the First Three), contain only a minute fraction of the Desire to Receive found in the Lower Vessels, and thus the Light revealed by those Upper First Three Vessels is practically nonexistent. *Malchut*, however, possesses more Desire to Receive than all of the other Vessels combined, and is thus capable of creating, by far, the greatest revealment of Light.

This is not to say the Light is increased by the Vessel, only that more of Its infinite Illumination is revealed. Light can neither be increased or decreased by the Vessel. Each Phase of Emanation (each of which is a Vessel by virtue of its Desire to Receive) represents both an increase in Desire to Receive and a decrease in Illumination—but only from the finite point of view. From the Infinite perspective the Light's Endless Presence does not decrease even slightly. The spiritual darkness perceived by those of us who have chosen at this time to dwell in the Kingdom, is an illusion that prevents our reasoning consciousness from experiencing the Light that fills us and everything around us.

Light is everywhere—and where could something that is everywhere possibly go that it would not already be? And so, while it may be a convenience to think in terms of the Light moving through the various levels of Emanation, in truth, Light, does not move. Why should it? Light lacks nothing, it needs nothing, it wants for nothing, it has no need or desire to do anything but share Its endless beneficence.

This is what the Ari meant when he stated that there is no disappearance of Spiritual Substance. What is Spiritual Substance? Spiritual substance is all that is of the Light, which, of course, includes everything that is, was, or ever will be—except for one exception: The illusion of lack.

Lack and Desire to Receive are synonymous, inseparable. Like space and time, energy and matter, one cannot exist without the other. Yet, both are illusions. Only from our finite perspective do they seem all too real. The Light has but one aspiration, which is to give of Its Infinite abundance. It is only we, the Vessels, who are motivated by the illusion of lack and saddled with the Vessel's constant companion, Desire to Receive. In truth, meaning from the infinite perspective, we lack nothing. It is only from the finite perspective that we seem to lack the fulfillment that comes from separation from the Infinite Light.

Everything in this world, physical and metaphysical, was born from the Light. All substance is spiritual. Even matter, at its essence, is Spiritual Substance. Matter is only a temporary alignment of an atomic structure. The subatomic basis of matter is not of a material nature and is therefore not influenced by physical laws. Subatomic units, are called quanta meaning "things," but are more accurately described as tendencies to become. And who can touch, taste or see a tendency?

Only an infinitesimal fraction of matter falls under the jurisdiction of gravity and the laws described by the physical sciences. This small quantity of matter, from the finite perspective, is deemed non-spiritual. Only that which is encompassed by Desire to Receive and must suffer through the constant illusion of lack is subject to transformation and seeming evaporation, the Light is constant and never changing. Spiritual Substance never disappears.

SPACE AND DIMENSION

So ensconced have we become in the world of illusion; so accustomed are we to thinking in terms of time, space and dimension, that it is impossible to rationally grasp a reality in which dimensions do not exist. Only by transcending rational consciousness can the higher realms of existence be perceived.

The study of *Ten Luminous Emanations* does not pertain to space, time, and dimension. It is only the inadequacy of language, coupled with the shortcomings of rational consciousness, which caused the Ari to describe the information that was channeled through him in words that seem to indicate that metaphysical activities evolve in terms of time, space and the linear proportions.

Thus, when the Ari taught us that the Line, a straight illumination, acts as if it breaks the roofs of the Circles as it passes through them, and that It (the Light) "descends" and is "drawn to the end," which is the Middle Point, he was speaking of something that was well beyond the range of what those words normally imply.

Unquestionably, that which happens Above, meaning the metaphysical world, mirrors perfectly that which occurs Below, in the realm of the physical, but in Reality, meaning from the Infinite perspective, the metaphysical and the physical components cannot be separated, for indeed they are one and the same. The physical is to the metaphysical as one side of a coin is to the other, apart, yet at the same time together.

Hence the student of Kabbalah should be ever wary of words that seem to imply space, time, and motion, and to remind him or herself of the two perspectives, finite and Infinite, from which all kabbalistic concepts must be viewed. Only from the finite or so-called rational perspective, meaning as things are seen from the standpoint of this illusionary world, do words such as, "time," "space," "upper," "lower," "above," "below," "ascent," "descent," "physical" and "metaphysical," have purpose and function. From the Infinite perspective there are no distinctions, no differentiation, no time, space, no restriction of any kind. All that exists from the Infinite point of view is cause and effect, the cause being the Light, the desire of which is to share, and the effect being the Vessel, the desire of which is to receive.

Chapter 9

Mirrors of Redemption

The Kabbalistic term for the supreme presence is *Or Ein Sof,* the Light of the Endless. When the kabbalist speaks of Light, with a capital L, he or she is alluding to that which is Infinite and never changing, for such is the nature of the *Or Ein Sof.* A lower case l is used when referring to sunlight or artificial light, which are finite.

The only light that we see, and the only *Or Ein Sof* that we perceive and experience is reflected. Both upper and lower case Lights or lights require resistance or restriction in order to be revealed. Like Light itself, resistance takes two forms, involuntary and voluntary. Sunlight and artificial light are revealed through automatic, unintentional resistance, whereas conscious, voluntary reflection is required to reveal the Infinite *Or Ein Sof.*

Involuntary functions are rooted in the finite Lower Seven of the Line. Rocks, trees, the Earth, and the animals are not required to exercise deliberate opposition to manifest the light of the sun. Obviously, a mirror is not obliged to consciously reflect the light that comes toward it. Our bodies, these finite vessels, are likewise visible without our having to constantly will their physical appearance, nor do we have to tell our hearts to pump, or remind our lungs to continue breathing. We are, however, required to impose conscious resistance in order to reveal *Or Ein Sof.*

Of all that exists on this Earth, only the human species is obliged to exercise deliberate resistance to reveal Light. The reason that we are required to act intentionally to resist the Light is, as has been well established, for the purpose of allowing us the opportunity of removing Bread of Shame. The *Or Ein Sof* permeates all existence, but like sunlight it only becomes visible when reflected. To reflect the Light is to reveal Infinite Energy-Intelligence; to not reflect It means remaining in spiritual darkness. The paradox is that by rejecting the Light one receives It, but by accepting the Light that is constantly and freely offered, one is deprived of Its endless beneficence.

Concerning this enigma, a relevant physical analogy can be drawn between a black, absorbent surface, the motivating energy-intelligence of which is the Desire to Receive for Oneself Alone, and a white, reflective surface, the energy intelligence of which is Desire to Receive for the Sake of Sharing. The color black captures light, allowing as little light as possible to escape. So, too, does the greedy person, who is motivated by the Desire to Receive for Oneself Alone, hold captive the Light that comes into his life, consuming as much as is humanly possible while giving little in return. The color white, contrarily, reflects light, thus sharing illumination with any and all that happens to be in its immediate proximity. Thus, it is said that the person whose motivating energy-intelligence is the Desire to Receive for the Sake of Sharing emulates the white, reflective surface, accepting only what is necessary for sustenance and sharing all that remains, while the person who is controlled by the Desire to Receive for Oneself Alone may be said to imitate the color black.

This phenomenon becomes particularly dramatic (in the physical world) at sunrise and again at twilight when the sun is near the horizon. At such times dark surfaces and all that surround them become invisible, while light-colored surfaces and everything in their proximity remain distinctly visible. Spiritually, a similar situation exists relative to the individual whose primary motivating influence is the Desire to Share. By resisting the Light, reflecting It, his or her inner motivation is recognized by all who bask in the nimbus of Light that is created by their resistance, while the opposite is true of the person whose motivating energy-intelligence is the Desire to Receive for Oneself Alone, for he or she reflects no Light and thus becomes spiritually invisible in dark shadows of his or her own making.

Hence, the kabbalist acts always in the manner of a reflective surface, resisting and opposing that which he or she most desires, holding up a mirror of redemption so that the Light may be revealed.

THE BIRTH OF DESIRE

When the Creator withdrew He created a vacuum, a dark, negative void that demanded to be filled. Of necessity, this vacuum manifested itself in every phase and facet of the physical aspect of existence. And since that time, no Light is revealed in the created world (from the finite perspective) without a Vessel, the motivating influence of which is the Desire to Receive.

We are creatures of the Light. We were born from Light and to Light we must one day return. And therein lies the key to understanding Desire. All that materialized at the *Tzimtzum*—every speck of matter and cosmic dust—emerged with a need, a void that demands fulfillment. This void is the essence of all Desire. And the need to fill the void that exists between ourselves and the Creator is the basis for all yearnings, whether psychological, physical, emotional, and spiritual.

We all have a vacuum in our lives, an emptiness that cries out to be filled. Is this any wonder? Having known unity with the Source it is only natural that we can have no rest until we are again united with the Light.

How is this accomplished?

Remember the vacuum was an illusion created by the Emanator to give us the opportunity of absolving Bread of Shame. In Reality, nothing was changed by the *Tzimtzum*, except for the illusion—that which is seen from the dark side of the Curtain. From the Infinite perspective, the vacuum, the space (all space), does not exist. We have no lack. There is no void to fill. Only from the finite perspective does the vacuum sometimes seem to exercise power over us. From the Infinite perspective we are still, even now, filled with Endless abundance.

The key, then, is to understand the ephemeral nature of Desire and to deny it access into our lives. The method by which this is made possible begins and ends with voluntary resistance. Seeing the illusion of lack for what it is, a temporary apparition that disappears when confronted with the Infinite Reality, we must act always in the manner of a Third Column, an intermediary between the darkness and the Light.

Chapter 10

Keter, Chochmah, Binah, Tiferet and *Malchut*

KETER – CROWN

Keter means crown. The root of each level is called Crown from the word "crowning," meaning "surrounding," which is why *Keter* is said to surround the entire "face" or "countenance" from Above. *Keter* is the purest of all levels, and at the same time the most ambiguous. Ambiguous in the sense that from our limited perspective it seems to change from Light to Vessel and back again according to the point of view from which it is perceived. Like an optical illusion *Keter* is one thing and then it is another and though mentally we can easily grasp the fact that it is two things at once we are incapable from our finite point of view of encompassing both "realities" at the same time. For example in this image the viewer will either see two faces looking at each other or a vase, but will not be able to see both images at the same time.

When a king is wearing a crown we easily identify him as a ruler and thus impart to him the image of royalty, but without it, when he is walking among the common folk in common attire, we have no way of distinguishing him from any one of his subjects. Another analogy is often drawn likening *Keter* with the seed of a tree, in that it, too, can be seen as belonging conceptually in two places at the same time: The tree that was and the tree that is yet to come. *Keter*, because of this ambiguity, seems uncertain whether it is in its original domain or if it is part of the next generation, and we, from our limited perspective, have no way of making that determination.

A long-standing debate rages among kabbalists as to whether *Keter* should be considered Light or Vessel. If *Keter* is Vessel then it is the first Vessel and can be aptly likened to the first seed that creates the second tree, whereas if we say that it is Light then it is a pure, total energy force, something divorced entirely from the tree. It seems to hover, caught, so to speak, between two worlds, that of cause and effect, energy and matter, potential and reality.

Still, though we cannot learn a single thing by gazing at *Keter*'s outward manifestation—indeed it has none—we can, however, determine certain characteristics concerning this enigmatic phase of existence by viewing the effects or manifestations that it creates, a methodology that is best summed up by the old adage, "As above so below." For instance, when we see a man or woman sitting on a throne in a castle holding a scepter and wearing a crown we are fairly safe in assuming that he or she is descended from royalty, or, by the same token, when a seed we have planted grows into a tree that bears apples we can rest secure in the knowledge that it was an apple seed.

Using this same conceptual construct we can say with some degree of certainty that *Keter*'s primary Energy-Intelligence is that of sharing; this must be so for it displays no Desire to Receive. *Keter* reveals what to the naked eye appears to be a complete lack of motivation. Forces of restriction, the Line, must act upon a seed before it can manifest its full potential. Only after we see activity taking place, the beginnings of a sprout or the breaking of the pod's outer covering can we ascertain that the Desire to Receive has been activated—and then and only then can we call the seed a Vessel in the truest sense of the word.

And so it seems that the true nature of *Keter*'s existence is destined to elude our finite understanding. *Keter* is the paradox personified, the enigma of life, and perhaps, from our limited perspective, its seeming duplicity will forever remain its single most salient identifying feature. Let us then be satisfied in calling *Keter* the connecting link, for any time we speak of *Keter* we are referring to the root of one Phase and the Crown of the next, to the transference of energies, to the linking up of time and space, energy and matter, cause and effect.

CHOCHMAH – WISDOM

The First Phase of the Light's Emanation is called *Chochmah* or Wisdom because, in the words of the Ari, "From it is drawn all forms of wisdom found in the world." *Chochmah* is the purest of all of the Phases of Emanation. In the Phase of Wisdom, the Light is unadulterated, unobstructed by even the slightest tinge of negativity. Its Vessel is of such a transparent quality that it is almost non-existent, and of such an incorporeal and Infinite nature that its essence lies beyond even a master kabbalist's perceptions. *Chochmah*, like *Keter*, defies finite understanding, and so again, as with *Keter*, we must interpret its cause according to what we can ascertain by studying its effects.

The ancient saying: "Who is wise? He who sees what is born," speaks of the quality of Wisdom. Properly interpreted from the Lurianic perspective it means that a wise person is one who can look at a given situation and see all of its consequences, all of its Phases, possible outcomes and manifestations, from the end to the beginning, the beginning to the end. As Rav Ashlag puts it, "...he sees all future consequences of the thing observed, to the very last one." And in reference to this he continues: "Every definition of complete wisdom is simply a form of 'seeing what is born,' from each and every detail of existence, right to the last result."

Unlike *Keter*, of which we can speak only indirectly, for the reasons previously stated, with *Chochmah*, we at least have some first hand or direct experience. Sudden inspirations, flashes of intuition, these glimpses into our own unique fulfillment are the blessings of *Chochmah*, they are only gifts for those who are deserving of them.

The Line is sometimes referred to as the creative process. *Chochmah*, the Second Phase of the creative process, being one of the First Three, operates in a state of metaphysical potential, establishing contact on a metaphysical level with *Chochmah* of the Circles (our inner Encircling Vessels) and causing in them a re-awakening. The *Chochmah* of the Line arrives without our knowledge and stimulates the Light of *Chochmah* within our Infinite Encircling Vessels.

All of the events, manifestations, and transferences of energy of which we are now speaking occur beyond the dimension of space and time. When we talk of cause and effect in the metaphysical realm, we are speaking of one energy following another, but not in space-time. Remember that all of the Endless is in constant, instantaneous contact with Itself, everywhere. Only when the Fourth Phase, with its inherent Desire to Receive is aroused does time begin to take on a more finite, or linear quality. Before the Fourth Phase is awakened, everything exists within one, all-encompassing dimension, a dimension that might be best visualized by imagining an Infinite sheet of paper on which the entire macrocosm of history, past, present, and future, can be gazed upon at one time.

Notice now how the reality suddenly and irrevocably changes when the perspective from high above the paper is shifted down, let us say, to the ground level of the paper. Here, the viewer sees only a minute fraction of the real picture. From this limited perspective the viewer has nothing to connect with other than the illusion (as it relates to the broader, higher, more complete perspective from above) and thus is apt to entertain nothing, no thought, idea, or physical manifestation, that does not occupy his immediate, limited visual scope and physical surroundings.

Does the reader now understand how a single "reality" changes entirely according to the perspective from which it is viewed?

Hence we say that *Chochmah* follows *Keter*, but not within the aspect of time. In the Upper Worlds everything happens instantly. Events that seem to take time on this finite, linear dimension are, from the perspective of the worlds above, undifferentiated aspects of the grand continuum. As with all kabbalistic truths, the person who wishes to grasp this concept must make a perceptual leap across the space, the chasm of illusion that separates us from the metaphysical reality.

BINAH – INTELLIGENCE

The nature of the Second Phase, *Binah*, is the awakening in the Vessel, the emanated being of the Desire to Share. As *Binah* is a phase of exertion and therefore deemed feminine we might say that She is blessed with a gift from the Endless, a gift for which She has no desire. The simple reason for this is that the Energy-Intelligence of receiving has not yet been activated, because the Desire to Receive is awakened only in the Fourth Phase. And because the Desire to Receive has not yet been aroused in *Binah* we find that while Her Vessel is filled with the Light of Wisdom, which is the Light of the Endless. This Light which she would dearly love to share, this gift from the Endless that was inherited by her through the Phase of Wisdom, can be shared with no one, for there has as yet been no awakening of the Energy-Intelligence of receiving.

At this point in the metaphysical evolution the options open to *Binah* are scant in the extreme. Here, She has been bestowed with a gift of unendurable majesty, but the Energy-Intelligence of receiving has not yet been awakened. In *Binah* there is no restriction, no Bread of Shame. She is, in this respect, a Vessel that does not want to be one. Her sole desire is to share, to abandon Herself unequivocally to the Light of Creation, but though She yearns for nothing more than to create such empathy with the Creator as to lose Herself completely, She cannot merge with the Endless without forsaking Her own existence.

Binah has no Desire to Receive; that grade or Phase of Will has not yet revealed itself. The Desire to Receive arises only to fill a need, as will soon be made clear. At this stage of metaphysical evolution *Binah* has no desire to receive the Light and because of Bread of Shame She cannot keep the gift of Wisdom extended to Her by the First Phase. Only one option remains available to *Binah*, and that is to establish complete affinity with the Light, but this can be accomplished only by cancelling out the thought activity of the Vessel, which is tantamount to nullifying Herself.

Binah has no choice; She must surrender. Thus, in the way that a young child abandons all pretense of individuality when lost in the arms of her mother, *Binah* seeks to satisfy Her one desire, which is to relinquish Her own identity and merge with the Light of Creation. Having no one with whom to share Her Wisdom, *Binah* disavows Her very existence.

This First Phase of exertion or conscious activity on the part of the Vessel is associated with *Binah*, and that consciousness itself is the root cause for the manifestation of a new transformation of Light. *Binah's* dramatic enactment represents a form of self-awareness that did not exist before. It is through this very cognizance of Her own being and giving that *Binah* transforms the Light of Wisdom into a Light of a wholly different and inferior expression, the Light of Mercy.

Each exertion on the part of the Vessel creates a denser atmosphere around the Light, and thus the Light found within each Phase of the Vessel is said to be inferior to the Light of the Vessel before—though that adjective does not speak of the Flawless Light of the Endless found within the Vessels, but solely of the nature of the Vessels themselves and more specifically of the degree of Light that each is capable of revealing.

The Vessel, as it passes through the Second Phase, which is the first arousal, *Binah*, though conscious, is not thought of as acting consciously—at least to the extent that a Vessel can truly be considered a Vessel only after the Fourth Phase has awakened in it the Desire to Receive. The first Three Phases activate only the potential of the Vessels, the Fourth Phase or grade of will, Kingdom, is the Phase of the Light's revealment.

The yearning succumbed to by *Binah*, which leads her to act in supreme self-deprivation, is itself a negative Energy-Intelligence in that it serves only to separate her still further from the Light of Creation. Though *Binah* displays only Desire to Share—a seemingly benign and selfless characteristic—by simply emulating the Light, *Binah* is enhancing in Herself an awareness that by virtue of her Vessel She is different from and can never achieve parity with the Creator—so by merely experiencing herself *Binah* is changing her essence.

It is said that *Binah*'s nature is to become and that her consciousness is the thought of transformation. *Binah*, then, purely by virtue of her self denial, causes a transformation in the Light, which results in an Energy-Intelligence that is changed to such a significant degree, so far removed, hence so inferior to the Light of Wisdom, that it merits a separate identity. The Ari named this transformation, Light of Mercy.

That this Light (Mercy) represents a significant lessening of the original Light of Wisdom, should in no way be misconstrued to mean that the Light of Mercy is comparable to the degree of Illumination manifested by the Fourth Phase, for the Light revealed in the Phase of Kingdom is minuscule by comparison. No, *Binah*'s is an awareness, an Energy Intelligence of such a high order that conscious entry into the Phase of *Binah* is considered the ultimate state of metaphysical awareness that any emanated being can hope to achieve in this world—an altered state of almost total purity that can be attained only by an Energy-Intelligence that is completely devoid of any trace of Desire to Receive.

TRANSFORMATIONS

The first extension of the Light of the Endless is called *Chochmah*, the Light of Wisdom. The Light of Wisdom emanates in a flawless state directly from the Endless. It is the essence of the Light of Creation and the root of all of the Light's subsequent transformations. *Chochmah* has only one aspiration, to spread the Light of the Endless, and hence it is deemed to be the pure driving force behind all existence.

No thought ever occurs whose essence is not of the Light of Wisdom. *Chochmah*'s Light (Wisdom) is the sudden flash of inspiration, the brainstorm, nirvana, satori, the highest state of meditation of which the most spiritual person is capable, the absolute joy of existence that sometimes comes over us for seemingly no reason at all. The Light of Wisdom contains both Desire to Share and Desire to Receive, though neither aspect is awakened until the Second and Fourth Phases respectively when *Binah* arouses the Desire to Share and *Malchut* awakens the Desire to Receive. Only when both Phases of Desire have been animated can the Vessel truly be said to be complete.

The First Phase, *Chochmah*, the essence of primal perfection, represents, we might say, the Light "personified." He is driven by a Divine inner dynamic of expansion. His one aspiration is to extend the Light to all Phases of Creation. Hence, He has no reason or desire to transform Himself. In this respect He differs from the Second Phase, *Binah*, whose nature is to change Her essence from the Desire to Receive into the Desire to Share, which She does with the intention of creating total affinity with the Light.

The Light of Mercy, the Second Phase of Emanation, results from the influence placed upon the Light by the vessel, *Binah*. Thus, while *Chochmah* is said to be an "extension" of the Light, *Binah* is named the first "exertion." In *Binah* the Vessel attempts to achieve parity with the Creator. *Binah* is possessed of a cognizance of Her own purpose that was not present in *Chochmah*, and it is this very self awareness, as was expressed in an earlier chapter, that causes the Light to be diminished. As a consequence, the new Light (Mercy) borne from the exertion of *Binah* is of a lesser magnitude than that which emerged from *Chochmah*.

Binah, merely by virtue of her own self consciousness, the awareness of her own being, decreases the Light to such an extent that the Light that eventuates from her exertion is said to be a "transformation" of the original Flawless Light of *Chochmah*, even though the Light embraced by both Vessels (*Chochmah* and *Binah*) is the same Light (*Or Ein Sof*) of the same Infinite intensity as that which passed through *Chochmah*. Thus, it is said that the Light of Mercy, is the same Infinite Light of the Endless transformed by the Vessel for the Sake of sharing.

TIFERET – BEAUTY

The Third Phase of the Light's emanation has many names. It is called, The World of Formation. It is called the second extension of the Light—the Phase of *Chochmah* (Wisdom) was also an extension, and is therefore defined as being masculine. The Second and Fourth Phases, you will recall, *Binah* and Kingdom (*Malchut*), are known as "exertions" and defined as being feminine. *Tiferet* (Beauty), the Third Phase of Emanation, is also called *Zeir Anpin* Small Face, because, like the moon reflects the sun, *Tiferet* is a reflection of a higher truth, the Light of the Endless.

In the Small Face—which is said to comprise two triads of emanations, the Six *Sefirot, Chesed* (Mercy), *Gevurah* (Judgment), *Tiferet* (Beauty), *Netzach* (Victory), *Hod* (Glory) and *Yesod* (Foundation)—is an extension of the Light of Mercy that emanated from *Binah* (Intelligence) by which the Light of Wisdom is again made manifest. This Third Phase represents a spreading out and hence a dissipation of *Binah's* Light (Mercy) the thought or energy-intelligence of which was to transform the Vessel back into the Light. *Binah's* exertion, you will recall, transformed the Light of *Chochmah* (Wisdom) into the Light of a separate description, the Light of Mercy.

As the student is by now aware, the Divine Light of the Creator was not concealed and therefore revealed in one action, but was transformed by a number of stages. The First Phase, *Chochmah* (Wisdom) had no consciousness of itself. *Binah*, awakened the Desire to Share, but concealed the Light of Wisdom through her desire to emulate It, and thus gave birth to a new transformation of the Light, the Light of Mercy. In *Zeir Anpin* (Small Face) the total negation of Vessel as vessel is carried over from *Binah* whose desire was to surrender Herself completely to the Light, but here in the Third Phase there is an added enclothement of the Vessel. Just as we must dress our vessels, our bodies, in order to make our presence felt to others, the Small Face enclothes the Light still further so that Its Divine Presence, too, in a manner of speaking, can begin to spread Its message to the physical world.

The Third Stage of the Light's emanation, *Tiferet* (Beauty), the Small Face, may be seen, then, as the Phase in which the Light of Mercy spreads out, hence becoming further concealed and dissipated from the point of view of Light, but closer to revealment from the perspective of the Vessel—like the calm before a storm, the Third Phase of Emanation, represents a gathering of the forces of the universe in preparation for the tidal wave of revealment that is about to follow in the Fourth and last Phase, Kingdom (*Malchut*).

ZEIR ANPIN – SMALL FACE

The Desire to Receive is included within all levels and layers of created existence. It is essential that every Vessel possess a certain amount of Desire to Receive, for that which is lacking in some dynamic force of attraction could not possibly manifest or maintain any material shape or essence. Thus, even the First Three (*Keter, Chochmah, Binah*) must also include a certain minuscule allotment of Desire to Receive, otherwise those exalted *Sefirot* could not be called Vessels in the truest kabbalistic sense of the word.

Both the higher and the lower levels of consciousness are comprised of the same fundamental elements, Light and Vessel, the only difference being in the aspect of revealment. From the Endless right down to this World of Action, nothing changes other than the increasing illusion of Desire to Receive for the Self Alone. The negative aspect of Desire acts as a cloak by which the upper levels of our existence are obscured from what we might call spiritual view.

The Light of Wisdom is termed "Light of the Face," which according to the Ari reveals the hidden meaning of the verse, "A man's wisdom lights his face." Thus the First Phase, the Crown (*Keter*) of the world of Emanation, which is illuminated by the Light of Wisdom, is given the name, the Long Face (*Arich Anpin*) while the Third Phase, which is illuminated by the lesser Light of Mercy, which extends to the Six *Sefirot* of *Chesed* (Mercy), *Gevurah* (Judgment), *Tiferet* (Beauty), *Netzach* (Victory), *Hod* (Glory), and *Yesod* (Foundation), is named the

Small Face (*Zeir Anpin*). The Six *Sefirot* of the Third Phase, Small Face (*Zeir Anpin*), are the realms of consciousness entered into with the aid of meditation.

Descending through the Six *Sefirot* of the Small Face the influence of the Desire to Receive for the Self Alone becomes more and more pronounced. Each of the Six is endowed with both the positive and the negative aspects of the Desire to Receive. However, while a certain portion of the Desire to Receive for the Self Alone must of necessity be embodied within the Vessels of the Small Face, certainly this amount is infinitesimal compared to the negative aspect of desire that manifests in the Fourth Phase, Kingdom (*Malchut*) where the Light of all subsequent Phases is revealed.

MALCHUT – KINGDOM

Malchut reveals the Purpose of Creation. Here in the Fourth Phase the three previous Phases are transformed from potential to actual, the dormant is awakened, the hidden is exposed, the passive is activated, the immaterial is materialized. The Small Face dispersed the Light to such an extent that it caused a severe lack or deficiency in the Vessel, an unquenchable thirst for the completion it once knew. That need for re-fulfillment caused the arousal of the Desire to Receive in the Phase of *Malchut*.

Space—both in terms of the physical and emotional separation between people and the distance between objects and planetary bodies—is a product of the loss or deficiency experienced by the Vessel because of the diffusion of the Light that occurred in the Third Phase, Small Face. This "distance" between the physical and the metaphysical was placed between the Emanator and that which He had emanated in order to preserve the illusion of separation that was a prerequisite of Creation.

While the revealment of sunlight takes place as a result of an involuntary reflective action, the revelation of the *Or Ein Sof,* conversely, at least insofar as we of *Malchut* are concerned, manifests as a result of voluntary resistance. The Earth's primal motivating energy-intelligence, the Desire to Receive for Itself Alone, acts involuntarily in conjunction with nature's inborn restrictive mechanism (Curtain) to reveal sunlight. We, however, because of our wish for individuation, must reveal the Light through a conscious act of resistance or restriction so as to absolve Bread of Shame—for that was the Purpose of Creation.

Recall that no light materializes other than that which is reflected. As has been previously noted, sunlight is revealed only through an act of resistance (reflection). This fact becomes readily apparent by gazing into the night sky. Light does not manifest between the stars, planets, and heavenly bodies simply because there is nothing of a physical nature with which it can interact. Hence, having nothing to reflect from (other than nuclear particles that exhibit only a minute Desire to Receive) light cannot be seen.

No light, no sound, no thought, nothing comes to Light in this World of Restriction without resistance, and the greater is the resistance the more magnanimous is the outpouring of energy. We of *Malchut* must work to deactivate the Curtain and thus re-illuminate our Infinite Energy-Intelligence, which, from our necessarily limited perspective, lies dormant within our inner Encircling Vessels. Our separation from the Light, which was the purpose of *Tzimtzum,* served to differentiate between the Creator and that which He had emanated, thus providing us with the opportunity of alleviating Bread of Shame.

THE MIDDLE POINT

The Middle Point is *Malchut,* the point from which radiated all the Worlds of Emanation. It is the place of first resistance, the point at which the World of Creation begins. The Middle Point reveals the Infinite Circular Vessels from which we all emerged and to which we will all one day return. The irony is that the only way we can unveil that Infinite Circular Reality is through the finite creative process known to Kabbalah as the Line.

The Middle Point reveals reality. It is our place of infinite, internal fullness and ultimate fulfillment. To connect with the Middle Point is to reveal the Infinite Circular Vessels of our being. Unless one can reach the Middle Point of his or her own being, he or she is destined to remain always in spiritual darkness. For it is at the Middle Point that all Light is revealed.

If we feel sadness or depravation it means that we are ensconced in illusion. As mentioned previously, lack can take root only in the world of illusion, and only there can it survive. By attaching to the Infinite Middle Point of our beings we cause the illusion of lack to lose its purpose in the world of illusion and, thus, having nothing of a negative nature on which to feed, it must of necessity disappear.

The importance of connecting with the Middle Point, humanity's internal place of the Light's revealment, cannot be overemphasized. In fact, the Middle Point is generally accepted by kabbalists as being the fundamental difference between the spiritual and the non-spiritual person. For whereas the spiritual person understands that all blessings emanate from a single source, the non-spiritual person sees only random chance as the motivating influence of his or her life. Thus, while the spiritual person's life is anchored in the tranquil waters of Reality, the non-spiritual person is tossed about like a twig on a sea of illusion.

Chapter 11

Keter Versus *Malchut*

We are by now aware that *Keter*, being closely aligned with the Infinite, is considered by Kabbalah to be greatly purer, higher, and thus superior to *Malchut*. Yet, from the following imaginary discussion between two students of Kabbalah, we shall see that the two *Sefirot* are perhaps more intimately related than previously imagined.

Kabbalist One: *Keter* is higher.

Kabbalist Two: No, I say it is *Malchut* for without her there would be no revealment of the Light.

Kabbalist One: Yes, but without *Keter* there would be no Light to reveal.

Kabbalist Two: True, but both, after all, are Vessels—so how can you say one is higher than the other?

Kabbalist One: Which would you rather drink, sludge or distilled water?

Kabbalist Two: All right, so admittedly *Keter* is, shall we say, of a purer consistency, but it is *Malchut's* very density that allows her to reveal the Light, which was, you will remember, the Purpose of Creation.

Kabbalist One: Maybe so, but *Malchut's* main motivation is still the Desire to Receive for Oneself Alone, which you will remember is the epitome of evil and negativity.

Kabbalist Two: If that is so then why is it that only *Malchut* and not *Keter* can have a dialogue with the Creator?

Kabbalist One: Dialogue? *Malchut*'s only free will is restriction—saying no—is that what you call a dialogue?

Kabbalist Two: It is better than what *Keter* can do.

Kabbalist One: *Keter* does not have to speak. He communicates in other, better, more Infinite ways.

Kabbalist Two: Ways that no mortal can understand.

Kabbalist One: Only our finite aspect cannot perceive *Keter*, our Infinite aspect hears him loud and clear.

Kabbalist Two: Big deal. What good is that? What's the good of anything if it's concealed?

Kabbalist One: What good is the Creator, then, by that reasoning?

Kabbalist Two: That's not what I mean and you know it. I'm talking about here on *Malchut*. Thoughts, words, deeds—anything you can name—what good is it if it's not revealed?

Kabbalist One: There, you said the magic word, name—anything you can name. If it's got a name it is part of the creative process, in other words, the illusion.

Kabbalist Two: That's the paradox. The illusion is the only way the Light is revealed. Besides, *Keter* also has a name, so it too must be part of the illusion.

Kabbalist One: True, but less a part by far than *Malchut*. Even you must admit that.

Kabbalist Two: Maybe so, but without illusion we'd still be back in the *Ein Sof* trying to find a way to get rid of Bread of Shame.

Kabbalist One: Better that than being down here trying to get rid of the illusion.

Kabbalist Two: What's so bad about illusion? Books are illusion, records, plays, Alfa Romeos, bodies...

Kabbalist One: Hmmm. You've got a point there. Maybe illusion is not such a bad thing after all.

Let us leave our two students of Kabbalah to their discussion. Which one is right? There is only one possible resolution to this argument, the ultimate compromise: both.

THE FOUR PHASES

The emergence of the Four Phases of Emanation is often likened to the concentric circles that form around the point at which a stone is thrown into water. The First Extension of the Light, Wisdom (*Chochmah*), the potential Vessel, forms the outer circle that is said to "cause" the Second Phase, Intelligence (*Binah*), where potential is activated, which in turn causes Beauty (*Tiferet*), the first "state of arousal" (also called Small Face (*Zeir Anpin*), which is comprised of the Lights of Mercy (*Chesed*), Judgment (*Gevurah*), Beauty (*Tiferet*), Endurance (*Netzach*), Majesty (*Hod*), and Foundation (*Yesod*) which in turn causes the Fourth Phase, Kingdom (*Malchut*) where the Desire to Receive is fully awakened and all Four Phases are finally revealed.

The First and Third Phases are said to be extensions of the Light and are represented as being masculine while the Second and Fourth Phases are called exertions and are described as being feminine. The two extensions of the Light, Wisdom, the First Phase, and Beauty, the Third Phase, are each bestowed with Light extended from the Emanator—Wisdom with the Light of Wisdom, Beauty with the Light of Mercy—whereas the two exertions of will, Intelligence, the Second Phase, and Kingdom, (sometimes called "Queen"), the Fourth Phase, represent the striving capacity in the emanated beings. The First Exertion, Intelligence awakens in the emanated being the Desire to Share, the Second Exertion, Kingdom awakens the Desire to Receive.

Of course, all Ten *Sefirot* are included in each extension and in each exertion of the Light.

Nothing exists in this observable world that has not gone through Four Phases. Thoughts, words, deeds, growth, movement, relationships, the manufacture or evolution of physical objects, even our very lives manifest through Four Phases. Spring, Summer, Winter, Fall—there are seasons of thought, of growth, of consciousness. Like the four directions—North, South, East and West—none of the Four Phases can exist without the others.

The Crown (*Keter*), while it is the Root of all Four Phases, is not included among them. The reason for this is that the Crown plays no part in the actual emanation of the Light. Having no Desire to Receive its power must be activated by the Line. Wisdom (*Chochmah*), the First Extension of the Light, is closely bound up with the Endless in that it exhibits minuscule desire. Each of the subsequent Phases is said to become denser, by virtue of being further removed from the Light, and is hence deemed "lower."

The first Three Phases, Wisdom (*Chochmah*), Intelligence (*Binah*), and Beauty (*Tiferet*), being closely aligned with Crown (*Keter*), all exist in a state of potential until they are revealed through the exertion of this world, Kingdom (*Malchut*). While each extension of the Light includes the Desire to Receive, it is not until the Light reaches the Fourth stage, *Malchut*, that the Light is transformed from a state of potential into a state of revealment when the Desire to Receive is aroused by the emanated.

When the Emanator withdrew so as to create a separation between Itself and that which had been emanated, residual impressions remained in the Vessels, reminders of their former unity with the Light of Creation. The term Four Phases is generally used to refer to the Light within each of the Ten *Sefirot*, whereas the terms, Crown (*Keter*), Wisdom (*Chochmah*), Intelligence (*Binah*), Beauty (*Tiferet*), and Kingdom (*Malchut*) define the impressions or residues of Light that remain in the Ten Vessels after the *Tzimtzum* in the World of Restriction.

The elements of what were later to become distinctions in the Four Phases or grades of will must have existed in the Endless before the *Tzimtzum*, just as all the various separate nuances of a tree, the leaves, roots, and branches, must exist in the seed, but those differences are undifferentiated and beyond the realm of perception or observance, logic and reason.

Still, we can assume that the emanated, having once known complete and utter fulfillment, must have experienced an understandable lack or deficiency upon separation from the eternal majesty of the Endless Presence. Hence, the First Phase of the Light's Emanation, Wisdom (*Chochmah*), might aptly be likened to a child emerging from the womb to find itself in a strange, new environment and experiencing for the first time some sensation of individuation from the mother. Here, in a similar manner as Wisdom is still closely bound up with the Creator, the baby, who is still connected with the mother by the umbilical cord, desires only to be enveloped by and to merge into the arms of the mother, a bond that once secured can never be broken. In subsequent stages of development, as the baby grows into a child, the child into a man or woman, he or she becomes further removed from the parent mentally, emotionally, and physically, yet still continues to feel strong emotional and spiritual ties with the mother—even many years after the mother's finite form, her body, has completed the cycle of its existence.

Chapter 12

The Outer Space Connection

Here in *Malchut*, we are presented with only the illusionary nature of existence. The real world is hidden. The Endless Light, *Or Ein Sof*, all that is, was, or will be, is present in this world of illusion. The First Three are here—the Infinite Wisdom is within us and all around us, yet beyond the scope of our rational senses.

If Reality is here, why do we not experience It?

Kabbalah teaches that the Purpose of Creation was to conceal the Infinite so as to allow us the opportunity of consciously recreating a circuit of energy through positive resistance thus removing ourselves from the oppressive energy intelligence that we know as the Desire to Receive for Oneself Alone. Although we cannot see reality, taste, touch, hear, or smell it, we can, however, through positive resistance, reveal the Infinite Light and thus alleviate Bread of Shame. Our ability to transcend the illusion and connect with the Infinite Circular aspect of existence hinges on a three stage process of knowing, believing, and letting go.

Knowing makes metaphysical connections. Awareness that there is an alternate, Infinite universe, here in the same place as this finite world, opens the mind to new possibilities in much the same way as a perceptual connection is made between a climber and the crest of a mountain even before the first step is undertaken. Knowledge then, is the initial stage in the journey toward transcendence of this negative realm.

Believing that there are Infinitely higher and purer states of consciousness than those accessible to the mind that accompanies our daily routines, comprises the second level of cosmic awareness. Blind faith is not implied here, but rather a simple emotional experience borne from knowledge and by which one becomes closer to establishing the Reality of the higher Phases of awareness within one's own consciousness and sub-consciousness.

Letting go, the third and final stage in the journey toward the connection of our "inner space" or consciousness with "outer space," the *Or Ein Sof* around us, consists of breaking free from the constraints placed upon us by the material illusion. Apprehension often accompanies the introduction of the concept underlying this third stage in the quest for transcendence, for it is often misconstrued as meaning that attachment to the metaphysical realm requires the total abandonment of the physical world, when nothing could be further from the truth. Kabbalah teaches that we can transcend the illusionary physical world entirely and yet still function with elevated efficiency in our daily routines.

In fact, we all disengage from the negative physical world every day and every night of the week—we all meditate; we all transcend the world of illusion; we all experience altered states of consciousness—to not do so would be to court insanity. Music can place us in an altered state; thinking, working, dreaming, daydreaming, even watching television, all of these activities and more can provide us with opportunities for disengagement from this negative realm. The barber who gives a perfectly adequate haircut without any conscious knowledge of having done so, the doctor who correctly diagnosis an illness intuitively without aid from the conscious, rational thought processes, the driver who drives a hundred miles on automatic pilot, stopping, starting, changing lanes, and finally arrives safely at his destination without the slightest idea of how he got there—all of these are instances of disengagement from the physical world and connection with the metaphysical.

Hence we find that one of the principal differences between the kabbalist and the so-called "average" person who is caught up in the material illusion, is that the kabbalist is conscious of the process of transcendence and is therefore able to use this natural tendency to his or her best advantage whereas the average person is not. Whereas the rational pragmatist values highly and struggles always to maintain control of his or her logical, reasoning thought processes, the kabbalist freely abandons analytic sensibility in favor of reaching the higher realms of consciousness that are accessible only by transcending the rational mind.

Another key difference between the rationalist and the kabbalist is that the rationalist mistakenly believes himself to be the instigator of his actions, while the kabbalist, secure in the knowledge that no thought comes about that does not have a preordained solution, sees himself as a channel for energy rather than as a source of it. Having realized that cosmic sentience is Infinitely superior to rational consciousness, and being aware that the only act that can effectively be instigated by humanity is that of positive resistance, the kabbalist initiates situations by which his or her Vessel can be used as a conduit for the Infinite power of the *Or Ein Sof.*

Thus, instead of viewing sojourns into the higher states of awareness as being mere lapses of concentration, and berating him or herself for losing mental control—as does the rational pragmatist—the kabbalist welcomes and initiates opportunities for creative disengagement from the negative illusionary physical world, for by so doing he or she connects with the Infinite.

So conditioned are we to living under the iron hand of the material illusion that today we have come to serve the illusion that poses as reality and to pay tribute to its dominance, praying before the alter of the modern deities, Science and technology, bowing and scraping as the endless parade of material progress marches by. The great paradox and the irony of this age is that the so-called reality that we allow to rule us with seeming impunity is really an illusion, and the so-called fantasy world—the thought energy-intelligence of dreams, daydreams, and other right brain activities—so heartily maligned by the self-proclaimed realists, is the true Reality, the Infinite *Or Ein Sof.*

Thus we find that the realists, those who value logic, reason, and common sense above all other human traits and attributes, the drivers, and the hard-nosed pragmatists, the leaders, and the takers of initiative who mistakenly believe that they are in control of their destinies, are all living in and perpetuating an illusion, while the dreamers, the meditators, the poets, those who spurn the illusion that poses as reality, become, when seen in this new light, the true realists, for they are the ones who are connected to the Infinite Reality of the *Or Ein Sof.*

Resistance to the material illusion is the key to Reality. Through the three phase process of knowing, believing, and letting go of the material World of Restriction one transcends the illusion and creates a circuit with the alternate universe of the mind, thus becoming a channel for higher states of consciousness. This is true control; this, not the tyranny of the material illusion, is the root of real self-determination and the way by which one transmutes the negative aspect of desire into Desire to Receive for the Sake of Sharing. This, and this alone, is the way one establishes and connects with the Outer Space Connection.

TEN NOT NINE

The word *Sefira* signifies brightness and Infinite luminosity. It refers to Light and Vessel together, or, more specifically, Upper Light clothed within a Vessel. Yet it is said that no Light illuminates the tenth Vessel, *Malchut* (Kingdom). How, then, can Kingdom be considered a *Sefira* in the fullest sense of that word?

The ancient phrase, "Ten not nine," refers to this seeming contradiction in terms. The author of the *Book of Formation* (*Sefer Yetzirah*), Abraham the patriarch, wanted to make it perfectly clear that there are precisely ten and not nine *Sefirot*. Indeed, he went one step further in stating that not only is Kingdom a *Sefira*, but the most exalted of all of the Ten *Sefirot*.

For reasons well established, the Infinite luminosity contained within *Malchut* is concealed. *Malchut* is imbued with the same Infinite Upper Light that is embraced within the other nine *Sefirot*, the only difference being that *Malchut's* Endless Illumination is revealed only through the restrictive action of the Curtain. The Light repelled by the Curtain, Returning Light, binds with the Upper nine *Sefirot* in the reaction known as Binding by Striking. And so we find that were it not for *Malchut*, the Endless Light would have no way of binding with the Upper nine *Sefirot*, and therefore, because *Malchut* demonstrates this unique ability to manifest Upper Light, it must be considered to be the most important *Sefira* in the Light's revealment.

Thus, there can be no doubt that *Malchut* is composed of the Light of the Endless and must therefore be considered a *Sefira* of the highest order, which clarifies what is meant by the phrase, "Ten not nine."

Part Three

Expanding
Consciousness

Chapter 13

The Line

The linear, rational mind is not the real mind, but merely a channel, a tool, like a nail that is pounded into a two-by-four. The hammer does not pound the nail. Nothing happens on the physical level without prior activity on the metaphysical plane of thought-consciousness. It is said that the Line is the embodiment of evil, which is true from the negative perspective of *Malchut* and the Lower Seven, but from the positive Infinite perspective of the First Three the Line is illusion. The paradox is that the Line, the negative illusion, is our only link with positive reality, the *Or Ein Sof.*

Illusions are essential impediments to awareness. Words are illusions, but they often tell the truth. Books are illusions—sentences, paragraphs—are channels, nothing more, and yet they have the ability to arouse our curiosity, sharpen our intellects, and more importantly to lead us to a higher state of consciousness and greater awareness of ourselves. Music is illusion, but the emotions that it can arouse are real. Our bodies are illusions in the sense that they reveal nothing of the Infinite Energy-Intelligence within, and yet we are also personifications of Infinity. This whole world is an illusion, and yet it embraces a hidden aspect of reality and it is to this concealed Infinite Phase, the First Three, with which it is the kabbalist's task to aspire and to ultimately connect.

The creative process, came into existence with what, for the sake of utility, is described as being one percent of the Light's capacity: The Straight Vessels, the Line. The one percent is the Line. The other ninety-nine percent remains concealed. The Line, the one percent, embodies space, time, motion, the Curtain, *klipot*, the finite body, and all aspects of physical creation. It is the flaw, the gap, the necessary metaphysical distance between the Creator and us, the emanated.

We are the Line. Our bodies, these lines of limitation, stand vertical to this sphere, *Malchut*. Through resistance we can act as the wire, the filament, the Vessel that reveals the *Or Ein Sof* that, of necessity, remains concealed, and in so doing we can shed Infinite Light on humanity and also on ourselves.

And herein lies the extent of our free will: We can resist and act as channels to the higher realms of awareness or not resist and remain in darkness as we so desire. The Line, then, is the bane of humanity, but also our only source of beauty, for it is solely through the resistance intrinsic to the limited aspect of the Line that we can absolve Bread of Shame

THE LIGHTS OF LIFE AND SPIRIT

The Light of the Line was deemed by the Ari to be superior to the Light of the Circles. This may seem odd in view of the fact that the Light of the Circles was the source from which everything, including the illusionary Light of the Line originated. However, the Ari, in his abundant wisdom, realized that as the Circles receive their re-illumination solely from the Light of the Line, thus, from our finite perspective, it is the Light of the Line that must be considered by far the more important.

Indeed, were it not for the Light of the Line, the Infinite Circular Vessels would never be "drawn down" or "extend" from the Endless and thus would never be revealed. When viewed from this perspective it becomes readily apparent why the Ari felt obliged to make this important distinction.

The Ari called the Light of the Line, Light of Spirit, while to the Light of the Circles he gave the name, Light of *Nefesh*. In Hebrew the word, *nefesh*, meaning "crude spirit," was also applied by the Ari in describing the latter Circular Light, indicating the infinite Light's lesser importance to this world.

The Lower Seven of the Line serve as initiators in the process of the revealment of Light in the Circles. The Crown (*Keter*) of Circles must be illuminated before the Wisdom (*Chochmah*) of Circles can receive illumination, the Wisdom of Circles must be revealed before Understanding (*Binah*) of Circles can be re-illuminated, and so on. However, the Circular Vessels themselves are totally incapable of their own revelation. The Light of the Circles is revealed only when acted upon by the Light of the Line.

The Line, in other words, triggers all revelation in the Circular Vessels. And as the Light of the Line (Light of the Spirit) always precedes the Light of the Circles (Light of Crude Spirit (*Nefesh*)), at least from the finite perspective, the Light of the Line was considered by the Ari, to be superior to the Light of the Circles.

When we, the Vessels, refused to accept the Light's blessing and beseeched the Creator for a way by which to relieve Bread of Shame, the Creator withdrew the Light's Infinite Blessing and thus granted to man a form of equivalence with the Light. And so it is that since the Tzimztum the creator in this finite world is man.

So while it is true that the Circles are the epitome of infinite perfection, whereas the Line is finite, hence flawed, still we owe our entire physical existence to the Line. Were it not for the Line we would have no corporeal essence, no Desire to Receive for the Self Alone, no way of relieving Bread of Shame, and consequently no means by which to complete our *tikkun*, the soul's period of correction. With this in mind, it becomes a simple matter to understand why the Light of the Spirit is considered more important than the Light of *Nefesh*.

THE LINE CONNECTS THE CIRLES

All manifestations physical and metaphysical advance through Four Phases, each of which is comprised of Ten *Sefirot*. There is, however, an aspect of negativity in the finite, linear aspect of Creation (the Line) caused by the Curtain, which imparts the illusion of darkness to the Lower Seven of the Line. This negative facet is transposed to the Circles, giving them the illusion of having the same deficiency as that which is manifested by the Line. The reason for this, as has been explained, is that the Circles receive all of their renewed Illumination solely through the Line. Thus, we find that while the Circles are eternal and utterly devoid of space or illusion, both the Line and the Circle appear, from our limited perspective, to possess the same imperfection.

Given the illusion of darkness present in the Lower Seven of the Line, one might conclude that the Line is incapable of reactivating the Light that is held in suspended animation within the Encircling Vessels, but that would be an erroneous assumption. Each Phase requires a full aggregate of Ten *Sefirot* for its revealment, and the Line of *Keter* (also called the Ten *Sefirot* of Primordial Man) is the only method by which this re-illumination can be accomplished. Therefore the Lower Seven *Sefirot* of the Line can and must link, bind, and re-illuminate the Ten *Sefirot* in each of the Upper First Three *Sefirot* of the line that connect with the Ten *Sefirot* of each Circular *Sefira*.

Wisdom must be fully activated before the next Phase, Intelligence, can be revealed; Intelligence must be restored to its former Infinite splendor before Beauty can manifest; and all Ten Vessels of Beauty must be animated before Kingdom can be activated.

At each of the Four Phases of the Circles—each of which is comprised of Ten *Sefirot*—the majority of Light is repelled by the Curtain. The First Three (*Keter, Chochmah, Binah*) of each Phase of the Line enters each phase of the Circles in a potential state. Not until the Light touches the Curtain of each Phase are the Ten *Sefirot* of each corresponding phase re-illuminated, that is, the First Three of the Phase of Wisdom in the Line re-illuminates all Ten *Sefirot* in the Circular Phase of Wisdom before the Light passes downward to the next Phase. The Light reflected by the Curtain in each Phase then descends through the Seven Lower *Sefirot* of each Phase, after which the First Three of the next Phase strikes the Curtain of the Lower Phase and the same process is repeated.

The resistance of the Curtain, which is located after the Head (the First Three) but before the Body (the Lower Seven) of each Phase (in other words between *Binah* and *Tiferet*) represents the casting off of Bread of Shame that not only sheds Illumination outward and upward but also allows the Light's Blessing to descend to the next lower level.

The Light is greatly diffused by each subsequent Phase. This action can aptly be likened to the repulsion and diffusion of sunlight in the various layers of Earth's atmosphere, each of which reflects much of the light while allowing an ever decreasing quantity of the light's full spectrum to descend to Earth.

Please note that the above example, as with all physical comparisons, should not be taken entirely at face value. The student should be ever watchful of literal interpretations of kabbalistic material. Physical comparisons such as the one given above can be misleading. The phenomenon of which we are speaking occurs also on the metaphysical or potential level through the Phases of Crown (*Keter*), Wisdom (*Chochmah*), Intelligence (*Binah*), and Beauty (*Tiferet*). Only when the Light reaches the Curtain of Kingdom (*Malchut*)—where the Desire to Receive for Oneself Alone (which itself is analogous to the Earth's gravity) is fully aroused—does the Endless Light become exposed on the level of physical actuality and the true Purpose of Creation revealed.

Although correct from an objective point of view (perhaps rational is a better word, true objectivity being humanly impossible) the above example is not indicative of the entire process as described by Kabbalah. The teachings of Kabbalah must be viewed from various angles to be fully comprehended. So while we find that the above comparisons hold true on their intended physical (sunlight) and metaphysical (spiritual/thought) levels, it is of utmost importance to consider this Four Phase process of Illumination also from a personal perspective. In other words, the Illumination of which we are speaking is both physical as in the revealment of sunlight and metaphysical as it relates to the potential and thought realms, however it must never be forgotten that when the kabbalist speaks of *Malchut* he is also referring to the heart of man.

Let us, then, summarize the method by which the Light descends through the Four Phases. The Head of the Line enters the Circle of *Keter*. The Light strikes the Curtain and much of the Light is repelled. The resistant action of the Curtain (Binding by Striking) allows the First Three of the Line to Illuminate all Ten *Sefirot* of *Keter* of the Circles and also allows a lesser amount of Light to be drawn downward. The diffused Light descends, passing through the Lower Seven straight *Sefirot* of *Keter* and down through the First Three of the next Phase, *Chochmah*, where it strikes the Curtain of that Phase and the process is repeated.

Remember that the Light must pass through the Lower Seven *Sefirot* of each Phase before the Ten *Sefirot* of the Phase below can be manifested. Thus do the Lower Seven in the Line, though unrevealed themselves, still accomplish the unification of the Ten Upper Circular *Sefirot* with the Ten *Sefirot* in the Lower Ten Circular *Sefirot* of each Phase and descend to each subsequent Phase below.

HERE AND NOW

Rav Isaac Luria (the Ari), took great pains to be certain that his students understood that all phases of existence are connected by the Line that extends from the Endless. He explained in fine detail how the Light is drawn down through one circle after another until all of the Phases have been perfected and completed. He caused his students to examine thoroughly the exact method by which Light descends through one layer to the next, becoming more and more concealed until, at last, by the time it arrives at this lowest level, *Malchut*, It is almost totally devoid of revealed Illumination. The Ari was most meticulous, too, in his explanation of the process by which the Curtain, through involuntary resistance, allows all of the Three previous Phases, plus *Malchut*, the Phase of Revealment, to become animated, but how we, the emanated, can attain contentment only through conscious restriction. Why should the Ari have considered it important to place so much emphasis on that which to some might seem at first glance to be picayune technicalities?

The Ari was imparting to us what might be described as the pantheistic perspective of Kabbalah, which posits that the Force, the Light, pierces each and every stratum of existence, that the Emanator is all-embracing; that every molecule, atom, and sub-atomic particle in the universe is imbued with the power of the *Or Ein Sof,* that the Creator is within us and without us, a part of us, yet apart from us, and that everything in the universe is but an aspect of one, living, breathing organism.

Some spiritual teachings place the Creator high on a lofty ethereal pedestal, far beyond the reach of humanity. In some religions it becomes necessary to die in order to "meet your Maker." Other philosophies see the Emanator as having created the universe before moving on to bigger and presumably better things. By his thorough teaching the Ari was attempting to clarify the kabbalistic concept that the *Ein Sof* permeates every aspect of the universe and that this is true no matter how concealed the Light may seem to appear, from our limited perspective.

We will learn, in due time, how each subsequent Phase conceals the one that emerged previously. One of the many analogies drawn by the Ari explains this phenomenon in terms of the various layers of an onion, each of which tastes the same. Using this metaphor for the purpose of understanding the all-pervasiveness of the Light, the Ari pointed out that just as the essence, the taste of the onion is the same throughout all of its layers, so too does the Light, the essence of existence, permeate every aspect of material substance as well as the intangible aspects of existence with equal consistency.

The onion metaphor serves, also, as an apt illustration of what is meant, kabbalistically, by the terms higher and lower in the sense that the inner layers are no lower or less real than the outer covering, but only more concealed. So we find that while one level of consciousness may be higher than the next, in essence they are all identical. The only difference between *Chochmah*, the highest Phase, and *Malchut*, the lowest, is in the degree of revealment, *Chochmah* being revealed, *Malchut*, concealed, but in fact they both consist of the same *Or Ein Sof.*

Another example used by the Ari was that of a lantern covered with layer upon layer of thin fabric veils, each of which conceals the light still further. Imagine a scenario in which one person enters a room at the moment when another is placing the last of one hundred veils over a lantern. The lantern is there beneath the veils and its light is still as bright as ever, but the new observer sees no lantern and thus quite naturally, though mistakenly, concludes that the first person has nothing more than a pile of cloth before him. Such is the prevailing condition here in *Malchut* as it relates to the *Or Ein Sof.*

The Creator is here, the sages, the saints. The Upper Worlds are here along with the Lower. The negative is entwined with the positive, the high with the low, the dense with the fine, the good with the bad. The Light is here in all of its Infinite glory, but it must remain hidden from our finite aspect, the Lower Seven, for that was the prerequisite of our existence. Reality is here and now, within us and without us, but concealed by the space, the gap, the illusion, that was the sole imperative of Creation.

Chapter 14

On Restoring Light
to the Circles

After the *Tzimtzum*, a negative space was established in the Circles by the Lower Seven of the Line. Thus, from *Keter* to *Chochmah* there is a gap of seven empty stages; from *Chochmah* to *Binah* another gap of seven, and so on. Each of these negative spaces is an outgrowth of the illusionary process of Line. The First Three of each phase of the Line can fill the Ten *Sefirot* of each Phase of the Circles, but the Lower Seven of the Line do not have that ability. The Ari's book of meditations describes a specific method by which prayer can fill the gaps and restore Light to the Circular Vessels.

Just as the energy of the seed must first establish itself as a root before a trunk can come into being, and the trunk before the branch, and the branch before the leaf, so must the Light travel through the Lower Seven of each Phase before it can illuminate the adjacent level below. The Light, in other words, must pass through the Lower Seven *Sefirot* Straightness of *Keter* before *Chochmah's* Light of Wisdom can manifest; it must then pass through the Lower Seven of *Chochmah* before *Binah's* Light of Mercy can be revealed. The same process is maintained throughout the ten levels of all Four Phases.

In our examination of the filament of a light bulb, we learned that it is the filament's negative restriction that is responsible for the Light's revealment. So too, in this world of illusion, does the Light require *Malchut's* resistance to reveal Its supremely positive blessing. At all Phases it is the level of *Malchut* that causes the Light's re-illumination. *Malchut* has the unique ability of manifesting the Light. She alone possesses the Desire to Receive for the Self Alone and hence the restrictive capacity requisite for the Light's revealment. Only within the tenth and final *Sefirot* of each Phase, *Malchut*, does the restriction occur which provides the stimulus for the revelation of Light in each subsequent phase.

No evolution or revealment occurs in the Lower Phases, even in the Circular Vessels, unless and until there is a manifestation of the Seven *Sefirot* of Straighness of the Phase above. The Seven Lower *Sefirot* of Straightness of *Keter* link the ten Circular *Sefirot* of *Keter* with the Ten Circular *Sefirot* of *Chochmah*, and so from *Chochmah* to *Binah*, and so on in a like manner. The Circular Vessels of *Chochmah*, for example, receive illumination from the First Three of the Line of *Chochmah*; while the Circular Vessels of *Binah* receive their illumination from the First Three of the Line of *Binah*. This is what the Ari meant when he declared that the Lower Seven *Sefirot* of Straightness unify all of the Circular Vessels by virtue of the Line.

It may strike the reader as a discrepancy that the infinitely positive Light, the essence of Reality, requires negative illusion for its revealment. After all, did the Ari not teach us that Light is infinitely superior to and always supersedes darkness? Adding to this seeming contradiction is the fact that the Ari also taught us that no positive energy is revealed in this illusionary world without resistance, the energy-intelligence of which is inherently negative. No light, sound, thought, word, deed—nothing is revealed in this world of illusion without resistance. Positive cannot be revealed without negative, the Light needs the darkness. Such is the nature of the paradox of Returning Light. How, then, can we harmonize these seeming contradictions?

Because the Light requires negative resistance to be revealed in this world this should not be construed as meaning that the Emanator's beneficence is in some way limited by the Vessel. Like sunlight, the Light's beneficence is constant. Would it not be a mistake to say that the sunlight ceases to shine during the nighttime hours just because the dark side of the Earth happens for the moment to be facing away from the sun? Like the sunlight, the Light, *Or Ein Sof,* gives of its endless beneficence twenty-four hours of every day. That fact that we may not see the Light does not mean It is not within us and without us, endlessly sharing Its Infinite abundance.

From the Infinite perspective darkness does not exist. The Light, *Or Ein Sof,* is everywhere, constantly imparting Its endless blessing. It is only from our finite point of view that the Light appears to be concealed. This was a prerequisite of Creation in that it provides us with a way of earning the Light's blessing and thus removing Bread of Shame.

The Ari's example, mentioned earlier, involving the removal of the veils covering a lantern may help to clarify this matter. The light beneath the layers of veils never ceased to shine, but from the perspective of one who might have walked into the room at the time when the veils covered the lantern, the light would have seemed to not exist. So it is with the infinite Light of our beings. We must use voluntary resistance to remove the veils of illusion from the Lower Seven and thus again reveal the endless Illumination of our Circular Vessels. Restriction, the removal of the veils, reveals Light in the Lower Seven of the Line. By injecting restriction we transform the illusionary Phase of the Seven and change the darkness into Light.

The Seven of *Keter* create an illusionary gap, as do the Seven of *Chochmah,* and the Seven of *Binah,* and so on. Thus the Seven of each Phase remain dark and unrevealed. However, as strange as it may seem, the Ari taught us that even though the Seven may seem totally devoid of Light, whereas the First Three of the Phase below are illuminated, the Seven in the higher Phase are considered to be more exalted. The Seven of the Phase above, in other words, are deemed superior to the First Three of the Phase below because they are found in a higher frame of reference.

If Light is superior to darkness, does it not stand to reason that the Light found in the First Three of the Phase below should be superior to the darkness of the phase above? Have we not been told that Light always prevails over darkness? Why then should the Illumination found in the First Three of the lower Phase not be judged superior to the Seven of the Phase above which is cloaked in darkness?

The reason that this was not seen by the Ari as being an inconsistency was that the darkness found in the Lower Seven is an illusion. The Light is there in all of its infinite glory, but obscured from our view here in the illusionary realm. Thus the Light in the Seven of the upper Phases, though veiled, is still closer to the Source and must thus be deemed purer and higher by virtue of its closer proximity to the Endless.

Chapter 15

Activating the Central Column

T he universe operates on a Three Column System. Acting between the positive influence and the negative is the mediating principle known to Kabbalah as the Central Column. The Central Column is synonymous with the neutron in the atom and also with the filament in a light bulb. The Central Column represents the mediating principle that must bridge the two polarities, positive and negative, in order that energy can be manifested.

The Central Column can be likened to the moderator in a debate, a referee, a diplomat, or the arbitrator of any dispute. Just as the filament must exercise resistance in order to reveal light, so too must the arbitrator restrain his own particular opinions or beliefs in the interest of settling the conflict, whatever it may be. Like the intermediary, we all want to have our way, to Receive for Ourselves Alone. The paradox is that to accomplish this we must restrict what we want to receive, for it is only through restriction that energy is revealed.

Restriction is the energy-intelligence of the Central Column. By resisting what we want to receive we create the connection that gives it to us. How strange this concept seems at first glance, how backward, how thoroughly wrong-headed. Can the kabbalist seriously expect us to believe that to get what we want we have to reject it? That to arrive at yes we have to say no? Yes, as strange as it may seem, the principle of Returning Light dictates a situation such, that all energy that is revealed in this world of restriction is reflected (restricted) energy. Hence, if we want to receive (in other words reveal the energy we desire) we have to withhold our desire and thereby create a blockage to the actual receiving. The moment we say no the Central Column creates interference in the world of *Malchut* that allows the Light, the positive energy, to be revealed.

RESISTANCE

Students of Kabbalah generally have no difficulty understanding how the negative pole's resistance to the incoming electricity initiates illumination in a light bulb. Nor do they have the slightest problem understanding the concept of resistance when confronted with some of the myriad physical examples of this phenomenon in action. All one has to do is contract a muscle (resistance) to see that it grows. Compare a reflective light-colored surface with an absorbent darker colored one in strong sunlight—there is no question that the former sheds (resists) more illumination than the latter. By clashing one rock forcibly against another the concept of Binding by Striking flashes to life before our eyes. Yet, however easily one may accept physical examples of Resistance (Curtain) and Restriction (*Tzimtzum*) in exterior terms, still we struggle when attempting to apply this concept to our daily lives.

Modern nations, cultures and civilizations, were founded and built, we are told, by men and women who believed in a philosophy of setting goals and striving toward them. Every day in school, on television, in books and magazines, we are presented with examples of people who through their apparent dogged striving have made something of themselves. When at first we don't succeed, the prevailing wisdom goes, try, try again. It is little wonder, then, that when the kabbalist attempts to inform us that the greater is our desire to possess something the less likely will be our chance of acquiring it, and, conversely, that resisting that which we most desire is the surest way of getting it; our personalities—that body of knowledge perceived by the senses and learned from birth—cry out in protest. This seeming contradiction rubs against the grain of all that we have ever learned. How are we expected to "get somewhere in this world" if we reject that which we most desire?

It is one thing, after all, to look at physical examples of resistance in action, and quite another to adopt it as a way of life. One important obstacle to contend with is the bias of Newtonian physics. Newton believed that nature is governed by absolute laws that operate totally apart from the consciousness of man. The Newtonian perspective, acquired by all who attend our schools, conditions us to believe that we can study nature without considering ourselves as part of the equation. So seemingly universal is this misconception that it is generally accepted without question.

Kabbalah, on the other hand, teaches that man is a participator in nature and therefore cannot possibly study its laws without also studying himself. Hence, the kabbalist merely by observing the laws that govern the external physical world—such as Binding by Striking— concludes that the same laws must also be acting internally within each of us. Resistance, then, being the *modus operandi* in the physical world, must also rule the realm of the metaphysical, including our emotional lives and even our thoughts. As basic and utterly sensible as this idea feels when it is expressed in simple terms, it still escapes the vast majority of people—expressly for the reason stated earlier that most people perceive nature as something apart from themselves.

Given these prevailing cultural perspectives and educational conditions, it is little wonder that the student of Kabbalah cannot grasp, at first, and therefore will not embrace wholeheartedly the concept of resistance. It is not easy, after all, to break the bonds of teachings so deeply ingrained. The verity of resistance, this most elusive element of kabbalistic thought, must be approached from various levels and angles, mentally, emotionally, and physically if it is to be fully comprehended and utilized to best advantage. As is the case with all kabbalistic truths, the idea of resisting that which is most desired cannot be perceived by means of logic alone—it must be experienced. Rational thinking is a tool, but like any tool it has its limitations.

Concerning this seemingly enigmatic kabbalistic concept, it should be remembered that it is not the Light that the kabbalist asks us to reject, but the obstruction of Light, the Desire to Receive for Oneself Alone. By resisting that which we most desire we create an altered state of consciousness, which though admittedly paradoxical from the standpoint of logic and common sense (as those words are commonly perceived), satisfies all desires. Self depravation plays not the slightest part in the kabbalist's resistance and denial. It is simply that by reenacting *Tzimtzum*, the original act of creation, he or she creates affinity with the Light and achieves union with the *Or Ein Sof.*

THE FILAMENT

In our discussion of the filament of a light bulb we learned that the negative pole and not the positive initiates any and all circuits of energy. The Line makes contact with the Circle thereby creating the circular condition necessary for the Light's revealment. The resulting circuit satisfies both the desire of the Line, to receive, as well as that of the Circles which is to share.

The brightness of a light bulb is determined solely by the size of the filament, not by the current that runs through the wiring system. The current is the same no matter what appliance is plugged into it, whether it is an air conditioner, the demands of which are great, or a five watt bulb, the desire of which is small. In a similar manner as a light bulb produces only that amount of light which its filament is capable of generating, so too can we manifest only that exact amount of Light, which our filament (our capacity for restriction) allows our inner Encircling Vessels to reveal.

RETURNING LIGHT

Lurianic Kabbalah classifies Light according to two divisions, Straight Light and Returning Light. From the human perspective the latter is by far the more important. This becomes apparent by simply examining these two aspects of Light relative to the physical universe. Straight Light becomes manifested only upon contact with resistance. Sunlight, the corporeal equivalent of Straight Light, is revealed only when it reflects off something physical—evidence of which is readily available by gazing into the night sky where no light is manifested between the planetary bodies. The light that is reflected is given the name Returning Light. Hence, because Straight Light is invisible the greater importance of Returning Light over Straight Light is indisputable, insofar as we of *Malchut* are concerned, for the simple reason that Returning Light is the only light that is revealed and is thus the only light we ever see.

Because non reflected light is not physically manifested is not proof that it does not exist. Light is everywhere, in the air, the water, and even in the center of the Earth. The Infinite presence of the *Or Ein Sof* permeates that which is physical and that which is immaterial with equal intensity, as does the light of the sun. The paradox is that no light is revealed unless by an act of resistance. And therein lies the essential difference between Straight Light and Returning Light, the latter reveals everything, the former, nothing.

An earlier chapter advanced what to the rational mind might seem like a ludicrous notion, namely that every wish is potentially granted, every desire is already fulfilled. From the kabbalistic perspective this concept makes perfect sense, for no desire can possibly arise, the fulfillment of which has not been attained on a metaphysical level. Nothing is manifested in this World of Restriction without there having existed a previous thought for the simple reason that nothing, but nothing, exists today that did not exist in the *Ein Sof* before the Thought of Creation—no thought, no deed, no aspiration or Desire.

Recall that the greater the capacity for reflection (resistance) the greater is the revealment of light. A white surface, for example, reflects more light than a dark one, a hard, shiny object such as a mirror more than a porous object such as a rock; which is precisely why Desire to Receive for Oneself Alone, being the epitome of absorbency, reveals nothing, while the Desire to Receive for the Sake of Sharing, being of a reflective nature, reveals all that can be revealed. The same holds true on the levels of the metaphysical, and even, as we shall now examine, on the most mundane levels of human experience.

What follows are a few examples of how the concept of Returning Light might apply to our everyday lives.

Two businessmen shake hands, one offering a firm grip and a smile, the other a passive grip with no facial expression.

Result: No deal.

Union demands new contract, management stalls.

Result: Strike.

Mother serves sumptuous meal to unappreciative children.

Result: TV dinners

Professor tutors student who does not listen.

Result: The purpose of both is defeated.

Wife attempts to communicate, but husband watches football on TV.

Result: Husband loses TV in divorce settlemen

Conscious restriction is not required on the part of the Earth, the moon, or other planetary objects in order to reflect the light of the sun. Nor is a body of water or any other physical object compelled to voluntarily reflect sunlight so that the light may be revealed. Light reflects from a mirror without the mirror's conscious intervention. The filament repels electricity with no act of awareness. Only humanity must exercise voluntary resistance to reveal Light. Failure to restrict or otherwise reflect the Light that is freely offered can result in enmity, financial disaster, lack of order and communication, obesity, alcoholism, and a host of other problems, whereas voluntarily resistance allows us to fulfill our true purpose which is to achieve affinity with the Light through the removal of Bread of Shame.

FREE WILL OR DETERMINISM

Free will is a privilege reserved only for those who choose to exercise it. The Ari taught us that the extent of man's free will rests in his ability and willingness to restrict the negative aspect of desire. Either we resist the Desire to Receive for the Self Alone and thus reveal the Light that lies dormant within us, or we do not restrict and remain submerged in the illusion. Failure to engage the system of restriction that grants us free will causes us to be ruled by the same deterministic system that causes a rock to fall to the ground or a planet to revolve around the sun.

A rock has no free will. Neither does a man who does not exercise resistance against the Desire to Receive for the Self Alone. Consciousness requires a ceaseless effort at resistance. By choosing not to restrict the negative aspect of desire we give up the one prerogative that was granted to us after the *Tzimtzum*, namely, the right to alleviate Bread of Shame. By restricting the negative aspect of desire we pay tribute to that original act of Creation and thus reveal the Light.

Chapter 16

The Good Fight

Merely to list, let alone recount, all of the atrocities committed by men and women in the name of goodness, truth, and righteousness would require a million megabytes of computer memory. All wars, all battles, are fought, supposedly, with the intention of eradicating some evil, righting some real or imagined wrong. This continuing cycle of violence in the name of high virtue has been with us since the earliest days of civilization and it will no doubt continue for some time to come.

Hypothetically, violence might be justified, from the kabbalistic perspective, in the unlikely event that the combatants were attempting to create affinity with the Light and thus restore the Circular integrity of humanity and all that exists on this planet. That would be a good fight, a fight worth winning, a fight worth "dying for." Of course no one fights to preserve the Circular aspect of humanity. In truth, the vast majority of wars, battles, and arguments, are fought by combatants who desire nothing more than to safeguard their own selfish self interests.

Politicians and world leaders may pay lip service to such concepts as world peace, but in the final analysis, when push comes to shove, almost invariably their true colors show through the veneer of illusion by which they surround themselves, and we see that greed, Desire to Receive for Oneself Alone, is their real motivating factor.

In short, they are fighting to preserve an illusion. Neck hairs bristle when this kabbalistic concept is expressed, throats are cleared, blood comes to faces—egos get fighting mad. All of us have known people, good people, loved ones, who have died protecting what the kabbalist so glibly, it seems, calls an illusion. What of World War Two—was that not a classic example of a good fight of truth conquering evil? Who among us does not cherish the memory of someone, a family member, a compatriot or loved one, who died protecting a beloved homeland or way of life? Does the kabbalist have the temerity to suggest that all of those precious lives were sacrificed in vain?

Naturally, from that standpoint of reasoning, anyone who is not ready to shed his or her blood; or better yet the blood of others, to protect their "God-given" homelands and cherished ways of life is, at best, a coward. It is precisely this mentality that sends young men off to war. Only later, when the war is over and carnage is complete and the battlefields are strewn with blood and body parts, and nothing, but nothing has been accomplished, do a few people raise their voices to decry the utter futility of it all—and perhaps for a brief moment someone hears those voices before the cycle of violence begins anew.

War is an aspect of the Line, and therefore, kabbalistically speaking, illusionary. In the grand Circular scheme of things there is no difference between Arab and Jew, Catholic and Protestant—these differences are temporal in the sense that we possess them only for the speck of time that each of our finite lives encompasses.

Yet, in spite of war's illusionary nature, the kabbalist does not contend that those who die in war necessarily do so in vain. War is an illusion, make no mistake about that. Still, as are all aspects of this illusionary finite existence, it can also be an opportunity for correction—not religious, political, or planetary correction (in that respect wars solve nothing) but personal, karmic correction.

Consider, then, the possibility that our beloved ancestors, who sacrificed their finite vessels in war, did not do so in defence of imagined differences and false beliefs. Perhaps they were motivated by a purpose higher than the mere preservation of some illusionary doctrine, religion, or the "ownership" of some piece of ground. Perhaps they died, rather, to complete a phase of their spiritual correction. Using this reasoning we find that even war, man's most senseless and futile illusionary gesture, can be resolved within the Infinite Circular perspective.

THE GLOBAL VILLAGE

Only recently has the concept of world citizenship reached the feathered edge of the collective consciousness. Today many people, if pressed for an opinion, would agree, at least in principle, with the concept that the world might be a better place if it were governed by a single international ruling body. Yet, as with so many altruistically motivated ideas, few people, no matter how humanitarian their intentions, can agree even on what such a forum might realistically accomplish, much less on how a plan of this nature might be implemented.

If such a body politic existed, how would it function?

Some see the world government as being an outgrowth of the United Nations. The current organization, they maintain, could be expanded to include all of the world's nations and territories, and U.N. decrees, instead of being elective, would become mandatory. Certain economists, on the other hand, contend that only free enterprise could be the catalyst for such a plan. If all of the world's economies were inextricably bound up with one another, they reason, there would be far less incentive for one country to wage war against another. Many military men insist that a strong nuclear arsenal is the way to bring peace to the world. The threat of nuclear carnage, they tell us, is the only reason we are not at war today. Certain evangelists agree, insisting that only religion—meaning the fear of God—coupled with a fearsome nuclear retaliatory capability, can save the world.

Of course, there is a large contingency of detractors who maintain that nothing short of an all-out invasion from outer space could possibly bring all of the nations and the people of the world together. Even this argument is not without merit. Indeed, given the current state of world affairs, it is difficult to imagine five human beings coexisting peaceably, let alone five, or more, billion.

Those who vehemently oppose the idea of a unified world government point to the dullness of a homogenized world in which everyone would be the same. Detractors argue that cultural identities would be lost, racial and religious distinctions obliterated, and we would be left with the blandness of a vast, homogenized cultural wasteland. And, certainly, this argument, too, warrants consideration—at least from the point of view of those who believe it to be true.

The point is that even among those who doubtlessly agree with the basic concept of a single international ruling body, no one has yet to, or is likely to, it seems, given prevailing world tensions, advance a formula as to how such a scheme might plausibly be brought into being. It seems that an almost insurmountable obstacle faces the idea of a One World government. For such a forum to be effective, a quality would have to be exercised rarely found in human interactions, namely, selflessness. This fact leads many people, even supporters of the One World cause, to conclude that the idea of a united world is doomed to failure.

Not so the kabbalist. Kabbalists have long maintained that world unity will one day be a physical reality. It is the kabbalist's belief that a millennium of world peace will precede the final emendation. Even here, today, in this chaotic riot of insanity that we mistakenly call the real world, the careful observer can perceive the emergence of a seed of changing awareness in this transitional period in humanity's tumultuous, yet curiously static, cultural evolution. The very fact that certain people are thinking, speaking, even raising their voices in behalf of One World is evidence of the vast, sweeping reformation that is to come. As always, the metaphysical realm of thought is the harbinger of what will one day become reality on the physical level.

In Reality, meaning the Infinite Reality of the *Or Ein Sof,* we are all cut from the same cloth. Each of us holds a share in a common stock, a stock that might be aptly named, Survival International—and the price of that stock is rising daily. In terms of the Endless Reality, the Infinite recognizes no distinction between the weak and the strong, poor and rich, Arab and Jew, commoner and king. In the grand scheme of things, we are already intimately entwined within a vast, never changing fabric of universal peace.

Assuredly, here in this Fourth Phase of existence, the fighting continues, the torture, the selfishness, the seemingly perpetual bickering, but this is of circumstance only in the transitory world, the World of Illusion. Outward appearances only appear to make us different; customs and languages only seem to separate us. Kabbalists see cultures, races, religions, and political movements as being of consequence only in the illusory world—hence of no consequence at all. These ephemeral distinctions play not the slightest part in the great, unchanging and ever peaceful design.

All that exists within a life cycle having a beginning, middle, and an end, is considered by the Kabbalah to be part of the illusion. Physical differences, being of a finite nature, are illusionary. Our bodies, these Vessels of limitation, with which we maneuver through the various Phases of the Earthly cycle of correction, are here today and gone tomorrow, and hence must also be considered illusion.

Kabbalistically speaking, only that which is permanent and never changing is real. Nothing ever changes in the *Or Ein Sof.* It is Endless, and, as such, it was, is, and forever will be endlessly peaceful, timeless, and perfectly still. Our souls live forever as part of the Endless Circle of

Infinity—thus, only they, of all human attributes and characteristics, are deemed by Kabbalah to be *bona fide* expressions of Reality.

Admittedly, the possibility of all of the world's politicians, economists, religious and military leaders suddenly agreeing to abide by the dictates of a single international ruling body, seems, from the finite perspective, to be remote in the extreme. However, from the Infinite point of view, those who aspire toward a One World government have just cause for celebration. For whether they know it or not, their wish has already been granted. From the Infinite outlook, the universe and everything in it has always been and will always be a single unified entity. The world is One.

In the real, the Endless World, peace already reigns supreme. As difficult as it may be to imagine, experiencing, as we do, only the underside of reality, it is just a matter of time (another illusory concept) before the aspiration for a united world becomes reality here in the World of Illusion.

Even today, the world operates under the auspices of a single authority, a unified Energy-Intelligence, the *Or Ein Sof.* Even in this violent, transitory, tumultuous sphere of illusion there is an all embracing aspect of harmony, peace, and unanimity with which each of us can connect. Thus, when seen from the kabbalistic point of view, the concept of a global village, as expressed by the late visionary and architect, Richard Buckminster Fuller (July 12, 1895–July 1, 1983), becomes not some tangled, international impossibility, but an intimate matter of personal choice and individual commitment.

Chapter 17

Tikkun, *Tzadik*, Coming Full Circle

Throughout the ages, writers, physicians and metaphysicians have been holding out to us the tantalizing proposition that a medicinal formula might one day be discovered that will once and for all put an end to human suffering. Alchemists searched for centuries for an elixir that would give us all eternal youth. Theirs and other utopian worlds of the imagination have played a large part in the continuing drama of the human psyche for they offer hope of a better world. Aldous Huxley (26 July 1894 – 22 November 1963), imagined such a panacea in his novel *Brave New World*. Many have dreamed of such a world, but from the kabbalistic perspective the discovery of a panacea that would end all human suffering would result in a human tragedy of unparalleled magnitude, in some ways worse than all wars, famines, epidemics, and atrocities combined.

What reason could the kabbalist possibly have for making this seeming outlandish declaration? Is it that the world population would skyrocket to such an extent that people would be fighting over every scrap of food? No, that problem could easily be alleviated simply by switching to a vegetarian diet. Cattle require an inordinate amount of grazing land that could be utilized in more productive ways. Nor does strange assertion have anything to do with either the problem of overcrowding or with energy. Solar, wind, wave energy, and other alternative sources could be employed to fill energy needs, and even today it is within the range of possibility that undersea or space stations could be developed to handle excess population. The real grounds for the kabbalists opinion that a life-extending elixir would result in a major disaster is precisely for the reason that it would end all Earthly suffering, which would only serve to prolong the spiritual suffering of humanity, thus extending our *tikkun,* the corrective process.

We are here to make adjustments, corrections, amendments to our finite constitutions, and these changes come about through resistance, discomfort and suffering. Each lifetime brings us closer to our goal of one day being reunited with the great Circle of Endlessness from which we came. This corrective procedure is called *tikkun.* The Line, the creative illusion, and the Lower Seven of the Line are all names for the same process of spiritual modification. Finite existence, this life in the Lower Seven, provides us with the opportunity of expelling Bread of Shame. Through resistance the soul is purified, bringing us closer to the Circle of beneficence that is the birthright of us all. Thus it becomes apparent why a magical panacea that would remove all suffering would turn the human drama into a tragedy for the simple reason that it would only prolong the agony of finite existence.

Our souls are like streams that can never rest until they once again mingle with the Infinite Sea. Until that time comes we meander, trying out new channels, new lines of least resistance. Sometimes the stream of life swells and rises, sometimes it cascades down like a waterfall. At times the water is shallow, at other times deep, sometimes dark and murky, sometimes pure and crystal clear. At times we enter lakes of the spirit that are so large and still that they deceive us into thinking that we have reached the ocean of endlessness that we have sought so long. Sometimes we are lured by gravity into swamps of uncertainty, sometimes we are trapped in tidal pools from which we fear we might never escape. From lifetime to lifetime the stream goes on, searching, suffering, pursuing the Infinite reunion.

We each have but one true aspiration and that is to return to the Light, the same Light that once filled us in the *Ein Sof* before the Thought of

Creation; the same Light that left its impression in our Encircling Vessels. Life, this finite existence is a Line, a channel, a stream, that was once a part of the great Circle of Infinity and to the Circle it will one day return. And so while it is true that from our finite perspective, suffering has nothing whatever to recommend it, and thus a magical life extending elixir would seem like a glorious blessing. But, from the Infinite point of view we see that suffering is a necessity, for it is only through the process of correction (*tikkun*), that we can ever return home to the state of blissful beneficence from which the stream of life originated.

THE MOTHER OF INVENTION

Consider a hypothetical situation in which an intrepid sea captain from, let us say, Moravia happens upon a deserted shore of the United States, plants firm the Moravian flag and declares this country to be the exclusive property of the Moravian king—an absurd proposition to say the least. Yet how closely it resembles, in some respects, the landing of Christopher Columbus on soil that had for millennia been inhabited by Native Americans. Is it not ironic that some five centuries later, we still honor Columbus as the "discoverer" of America when, in fact, he did no such thing?

We believe that our actions initiate results; that inventors invent, that composers compose, that discoverers discover. According to kabbalistic philosophy, this is a fallacy. Kabbalah teaches that the most anyone can hope to do is to reveal what already is. As the old saying tells us, "there is nothing new under the sun." Everything that ever was or will be must of necessity have been present in the *Ein Sof* before the Thought of Creation. The seeds of all ideas and inventions great and small are therefore around us and within us, awaiting revealment. Thus, by aligning our thoughts and actions with the needs of our time we can make ourselves worthy of being channels through which some truth or great discovery might be expressed.

GROWTH

What causes growth? Why do seeds become trees? Why is the physical universe expanding? In a word the answer is desire. Desire draws energy to itself. The only time there is a lessening of expansion is when there is a lessening of desire.

There is no physical connection between the seed and the root of a tree, the root and the branch, the trunk and the leaf. Yet obviously there must be a relationship of some kind between these various elements, a bond that must somehow be enclosed within the makeup of the seed. The seed is the blueprint for the tree. The tree exists within the seed. The entire growth cycle of the tree, from birth through death, is included in the seed. The same may be said of the *Ein Sof,* which is the seed of physical Creation.

Just as the seed cannot jump to a branch, nor can the First Three of the Line (*Keter, Chochmah, Binah*) of the Phase of *Chochmah,* reveal the Ten *Sefirot* of *Chochmah* of the Circular Vessels because the injection of empty space of the Seven Lower *Sefirot* have become part of the growth. The Seven of *Keter* precedes the First Three of Line of *Chochmah.* Consequently these Seven fill the gap between *Keter* of the Circular Vessels and *Chochmah* of the Circular Vessels. The Fourth level of each Phase (*Malchut*) provides the impetus for the evolution of each subsequent Phase.

Growth is something we share with all things physical. Spiritual and intellectual, growth is our only method of relieving the burden of Bread of Shame. Thus, the kabbalist strives to close the gap between him or herself and the Light within. To not do so is to remain in the illusion of darkness.

Physical birth, growth and death, according to the kabbalistic wisdom, are of consequence only in the realm of the illusion. The death of the body's desire has no affect whatever on the soul, the striving and spiritual growth of which must continue through various lifetimes until the soul's corrective process (*tikkun*) is completed.

All that exists in the universe and all that ever will exist was included in the Endless before the *Tzimtzum* and will remain after all growth and expansion and Desire to Recive for oneself alone no longer serve a useful function. Thus, from the kabbalistic perspective, growth like time, space, and matter is an illusion, though, of course, a necessary one.

Desire to Receive for Oneself Alone, itself is a product solely of the illusion, only of the Line. According to the kabbalistic tradition, that which is temporary, meaning all things physical, including striving (Desire) and growth, are considered mere blips on the endless, timeless, unmoving grid of Infinity.

Thus growth is of vital importance to us. Indeed, if it were not for the striving that manifests as growth in this World of Action, we would have no way of completing our soul's *tikkun*, which is the very purpose of our physical existence. Indeed, all of the Encircling Light that we can ever hope to reveal in this realm of illusion manifests as a result of the interaction between the Light and our receiving mechanism (Desire to Receive), which by its nature engenders growth.

TZADIK

The term *tzadik*, meaning righteous, is reserved only for a blessed few. A *tzadik* is a holy man, a person of knowledge. Moses was a *tzadik*, as were all of the patriarchs. Rav Shimon ben Yochai and Ravi Isaac Luria also share that blessed name. A person who aspires to be a *tzadik* denies the world of illusion, rejects totally the Desire to Receive for Oneself Alone, and resists the yearnings of the body, favoring instead to follow only the mandates of the soul. Such people are so completely devoid of the negative aspect of desire that when the body of a *tzadik* expires it is said to remain in a state of almost perfect constitution.

As with any physical object on Earth, the human body is subject to gravity, which is the manifestation of Earth's primal motivating influence, Desire to Receive for Itself Alone. The soul, however, operates beyond gravity's jurisdiction and hence is free to travel in its quest to complete the cycle of its correction, or *tikkun.* Thus, while the body's natural inclination is to succumb to gravitation and remain inactive and rooted to one spot, the tendency of the soul is to travel in its quest for restoration with the infinite Light, the *Or Ein Sof.*

Above the atmosphere, beyond the realm of gravity, everything becomes weightless. In space, it is the natural inclination of any physical object, given even so much as a modicum of momentum, to continue to move until such time as it falls under the influence of another, larger planetary body. In fact, removed completely from any gravitational influence, the object in question would travel for light-years without changing direction or speed. By transcending the Desire to Receive for Oneself Alone, the *tzadik* connects with an altered state of consciousness that is spiritually comparable to that weightless condition, in that his consciousness is no longer anchored by the negativity that is the motivating influence in the world of Restriction.

The *tzadik,* at every opportunity, resists comfort and complacency, for those are aspirations of the body caused by the Desire to Receive for Oneself Alone. Because of this, people whose concerns are only physical, meaning that they are ensconced in the Desire to Receive for Oneself Alone, may look at a *tzadik* and mistakenly believe that he is suffering, when nothing could be further from the truth. The *tzadik,* by denying the trappings of comfort, rises above the world of personalities, illusion, and outward appearances, and connects with a higher consciousness which is activated by the Positive aspect of desire, namely, Desire to Receive for the Sake of Sharing.

The *tzadik's* voluntary resistance causes a cancellation of the Desire to Receive for Oneself Alone, which, of course, is the root of all wrongdoing, and thus is he able to transcend the negative realm. By transforming the Desire to Receive into the Desire to Receive for the Sake of Sharing, he rises above what kabbalists for convenience call the negative one percent, which represents the illusionary reality with which we are presented on a day-to-day basis, and unites with the ninety-nine percent, which is the true, Infinite Reality of the *Or Ein Sof.* When the negative one percent has been transformed by sharing, the *tzadik* is no longer affected by the negative acts of mankind.

The *Sefirotic* triumvirate of *Keter, Chochmah,* and *Binah,* the First Three, which are synonymous with the soul, are governed by the laws of gravity only insofar as they are housed within the physical body. The soul operates beyond the laws of time, space, and motion. Only humanity's finite Lower Seven *Sefirot* (the body) are subject to the laws that govern the physical world. Only the Lower Seven are constrained by gravity, air pressure, and the aging process. Removed from the confines of the body, our Infinite aspect is capable of infinite movement at infinite speed.

When negativity, the *klipot* that manifests as a result of the Desire to Receive for Oneself Alone, has been converted to the positive energy through an attitude of sharing, one no longer is affected by negativity. Thus transformed, the *tzadik* exists on a level of consciousness that is by far higher than that which is experienced by the so-called average person, though in all respects but one, the former and the latter are the same. The only difference being that the so-called average person's consciousness is tuned in to the lower frequency (the Lower Seven) while the *tzadik's* receiving mechanism is set on the higher frequency of the First Three. True, the body of a *tzadik* exists, like everyone else's, in the World of Restriction, but his consciousness remains above the petty machinations of negativity caused by material existence.

Only in the consciousness of this World of Restriction does chaos reign supreme. Above that lowest state of body consciousness, there exists the Infinite, Endless, true Reality of the *Or Ein Sof,* the Reality with which the *tzadik* is continually connected. Thus, the *tzadik*'s self denial should in no way be mistaken for suffering. The *tzadik* denies the body's desire for comfort and complacency in order to satisfy the much stronger and more important directives of the soul. Not unlike the negative pole of the filament of a light bulb, which denies electricity and thus produces light, by resisting the negative, represented by stasis and complacency, the *tzadik* reveals the positive, eternal, infinite Light of his own existence. For whereas the Lower Seven, being of a finite nature, can never achieve more than a transitory fulfillment; the connection made by the *tzadik* through positive resistance is with the Eternal.

COMING FULL CIRCLE

From the Infinite perspective, we are, each of us permeated, filled to the capacity, with endless illumination. Spiritually, we lack for nothing. Lack is an illusion, though a necessary one, for it gives us our only opportunity of relieving Bread of Shame. This fact alone, however, does not oblige us to grope blindly in spiritual darkness. The purpose of the original restriction was to impart to man an element of free will sufficient for the removal of Bread of Shame. We have a choice in the matter of spirituality, the extent of which rests in our ability to recognize the negative Desire to Receive for the Self Alone and consciously act against it.

Spiritual circuitry requires conscious resistance. Either we restrict and reveal the Light or we do not restrict and remain in darkness. Unless, by his voluntary resistance, man acts contrary to the negative aspect of Desire, the purpose of his existence will never be revealed. This principle of kabbalistic metaphysics was established at the *Tzimtzum* and it will remain with us until Bread of Shame has been completely alleviated and the *tikkun* process, the cycle of spiritual correction, has come full circle. Only then will we as a species again receive the Light's blessing without the need for our conscious intervention in behalf of the Light.

Unlike the negative pole of the filament of a light bulb, man has the option of restricting in order to bring forth the unique Light of his existence. Thus, the kabbalist adopts an ongoing attitude of restriction, because by so doing, he or she dispels the illusion and brings Light to himself and the world. When one consciously resists the negative impulse of Desire to Receive for the Self Alone, a new and blissful state of consciousness is achieved in which the negative aspect of Desire is converted into the positive Desire to Receive for the Sake of Sharing. This simple mechanism has the unique capability of erasing all illusions.

Just as the positive polarity seeks to fulfill the desire of the negative, the Emanator wants nothing more than to satisfy our every desire. In fact, kabbalists believe that every wish is immediately fulfilled on the level of the metaphysical and that all one must do to receive the benefit of that wish is to reject the impulse which first brought it into being. The paradox is that when man's negative polarity, which is expressed as the illusion of lack, accepts the Light which is freely offered, none of his spiritual potential is revealed, but if he rejects the Light then, contrarily, all of his potential is manifested.

The moment we experience the illusion of lack, the moment we feel deprived of love, of companionship, of money or creature comforts, and we are conscious of it, that is the moment to exercise voluntary restriction, for by so doing the illusion of lack is dispelled. Conscious resistance of this nature establishes a circuit with the Light that banishes the illusion of darkness to the nether regions of one's existence.

Consciousness, from the kabbalistic viewpoint, consists of a concerted and continuous effort to restrict the negative Desire to Receive for the

Self Alone so as to convert it into the positive Desire to Receive for the Sake of Sharing. This, and not some misplaced need for self-depravation, is the reason why kabbalists restrict the impulse to accept for selfish reasons the Emanator's Endless Blessings. By refusing to succumb to the Desire to Receive for the Self Alone the kabbalist creates the circuitry necessary for his own unique fulfillment.

A WORLD OF DIFFERENCE

The original text in which the Ari's disciples first described the principles of what would later be known as Lurianic Kabbalah contains reference to the Light "moving down" through the Four Phases of Emanation. Today, the extension of the Upper Light through the Phases of Emanation is similarly termed descent, which refers to the process by which the Light becomes increasingly denser, or we might say more obscured by the illusion, as it extends from the *Ein Sof.*

Also, that which is Above, meaning closer to the *Or Ein Sof,* was designated as being purer than that which is Below, or closer to the level of consciousness found in this Fourth Phase, *Malchut,* the World of Action. Thus, we say that the Light descends through the Four Phases from Above to Below, the higher, or purer levels being closer to the source, *Or Ein Sof.* The lower or denser levels being closer to the Curtain of this Fourth Phase, is the Middle Point where all Light is revealed.

To put this into a more functional perspective, let us consider a situation in which information is passed from one person to another, who then passes it on again, and so on. Generally speaking, each person, consciously or otherwise, modifies the information, embellishes and diminishes it, until eventually the original ideas can hardly be recognized. The information becomes clothed, we might say, or obscured as it extends from its original source and passes through the various Vessels, the people through whom it is passing.

Fortunately, not all of our words and ideas are destined to descend into obscurity by the process of passing them on. Some might actually be improved and elevated, if those to whom we are speaking are motivated by Desire to Receive for the Sake of Sharing. In such instances, the illusionary process is superceded through the principle of Returning Light.

Take for example the so-called "think tanks" in which scholars meet to formulate new concepts, or the simple brainstorming sessions in which friends get together to create something for the common good. In situations such as these, the participants sometimes speak in terms of bouncing ideas off one another, a concept that demonstrates the kabbalistic principle of Returning Light.

When we are motivated by Desire to Receive for the Sake of Sharing we trigger the principle of Returning Light and instead of becoming more dense or clothed with illusion our ideas can become elevated by the process of reflective interaction. In our think tank example the motivating influence of the people involved is more likely to be Desire to Receive for the Sake of Sharing than the negative Desire to Receive for the Self Alone and thus the participants are apt to be rewarded with results that surpass their original intentions. Whereas when little or no resistance is established, such as in our first example, the original ideas are apt to be lost as they descend into what we might call an ever deepening abyss of illusion.

In this world of illusion everything must go through process of descent, meaning that it must traverse the gap between the positive polarity and the negative. The extent of our free will rests in our ability to exercise the principle of Returning Light, such as in our example of the brainstorming session, and thus remove ourselves from the illusion by relieving Bread of Shame. *Or* we can exercise no resistance, such as in our first example, and remain in the world of illusion.

The Light's only aspiration is to fill us with its endless abundance, to restore to us a condition of complete spiritual and also of material contentment. However, the Light relinquished the ability to reveal its endless blessing at the time of the *Tzimtzum*. Had it not done so we would have no way of relieving Bread of Shame. And that is why it is up to us to reveal the infinite Light of our beings and to bring spiritual and material abundance to our lives. With an attitude of restriction, meaning resistance to the Desire to Receive for the Self Alone, we can defeat the illusion and reveal the Light within.

Part Four

Art of Living

Chapter 18

The One Percent Solution

Only a minute fraction of physical reality, let us for the sake of this discussion say one percent, is dominated by Desire to Receive for the Self Alone. The other ninety-nine percent, which represents that aspect of existence that we share with all things animal, vegetable, and mineral, is not influenced in the least by the negative aspect of desire. The one percent is the source of all of our problems. It is the one percent that harbors all of our illusions. And thus it is only that one percent which we must restrict in order to reveal the totality of our endless illumination.

According to the ancient kabbalistic wisdom, the animal, vegetal, and mineral kingdoms are essentially the same, the only difference being that the higher levels of the chain of life possess more Desire to Receive than the lower levels. Unlike the animal, vegetable, and mineral kingdoms, man alone has the ability, and it might be said the burden, of having to turn on the switch, so to speak, to reveal Light. All other beings and inanimate objects have an instinctual mechanism with which to reveal Endless Illumination.

All matter possesses Desire to Receive. Yet man, and man alone, is obliged to restrict the negative facet of Desire to alleviate Bread of Shame. The difference between a man and an animal rests solely in man's ability and obligation to restrict the minuscule fragment of his existence (the one percent), which is dominated by the negative aspect of Desire. Man can switch it on or off, meaning he can either restrict, thereby creating a circuit, or he can succumb to the Desire to Receive for the Self Alone and remain in spiritual darkness. Only when we trigger the energy-intelligence of restriction does our Light become revealed.

99.44% PURE

A certain soap commercial attests to its product being 99.44% pure. And yet it is quite amazing how many people are allergic to that product and break out in hives every time they use it. Such is the nature of impurity. A speck of dirt can, for some people, make a bowl of soup unappetizing. A spoonful of PCB's can contaminate an entire reservoir, making millions of gallons of water undrinkable.

A little impurity goes a long way.

A similar situation exists in the world as it relates to the illusion. The illusion of darkness comprises only a tiny fraction of the entire cosmic picture, let us say one percent. The other ninety-nine percent is Light, the true Reality. However, the vast majority of people live in only the illusion. Where there is Light, they see darkness; where there is good, they see evil; where there is truth, they see only fiction.

Why, if there's so much reality around are we so blind to its presence?

The answer, of course, like the answer to every question, can be found in the *Ein Sof* before the Thought of Creation. Remember, it was we who asked to share in the process of Creation and by so doing caused the reign of darkness to prevail. Thus we have no one to blame if we are slaves to the illusion and darkness rules our lives.

Evil is an illusion that is animated by our failure to act against it. Through resistance, we can liberate the Light and in the process free ourselves. When the one percent is dominated by the energy-intelligence of the Desire to Receive for the Self Alone darkness seems to encompass everything, even the ninety-nine percent, which is the Light. This, of course, is an illusion. No negative impulse can exist in the Endless presence of the *Or Ein Sof*. By succumbing to the negative aspect of Desire we allow the darkness to triumph over the Light.

Contrarily, by converting the negative aspect of Desire, the Desire for the Self Alone into the positive, the Desire for the Sake of Sharing, we end the reign of darkness and the Light is again revealed.

In the Messianic Age, much will change as a result of a simple conversion of energy. The Desire to Receive for the Self Alone will be converted into the Desire to Receive for the Sake of Sharing. Thus the fraction of Reality that is now obscured by illusion will disappear. For some that age is here today. For those who understand and exercise the principle of resistance in their daily lives, the illusion of darkness holds little sway. The object, then, for the kabbalist, is to achieve an altered state of consciousness by which he or she can remove the illusion and again unveil the Light.

THE SHORTEST DISTANCE BETWEEN
TWO POINTS

According to the laws of geometry, the shortest distance between two points is a straight line. This is true in the world of illusion. In Reality, however, meaning from the Infinite perspective, the shortest distance between any two points is a circle. By creating a circuit of energy, meaning a circular connection with the Light, one is instantly connected with everything, everywhere, which, according to Kabbalah, is not only the shortest distance between two points, but the only connection truly worth making.

SUCCESS AND FAILURE

The Desire to Receive is comprised of two aspects: Desire to Receive for Oneself Alone and Desire to Receive for the Sake of Sharing. The former is a byproduct of the Line, the latter emerges from the Circle. Kabbalah, therefore, designates the former as illusionary while the latter is deemed real. Of all the life forms and energy intelligences in the animal, vegetable, and mineral kingdoms, we (mankind) alone are subject to the snares and entanglements created by false desires stemming from the impure, linear illusion, for only we have been given the opportunity and the responsibility of alleviating Bread of Shame.

No thought, deed, or endeavor will ever succeed on anything other than the illusionary level if it is based in the impure aspect of Desire to Receive. Those ventures that are motivated by false desires lead inevitably to failure. Therefore, one may look at almost any failure, defeat, or lack of attainment and instantly conclude that it was borne of an impure (false) cause.

Yet personal failures should not necessarily be looked upon with regret. They can be viewed as lessons, opportunities for correction, re-connecting mechanisms in the circle of spiritual adjustment, transformation and reincarnation. Kabbalistically speaking there is only one true criterion for the measurement of success or failure and that is how well one succeeds in determining and applying the singular activity by which each of us recreates affinity with the Light.

How is it that some people seem impervious to their failures while others are totally debilitated by them?

Those who measure themselves according to standards prescribed by others, by the media, by the educational system, by conventional societal dictates or the narrow precepts imposed by dogmatic religious beliefs are far more apt to suffer as a result of failure than are those who measure success and failure according to their own unique requirements. Inevitably those who succeed must meet certain personal prerequisites, but certainly these have little or nothing to do with the conventional injunctions foisted upon us by the illusionary material dream. It means nothing to succeed according to the standards of others if one does not also succeed according to his or her own ethics and principles.

The moment we acknowledge a failure as something other than a lesson and an opportunity for correction we give it credence and establish it as a reality. And so we find that measuring ourselves against the standards set by others makes us immediately susceptible to this debilitating syndrome. Kabbalah teaches that one should never see oneself as lacking in anything for the very acknowledgement of deficiency creates deficiency, as does the acceptance of failure establish failure. Is it not more prudent and desirable to avoid, as much as possible, the debilitating carousel of self depravation that revolves around false comparisons?

The only reality in this world is the eternal aspect that results from restriction. Thus the kabbalist restricts lack and resists deficiency, because by so doing he or she creates affinity with the first act of Restriction, *Tzimtzum*. The *Or Ein Sof* is immeasurable in its perfection. We, too, have an element of perfection, an Infinite aspect that transcends finite comparisons and limited rational understanding. Only the finite, limited, corporeal aspect of ourselves is imperfect, and that facet of our existence, as has been well established, is illusion. Therefore the only success that can be gained by gratifying false linear (finite) desires is false success that, by any real standard, can only be deemed failure.

PERMANENT AND TEMPORARY REMNANT

The Ari stated that, "... in the matter of the devolvement of the Light from place to place, there are two forms of remnant in the places traversed: The first is permanent remnant, which means the mixing and binding with the Light already found at the level—the two lights becoming one as if they had always been one; the second is merely a temporary remnant, in other words there is no mixing and binding with the Light found there. The Lights remain distinct." He further stated that, "... the Light of the Line, which traverses the levels of Circles, does not do so as a permanent remnant but merely as a temporary remnant, to teach us that it is not mixed with the Light of the Circles to form one Phase, rather it is found there distinct and in its own Phase."

This abstruse-sounding text, when deciphered, reveals a number of kabbalistic truths and has various practical applications. First, though, let us attempt to explain or otherwise allay such questions as might be raised by the language of what has been stated thus far. What did the Ari mean by words such as traverses, passes, and devolvement? Was he not speaking of Light that kabbalists believe to be Endless, timeless and perfectly still? If, as the kabbalists say, the Light is everywhere, how can it possibly traverse anything? And if It is eternal and Infinitely abundant, how can It accurately be spoken of in terms of devolvement, and moving from place to place?

Again we confront the difficulty in attempting to describe deeply spiritual images with common language. Only from the illusionary, finite perspective does movement of any kind seem to occur. From the Light's perspective, nothing moves from place to place, or devolves, or diminishes through the successive stages of Emanation. Light is everywhere, at the center of the Earth, at the bottom of the sea, in darkest space, in the marrow of our bones. So in Reality, meaning from the Infinite perspective, nothing whatever happens to the Light; Its energy is ubiquitous and never changing.

What the Ari is attempting to impart is that the Circular Vessels, which might aptly be described as "the real me," encompass everything that one will ever acquire in the way of knowledge, but because of the *tikkun* process and our need to absolve Bread of Shame, the Circular Vessels, of necessity, although they are here, ever-present, and although they completely permeate every level of Earthly and metaphysical existence, must, because of the illusionary process, appear from our limited, finite perspective in the illusionary world as if they do not exist.

By passing the Ari was referring to information of any kind that fails to make an impression upon us. Obviously some information makes a distinct impression upon us while other information passes as we say "over our heads." Some knowledge is "etched" into our memory banks, while other knowledge "goes in one ear and out the other." That information which seems to "pass through" is termed temporary remnant, while that which remains, becoming a permanent part of our finite consciousness is termed by the Ari to be permanent remnant.

The Circular Lights, our inner Encircling Vessels, contain all of the information, all of the knowledge and the wisdom that one can ever hope to possess. In terms of the Infinite picture, the Light of the Circles certainly preceded the Light of the Line (everything originated from the Circular Light), however, from our limited perspective the opposite is true: It is the Light of the Line that precedes the Light of the Circles, for only when the latter connects with the former is any Infinite Illumination revealed to us. The Light of the Circles is always here. It is simply concealed from our view until it is acted upon by the Light of the Line.

As to the matter of permanent and temporary remnant, we all realize that certain information remains with us while other information seems never to become embedded in our consciousness and subsequently seems to disappear. Does this have anything to do with the information or the medium through which the information was coming to us? For instance, if a good teacher makes an important point while we happen to be daydreaming, is this any fault of the teacher? Of course not. Is the information the teacher is trying to impart in any way lessened by our failure to listen? Yes, but only from our point of view. For another example let us examine a situation in which the sun is shining but we choose to remain in the shade of an umbrella. Is the sun in any way affected by our decision to remain hidden from it? No, only from our perspective beneath the umbrella does the light of the sun seem to be diminished. It is this same phenomenon that the Ari is referring to when he makes the distinction between permanent and temporary remnant.

An old kabbalistic saying serves as an apt illustration of permanent and temporary remnant. "Some people live seventy years as one day, others live one day as seventy years." Except in the case of *tzadikim,* such as Moses or the Ari, who are totally connected to the Light and thus require no spiritual correction, a life without change is a life not worth living. If no change takes place in a person's life, meaning that if a person goes through life without making any attempt to connect with the reality, the Circular Light of his or her inner being, there can be no spiritual correction, which after all is the purpose of our Earthly existence.

It is up to us to consciously form connections with and thus reveal the permanent remnant within us. To not do so is to derive no more from our lives than if we had lived only one day. Light is revealed through the illusionary process; for that is the world we exist in. We must make every attempt to capture the Light of the "real me," otherwise life passes by and we reveal nothing of our Infinite nature.

This is what the Ari is referring to when he states that, "The Light of the Line that traverses the levels of Circles does not do so as permanent remnant, but merely as temporary remnant. The Circles are within us, and they contain everything that the Line will ever provide them with, but unfortunately we need the illusionary process because that is our only way of removing Bread of Shame. It is for this reason that kabbalists consider the Light of the Line to be of far greater importance than the Light of the Circles.

So it must be until that day when the cycle of our spiritual correction is complete and we return to our place of ultimate spiritual fulfillment within the Endless Circle of the *Or Ein Sof.*

ALL VIBRATION IS MUSIC

Like life itself, sound contains many levels and frequencies, some which are beyond the range of our perceptions, others which are not. Each of us listens at different emotional, intellectual, and spiritual frequencies, depending on various factors and variables. Our mood can play a part in what we hear, our attitude, our frame of mind, what kind of day we've had, what kind of pressures we are experiencing in our lives.

A hundred people may attend a lecture and each will come away with a different perspective on what the lecturer was attempting to say. Some will feel uplifted by the presentation, others may feel defeated. Also it is quite possible for a speaker to be sending messages that he or she had no intention of sending but that can still be readily comprehended by someone who is listening on a different frequency.

What we hear, then, depends largely on how we listen, and what we are able to perceive has less to do with the words that are spoken than on the direction and focus of the listener's ear. For example, some people have the unfortunate tendency of attempting to manipulate everything they hear so as to make it fit a certain ideology or obsession that, for selfish reasons, they happen to be attached or to which they are habitually tied. These people are not really listening and hence they do not really hear.

Sound, all sound, because it is ephemeral, is considered from the kabbalistic perspective to be illusionary. However, as with all that is of this World of Action, sound, too, embodies a large measure of Infinity. Thus if one listens intently, and if one's Desire to Receive is properly aligned and focused, and if one makes no attempt to manipulate the sounds that he or she is hearing so as to fit a selfish preconception, there is no reason why one might not find infinite delight in virtually any sound, from the babbling of a brook, to the ranting of an idiot, or even in the barking of a dog.

This is why it is possible for a wise man to listen to the words of a fool and hear wisdom, while another who may possess a genius I.Q., but who is motivated by the Desire to Receive for the Self Alone, may sit for years at the feet of an intellectual or spiritual master and not understand a single word. For the kabbalist, every sound holds the potential for union with the highest states of his or her spiritual existence.

CREATIVE DISENGAGEMENT

So conditioned have we become to living under the iron hand of the material illusion that today we serve the illusion that poses as reality and to pay tribute to its dominance, praying before the alter of the modern deities, Science and technology, genuflecting as the seemingly endless parade of material progress marches by. The great kabbalistic paradox, and one of the more lamentable ironies of this modern age, is that the so-called reality that we allow to rule us with impunity is a total illusion, whereas the so-called fantasy world of thoughts, dreams, daydreams, imaginings, meditation, so soundly maligned by many self-proclaimed realists, is much closer to being real.

According to the ancient wisdom of Kabbalah, reality diminishes in direct proportion to physicality. Thus, resistance to the finite material illusion is the key to unlocking the door to the gates of the only true Reality, that of the Infinite. By challenging the material illusion, one creates a circuit with the alternate universe of the mind and becomes a channel for higher states of consciousness. This is true control; this, not the tyranny of the material illusion, is the root of real self-determination and the way by which to transform life's negative polarity into the positive.

That which you resist you draw to you, that which you resist you become.

ON DEATH AND DYING

Did Moses die? The Bible says yes; the Kabbalah, however, says no. How can this seeming discrepancy be reconciled? The answer is that both opinions are correct, depending on one's point of view. From the finite perspective (meaning the limited vista seen from the illusionary world), yes, it is true that Moses died. From the Infinite perspective, however, he is still alive. The death spoken of in the Bible is the death of the illusion, the Desire to Receive for the Self Alone.

Friction, gravity, and air pressure will eventually cause a top to stop spinning. Consider, though, the possibility that the thought that sets a top in motion might continue on even after the body of the top has ceased turning, even for all time. In a frictionless environment a top would presumably spin forever. The spiritual realm is impervious to friction. Being without material substance, the Light of our beings is the state of the art in perpetual motion. Like a top set spinning in space, it is not subject to physical tribulations.

The part of us that is of the Light is not prone to change or decomposition. Only the body, the intelligence of which is the Desire to Receive, is susceptible to aging and death. The body dies, but the Infinite aspect of a person lives on in circles of return.

To die, then, is merely to shed that which is influenced by gravity and friction, namely the Desire to Receive for the Self Alone. Disease can kill a body, not a soul. Accidents, pain and suffering, catastrophes, chaos and confusion are all of the physical world. The world of the spirit, though it is in the same place as this world, functions in a state of utter stillness and tranquility, far beyond the stifling influence of gravity and other physical limitations.

That is not to say that the physical aspect of humanity is not also of the Endless. All that was of the Endless still is of the Endless. Every speck of matter is endowed with the Infinite Presence and also with the Desire to Receive for Itself Alone. Everything in this world has its roots in the Endlessness, and to the Infinite it will always belong.

Certainly it is true that the physical body decomposes upon death, but the material constituents of the body do not expire or disappear. The material merges with other components to form new objects and organisms. Nothing happens to the material itself. Change occurs only within the shaping influence that keeps each object or organism in its present form, namely, each individual organism's Desire to Receive for the Self Alone.

Physical death, then, is the dissolution of the body's Desire to Receive— this and nothing more. Only that which is negative, meaning controlled by Desire to Receive, is subject to change. However, although it is negative, Desire to Receive for the Self alone, also affords us our only opportunity to relieve Bread of Shame. Until one sheds all Desire to Receive for the Self Alone, he or she is obliged to return to this world of illusion to continue the process of correction.

Did Moses die? Yes and no. His body ceased to function as a Vessel for the Desire to Receive, but his spiritual legacy, his energy, that which transcended the Desire to Receive for the Self Alone, lives on. To the extent that Moses was physical, to the extent that physicality includes the Desire to Receive for the Self Alone, Moses died, but that part of him that transcended the Desire to Receive lives even today.

Rav Ashlag, in his translation of the *Zohar*, spoke eloquently of the death of Moses when he wrote that, "By his death he added more light, more life to the world."

TWO POINTS OF VIEW

Let us, for the sake of argument, pit the pessimist's view of life against that of the optimist.

The pessimist tells us that war and deception, death and duplicity, nationalism, ethnocentrism, terrorism—the trademarks of this modern age—are manifestations of the true nature of humanity. Man, he tells us, is an irredeemable villain, an incorrigible criminal, a rapist, a killer, a liar, and a cheat. He asserts that the world is populated by a virtual gang of thugs called the human race, most of whom would just as soon stab you in the back as give you a second glance, and concludes his argument with a statement to the effect that the living hell of violence, torture, starvation and terminal disease that man is harvesting is the price he must pay for the seeds of evil he has sown—a retribution for which he is only too well deserving.

Next the optimist stands before us holding up a sprig of leaves. He challenges us to look closely at the miracle that is a leaf and then try to tell him that this world is not a wondrous place. Life, he tells us, is two lovers on a sun drenched meadow, it is a drop of dew on a cactus in the first light of a desert morning, it is a river that runs to the ocean, it is the miracle of procreation. Love, he asserts, is the motivating force in the world. Yes, bad things happen, unfortunate, isolated incidents, but the bad is far outweighed by the good. The optimist assures us that people, at the core, are good and honest. In conclusion he states that we should be grateful for this life—for each day is a joy and a blessing, and each and every one of us is a jewel of creation.

Which one are we to believe?

Of course, by now the student of Kabbalah is aware that the chasm between ourselves and the Light of Creation was of our own making, because by demanding individuation from the Creator we also inherited the responsibility of re-illuminating our Encircling Vessels and thus absolving Bread of Shame. The separation between ourselves and what kabbalists call the real world—meaning the world of the Endless—causes us to be oblivious to the Infinite Light around us. While the world we do see, the negative world of Illusion and Restriction, represents only the smallest fraction of the big picture—the grand scheme of things—it is still the world that most of us deal with exclusively.

So who is right, the pessimist or the optimist? Is this world a living heaven or a living hell? It all depends on one's point of view. From the perspective of the Lower Seven we see the negative side of existence; from the point of view of the Upper Three we see the positive. The kabbalist seeks to bridge the gap between the two through the art of well tempered resistance.

Chapter 19

Crime and Punishment

ANSWER TRUE OR FALSE:

A. Crime pays.

B. Most crimes go unpunished.

C. The more selfish one is, the more cutthroat, the higher one will be able to climb up the ladder of success.

D. Some people get away with murder.

E. It is sometimes possible to cheat the system of restriction and Receive for the Self Alone.

If you answered false to all of the above questions you are well on the way to becoming a kabbalist. No crime goes unpunished, no sin escapes retribution.

Ridiculous, you say? Outrageous! What about the thieves who are never caught? Look at all the loan sharks and black-marketeers who amass fortunes through their shady dealings. Look at the risk arbitragers who make hundreds of millions trading on insider information. And what about the cocaine barons who have all but wrested control of certain South American governments?

True, in light of the evidence it would seem that no sane person could possibly deny that many people get away with all sorts of crimes, even murder, every day of the week. Many people profit from crime, but only from the perspective of the illusion. In reality, meaning from the infinite perspective, the builder who cuts costs on hidden corners, the businessman who skims profits, the broker who trades on inside information, the thief, the killer, or anyone who benefits at the detriment of others, may achieve windfall profits and certainly have the ability to amass a mountain of material possessions, but if his or her actions were motivated solely by Desire to Receive for the Self Alone he or she will receive only the outward appearance of those acquisitions, the title to the goods, but not the goods themselves, the things, but not their intrinsic value.

The material trappings accumulated by the person who is motivated by Desire to Receive for the Self Alone will be just that—traps, prisons from which the only escape is restriction. Instead of enjoyment, they will give him only grief. He may own many homes, but he will never feel at home in them. He may possess beautiful and priceless art objects, but they will impart less true pleasure to him than if they were dollar signs scrawled on a wall. As much time and effort as he might have expended, as difficult as his task might have been, as materially prosperous, as brilliant and incisive as his actions may have appeared to others, the person who is inspired by the negative aspect of desire will receive no lasting satisfaction from the spoils of his greed motivated labors.

Ironically, all of the acquisitions accumulated by greedy people only cause them greater discomfort. If the same people were to restrict and thus remove the illusion, they would acquire the contentment that eludes them. That is the paradox of Returning Light: By saying yes to the impulse to Receive for the Self Alone we get nothing, whereas by saying no to that same impulse we can, quite literally, "have it all."

When one negates the body's desire for comfort (especially in the form of luxury and opulence), one gives comfort to the soul. By choosing to remain in a state of unfulfillment the kabbalist acts as a filament, a

Third Column mediator, and thus is able to establish a circuit with the Light.

No doubt this concept would be scorned as something akin to blasphemy by the growing segment of the population that deifies money, worships at the feet of the rich and famous, and has made a religion of material acquisition. Today, the prevailing attitude seems to be that any means is justified if it comes to a profitable end. And, indeed, statistics seem to bear out the fact that the majority of crimes do go unpunished. And certainly we can all cite examples of criminals and businessmen who have made millions by taking advantage of those less fortunate than themselves. Nonetheless, it is a fallacy to think that money and material possessions will automatically bring us fulfillment. The only act that imparts true contentment is restriction.

The illusion is given weight and substance by our thoughts and actions. By accepting the illusion as our reality we make it real. The thief sustains the illusion, as does the cocaine baron, the inside trader, and all people who better themselves at the expense of others. The person who succumbs to the negative aspect of desire perpetuates the illusion, whereas the kabbalist, by his or her resistance, destroys the illusion and reveals the Light. The difference between the kabbalist and the person who is motivated by the negative aspect of desire is that whereas the latter, the thief, the inside trader, the greed motivated businessman, attempts to achieve fulfillment by satisfying the Desire to Receive for the Self Alone, the kabbalist achieves true fulfillment by rejecting that same impulse.

Failure to restrict the negative aspect of desire produces a short circuit which causes one to remain in a state of robotic consciousness. Surrendering to the illusion perpetuates the darkness and imparts pleasure to no one. The conscience of the person who is motivated by the negative aspect of desire carries a heavy burden, the weight of illusion, the darkness, the blindness that is the constant companion of the Desire to Receive for the Self Alone. The kabbalist, contrarily, has no excess freight to carry; his conscience is clean, his vision unobstructed.

Fulfillment exists only in the real world, the endless world in which the Desire to Receive for the Self Alone has absolutely no influence. Desire to Receive for the Self Alone preserves the illusion; voluntary resistance destroys it. Restriction creates an altered state of consciousness by which to bridge the gap between ourselves and the Light.

The Creator restricted His benevolence so that we, the emanated, would have a way of absolving Bread of Shame. Through conscious, voluntary resistance we impart pleasure to the Creator and also bring Light into our lives. By paying tribute to the original act of Restriction, the *Tzimtzum*, which we do when we resist and thus expose the illusion, we enable the Light to be revealed. For illusion cowers in the presence of Reality; darkness cannot exist where there is Light.

The goal of the kabbalist, then, is to redirect his or her thought processes in such a way as to bring about the end of the reign of the illusion and restore illumination to the world and also, as a consequence, to him or herself. This may strike the reader as being at best a difficult, if not an impossible, task until one considers that despite its seeming omniscience, the one percent that is illusion has a very tenuous existence that even a small degree of resistance can easily destroy. Even a little resistance can illuminate a large, dark space. Light a match in a totally darkened airplane hangar and every corner will, at least to some small degree, be exposed.

Such is the beauty of Returning Light.

Thus, through conscious resistance, does the kabbalist serve the needs of both Light and Vessel. By transforming the negative aspect of desire into the positive he or she exposes the illusion of darkness to the Light of reality. The Light is everywhere, ready, willing, and able, at the slightest provocation (resistance), to reveal its endless presence. Through conscious resistance to the Desire to Receive for the Self Alone the kabbalist acts in the manner of a match in an airplane hangar, or the filament in a light bulb, establishing a circuitous flow of energy, which in turn creates a wide circle of Light, even from a small amount of resistance.

This considered, let us return to the question: Does crime pay? No, those who engage in crime merely serve to perpetuate the illusion. The same is true of all those who succumb to the Desire to Receive for the Self Alone. While it may seem as though the criminal is escaping punishment for his crimes, and the shrewd captains of commerce and industry, who seemingly let nothing or no one stand in their way, are prospering at the expense of others, in reality, the thief is stealing from himself, the killer is committing suicide, the inside trader is trading in his soul. In the real world no crime goes unpunished, no sin escapes retribution.

A FABLE OF TWO BROTHERS

Long ago, there lived two brothers who were as different as two people could possibly be. In fact, you could search the whole world over and be unlikely to discover two young men with so little in common. For whereas the elder was studious, the younger cared nothing for books and learning; and while the elder was courteous, the younger tended to be quite rude; and though the elder ate and drank moderately, the younger ate gluttonously and drank like a proverbial fish.

The elder brother aspired to be a *tzadik*, a righteous one, and to that end he applied himself with unmitigated diligence. Early in life, he had been called by some deep, inner longing to live an austere and ascetic existence. And so, in deference to those whom he considered his spiritual forbears, the righteous ones of old, he prayed and studied the ancient wisdom, resisted comfort and complacency, and avoided, as much as was humanly possible, all Earthly pleasures—all, that is, save one. The sole diversion he did allow himself, if it could be called that, was to sing a single hymn of jubilation, each evening.

The positive example set by the elder brother was, needless to say, not for a moment emulated by the younger. Quite to the contrary, the only mandates that the younger brother was interested in fulfilling were those of his untamed libido. Indeed, it was with deliberation equal to that of his older brother's piety and goodness that the younger engaged in all manner of hedonistic and reckless pursuits. His profligacy had made him a local legend, and, verily, the infamy was well deserved. He could eat any three men under the table, and was sometimes heard to threaten that he might one day drink the entire county dry—a threat that was not lightly taken. The life of any party, and quite a lady's man, too, the younger brother was always accompanied by a coterie of woman and a cluster of friends and hangers-on.

For fear that the reader might credit the younger brother's popularity to wit, charisma, charm, or even to his vainly handsome appearance, it should be explained that such was anything but the case. Nor should the younger's renowned generosity be mistaken as an emblem of a compassionate heart. No, alas, neither was the circumstance. In truth, the state of affairs that existed then are no different from the one that endures to this day; it has never been terribly difficult to find those who will gladly assist one in squandering an inheritance, no matter how meager it may happen to be. And as for the younger's generosity, it was born not from kindness, but rather from guilt, so deeply ingrained that it was not even perceived by him, much less admitted to. For, unlike the elder brother who had been a good and dutiful son, the younger had rarely lifted so much as a finger on his late father's behalf.

Additionally, lest the reader be inundated by mistaken impressions, it must also be clarified that the notable contrast in their personalities caused the brothers to harbor no great animosity toward each other. Despite their differences, there was, in fact, hardly a morsel of enmity between them. Their upbringing by a recently deceased , kindly merchant, and a loving, doting mother instilled in them tolerance and a disposition to live and let live, and, accordingly, they got on well for the most part—though, to be sure, neither approved of the other's protocol and they did have their share of arguments. Always, though, in the end, when the heat of the battle cooled, all was forgiven.

So it came as no great surprise one sunny morning in the late spring of the year 1653, when the two brothers bid farewell to their separate circles of friends, and gave their mother goodbye kisses and numerous assurances of their safe return, and set out walking toward a distant mecca of art, commerce and culture. Nor should it strain any reasonable reader's credulity to discover that their intended aims and expectations for making this journey, like the brothers themselves, were as different as darkness and light. For whereas the elder brother hoped to find a certain *tzadik* who was rumored to be seeking a spiritual apprentice, and whom he would humbly beg to aid in his quest to become a righteous one himself, contrarily, the younger brother had heard tales of the city's many lewd and lascivious pleasures, of which he hoped to sample but a few.

The days passed amicably. Mile after mile, village after village, county after county, they walked, conversing and arguing good-naturedly, occasionally pausing to gaze upon some uncommon sight, to hear some unusual sound, or to rest and eat by the banks of an algae-laden pond or a fast running brook. By night, though, they went their separate ways. While the elder brother read the Bible by firelight, meditated, and sang his nightly song, the younger brother, depending on their proximity to a town or village, would either eat and drink himself into a stupor, or, in the event that a town was nearby, would go off in search of wine, women and song.

A week passed and the better part of another. The halfway point was well behind them. The elder brother felt thoroughly invigorated. Not so, the younger, whose constant drunkenness and nightly bacchanalia were taking a heavy toll. Mornings were most difficult. He detested mornings to begin with, and at normal times he did his best to avoid them, often not rising until the sun's disagreeable glare had begun to wane in the evening sky. On the road, however, it was imperative to put in as many miles as possible during daylight hours.

Rather than admit to the adverse effects of his over-indulgence, the younger brother would always bravely rise at the elder's prodding, laugh off his aching head and pretend that all was well. Thus, he would stoically sally forth with throbbing temples and squinty, dark rimmed, bloodshot eyes, a dull ache in the pit of his stomach, and a sour aftertaste left over from the previous evening's revelry that often would linger through most of the day.

As might be expected, the younger brother soon tired of this facade and so he was greatly pleased and relieved when a fierce storm struck one evening at a time when they happened to be in sight of a rustic, though agreeable looking village inn, which would, he hoped, afford him a quiet room, a hot bath, and a chance to recuperate from the past fortnight's dissipation. His expectations, however, proved ill-founded. When the two brothers inquired as to the availability of lodgings, the innkeeper, though seemingly sympathetic, informed them that several other travelers before them had sought shelter from the storm, the result being that every room was taken. After seeing the younger's debilitated condition, though, the innkeeper did offer, for a modest sum, to set up two cots in a corner of the room that was used by the inn's patrons for eating and imbibing alcoholic beverages.

While in no sense an ideal situation, the brothers considered the cold, wet alternative and accepted the innkeeper's offer, the elder thinking that perhaps fate had brought him here with the object of furthering his spiritual education, the younger having no thoughts whatsoever other than to rest his aching head and weary bones. While he was loathe to admit it, the younger brother was feeling more flushed, feverish, and utterly wretched with every passing minute and wanted nothing more than to sink into oblivion.

Ruddy, rowdy, Brueghel like figures crammed the smoke drenched dining room. Townsfolk, farmers, peasants, and travelers were talking, smoking, drinking, laughing, all of them seemingly intent upon making as much noise, while consuming as much as was humanly possible. These were the younger brother's kind of people, and on any other night he would have joined the festivities, but on this particular evening the very sight of so much gusto was enough to cause his head to spin and his stomach to do lazy cartwheels in sympathy.

While the innkeeper and his wife were setting up two cots in a shaded corner of the room, three of the patrons, thick of hand and of girth, called over to the brothers in drink thickened voices, offering to buy them a drink. The brothers smiled politely, waved across the noisy, smoke filled room while patting their lumpy, hay filled mattresses, as if to say, "thanks but no thanks."

At the younger's request, the elder took the cot nearest the wall, while the younger occupied the one closest to the night's cacophonous proceedings—the younger's logistics being based on the possibility that his dizzy head and churning stomach might give him cause to effectuate a hasty retreat out of the thick, unpainted, weathered hardwood door. Thus, they settled in, as best they could, to sleep.

The elder brother had not the least difficulty getting to sleep. Only minutes later, when the younger groaned to him about the noise and the smoke, the elder, who was facing the wall, snoozed heavily in reply. For the younger, however, sleep was as elusive as a swarm of fruit flies. The din, the smoke, and the laughter, seemed, in his increasingly feverish condition, to be conspiring against him. The evening's revelry seemed, at times, to be going on right inside his skull, his nerve endings, and in the very marrow of his bones. At other times, the babble of voices no longer seemed human, but like the barking of a kennel full of rabid strays. He tossed and twisted, stirring restlessly for an hour, maybe two, before falling into fitful, though blessed, insensibility.

About the same time as he fell asleep, it dawned upon the three thick-set revelers, who had earlier asked the brothers to share a drink with them that perhaps the two strangers had refused them not out of simple fatigue, as their motions had seemed to suggest. One of the three suggested that the brothers' refusal to drink with them might have been the result of just plain high-and-mightiness. Perhaps they thought themselves too good to drink with three men who made their living by the sweat of their brows and the strength of their backs and hands. In no time, the brothers' simple gesture of refusal, in the hazy brains of the three muscle-bound drunkards, had been blown all out of proportion, taking on the dimensions of a hard slap across the face.

With this in mind, the three ruddy-faced drunkards arose laboriously from their overburdened chairs and wobbled over to have a closer look at the two insolent toplofty snobs who had the temerity to judge good men based upon the sketchiest evidence. They loudly cursed the audacity of those who would spurn and then rudely sleep through such a glorious festival of over-indulgence as they, out of the goodness of their hearts, had offered to share with these two sleeping ingrates.

Being that the younger brother's cot was positioned nearest them, it was he upon whom the brutes started beating. A hand must have instinctively leapt out as he was waking and struck one of his attackers quite forcibly on the cheek—at least that was one of the complaints lodged against him as they hauled him from his bed, still half asleep, and commenced to push him around and then to slap him and then to pummel him with blows to his body and his undefended face and head.

As for the possibility of extricating himself, there was none. As for reasoning with them, that too was impossible. His protests fell on deaf ears. As for why they were doing this, he had not the slightest idea. All he did know was that three vaguely familiar brutes with hot, stale breath, scowling red veined faces, and anvils where their hands should have been, were beating him half senseless for no apparent reason. Worse, his fever and depleted condition gave him neither the strength nor the conviction to give back even half so good as he was getting. So, there he was, poor fellow, hardly able to defend himself, and without even the benefit of his customary instinct for self-preservation, which under normal circumstances was quite considerable.

Fortunately, for the sake of our young casualty, the innkeeper intervened to mediate on his behalf before the brutes had damaged him too seriously. This act of sensible interposition, however, was hastily nullified by other deeds which were, to the victim's way of thinking, outright travesties. Instead of having the louts arrested, as the owner of any respectable establishment would have done, or at very least treating the drunkards to a bum's rush into the cold night, the innkeeper verily coddled the thugs instead and called them all by name. He gently chided the drunken brawlers in a tone that carried no more indignity than one would use on an errant child who had purposefully spilled a glass of milk.

Contempt gave way to bitterness, pain to self pity as the younger brother sat on the lumpy mattress and nursed his wounds. He had a split lip, a lump on his head, possibly a cracked rib, or worse, and his attackers were back at their seats, ordering another round, and being treated as if they had created no more than a minor annoyance. Where was the justice?

And where had his brother been while all this was going on? Hard though it was to imagine, the man had been, and still was, deep in slumber. A wave of incoherence suddenly came crashing over the rocky shore of his inner being, causing him to conclude, unreasonably, that somehow his sleeping brother was to blame. Whereupon, he leaned over and shook the elder roughly.

The elder awoke to a barrage of harsh criticism for not having risen to the younger's defense. Seeing his brother's condition, of course, he felt only sympathy for him and not the slightest contempt. Indeed, his compassion grew more empathetic with each passing affront and insult. And nor did he make any attempt to defend himself against the tirade—for the poor man had obviously reached his breaking point. Finally, with quite words of comfort, he managed to calm the younger down, and to convince him that he should try to go back to sleep. The younger agreed to this suggestion in principle, but fearing a repeat performance by the brutes, he asked that the elder switch beds with him. And as many a loving brother would have done under similar circumstance, the elder more than gladly complied.

Be not mistaken as to the nature of the motivations of those who aspire to become *tzadikim*. While it may be true that a *tzadik* does not shy away from life's hardships and uncertainties, and it is true that he denies bodily comfort, he does so not out of some masochistic yearning, but for the purpose of achieving the greater pleasure that can be derived by completing the soul's cycle of correction. Thus the elder welcomed the opportunity to place himself between the thugs and his errant brother, but not because he had any desire to have the stuffing beaten out of him. If, however, his body did receive a pummeling, well so be it. Certainly, it would be for a reason. Perhaps some wrong deed in a previous life demanded retribution. At all events, he would accept what fate or providence had in store, firm in the conviction that the pain suffered by his body would be serving a higher purpose, namely, the purification of his soul. And so it was that the two brothers traded places, and, eventually, they drifted off to sleep.

Sure enough, later in the evening, as fate would have it, it dawned upon one of the three thugs that they had attacked only one of the impudent strangers, while sparing the other. This, in his inebriated judgment, did not seem equitable. Both were guilty of the same holier-than-thou impudence. Both had demonstrated equal conceit by refusing to share drink with them. Should they not, then, he asked his companions, mete out equal treatment to the other? The brutes agreed. In good conscience, they could not beat upon only one of the haughty newcomers and let the other off scot free. Justice demanded that the other receive equal retribution. The incident, long forgotten by the brothers, in the benumbed brains of the three brutes, had become a matter of honor, principle and integrity. There was no question that the other traveler, too, would have to be punched, kicked, and viciously cudgeled. Fair, after all, was only fair.

The brutes rose from their seats and lumbered over to the shadowed corner in which the two brothers were sleeping, both of them facing the wall. The thugs, of course, had no idea that the two brothers had switched beds, so quite naturally it was the man who was sleeping in the bed closest to the wall who was the target of their animosity. As it turned out, the ruffians did at least possess a grain of decency. Thinking that the man closest to them had already received his comeuppance, they took great pains not to disturb him. And that is how the younger brother came to be dragged out of bed a second time and given a thorough thrashing, while the elder slept.

A strange sensation overcame the younger brother as his body was suffering that second attack. Attribute it to fever, if you will, sickness, a concussion, or merely the utter absurdity of the situation, but he hardly felt the blows that were hailing upon him from all sides and angles. Whatever the cause, he was suddenly catapulted into an exquisite state of awareness, higher, purer, more lucid by far than any he had previously imagined. In those moments of mystical recognition his life came into clear and perfect focus. The facade of illusion with which he had always protected himself began to crack and then to crumble, leaving him alone with the naked reality of his empty existence. He saw it all: The futility of his hedonism and ribaldry, the price of his physical dissipation, and the true agony of his moral decay.

Those few seconds of mystical revelation taught him more than a lifetime of self-indulgence. And to whom did he owe this transformation if not the brutes? He laughed! How he laughed! Which, as it happened, did much toward lessening the severity of the beating. So uproarious did his laughter become that the oafs lost the thread of their concentration and became confused and disoriented. Little pleasure can be derived, even of the most brutal and vulgar kind, from striking a defenseless madman, especially one who takes pleasure in the beating!

The elder brother awoke to the sound of laughter—not just that of his brother, but others had also been bitten by the mirthful contagion, including the brutes, themselves! At that moment, he too underwent something of a transformation, for he understood what had happened and immediately realized that indeed fate, or some power higher than themselves had guided them to this inn on this rain swept night.

The two brothers never did complete their journey to the city. They had no need to. In that one evening, they had transcended any further need for restless wandering and the visceral agonies that pass for worldly experiences. And so it was that they returned to their village—two brothers who had become tzadiks. They lived long, productive, loving lives in the village and through the years many seekers traveled from far and wide to request their counsel or simply to pay respects.

In their later years, the two wise *tzadiks* would sometimes recall with fondness the night in the village inn, and remember the two beatings that the younger had suffered at the hands of those three brutes. And, as always, they would smile, bless the brutes, and thank them in their evening prayers.

Chapter 20

Victim of Circumstance

A common excuse for failing to live up to one's full potential is often stated with words to the effect that one has to make a living. Certainly, everyone must earn his keep in this world and everyone has an obligation to do all that one can to maintain and improve the living conditions of his or her family. Yet, this concept of "making a living" can be used to conceal or otherwise excuse a multitude of responsibilities, spiritual, emotional, and intellectual.

"A man's got to make a living." What is the habitual user of this old chestnut really saying if not ... it's out of my hands... it's not my fault... I'm a victim of circumstance? The very words make a living seem to denote something that is one step removed from living. In fact, it might be said that one whose energy is completely taken up in the making and not the living is not really living at all.

The concept of making a living can hide a multitude of emotional insecurities. It can be used as justification for a stock broker or other professional person to work ninety hours a week and rarely see his or her family. It can give one a reason to remain in a job that is neither enjoyable nor challenging. It can allow one to be obstinate and unforgiving, and absolve one for being complacent and emotionally unresponsive.

Did the Emanator place us here to engage exclusively in hand-to-mouth survival? Is material acquisition a fitting foundation on which to build a life? Are we merely slaves to the system, gears in government, corporate, or religious machinery, cogs in wheels of progress? Is life nothing more than a string of days for mindlessly, dutifully trudging through?

Kabbalah teaches that there is no such thing as a victim of circumstances. If we are victims it is of our own minds, our own patterns of thinking and perceiving. There is no empirical criterion by which to determine success or failure. The value of a person is internal and cannot be measured solely by his or her position or monetary worth.

An old parable tells of a holy man named Yohan, who earned his living as a cobbler. It is said that so completely had Yohan transcended the Desire to Receive for Oneself Alone that to wear his shoes was to feel shoeless, as if one were walking on air. Many people wondered why a man of such obvious gifts chose to remain a humble shoemaker, but Yohan had transcended his work entirely, transforming what for others appeared to be a menial task into an endeavor of the highest spiritual order.

According to the kabbalistic teachings, past incarnations determine the amount of desire possessed by each of us. We are born with a certain degree of longing that does not increase or diminish throughout each lifetime, but, regardless, the desire one is born with is always sufficient to meet one's spiritual needs. People who are born with a greater degree of desire have more spiritual ground to make up, so to speak, and therefore feel compelled to excel, to accomplish more than others. The reason that certain individuals who are born with blazing desires fail to achieve their full potential, while others who are born with comparatively little desire prosper, emotionally, spiritually, and financially lies in the ability of the person with the lesser desire to transform his or her Desire to Receive for Oneself Alone into a Desire to Receive for the Sake of Sharing.

The true measure of a person's worth lies not in the magnitude of his or her inborn desire, but in how positively or negatively one implements his or her inherent aspirations. No amount of ambition, if it is rooted in the negative aspect of desire can lead one to spiritual fulfillment. However, by transforming the negative aspect of desire into the positive aspect, work can then have the opposite effect of challenging a person to reach his or her full spiritual, emotional, and intellectual potential.

Thus, to the kabbalist's way of thinking, the choice between the Desire to Receive for Oneself Alone and the Desire to Receive for the Sake of Sharing is reduced to one of absurd simplicity. For whereas the person who is immersed totally in the Desire for Oneself Alone will never be satisfied in his or her work, the person who can transform his or her Desire to Receive for Oneself Alone into the Desire to Receive for the Sake of Sharing will find fulfillment in almost any non-violent occupation. And while those who are motivated by the negative aspect of desire can expect nothing more than material acquisition; those who are motivated by the positive aspect of desire can transcend negativity and achieve Infinite contentment.

WHAT IS LOVE?

This question elicits as many responses as there are people who care to formulate a response. Kabbalistically speaking there are only two kinds of love, illusionary and real, false and true. Let us examine the former for in this world it is by far the more prevalent.

False love is jealous.
False love tells lies.
False love is smug.
False love is boastful.
False love pays lip service.
False love is insecure.
False love deceives.

False love is greedy.
False love makes demands.
False love clings.
False love smothers.
False love is guilty.
False love "turns me on."
False love is placed on pedestals.
False love is paid for with dead mink.
False love divorces.
False love complains.
False love is convenient.
False love looks out for number one.
False love reads like a grocery list:
False love runs on empty.
False love is hate.

As elusive as a sub atomic tendency, as cranky as a wounded bear, as complicated as a Mack truck's transmission—false love eludes, frightens, and confuses us.

True love is sublimely simple, for unlike false love that has many desires real love has but one aspiration: To Share.

LACK

Kabbalah teaches that we lack nothing, that any deficiency we may experience is an illusion derived from the Lower Seven, the creative process of the Line. Does this mean that sadness is non-existent; that anger, confusion, desperation, the great chasm that separates us from ourselves and from others, is all just a figment of unreality? In a word, yes. According to Kabbalah, the Infinite aspect of existence, and hence of humanity, the First Three, is totally fulfilled. The lack we feel, the emptiness and alienation, the anger, the greed and envy are aspects of the Line, and the Line, as we have determined, is an illusion that was caused by the *Tzimtzum* and manifested in the Lower Seven of the Line.

The Creator's only aspiration is to share Endless beneficence. It was we, the emanated, who demanded free will sufficient to alleviate Bread of Shame. The reason we feel unfulfilled is that the Line transfers the illusion of space, the gap inherent in the Lower Seven, to our Infinite Encircling Vessels, the Head or First Three. The only reason we think we are not fulfilled is not because the Ten Vessels of the Circles, the Infinite aspect of existence, are unrevealed, but rather that the creative process of the Line creates a consciousness of depravation within the Circular Vessels, but only from the perspective of the Line.

The challenge faced by the kabbalist is to redirect his or her consciousness from the Lower Seven and raise it to the level of the Upper Three. Lack exists only in the world of illusion. Failure to restrict causes an individual to remain in the illusionary realm. Through the practice of positive resistance, the kabbalist transcends the negative aspect of the Curtain and rises to a state of consciousness that is impervious to the illusion presented by the Lower Seven, the Body of the Line.

The separation of the First Three from the Lower Seven was the primary qualification for the establishment of Creation, for without the aspect of voluntary restriction we would have no way of removing Bread of Shame. Such is the nature of the paradox that Light is brought into this world. Reality, the Circular and Infinite aspect of existence, must remain hidden to allow us the opportunity for correction. The constant sense of depravation, the personal and cultural alienation experienced by so many people in this world of unremitting stress and friction is a product of the Line, the illusion, but like any illusion it pates, cowers and finally surrenders when confronted by the face of Supreme Reality in the manner that darkness is always defeated when challenged by light.

From the perspective of the Higher Realms of awareness lack does not exist. When one has risen above the illusionary state of consciousness the negative babble of this world of resistance becomes interesting possibly, but seldom engaging emotionally. Yet, the fact that the kabbalist disconnects totally from this unreal world should not be taken to mean that he or she runs away or hides from negativity. It is not necessary to become a recluse or withdraw physically from society and civilization to transcend negative existence. Rather it is by confronting the darkness that the Light is revealed. The kabbalist meets reality, so to speak, head on, face to face, for it is through resistance that the Light is brought out of hiding. Thus does the kabbalist rise above the illusion of lack that is both the boon and the bane of humanity (in the sense that it tortures us while at the same time offering us the opportunity for correction) to again defeat the paradox and lift from his or her shoulders the negativity that is the burden of this realm.

AMNESIA

Let us briefly examine the cause of lapses in memory and the constant interruptions that break the continuity of our daily lives. Why do we lose our train of thought? Why do we go off on wild tangents in our conversations? Why must we put up with a constant stream of petty disturbances? Why are we subject to sudden mood swings that can take us from bliss to sadness in a matter of seconds?

The answer is that the Line is continually exerting its influence into every aspect of our lives. The Line injects space, the gap, into everything we say and do. Were it not for the Lower Seven of the Line our lives would have total coherence. No longer would we be subject to trivial disturbances; no more would we have trouble seeing things through from beginning to end. However, as desirable this may sound, total continuity would completely obscure and negate the very purpose of our existence which is, of course, the removal of Bread of Shame.

LIMITATION

Man cannot cause chaos in the Upper (inner) levels of his own or of cosmic experience. Fortunately, the negative activity of man does not reach beyond the level of *Malchut*. He can, however, wreck havoc in the seven of the Line. Only *Malchut* is subject to Desire to Receive for the Self Alone. Through restriction we convert the negative aspect of desire into the positive aspect and thus tap into the state of consciousness which is above and beyond the realm of illusion.

The vacuum created at the time of the *Tzimtzum* caused the illusion of the Line to descend without interruption. Thus, from the finite (illusionary) perspective, there is an empty space between each of the Ten Circular *Sefirot* which is imparted to the Circles by the Line, but there is no such gap between the Ten *Sefirot* of the Line which begin from the Endless and extend unobstructed to the Middle Point of *Malchut.*

The Line, in other words, is a total illusion and thus the gap in the Circles is itself illusionary. However, from our finite perspective, it is the Line that appears real while the Circle seems to be illusionary.

There is total continuity between the First Three of the Line and all Ten *Sefirot* of Circles. Only from our finite perspective does the illusion appear to be real. The Lower Seven of the Line causes all of our problems and difficulties, chaos and disorder, but the moment we inject conscious, voluntary restriction into the equation we remove the illusion and reveal the Light. This occurs not only in the normal process of the First Three, which automatically reveals Light because there is no Curtain in the Circles, but also in the Lower Seven of the Line, which are obscured by a Curtain.

We must remember that while the physical universe is affected by whether or not we are converting the negative aspect of Desire into the positive, nevertheless there is a certain component of the universal order that we have absolutely no control over. While we are certainly capable of molding, shaping, even transforming, the illusion of the Lower Seven, nothing we do has the slightest effect on the infinite reality of the Upper First Three.

Above *Malchut* negativity is capable of no influence, for the illusion of darkness can never exist in the presence of the all embracing Light. By injecting the aspect of restriction we create affinity with the Light, thus obliterating the illusion of darkness within the Circular *Sefirot* and also in the Lower Seven of the Line.

Negative activity has no effect on the man or woman who has converted the Desire to Receive for the Self Alone into the Desire to Receive for the Sake of Sharing. By connecting with our Infinite aspect we reveal the Light, whereas a failure to exercise restriction causes us to remain submerged in spiritual darkness and limitation.

ON BECOMING UNREASONABLE

Rav Moses ben Maimon (Maimonides, also known as the Rambam), whose *Mishnah Torah* (Copy of the Law) was the first systematic exposition of Jewish Law, was obviously a man possessed of remarkable reasoning capabilities. His *Articles of Faith* are quoted in most Jewish prayer books, and his main philosophical work *Moreh Nevukhim* (*Guide for the Perplexed*) strongly influenced all philosophical thinking of his era. He also wrote, *Yad haHazakah* (*Strong Hand*), which restructured the entire content of the Bible. Yet, he once compared himself seemingly unfavorably with the Greek philosopher Aristotle saying that Aristotle's deductive logic far exceeded his own. In fact this seeming compliment carried more than a shadow of irony, for Maimonides actually considered the rational mind to be an impediment to true awareness, meaning that while, from the terrestrial perspective,

Aristotle's reasoning capacity may have been greater than his own, speaking from a celestial level (the First Three) it was Maimonides whose mental acuity was superior.

Albert Einstein, also indisputably a man of tremendous analytical endowments and rational cognizance, frequently credited leaps of intuition with his greatest discoveries and mental breakthroughs. He was quoted as saying, "To imagine is everything; The gift of fantasy has meant more to me than my talent for absorbing positive knowledge." However, later in life Einstein took an intransigent position with regard to quantum mechanics. His total inability to accept certain precepts of quantum theory so infuriated Niels Bohr, the Father of Quantum Mechanics—that the latter would later accuse Einstein of no longer thinking, but of just being rational.

The rational, reasoning mind accounts for but a minuscule fragment of our true mental potential. Contrary to what is believed by most Western educators who place great emphasis on mindless regurgitation of rote learned facts, tests, grades, and IQ examinations (all of which are concerned only with the rational mind), by far the greater measure of human mental aptitude rests hidden, clothed in darkness, dormant and unrevealed until such time as the higher realms of consciousness are aroused and re-illuminated through a continuing attitude of positive resistance.

Post Scrip
I'll Take the High Road

Two forces exert influence on humanity. Two energy-intelligences, positive and negative, battle constantly for dominance over the minds and hearts of man. The positive aspect we will call "the high road," from the old Scottish folk song, and, accordingly, the negative aspect we will give the name "the low road." They are two roads, yet one; the same, yet different.

Getting to the low road is a proverbial breeze. Unlike the high road, the low road is wide, smooth—a freeway—or so it seems. Certainly, of the two roads, the low road is the one well-traveled. One can coast down the low road, secure in the knowledge that he or she will never be alone. The vast majority of people choose the seeming comfort and convenience of the low road, little knowing that what appears at first to be the easier way inevitably proves, in the long run, to be the more arduous and demanding.

Being elevated, the high road remains out of sight, above the range of the senses, invisible to the naked eye. One must therefore have a certain sense of adventure, faith, and optimism before embarking upon the high road, a feeling that something positive will result from the long uphill climb. The high road is the path of the *Sefirotic* triumvirate—the Head or First Three. The First Three, synonymous with the soul, must remain obscured from common view. Otherwise, we would revert back to the condition before the *Tzimtzum* with no way of ridding ourselves of Bread of Shame.

When the Emanator restricted to allow for the emergence of free will and its faithful associate, the Desire to Receive, necessity dictated that the high road be an uphill climb. At the *Tzimtzum*, when the Endless imparted free will to the emanated creations, It initiated a situation whereby human energy-intelligences would be obliged to choose between the high road, the positive path, and the low road, the negative. This, however, was not the will of the Emanator, but of the emanated. For as has been often repeated, the Emanator's only aspiration was, is, and will always be to share.

The Emanator has no intention other than to impart Endless benevolence. But as much as the Emanator desires to extend Light to the Vessels, the souls of man, we cannot receive the Light in good conscience without relieving Bread of Shame. A gift imparts no joy to the giver if there is no one to receive it. There must be a Vessel for the Light to be revealed.

Just as there is no light in the cold, dark reaches of space because the light has nothing there to reflect from, so to do the dark places in the consciousness of humanity remain in darkness until positive resistance is exercised. Conscious, positive resistance is the mediating principle between the high road and the low road, the positive and negative aspects of our existence. Resistance reveals Light, which obliterates darkness. The paradox is that by resisting the Light, the gift we most desire, we receive; but by accepting it (like the darkness, it envelops the sunlight allowing it no opportunity for revealment), we too remain in spiritual darkness unless and until we exercise resistance and thereby alleviate Bread of Shame.

The high road is there always, quietly impelling us to resist the negative pull of the Lower Seven, which is a constant in this finite World of Restriction, and to choose, instead, to walk in the Light of the Infinite First Three. Of course, in the Infinite sense, the high road is the only road. In the long term, it is the path that we will all one day follow. In the short term, however, when we are speaking only of life in this finite world, the low road is by far the most frequently taken. The choice is ours. The high road leads to truth, the low road to illusion. The high road leads to sublime contentment, the low road to hardship and worry. Those who choose the high road walk in Light, those who choose the low road have darkness as their constant companion.

Appendix

GLOSSARY OF KABBALISTIC TERMINOLOGY

ABSOLUTE FARNESS - The condition resulting when a change of form is so great as to become an opposition of form.

***AKEDAT YITZCHAK* (THE BINDING OF ISAAC)** - The containing of the negative energy, left column, of the *Sefira* of *Gevurah* (Isaac), in order to bring about harmony with the positive, right column energy of the *Sefira* of *Hesed* (*Abraham*).

AROUSAL - Awakening in the vessel of desire to impart and receive.

ASCENT - Purification. The purer is higher, the impure (thicker) is lower.

BAR/BAT MITZVAH - The time at which the aspect of imparting in the soul awakens; age thirteen in the male and twelve in the female.

BEGINNING OF EXTENSION - The Root of all extension of Light. Also called Crown (*Keter*).

BINDER - The Kingdom of an Upper *Sefira* becomes the Crown (*Keter*) of a Lower *Sefira* thus each Kingdom (*Malchut*) binds every Upper *Sefira* with the one below.

BINDING - The enclosing of the Ten *Sefirot* of the Head in the Ten *Sefirot* of the Returning Light.

BINDING BY STRIKING - The action of the Curtain that repels the Light and hinders it from entering the Fourth Phase.

BOUNDARY - The Curtain at each level stretches out and makes a boundary.

BREAD OF SHAME - Shame at receiving that which is not earned.

CABLES - Various means for the transference of positive meta¬physical energies to man (such as, prayer, meditation, Shabbat, the Festivals, etc.).

CAUSE - That which brings about the revelation of a level.

CENTRAL COLUMN - Synthesizer and synthesis of the Left and Right Columns (negative and positive energies).

CIRCULAR CONCEPT - The balance between Left and Right, negative and positive, brought about by use of restriction. Central Column.

CONCLUSION - The Fourth Phase.

CORPOREALITY - Anything perceived by the five senses.

CORRECTION (*TIKKUN*) - The task of bringing the universe to a state of perfection.

CREATOR - The source of all positive energy.

CROWN (*KETER*) - The purest of all levels.

CURTAIN - The power of future restriction (additional to that of the *Tzimtzum*) that prevents Light from entering the Fourth Phase.

DESCENT - Impurification. Descent from a level. Thickening.

DESIRE TO RECEIVE - Negativity. The aspect of drawing or taking. In our universe all is made up of the Desire to Receive. On the physical level, a Desire to Receive for Oneself Alone, characterized by selfishness, egotism, materialism in man must be transmuted to a Desire to Receive for the Sake of Sharing—a balance and harmony between receiving and imparting permitting the individual to draw into himself the positive Light of the Creator.

DESIRE TO IMPART - Positivity. The aspect of giving characteristic of the Creator (See above: Creator, Desire to Receive).

DEVEKUT (CLEAVING OR UNIFICATION) - Fulfillment of the circular concept whereby union is brought about between the Light of God and man.

DIN (JUDGMENT) - Energy drawn by the Left Column without the use of the Right and Central Columns, causing a metaphysical imbalance or spiritual disharmony in the individual.

DRAWN - The descent of Light brought about by the power of longing (impurity) in the Emanation is said to be drawn down.

EMERGENCE TO THE EXTERIOR - A change in the form of spiritual substance.

ENCIRCLING - That which brings about the revelation of a level is said to surround or encircle that level.

EIN SOF - Endless World, World of the Infinite, The first world from which sprang all future emanations. The primal world in which the souls of man were in perfect harmony with the Crea¬tor. A complete balance between the endless imparting of the Creator and the endless receiving of his creations the souls of man.

ERECT HEIGHT - When the Lights of the Head are clothed in the Vessel of the Head we speak of the Countenance as being of "erect height."

ESSENCE - The Light of Wisdom is the Essence and life of an Emanation.

FAR - An extensive change in form.

FROM ABOVE TO BELOW - Straight or Direct Light extending in the Vessels from higher to lower (purer to impure) levels is described as descending "from Above to Below."

FROM BELOW TO ABOVE - Returning Light drawn in order of levels from lower to higher (impure to purer) is described as ascending "from Below to Above."

GEMATRIA - System of numerology used for biblical interpretation and mystical enlightenment of the more hidden aspects of Bible.

GEMARA - See "*Talmud.*"

GOD - Source of all positivity.

GEMAR HATIKKUN - The Final Redemption of humanity—ultimate peace through harmony in the world. (See Correction.)

GROUND or FLOOR - The Kingdom (*Malchut*) of each level or World is termed the "ground" or "floor" of that level or World.

GEVURAH (JUDGMENT) - Power or might. The second of the Seven Lower *Sefirot*. Left Column; Chariot of Isaac.

HALACHA (CODE OF LAW) - The system through which humanity can attune him or herself to the true flow of spiritual energies of God.

CHASSIDISM - A movement founded by the 18 century Kabbalist Rabbi Israel ben Eliezer (*Baal Shem Tov*) on kabbalistic principles. The key to all of life and worship of God is through joy and happiness.

CHIYA - Fourth level of the soul of man.

HEAD - The Three *Sefirot* of the Upper Light.

CHESED (MERCY) - First of the seven *Sefirot* - Right column; Chariot of Abraham.

HOD (SPLENDOR) - Fifth of the Seven Lower *Sefirot* - Left Column; Chariot of Aaron.

IDRA RABBA (GREATER ASSEMBLY) - The meeting of Rav Shimon bar Yochai, his son, Rav Elazar, and eight disciples. The first instance in history of a group of people learning Kabbalah together. From this group came the *Sefer HaZohar*, the book of the *Zohar*.

ILLUMINATION FROM AFAR - Light that is unable to enter the *Sefirot* but surrounds it from a distance.

INDIVIDUAL - Light clothed in the *Sefira* of the Crown (*Keter*).

INNER LIGHT - The Light inside each *Sefira*.

IN PASSING - Each *Sefira* contains two kinds of Light, the Light that is indigenous to it, and the Light that is left there when the Light of the Endless passes through it. The latter is said to remain there "in passing."

IMPURITY - A strong Desire to Receive. Thickness.

INTELLIGENCE - Reflection on the ways of cause and effect in order to clarify the final result.

JUNCTURE - Equivalence of form between two spiritual substances.

KINGDOM (*MALCHUT*) - The Fourth and last Phase. The tenth and final *Sefira* from *Keter* in which the greatest Desire to Receive is manifested and in which all correction takes place. The physical world.

IDRA ZUTA **(LESSER ASSEMBLY)** - Day of death of Rav Shimon bar Yochai.

KASHRUT - Dietary laws to keep metaphysical and spiritual harmony.

KLIPOT - Shells, evil husks created by man's negative deeds that "cover" and limit man in his spiritual development. The barriers between man and the Light of God.

LAG B'OMER - Day of the death of Rav Shimon bar Yohai. Thirty-third day of the *Omer*. This day coincides with the cessation of the plague that killed 24,000 disciples of Rav Akiva. *Hod* of *Hod* of the forty-nine *Sefirot* between *Pesach* and *Shavuot*. (See *Sefirot Ha'Omer*)

LEFT COLUMN - The column (channel) through which are drawn all metaphysical energies. (See Desire to Receive.)

LENGTH - The distance from the purest Phase to the impurest Phase.

LIFE - Light that is received from the next highest level and not from the Endless, is called Light of Life or Female Light.

LINE - The Light found in the Vessels of Straightness. Also denotes finitude.

LIVING - The Light of Wisdom.

LOWER VESSELS - the Vessels having the larger Desire to Receive.

MALACH - Supernal Angel or energy force devoid of any physical manifestation of the Desire to Receive.

MALCHUT (KINGDOM) - The tenth and final *Sefira* from *Keter*. The *Sefira* in which the greatest Desire to Receive is manifest and in which all correction takes place. The physical world.

MATERIAL - The impurity in the Countenance (*Partzuf*) from the Fourth Phase of Desire. Analogous to physical matter.

MAYIM CHAIM (LIVING WATER) - Springs, rivers, etc. The water of the *Mikveh* is an extremely powerful channel for positive energies.

MERKEVAH (CHARIOT) - Abraham, Isaac, Jacob, etc. with the metaphysical ability to combine metaphysical forces with mundane, physical entities.

MESSIAH/THE AGE OF THE MESSIAH - The end of the period of correction and the beginning of an era of universal peace and harmony. The Messiah is the symbol by which man is shown that the correction has been completed and is not, as in the common misconception, the means to the correction itself.

MIDRASH RABBA - Collection of interpretations, poetic reflections and homilies on the Bible and the Five Scrolls.

MIDDLE POINT - Name of the fourth phase of the En Sof. Called the middle point because of its absolute unity with the infinite light of G d (Ha Shem).

MIKVEH - A body of water through which the individual enclothed in Judgment is brought into spiritual balance. More specifically for women after the time of *Niddah*. Also used by men to remove *klipot* and thereby further their spiritual development.

MISHNA - Oral teachings. he collection of writings of the *Tanna'im*.

NEAR - Closeness of one form to another.

NEFESH - Lowest of the five levels of the soul. Correlated with the *Sefira* of *Malchut*.

NESHAMAH - Third of the five levels of the soul. Correlated with the *Sefira* of *Binah*.

NETZACH (VICTORY) - Fourth of the Seven *Sefirot*. Chariot of Moses.

NIGI'EH - Revealed. Specifically the revealed aspect of the Bible, Talmud, etc.

NISTAR - The concealed, hidden wisdom of the Bible.

NOT JOINED - Changes in forms causes them to be not joined to one another.

NULLIFIED - When two spiritual substances are equal in form they return to one substance, the smaller being nullified by the larger.

OLAM EIN SOF - The World of the Endless Light

OLAMOT **(WORLDS)** - Frameworks of reference used in the study of Kabbalah; usually connected with various degrees of the Desire to Receive.

ONE WITHIN THE OTHER - An outer Circle is defined as the cause of the Circle within it. One within the other points to a relationship of cause and effect.

OR **(LIGHT)** - The Supreme emanation of the Creator.

OR EIN SOF - Light of the Infinite, Endless.

OR MAKIF **(ENCIRCLING LIGHT)** - The spiritual Light surrounding every individual. It is the task of each person to draw this encircling light into himself and thus spiritually elevate himself.

OR PENIMI **(INNER LIGHT)** - The inner energy of a human being that maintains him physically. The energy responsible for all physical growth.

OUTER - The purer part of each Vessel is distinguished as the outer that is illuminated by Surrounding Light from afar.

PASSING - The Light that passes through the *Sefirot* is called "passing" Light.

PARTZUF - Complete structure, also known as Countenance or Face

PIPE - Vessels of Straightness are termed "pipes" since they draw and confine the Light within themselves as a pipe confines the water that passes through it.

PRIMORDIAL MAN (*ADAM KADMON*) - The First World. Also called a Single Line. The root of the Phase of man in this world.

PURIFICATION OF THE CURTAIN - Purification of the impurity in the Fourth Phase brought about in direct proportion to the Desire to Receive.

RETURNING LIGHT - Light that is prevented from entering any world by the Curtain.

RIGHT COLUMN - Column that draws the energy of imparting the positive force. The aspect of the Desire to Impart or Share.

SEFIROT - The Vessels through which the light of the Creator is emanated to man.

SEFER YITZIRAH (BOOK OF FORMATION) - First known kabbalistic work containing in concise, highly esoteric language, the entire teachings of Kabbalah. Attributed to Abraham the Patriarch.

SEVEN LOWER *SEFIROT* - The Seven *Sefirot*; Mercy (*Chesed*), Judgment (*Gevurah*), Beauty (*Tiferet*), Lasting Endurance (*Netzach*), Majesty (*Hod*), Foundation (*Yesod*) and Kingdom (*Malchut*), comprising the Body of the Countenance.

SHABBAT **(SABBATH)** - The final day of each week (Saturday) in which humanity is enclothed solely in positivity.

SIMILARITY OF FORM - When the Desire to Receive is in balance with the Desire to Impart, there is then a situation whereby the individual is receiving for the sake of imparting. Therefore, a similiarity of form comes about with the imparting of the individual being similar to the imparting of the Creator, and thus a union can take place between the individual and the light of God.

SITREI TORAH **(SECRETS OF THE TORAH)** - The deepest hidden teachings of the Bible received only through divine revelation.

SOD - Secret, inner meaning.

SOUL - The Light clothed in the Vessel of Intelligence.

SPIRIT - The Light clothed in the Vessel of the Small Face.

SPIRITUAL - Devoid of material attributes, place, time and shape.

STRAIGHT - The descent of the Upper Light to the impure Vessels of the Fourth Phase is described as being Straight. Compare the swift straight descent of a failing stone with the slow meandering descent of a failing feather. The Earth's gravity (Desire to Receive) exerts a more direct influence on the stone. In a similar manner do the Vessels of Straightness, whose longing is strong, cause Light to descend swiftly in a Straight Line.

SURROUNDING LIGHT - The Light that surrounds each *Sefira*, the illumination of which is received from the *Ein Sof* flat a distance."

***TA'AMEI TORAH* (TASTE OF THE TORAH)** - The reasons of the Bible. The teaching through which one reaches the true Inner meanings of Torah and thereby elevates oneself to the highest degrees of spirituality.

TALMUD - The written form of the oral law. The main work of spiritual studies. A compilation of *Mishna, Tosefot, Gemara.*

TALMUD ESER SEFIROT (TEN LUMINOUS EMANATIONS) - A study of the emanations of the *Sefirot*, vital for any deep understanding of the workings of our universe. Written by R. Yehuda Ashlag.

TANNA'IM - Teachers of the law in the First to Third centuries. Their teachings are known as the *Mishna.*

***TEFILLIN* (PHYLACTERIES)** - Small black boxes containing certain Bible portions. *Tefillin* are placed on the left arm and head. The *Tefillin* of the arm is to bind and contain the Left Column energy of the Desire to Receive for the Self Alone—to transform this to a Desire to Receive in for Sake of Imparting—a balance of Left in harmony with Right. The *Tefillin* of the head is to connect with the positive energy and subsequent cosmic consciousness and pure awareness.

THE ENDLESS (*EIN SOF*) - The Source of the Vessels of the Circles.

THE FIRST THREE - The First Three *Sefirot*: Crown (*Keter*), Wisdom (*Chochmah*), and Intelligence (*Binah*). Also called the Head of the Countenance.

THE LARGE FACE (*ARICH ANPIN*) - The Countenance of the Crown (*Keter*) in the World of Emanation, its essence is the Light of Wisdom.

THE PURPOSE OF ALL OF THIS - The Fourth Phase of the Fourth Phase.

THE SMALL FACE (*ZEIR ANPIN*) - Six *Sefirot* of the Third Phase whose essence is the Light of Mercy, containing illumination from Wisdom (*Chochmah*) without its essence.

TIKKUNEI HAZOHAR - Separate section of the *Zohar* by Rav Shimon bar Yohai, not contained in the main body of the *Zohar* itself. Its teachings are specifically geared to the Age of the Messiah.

TORAH (BIBLE) - In its broader sense, the entire doctrine of humanity, written and oral, including all commentaries, past and future. In its restricted sense it refers to the *Pentateuch*, the Five Books of Moses.

TOSFAT SHABBAT - The extra soul one receives on Shabbat in order to enable him to reach a higher state of spiritual con¬sciousness. Through the *Tosfat Shabbat* humanity's vessel for receiving is vastly enlarged enabling him to draw forth more positive energies than would normally be possible.

TUMAH - Unclean, impure. A state of total metaphysical imbalance. When there is a manifestation of the Desire to Receive for Oneself Alone, the resulting imbalance is the energy of *Tumah*.

***TZIMTZUM* (RESTRICTION)** - The voluntary rejection or restriction of the Divine Light in the *Olam Ein Sof* due to the aspect of bread of Shame and the desire to identify with the aspect of sharing and imparting. In the Lower Worlds this restriction is no longer voluntary but imposed and constitutes one of the basic rules by which our mundane world must operate.

VEILS - Metaphysical barriers brought about by our own negative actions. The veils refuse entry to the Light of the Creator and completely limit the individual's spiritual potential.

VESSEL - Containers of the Divine Light derived from the Desire to Receive and growing in thickness from level to level until they are co-terminous with the world of the senses where the Light is practically invisible. Also referred to as "bottled up" energies.

WATERS OF LIGHT - Light that descends from its level.

WHEEL - The *Sefirot* of Circles.

WISDOM - Knowledge of the final ends of all aspects of reality.

YECHIDA - Highest level of soul. Total oneness—union with the Light of God. A level unobtainable until the coming of the Messiah. Correlated with the *Sefira* of *Keter*.

YESH ME'AYIN - (Something from Nothing). See Appendix   Creation.

YESOD **(FOUNDATION)** - Sixth of the Seven *Sefirot*. The *Sefira* through which is emanated all light to our world. Chariot of Joseph.

YETZER HARAH - Man's evil inclination. The Desire to Receive for Oneself Alone.

More Ways to Bring the Wisdom of Kabbalah into your Life

The Holy Grail: A Manifesto on the Zohar
By Rav Berg

The Holy Grail is a mystical legend that dates back before Christianity. Believed to have magical influences, the Holy Grail is widely known as possessing the ability to endow infinite knowledge and power upon the person who has earned the right to discover it through spiritual work.

Here in this unique short form, Rav Berg explains what the kabbalists have said for centuries—the *Zohar* is the Holy Grail. In clear modern language he explains how the *Zohar* can empower anyone, with an open mind and an open heart, who studies from its pages to leap from the world where we experience ups and downs, good and evil, to a parallel universe in which all is good.

God Wears Lipstick
By Karen Berg

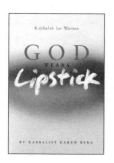

This groundbreaking and bestselling book reveals the power that's innate to every woman. From a Kabbalalistic perspective, Karen Berg outlines life's deeper meaning, and gives tangibles solutions to issues women face today. She delves into the spiritual purpose of relationships—to reach our highest potential—and the way to enrich our connection to our self, our mate, our children, and God.

The Power of Kabbalah
By Yehuda Berg

The familiar reality is the physical 1 percent material realm in which we live, yet there is another dimension—the world beyond our five senses. According to Kabbalah, this is called the 99 percent realm. Everything we truly desire: love, joy, peace of mind, freedom, is available when we connect to the 99 percent reality. The problem is that most of us have inadvertently disconnected ourselves from this dimension. Imagine if we could access this source at will, and on a continuing basis. This is the power of Kabbalah. This foundational text features new content and is more accessible for meeting today's current challenges. Use the exercises included to break free of prevalent beliefs and habits which lead to negativity. Readers will discover how to align their actions with their higher purpose, and become conscious of the unlimited possibilities in their own life.

Secrets of the Bible
By Michael Berg

The Secret of the Bible is a lifelong pursuit and there are many teachings within its veiled text. Bringing forward a fresh and relevant message about our purpose, and how to make life better, kabbalistic scholar, Michael Berg, imparts wisdom from decades of research and sources unique to his lineage. Gems of insight from the *Zohar*, Rav Berg, Rav Ashlag, Rav Isaac Luria (the Ari) as well as other known kabbalists are complemented by lessons from the ages. Kabbalists believe that the Bible is not just a book of stories or an historical archive of events: It is a guide to understanding the nature of this world, of life, and of the planet. Although these events physically took place thousands of years ago, there are transcendent fundamentals hidden within each tale. Michael drills through complex concepts to reveal essential truths. He utilizes biblical texts to expand our perception to see God in everything and everyone. Although Michael shares ideas that can awaken a desire for transformation, the gift he offers is another view of the Bible and its secrets.

The *Zohar*

Composed more than 2,000 years ago, the 23-volume *Zohar* is a commentary on biblical and spiritual matters written in the form of conversations among teachers. It was given to all humankind by the Creator to bring us protection, to connect us with the Creator's Light, and ultimately to fulfill our birthright of transformation. The *Zohar* is an effective tool for achieving our purpose in life.

More than eighty years ago, when The Kabbalah Centre was founded, the *Zohar* had virtually disappeared from the world. Today, all this has changed. Through the editorial efforts of Michael Berg, the *Zohar* is available in the original Aramaic language and for the first time in English with commentary.

We teach Kabbalah, not as a scholarly study but as a way of creating a better life and a better world.

Who We Are:

The Kabbalah Centre is a non-profit organization leading the way in making Kabbalah understandable and relevant in everyday life. The Centre was founded by Rav Yehuda Ashlag in 1922, and now spans the globe with brick-and-mortar locations in more than 40 cities as well as an extensive online presence. Our funds are used in the research and development of new methods to make Kabbalah accessible and understandable.

What We Do:

We translate and publish kabbalistic texts, develop courses, classes, online lectures, books, audio products; provide one-on-one instruction, and host local and global energy connections and tours. As the principles of Kabbalah emphasize sharing, we provide a volunteer program so that our students can participate in charitable initiatives.

How We Teach:

For every student, there is a teacher.

Our goal is to ensure that each student is supported in his or her study. Teachers and mentors are part of the educational infrastructure. Many of our classes take place in physical locations around the world; however, with today's increasing need and desire for alternative ways of learning, The Kabbalah Centre also offers instruction by phone, in study groups, and online through Webinars and classes, as well as self-directed study in audio format.

Student Support:

Because Kabbalah can be a deep and constant study, it is helpful to have a teacher on the journey to acquiring wisdom and growth. With more than 300 teachers internationally serving over 100 locations, in 20 languages, there is always a teacher for every student and an answer for every question. All Student Support instructors have studied Kabbalah under the supervision of Kabbalist Rav Berg. For more information call 1 800 Kabbalah.

Kabbalah University (ukabbalah.com):

Kabbalah University (ukabbalah.com) is an online university providing lectures, courses, and events in English and Spanish. This is an important link for students in the United States and around the globe, who want to study Kabbalah but don't have access to a Kabbalah Centre in their community. Kabbalah University offers a library of wisdom spanning 30 years. This virtual Kabbalah Centre presents the same courses and spiritual connections as the physical centers with an added benefit of streaming videos from worldwide events.

Kabbalah Publishing:

Each year, we translate and publish some of the most challenging kabbalistic texts including the *Zohar*, the *Writings of the Ari*, the *Ten Luminous Emanations* and essays from Rav Ashlag. We synthesize this wisdom into beginner and intermediate level books, which are distributed and published in more than 30 languages.

Kabbalah Museum:

We gather and preserve original kabbalistic texts and rare manuscripts that are housed in Los Angeles. We make these texts available online for students and scholars to view. These important texts enable us to continue to lead the way in the education of Kabbalah

I dedicate this book to all those near and far that
have helped me on my journey
and were always there for me unconditionally.
May the Light and wisdom of this book
protect and guide
Michael, Michelle, Matthew, Andrew and Jeffrey
always and forever.

Neil

נחום בן יעקב יוסף